The Mafia

The Mafia

The First 100 Years

William Balsamo &
George Carpozi Jr

Published by Virgin Books 2009

4 6 8 10 9 7 5 3

Copyright © William Balsamo and George Carpozi Jr 1988

William Balsamo and George Carpozi Jr asserted their right under the Copyright, Designs and Patents Act 1988 to be identified as the authors of this work.

This edition first published in Great Britain in 1997 by
Virgin Books
Random House, 20 Vauxhall Bridge Road,
London SW1V 2SA

Reprinted 1997, 1998, 2000, 2001 (twice), 2002, 2003, 2004, 2005, 2006, 2007

First published in Great Britain in 1988 as Crime Incorporated by W.H. Allen & Co Plc

www.virginbooks.com
www.rbooks.co.uk

Addresses for companies within The Random House Group Limited can be found at:
www.randomhouse.co.uk/offices.htm

The Random House Group Limited Reg. No. 954009

A CIP catalogue record for this book is available from the British Library

ISBN 9780753518205

The Random House Group Limited supports The Forest Stewardship Council (FSC), the leading international forest certification organisation. All our titles that are printed on Greenpeace approved FSC certified paper carry the FSC logo. Our paper procurement policy can be found at:
www.rbooks.co.uk/environment

Typeset by TW Typesetting, Plymouth, Devon
Printed in the UK by CPI Bookmarque, Croydon, CR0 4TD

Contents

Introduction

An invisible government under the whip of the Mafia – the
government of syndicated crime – has enveloped much of the
Western world like a cancerous growth, stubbornly defying the
prognosis and treatment of law enforcement agencies.

It is a government so insidious that it has subjugated millions
of innocent persons to servility.

The plunder cascading into the coffers of this empire amounts
to as much as ten percent of the national income.

Millions of Americans – knowingly and unknowingly –
are compelled to contribute a part of their hard-earned wages or
income to the big business of international crime.

The public pays its tribute to the sprawling, voracious monster
of syndicated crime in many ways: in the clothes it wears, in the
food it eats, in the union dues it pays, in the music it listens and
dances to, in the cigarettes it smokes, in the gasoline that fuels its
cars, in the shipments of its merchandise and parcels, in the
buildings and bridges it erects. In innumerable other ways the
public is made a helpless sucker by the common denominator of
greed and avarice upon which this invisible government gorges
itself.

Organised gangs operate largely unmolested in interstate
commerce and industry. The criminals behind this vast conspiracy are descendants of the underworld wars of the Prohibition

1

Era; they are people of varying talents, qualities, and responsibilities banded together in a surreptitious conspiracy which, for the most part, is run like many large, diversified industries or businesses.

Unlike the old, bloody roaring twenties days when bootlegging was one of the chief sources of income for the Mob and gunfire tattooed the syndicate's enforcement aims, today's organised criminals shy away from violence and murder as much as they can.

Rather than engage in blatant and belligerent lawbreaking, today's underworld take refuge in the self-respecting guise of legitimate entrepreneurs; they have ably organised themselves in much the same manner as giant corporations.

In the great complexity that is organised crime, one ruling body stands firmly entrenched at the top of the enormous roster of mobsters. It imposes onerous rules and regulations; it exercises tremendous pressure to maintain control.

This is the Mafia.

No single underworld group has survived the ravages of time nor the onslaught of crime fighters as well as this, most extensive, most effective criminal body in the world.

There are many who feel that the power of the Mafia does not prevail any longer, that 'Mafia' is just a word loosely used by sensationalist headline writers to boost the sales of newspapers, magazines and books, to boost box office sales, and to hype the Neilsen ratings for network television shows.

The authors maintain that the Mafia does exist. The chapters that follow will chronicle the rise, and rise, and rise, of this sinister underworld government. It does not exist as a colossus of crime with branch offices in every major city. Nor does it work with IBM or push-button efficiency, as some may envision.

The Mafia today is a relatively loosely knit group who work together for their mutual well-being and continued dominance of criminal objectives and who share in a way of life that brings its followers an understanding of trust for one another.

Their efforts are concentrated, to a very large extent, in narcotics. The Mafia is the principal and dominating agent in drug trafficking, and the rise of such Johnny-come-lately dealers in opiates and sopophoric agents as Columbians, Haitians, Puerto Ricans, Chinese, and other newcomers to the field, have not lessened its domination.

The Mafia is also deeply involved in illicit activities such as gambling, the coin machine rackets, juke box businesses, pizza parlor operations (which are also used as fronts for drug trafficking and money-laundering), prostitution, extortion, smuggling, and counterfeiting.

Then, too, the Mafia has become deeply entrenched in the control over such lucrative legitimate ventures as trucking, restaurant supplies, laundry services, restaurants, night-clubs, labor unions, garbage hauling, beer and soft drink distributorships, garment manufacturing, ready-mix concrete and many others.

They have intruded into the world of sports. Men from the crime kingdom exercise powerful influences over boxing, harness racing, dog races and other professional sports.

As the Mafia spreads into each new area, the tribute to it grows accordingly – at the expense of average, law-abiding citizens.

The Maffia (as it was originally known) did not begin as a criminal agency. Its infamous web has only been spun over the last century. Prior to then, it was an underground patriotic society, born more than six hundred years ago on the Mediterranean island of Sicily, the 'toe' of Italy's 'boot'.

It rose to prominence in the thirteenth century as a resistance group to foreign oppression. Through the centuries Sicily had been invaded repeatedly – by Arabs, Normans, Germans, French, and Spaniards. The underground organisation was formed to conduct warfare against these intruders. For hundreds of years the society was held together only by an indomitable spirit of patriotism to repel all foreigners.

We chronicle the transformation of this early organisation, banded together by a sense of nationalism, into its present-day configuration as a criminal colossus unmatched by any other body of criminals anywhere.

The advent of Prohibition in 1920 gave rise to the Mafia as we know it today in the United States. Many Mafiosi who had emigrated here since the turn of the century and dealt in shakedowns and extortion of the hapless Italian newcomers became aware of the lucrative rewards in bootlegging and rum-running, which opened the way to a climb to power. Many of the hardy survivors of those early roaring twenties days of mobsterism emerged as overlords of organised crime in the thirties and kept their power into the forties, fifties, sixties, and even the seventies.

Among them are: Frank Costello, Vito Genovese, Michele 'Mike' Spiranda, Tony Accardo, Joseph Profaci, Michael 'Mike' Spinella, Joseph 'Joe Adonis' Doto, Thomas 'Three Finger Brown' Luchese, Anthony 'Tony Bender' Strollo, Albert Anastasia, and Anthony 'Little Augie Pisano' Carfano.

Contrary to general belief, the Mafia in the last sixty years has not restricted its membership to Sicilian emigrants or their descendants, nor even to those of Italian extraction. Members of today's Mafia hierarchy include, for example, Meyer Lansky and Abner 'Longie' Zwillman.

Membership in the Mafia is achieved through diverse ways: by birth, marriage, or through the sponsorship of relatives or close friends.

Members are selected for their particular aptitudes and abilities in the toils of the underworld.

Those with unusual talents who can serve to further the Mafia's aims and controls in the rackets are initiated as 'brothers' regardless of national origin. Nationalistic sentiment is set aside for someone with a genius for extending the perimeters of the Mafia's racket preserves and enriching its coffers.

Gaining acceptance in the Mafia is a slow, gradual process. A candidate no longer goes through the ancient religious-flavored ritual of being transformed into a 'brother'; now he puts in a period of apprenticeship as a full-fledged member's stooge, moving with him in Mafia circles and lighting his cigars and cigarettes, running his errands, raking in his bets, collecting extortion, and carrying out murders.

The area of the underworld in which the candidate receives his experience depends upon his sponsor's particular specialty, which could be narcotics, prostitution, labor extortion, gambling, or any other unlawful arena in which the Mafia is entrenched.

When his protégé proves himself and is ready for full-fledged membership in the organisation, a sponsor will take him on as a partner or set him up with a racket operation of his own in a neighboring territory. Once thus established, the new member is eligible for all the protection, secrets, and privileges incumbent on the Mafia to provide its own. It is a union that can be dissolved only by death.

Deepest secrecy is the organisation's binding code, epitomised by the Italian *omerta*, a variation of *umerta*, a Sicilian word meaning 'humility' – a quality which every Mafioso must exhibit. In the primitive dialect, the word meant 'noble silence'.

This conspiracy of 'no speak to nobody', the traditional trademark of the Mafia, is rigidly enforced. Anyone who violates the code is certain to meet a swift and violent end, and the aggrieved members take their revenge by their own methods.

Although there's been considerable intermarriage among Mafia families that gives the organisation the specter of being a single far-flung clan, it seldom holds big meetings.

And when it did – it was the first time Mafiosi got together to talk things over in an open forum . . .

That meeting, held on the palatial hilltop estate of mobster Joseph Barbara in upstate New York's serene picturesque hamlet of Apalachin, degenerated into a colossal boner.

The infamous conclave finally gave credence and validity to the accumulating claims of one investigator after another that a super-government of crime – the Mafia – indeed exists.

That warning toll was sounded with electrifying reverberations on a rainy 14 November 1957, when Empire State troopers, led by Sergeant Edgar Crosswell, and United States Treasury agents invaded Barbara's mansion.

Crosswell's curiosity was first aroused by a procession of sleek, expensive cars with out-of-state and out-of-country license plates sweeping up through the tiny community (pop. 280) to Barbara's secluded fifty-three-acre estate.

5

At the first sight of the gray-clad troopers and Treasury agents in street garb, sixty-three impeccably tailored men deserted two hundred pounds of beef at the barbecue pit, grabbed their coats, and scrambled for the exits. The troopers managed to nail fifty-seven of them in different stages of flight – some at a roadblock, others tripping aimlessly on foot through the dense woods.

'The troopers on the raid had a field day when they went into the woods,' said Sergeant Crosswell. 'All they had to do was find the guys wearing the pointed patent leather shoes and they knew they had Mafiosi.'

When taken in for questioning, and asked who they were, where they came from, and why they were in Apalachin, the fifty-seven trapped delegates answered that they'd come to visit a 'sick friend' – Barbara – who, ironically, died just a few years later without a single Mafioso at his bedside.

While they gave their true identifies, none of the fifty-seven mobsters revealed the real purpose of the convention. Each held tightly to the secret, true to the Mafia code of *omerta*: 'talk and you die; keep your mouth shut and we'll take care of you and your family . . .'

The state and federal officials became frustrated in their efforts to learn what the meeting was about, but they did learn one thing: the Mafia 'grand council' apparently did meet periodically. Its purpose ostensibly was to deal with crucial problems and map ways of enhancing the organisation's holdings and wealth.

After Apalachin, the syndicate never let itself be caught in similar straits. If indeed they met again – and it's believed they've had many conclaves in the years since – they were careful not to send out any more telltale smoke signals of their get-togethers, such as a procession of expensive, out-of-state cars all heading to the same place.

The chapters that follow are a powerful portrayal of America's Mafia, shaped by the authors through research and investigation – as well as personal experience. We have chronicled in exacting detail every significant episode of the Mafia's underworld activity from before the turn of the century to the present day.

Chapter 1

Amorte . . . He Deserved It

4 August 1919 was an unbearably hot, muggy day. The temperature reached 95 degrees at high noon – just the time two sinister-looking figures, dapper in Palm Beach suits and Panama hats, strolled off busy Flatbush Avenue and entered the Mount Olympus Restaurant, in the heart of downtown Brooklyn.

'Hello, my good friends,' a voice encumbered by a heavy Greek accent greeted the two men, who needed no introduction to many of Nick Colouvos's gathering lunch crowd. Frankie Yale was one of the underworld's fastest rising gang leaders; his squat muscular companion and chief lieutenant, Anthony 'Little Augie Pisano' Carfano (also known as 'Augie the Wop') was equally well known.

'Here, let me give you a table near the big fan in the back where you will be cool,' Colouvos offered. The soft-spoken, personable restaurant owner had looked up to Yale as a hero since the dreary winter's night in 1918 when a young boy, no older than ten, hawking evening and morning newspapers from a makeshift stand outside the restaurant. That night the stacks of papers were still piled high at an hour when they should have been depleted. It was indoor weather and the streets were deserted.

Nick watched as Yale went over to the boy, bought out his newsstand with a crisp fifty-dollar bill, and commanded him to 'Go home to your mama.' Nick never forgot that episode. To the immigrant from a poor Spartan village who had known only poverty until he came to America and lifted himself up by his bootstraps by washing dishes, then working as a chef until he scraped enough savings together to open his own restaurant, the underworld hoodlum's gesture to the newsboy was an example of true generosity.

He sat his guests down and took their orders, then went off into the kitchen to make certain the meals were prepared to Frankie's and Little Augie's satisfaction. Nick wasn't his usual smiling ebullient self, Yale remarked to Pisano. 'Something is bothering him,' he said.

When Nick brought the food out and served it to his guests, Yale asked what was troubling him. Nick simply shrugged and said everything was all right. Yale didn't believe him.

'Nick, something is on your mind, my good friend. What is it? Somebody bothering you? You having trouble with the help around here?'

Nick shook his head. 'Nah, nothing like that. It's a personal thing . . .'

His voice trailed off and Yale sensed a deep problem gnawing at Nick.

'Let's go to the back room where we can talk,' Yale suggested. He stood up, dug a hand into his pants pocket, and pulled out a wad of cash. He peeled off a ten-dollar bill and dispatched Little Augie to fetch a bottle of Scotch from a nearby liquor store.

When Augie returned, the three retired to the back room. After the drinks were poured, Frankie and Augie settled back to listen to Nick's plight.

Speaking with considerable hesitation, Colouvos managed to say, 'It's . . . my daughter . . . Olympia . . . You know her, Frankie . . . You gave her twenty dollars two months ago for her birthday . . .'

Yale knew the girl. She had an angelic face and long auburn curls that hung down her back. He also remembered that she was eight years old.

Nick explained that for the past several weeks Olympia was extraordinarily melancholy, often crying for no apparent reason, refusing to eat.

'This is not at all like my daughter,' Nick said. 'We finally took her to the doctor, but he could find nothing wrong with her. He thinks she is going through a phase, but my wife and I just know something is not right.'

Lately the little girl was awakening in the middle of the night, screaming from nightmares. 'I can't see my child in tears,' Nick protested. 'It depresses me. And worse, she won't even talk about what is bothering her. We don't know what to do anymore.'

Yale thought of an immediate solution.

'You know what I'm gonna do for you?' He paused briefly to give emphasis to his words. Then, with a grand sweep of his hand, he laid out his blueprint to get into the little girl's head:

'I'll get Mary Despano to take Olympia to Coney Island this weekend. Maybe after she goes on a few rides and has some ice cream, she'll open up for Mary and tell her what's bothering her.'

Mary Despano, a saintly forty-five-year-old widow, lived alone in a tenement at the corner of Union and Henry Streets in the center of Brooklyn's Little Italy. Her husband and son were victims of the great flu epidemic of 1917 and since then Mary had worn nothing but black mourning dresses.

Children adored Mary and many of them made her their confidante. They could tell her things about their personal lives and their weightiest problems that they didn't dare discuss with their own mothers.

That Sunday Mary took Olympia to the famed summer playground on the Brooklyn shore where, after a round of rides, and hot dogs, French fries, frozen custard and cotton candy, the little girl's tongue loosened.

After depositing Olympia safely at home, Mary Despano sought out Yale and told him what had been causing Nick's daughter so much unhappiness and nightmares. Frankie shouted a litany of epithets and slammed his hand against the dining room wall with such force that the picture frames rattled and a crack was left in the plaster.

9

After Mary departed, Yale phoned the restaurant and asked Nick to have his wife prepare dinner for the following Sunday.

'I want to eat with you and Maria. And be sure to ask your brother George over, too. That is very important. But the children will not eat with us. Mary will take Olympia and your two sons to Coney Island for another treat.'

Nick's apartment was located in a brownstone on Clinton Street, not more than eight blocks from the restaurant. Nick greeted Frankie Yale at the door and ushered him into the living room where Colouvos's wife, Maria, and brother were already seated.

After a period of small talk, Mrs Colouvos excused herself to prepare dinner. Twenty minutes later she brought the roast leg of lamb and all its trimmings to the table, and summoned Yale, her husband, and brother-in-law into the dining room.

The conversation was simple and unencumbered during the meal. After she cleared the dinner dishes, Nick's wife served the traditional Turkish coffee, the Greek after-dinner delicacy, baklava, and little jiggers of ouzo.

Until this moment, none of the Colouvoses seemed to have an idea of why Frankie Yale had arranged this get-together. Then Yale took the last sip of his ouzo and turned to his host.

'Nick,' Yale began, with a grim face. 'I have very bad news about Olympia. The reason she has nightmares is because . . .'

Frankie's words trailed off. But only momentarily. His eyes were afire now and he could no longer hold back the stunning secret about Nick's daughter's problem that Mary Despano had unearthed.

'. . . Listen closely, Nick,' Yale began anew. 'I have very bad news for you about Olympia . . .'

Again Frankie hesitated as he spoke. He was measuring his words and seemed to want to deliver the message he had for Nick in precise language.

'Frankie,' Nick blurted after so much anticipation, 'what are you trying to say?'

'Okay, my friend, I will stop beating around the bush,' Yale rasped. 'I'm going to tell you what I found out . . .'

Yale turned and glared at Nick's brother George, little Olympia's uncle.

'This man,' Frankie said through tightly clenched teeth, pointing a finger straight at the now-startled George Colouvos, 'has been screwing your daughter – and that is why she has been having nightmares and been so depressed –'

Nick's face suddenly became a dark mask as he turned and glared at his brother in total shock and disbelief.

George sat bolt upright in his chair at the table, stupefied and speechless.

Before Nick could utter a word, Yale continued to relate what Mary Despano had learned from Olympia.

'This thing has been going on for two months – ever since your brother's ship went into dry dock for repairs and he came to visit you. Olympia told Mary how George lured her to the cellar with the promise of giving her chocolates. He did vile things with her. Then after he had satisfied himself with her he warned Olympia that he would kill her if she told anyone what he was doing to her.'

Nick again turned and glared at his brother in disbelief. George Colouvos became terrified. He leaped out of his chair and started to run for the door. He froze in his tracks when Yale yelled, 'Sit down, you *disgraziato degenerato* bastard!'

George obeyed, went back to his chair on trembling legs, and seated himself. He broke out in a cold sweat as he waited for Frankie Yale's next command.

His eyes popped wide open as Frankie opened his jacket and unlimbered a .45-caliber revolver from his hip holster.

Frankie cocked the trigger and aimed the barrel at George's head. 'You should not be so impolite when somebody is talking,' he snarled.

George sat back in his chair at the dining room table and submitted to the rest of Frankie Yale's narrative about Olympia's agonising experiences.

Nick and Maria were utterly devastated as Frankie went into the most sordid details of their daughter's abuse by her uncle, of his threat to kill her if she ever told anyone about what he was doing to her, and of how fright drove her to withdraw into a shell of fear and confusion.

When he finished Yale turned to Nick and placed the gun on the table before him.

'More than anything in this world, Nick,' Yale said in a slow, measured tone, 'I want to kill this degenerate bastard brother of yours. But I am not selfish. I do not want to deprive you of that honor.'

Nick gazed disbelievingly at Yale.

'. . . You want . . . me to . . . kill . . . my . . . my brother . . .' he stammered.

Yale's eyes narrowed to slits as he glared at Nick.

'I know you are a gentle, mild-mannered man, my friend. But I have not gone to all this trouble to find out what is bothering Olympia only to have your brother escape the punishment he deserves – from the only person who should give it to him. And that person is you!'

Nick's hand moved slowly toward the gun on the table. All the while George Colouvos, cringing in his chair, let his eyes follow his brother's movements.

As Nick palmed the gun, George suddenly cried out plaintively in Greek:

'*Adelphi, mou . . . oyi!*'

The plea, 'Brother of mine . . . no!' went unheeded.

Nick Colouvos, now as revenge-bent as Frankie Yale instructed him to be, aimed the .45 at his brother's sweating temple.

George pleaded again. 'Please, Nick . . . I couldn't help myself. I'm a sick man . . .'

Nick glared at George and screamed, 'I'm ashamed and humiliated to have a brother such as you. If Papa was alive he would kill you himself. But since he is not, I am going to do it . . .'

The dining room fell into an eerie silence, broken only by the condemned man's heavy breathing – and then by the two quick shots that Nick triggered at his brother's head.

Twin holes tore open George Colouvos's temple, and blood spurted in torrents from them.

Maria Colouvos screamed hysterically as her brother-in-law collapsed on the table, his head falling into the baklava.

As the echoes of the gunfire subsided, Yale moved quickly.

'All right, Nick, grab his feet and help me put the body on the kitchen floor,' he instructed. 'I don't want to get blood on the carpet in here.'

Taking hold of George's limp upper torso under the armpits, Frankie lifted the dead man out of his chair as Nick lifted his brother's feet off the floor. They carried George's body to the kitchen and laid it on the linoleum, which Olympia's mother later mopped to remove the blood that still trickled from the two head wounds.

At about nine o'clock that night, as darkness descended, Yale and Colouvos carried the blanket-wrapped corpse to the street, stuffed it into the trunk of Colouvos's sedan, and drove to the New Jersey ferry.

Their destination had already been mapped by the Mafia overlord: a weed-covered illegal dumpsite at Lyndenhurst close to the Passiac River. They sprinkled quicklime over the body. In just days, the flesh and bone totally disintegrated.

They drove home in silence and didn't get in touch with each other for a week – until Nick phoned Frankie.

'My very good friend,' he said. 'I want to tell you how much my little girl has improved. She is talking again and smiling like she used to. And she is eating once more. Most important, she does not have nightmares . . .'

Nick's voice went silent a moment as Yale listened. Finally, Olympia's father spoke again:

'Frankie, I want to thank you. I know what you did was because of your love for children – and that you hate to see them hurt in any way.

'You are a very fine man and on that account I am proud to call you my friend.'

Yale thanked Colouvos for those sentiments, then imparted a few words himself:

'Nick, I know you are sincere in what you just said and mean every word. And because you and I are such good friends, I want to give you this bit of advice:

'Never forget. We only kill if we have to. And they die – but only because they deserve it . . .

'And your brother – Amorte . . . he did deserve it!'

Chapter 2

Those Dirty Black Hand Ginzos

5 January 1920 was a Monday. A chill winter day.

The wind swirled in twenty-five-mile-an-hour gusts. The leaden gray skies threatened to disgorge the season's first heavy snowfall.

On the Brooklyn waterfront, crews of longshoremen were busily shifting crates and bales, loading freighters bound for foreign ports, unloading cargoes shipped across the Atlantic.

PIER 2. The new sign had just been hung over the long, rectangular, narrow-fronted warehouse jutting out over the East River from the foot of Furman Street. Bright red clock letters against a white background heralded the proprietorship of the Gowanus Stevedoring Company, a proud firm that had been doing business on the Brooklyn docks for more than fifty years.

Gowanus had just expanded its dock operations by taking over the Pier 2 warehouse. The new foreman, Jimmy Sullivan, was a monstrous man with huge forearms etched with gaudy tattoos of exploding bombshells – reminders of his hell as a doughboy in the trenches of the Marne and Belleau Woods during World War I. He was put into the job because he'd given honest sweat as a dockhand for Gowanus since 1902. When he'd come back from two years in the army the company needed a tough thumper to hustle the crews on the new pier. Jimmy was their boy. From his first day on the job, Sullivan showed who was boss. His thick, cracked lips and his squinting blue eyes never smiled. His flat face and the nose busted from countless pier brawls carried a message to the men: they'd better not mess with him.

At forty-eight, Jimmy Sullivan did not know what had to be done on the wharf. The respect he commanded from the dockers made him a good man to run Pier 2.

One of his duties as pier superintendent was paying the weekly extortion to Denny Meehan's White Hand collectors. Shelling out protection money was a way of life on the waterfront. It prevented the wholesale theft of cargo from the company's warehouses and spared their merchandise-laden trucks from hijackings.

The handful of companies that had balked at coming under Meehan's thumb were paying through the nose now. Cargoes were constantly pilfered from their piers and their trucks were constantly waylaid in the middle of the night.

Jimmy Sullivan liked everything about his job except handing over the weekly envelope to Meehan's torpedoes. Although it wasn't his money, Jimmy felt it was wrong. So did his boss, John O'Hara, the president of Gowanus. Jimmy's salary as pier superintendent was a respectable $150 a week, fifty percent more than he'd been making as a dock labourer. In a sense, then, the extortion O'Hara was paying to the White Hand gang was money coming out of his pocket – and the dockworkers'.

Jimmy never let on how he felt to Meehan's ambassadors. Generally he received them in his warehouse office – and always tried to get them out of his sight in as little time as it took to hand over the envelope containing the $1,500 in cash which O'Hara sent over early every Monday morning.

Pleasantries, if exchanged, were as short as Jimmy could cut them. He felt like taking Ernie 'Skinny' Shea and Wally 'The Squint' Walsh, Meehan's regular collectors, and pulverising them with his bare hands. He often wondered how two scrawny punks like these could fit into a group with such an awesome reputation as Denny Meehan's organised mob.

Shea got his nickname for a very apparent reason – he was five-foot-four and weighed in at under 120 pounds. He looked even skinnier: his high cheekbones and hollowed cheeks gave him the appearance of someone who routinely siphoned gasoline out of a car and drank it.

Jimmy Sullivan could swear he never got a glimpse of Wally Walsh's eyes. His gaunt, pale face didn't differ much from Shea's. But it had a distinctive feature: his eyeballs never showed. Even in Sullivan's drab office, where the forty-watt light bulb couldn't even make a bat blink, Walsh squinted as though the high-noon sun were blazing into his eyes.

It was eleven o'clock on that Monday morning of 5 January 1920, when Shea and Walsh arrived at Pier 2. Sullivan was standing on a crate which contained religious plaster of Paris statues of St Anthony shipped from Milan which had just been unloaded from a freighter.

As he shouted orders to the longshoremen to guide the boom lowering cargo from the freighter's hold, a corner of his eye caught the black LaSalle that had just pulled to a stop outside his office door.

'All right, keep the jig moving,' he shouted. He hopped off the crate and scampered into his office ahead of Shea and Walsh. Sullivan always tried to be sitting behind his desk when he encountered Meehan's collectors. It gave him a feeling of superiority.

'Hi, Jim,' greeted Shea as he entered the office.

'Yeah,' Sullivan shorted, opening the lap drawer of his desk.

Wordlessly, he handed the envelope with the $1,500 – in one-hundred-dollar bills – to Shea.

'No need to count it,' Shea said, his thin lips curling up to his ears in an ingratiating smile. 'The amount is always right.'

Sullivan had no doubt that Shea and Walsh knew that neither was half the man he was and that without those guns they carried they'd be nothing. He could crush the two bums with his hands, even with their rods on them. But he had no intention of going out of his way to make trouble with the men who represented the White Hand gang; it could be ruinous for his company.

'That's it, eh, fellas,' Jimmy said. He lifted himself from his chair behind the desk.

'Yeah, that's it,' echoed Walsh. 'See ya next week, okay?'

'Okay,' Sullivan said deadpan as he strode out of the office.

An hour and a half later Jimmy Sullivan was still directing the unloading of the Italian freighter when he spotted a black Model-T Ford pulling up to the dock. He concentrated his gaze on the three husky men who climbed out of the car and strolled toward him.

'You run the dock?' asked the one with blond hair neatly combed back from his narrow forehead. He had large, cold blue eyes and thin lips that twisted into a mean-looking smile when he spoke.

'Who are you? What do you want?' Jimmy demanded, annoyed at the interruption.

'I'm Willie,' the answer came.

A squat five-foot-seven, 170-pounder, Willie 'Two-Knife' Altierri carried the secret of where perhaps as many as thirty bodies were buried. None were in cemeteries. The final resting places were in weed-covered culverts, hastily dug shallow graves along the shoulders of deserted highways, and under the concrete poured for newly built roads. He was responsible for most of them. He was one of Brooklyn's most feared underworld hit men.

Willie Altierri's specialty was performed with two slivers of steel, never less than six inches long. He carried them in leather scabbards strapped to his waist by a thin leather belt. The knives were as much a part of Willie's body as any of his vital organs. Altierri couldn't function without the knives; it felt unnatural not to have the knives on him. He wore them when he slept.

There were times when Willie had to part with one of his knives; that was when, inadvertently or otherwise, he had plunged the blade so deeply into his victim that he couldn't pull it out. His technique had much to do with the high replacement rate for the tools of his trade. Willie invariably went for the heart and lungs, but he was seldom satisfied to merely stick the knife in and yank it out. He had a compulsion to twist the handle while the blade was still in his prey because it gave him special delight inflicting the horrendous pain that extra turn of the wrist caused his victim to suffer. But that technique very often got the blade caught in the rib cage and no amount of pulling could extricate it. So Willie would have to inter the victim with the knife embedded in the corpse.

Only once, it was said, did Willie lose both knives in carrying out an assignment for the Black Hand mob. That was when he knocked off Mario 'Greaseball' Pignatore, one of the gang's own. It was a very special rubout because Pignatore was suspected of squealing on the gang to save his own skin.

Detectives from Brooklyn's Butler Street squad had grabbed him from behind the wheel of a hijacked truck loaded with Fisk whitewall tires being delivered to the Bush Terminal docks for shipment to England. Mario's release on a piddling $500 bail by Magistrate Thomas Gibson was a dead giveaway that the Greaseball had become a pigeon for the Kings County District Attorney's office. No hijacker caught as red-handed as Pignatore ever broke away from arraignment for less than $10,000 bail. But that wasn't the only giveaway that the Greaseball might have become a canary.

One afternoon, one of Frankie Yale's boys, Joe 'Squats' Esposito, who worked inside keeping the books for the Mob, caught sight of Pignatore coming out of the elevator of the County Court Building in downtown Brooklyn. There was only one place that Squats figured Pignatore could have been in that building: the D.A.'s office. Perhaps even the grand jury room.

Mario Pignatore immediately became the very special referral for the honor of extinction which Altierri dispensed so professionally. And this extermination had to stand as an example to all the other members of the Mob. So Willie made it a showcase production. He not only jammed both knives into the Greaseball's ribs and twisted them; he added a novel and ritualistic touch by breaking the handles off while the blades were still buried in Mario. These were then presented to Frankie Yale as mementoes of that significant execution.

Yale had the handles mounted on a shiny foot-square mahogany board that had been beveled and made to look like a plaque, and it was hung on the wall of Yale's garage office at Fourth Avenue and Second Street in the borough's Red Hook section. A gold nameplate engraved by a local jeweler carried a simple but meaningful message to all who pilgrimaged to Yale's office on social or business calls:

IN MEMORY OF THE GREASEBALL

The jeweller who performed this engraving, gratuitously of course, was Robert Corn, whose store was on the east side of Columbia Street, between President and Union Streets, in downtown Brooklyn. Outside his store on the sidewalk next to the curb was a fifteen-foot-tall cast iron clock that was a landmark for more than a half century.

It was under this clock that the members of the organised crime gangs conducted their public assemblages for purposes of assigning 'hits' or whatever other business had to be dealt with in the protection rackets, bootlegging, and the other illegalities the Mob was engaged in. Standing there beside that sidewalk timepiece many of the roaring, raging episodes of Mob violence were masterminded or hatched by the Mob braintrusts.

'Two-Knife' was never long in getting a replacement when he lost a knife in the line of duty. For the distance between an empty scabbard on Willie's waist and the next knife that would supplant the one abandoned in a victim's rib cage was as far away as the trunk of his shiny black Model-T Ford. The brown leather suitcase that Willie kept in the back of his car didn't contain a wardrobe for travel, although he often took out-of-town assignments to Newark, New Jersey, Wilmington, Delaware, or Springfield, Massachusetts, among the other locales.

The suitcase kept his supply of knives near at hand. He never allowed the stock to dwindle to less than a dozen blades. When he ran that low, Altierri would put everything aside and drive to the Bowery in Lower Manhattan, where all the wholesale restaurant and hotel supply houses were situated, and replenish his store with a couple of dozen shiny paring knives used by butchers and chefs.

Jimmy Sullivan knew none of this that Monday afternoon when he first encountered the Black Hand's chief executioner. When Willie gave his name to the pier superintendent, the impatient Sullivan barked at him, 'What the hell do you want with me?'

Joe 'Rackets' Capolla and Joe 'Big Beef' Polusi flanked Willie in his confrontation with the pier boss. That didn't seem to faze Sullivan. He made no attempt to size up either the short, broad-shouldered Capolla, who in his mid-thirties already had the look of middle age, or Polusi, whose body build on a frame almost six feet tall made him look like the dockworker he'd been until the Black Hand recruited him as an enforcer.

Irritation burned in Jimmy Sullivan's intolerant stomach. He had a built-in prejudice against anyone Italian, and a mere glance at the trio that had interrupted his work routine grated him into an attitude of total belligerence.

'Get it over with, Mac,' Sullivan said raspily. 'I got too much work to do. Tell me what business you got coming to this dock.'

Altierri's hands fidgeted. He unbuttoned his heavy black overcoat, slipped his hands underneath, and placed them over his suit jacket around his waist. Sullivan could not know why Two-Knife's fingers were drumming nervously. Nor had he any awareness of the scabbards and the deadly instruments hidden under Willie's jacket.

'We come to ask you something,' Willie finally said slowly, every word measured and uttered with restraint. It was the way he spoke when his anger was aroused. Sullivan's gruff attitude didn't endear him to his visitors.

'Whaddaya want to ask me?' he snapped. 'I'm waiting. Ask me.'

Willie pointed toward the door of Sullivan's office.

'In there, if you'll be so kind,' Willie said. 'This is private.' His voice was commanding now. Sullivan wasn't frightened, but he sensed the authority that Willie carried. This guy and his pals were after something. Maybe it was a good idea to listen to why the hell they were there.

'All right,' the superintendent submitted. 'Haul your asses in there and I'll be with you. I got a couple things to do so my schedule doesn't get fucked up.'

Altierri, Polusi, and Capolla made their way into the office. Sullivan went back to the dock and checked on the progress his longshoremen were making. He glanced up at the sky and shook his head in disgust. It was starting to snow. He shouted commands. 'Hey, let's move it! We got to get these crates into the warehouse before we get buried under! Hurry it up!'

The forecast was for six to eight inches. The snow had not been expected until nightfall. But it had already begun, and Sullivan was afraid it would be a bigger storm. It would take at least another three hours to clear the freighter's hold, and the only way that could be done was by riding the men relentlessly.

Now he had an interruption. Those three Italians in his office, waiting to talk with him. About what? Well, he told himself resignedly, he'd go in and get it over with.

As they reached the office entrance, he turned for one last look at the dock. The crews were hustling, just as he wanted them to. Okay. The instant he slammed the door shut, Big Beef Polusi slipped behind him and turned the lock.

'What the hell you doing that for?' Sullivan demanded, whirling around and reaching to unlock the door. Before he could touch the lock, a piece of cold steel was slapped against the back of his hand.

'You want to lose some fingers, you put your fuckin' hand on that lock,' Altierri scowled.

Sullivan was courageous but he wasn't stupid. He didn't survive the Marne and Belleau Woods battles by scrambling out of the trenches and charging blindly into the Krauts' machine-gun nests. A well-aimed grenade was a much more sensible way to destroy the enemy than stupid bravery. The situation right now didn't differ from the battlefront. Sullivan was surrounded by the enemy.

Capolla, Polusi, and Altierri hadn't yet told the superintendent their business, but Jimmy had a good idea what he was up against. Big Beef and Rackets hadn't even introduced themselves by name to Sullivan, but the .38-caliber automatics they were pointing at him announced their occupations more clearly than the fanciest calling cards they could have presented.

Altierri had told Sullivan his first name was Willie, but no one had to tell him Willie's nickname after that introduction. The whack of steel against his hand followed instantly by the thrust of another sharply pointed blade against the side of his thick neck signalled to Sullivan in the clearest terms that he was up against a two-knife killer.

'Okay, tell me what you want,' Sullivan said. His voice was more respectful, meeker.

'We gonna give you protection because we hear somebody is gonna put the torch to this warehouse tonight,' Altierri said through clenched teeth. 'You catch?'

'What kind of protection?' Sullivan asked, not really surprised. 'We already have protection from Denny Meehan –'

Altierri, who had been holding the flat side of his knife against Sullivan's neck, suddenly turned the blade and pressed its razor-sharp cutting edge into the skin. The dock boss was gripped by palpable terror.

'Meehan can't protect you no more,' Altierri wheezed. 'That's why Frankie Yale sent me to see you. He wants you to buy insurance from him from now on.'

Altierri dug the edge of the knife deeper into the fold of Sullivan's neck. Jimmy knew that the slightest movement on his part would slit his throat down to his jugular.

'Look, gimme a break,' Sullivan pleaded, his voice almost a whisper. 'Take that knife away and let's talk this out . . .'

'No talk!' Altierri bellowed. 'We here to make deal. We make deal right away. You ready?'

'Yeah, yeah,' stammered Sullivan. 'But there's something I got to tell you first.'

Two-Knife relaxed the pressure. He turned the flat side of the blade against Sullivan's neck again.

'What you wanna say?' Altierri pressed.

'I gotta get the okay from my boss,' Sullivan said.

'Where is he?' demanded Altierri.

'At the home office – over on Pier 9.'

'You know the number or you want me to give you it?' Altierri asked snidely.

'Sure – sure I know it.'

'Then you call him right away, eh?'

'Okay, okay . . .'

Altierri took the knife away from Sullivan's neck and let him walk to his desk. Jimmy sat in the chair and picked up the phone.

'Operator, gimme President 0321,' he said nervously.

When O'Hara got on the line Sullivan explained what was going on.

'They're gonna kill me, John,' he said. 'They're also gonna burn the warehouse tonight . . .'

O'Hara was reluctant to capitulate but he could sense that his pier superintendent's life was in imminent peril. He asked what the 'insurance policy' would cost, a detail Sullivan had neglected to learn in his fright.

'The boss wants to know how much?' Sullivan said to Altierri.

'Two thousand a week,' Willie replied without looking up. He had holstered one of the knives by now and was cleaning his fingernails with the point of the other one.

Sullivan relayed the information to O'Hara. O'Hara hit the ceiling.

'Mr O'Hara says Denny Meehan is only getting fifteen hundred right now,' Sullivan told Altierri.

Willie stopped picking his nails. He edged over to Sullivan, wiped the point of the knife on the shoulder of Jimmy's red plaid lumber jacket, then stuck the knife against the flesh of his neck.

'Tell Mr O'Hara Meehan's policy doesn't cover death and fire,' Altierri said with a laugh that was joined in by Polusi and Capolla, who were standing in front of the desk with their guns still pointed at Sullivan.

The pier boss relayed Altierri's answer to O'Hara.

There was a long pause. Suddenly Sullivan's face brightened.

'He said okay,' Sullivan told Altierri. 'The money will be here tomorrow.'

'Smart man, that Mr O'Hara,' Willie smiled, taking the knife away from Sullivan's neck and slipping it into the empty scabbard at his waist.

'All right, all right!' He turned scoldingly to Capolla and Polusi, who had their gun barrels still trained on Sullivan. 'Dinja hear? They bought the policy. Put those heaters away, goddam ya!'

Altierri stuck his hand out to Sullivan. 'We shake,' he said. 'We make a good deal and now we be friends, right?'

Sullivan's stomach turned as he shook Altierri's hand, which felt soft and delicate, almost like a woman's.

Sullivan unlocked the door and led the pack of Black Handers out of the office. The snow was falling so heavily now that the booms and cranes were obliterated from view.

'Somebody come tomorrow for the first premium,' Altierri said before walking off with Polusi and Capolla to the parked Ford. 'Two o'clock sharp . . .'

'Yeah,' grumbled Sullivan as he headed out on the dock. More than anything now he wanted to speed up the unloading before the storm crippled operations.

At two o'clock the next afternoon, activity on Pier 2 was at a standstill. The snow had stopped falling several hours ago, but the eleven-inch white blanket had wrought total paralysis. While Sullivan had managed to get the freighter unloaded and the last of the cargo stacked in the warehouse early the previous evening, none of the cargo was on its way to the consignee. The storm had played havoc with traffic and not a single truck rolled onto Pier 2 that day.

The depth of the snow on the city's streets did not deter Benjamin 'Crazy Benny' Pazzo, Frankie Yale's ace 'collector', from reaching Gowanus Stevedoring's pier at two o'clock sharp. Nothing less was expected since Joe 'Frenchy' Carlino was driving the car. The number one wheelman in the Black Hand's ranks, Frenchy could be trusted to tool passengers to their destinations through fog and rain and sleet and driving snow. No element of nature could prevent Frenchy from making his appointed rounds.

His vehicle on this particular afternoon was a black Cadillac limousine, Frankie Yale's personal car. Frankie had put it at his henchmen's disposal because of the significance of their mission.

This was the Black Hand's first important breakthrough against Denny Meehan's gang in the brief war for control of Brooklyn's waterfront rackets. Although Frankie Yale had made progress in his attempt to break up the Irish underworld's hold on the docks, none of his gang's advances had achieved as dramatic a turn as the coup scored against Gowanus Stevedoring.

This, Yale felt, was to be a turning point in his drive to seize power on the lucrative waterfront from the White Hand gang. A $2,000-a-week payoff from Gowanus Stevedoring certainly was a signal step.

There was a hush on Pier 2 as Crazy Benny left the Cadillac and made his way to Sullivan's office. Even Denny Meehan and his two executioners in their somber black coats and black fedoras acted as though they didn't wish to disturb his tracks, for they walked alongside him, leaving their own impressions in the snow of their ripple-soled snap-buckle galoshes.

Three hundred and twenty-five feet: that was the distance to the end of the pier where the oil-slick East River rushes by in a seeming hurry to carry into Upper New York Bay tin cans, bottles, broken crates, and the rest of the garbage people dump into the water. Crazy Benny's last walk ended at the very ledge overlooking the water.

It is believed the expression, 'Why don't you take a long walk off a short pier?' evolved from this episode.

Crazy Benny made no attempt to postpone his death. He didn't want to die. He was afraid to die. But he also must have known how useless any plea would be. He faced his death with a grim look as Denny Meehan's executioners opened fire. The first .45 slugs tore through his overcoat and plowed into his chest. Benny slumped into the snow, his face expressionless. His eyelids closed. He was a man who seemed to have gone to sleep in the snow.

Few seconds were wasted. With a practiced motion the two executioners holstered their revolvers that had pumped fourteen bullets into Benny's body, then bent over, picked up Crazy Benny's body, and hurled it into the river with the deftness of longshoremen pitching a bale of fertiliser into an unloading net.

Benny's body floated several seconds on the surface amid the whitecaps. Its buoyancy lasted only as long as it took the water to soak into his heavy woollen overcoat. And then it disappeared into the murky surf. His body would not rise again until the gases that inevitably form by fermentation after death filled it like a balloon and brought it bobbing up to the surface once more.

'Very neat work, boys,' Denny Meehan praised his lieutenants of death. They were two of the most reliable gats in the White Hand organisation, William 'Wild Bill' Lovett and Richard 'Peg-leg' Lonergan.

Lovett cast a curious eye on the flattened snow where Benny had lain.

'Funny,' he said, 'there isn't a drop of blood. Do you think the guy ever bled . . .?'

As they walked back toward Furman Street, Meehan, Lovett, and Lonergan sloshed over the footsteps they'd made in the snow bringing 'Crazy Benny' to the end of the dock. They didn't disturb Benny's tracks. When they returned to the street, Meehan called Jimmy Sullivan out of his office.

'Com'ere. Jimmy,' Denny said. 'I wanna show you something.'

He took the pier boss to the dock and pointed at the only pair of footsteps that were still clearly visible in the snow.

Sullivan glanced at the impressions of what must have been a size-ten snowboot making one-way tracks the length of the pier.

'Crazy Benny ain't coming back this way,' Meehan said, slapping Sullivan on the back.

'I'll light a candle for him,' the superintendent remarked, and walked back to his office. He despised Meehan and the whole White Hand, but he was grateful for the service they had performed for Gowanus Stevedoring.

Frankie Yale was fit to be tied. He banged his fist savagely on the desktop in his garage office. Frenchy Carlino expected this reaction. The big coup that Willie Altierri had accomplished only the day before at Gowanus Stevedoring had been wiped out by Denny Meehan's swift, stunning reprisal.

Frenchy had been able to get back to the boss alive and well because of the head start Crazy Benny had gotten in leaving the car. That sixty-second delay gave Frenchy just the time needed to spot Denny Meehan and the two torpedoes approaching Benny. In fact, Frenchy saw the White Hand leader and his confederates even before they had turned the corner of the warehouse, which was when Benny first became aware of them. But it had been too late to shout a warning to Benny. So Frenchy took the only sensible turn under the circumstances: he drove away as quickly as he could, leaving Benny to his fate.

If Frankie Yale had any doubt as to what became of Crazy Benny, it was erased by the headlines of the morning newspapers of Saturday 10 January:

Benny's body had been trawled out of the Lower Bay off Hamilton Parkway in Brooklyn's Bay Ridge section, about ten miles from where the corpse was dumped.

The autopsy showed Benny had been struck by fourteen bullets, six of them had gone through the heart.

The newspaper accounts of Crazy Benny's demise were also read over at Denny Meehan's second-floor offices in a garage on Baltic Street. Denny Meehan and his boys grinned from ear to ear.

'I always said Crazy Benny had a stout heart,' Meehan laughed uproariously. 'With six bullets in it . . . hey, that gotta be a very stout heart.'

Levity had no place at Frankie Yale's office. Frankie mouthed maledictions at Denny Meehan for almost an hour, helped by a chorus of curses uttered by Two-Knife, Big Beef, Rackets, and some of his other boys.

Finally, Yale walked over to the plaque with the two broken knife handles.

'I swear on this fuckin' squealer's grave,' Yale snarled, slamming his fist into the wall. 'If Denny Meehan wants war, that's what the fuck he'll get!'

Chapter 3

'Buona Sera, Signore . . .'

A mean March wind whipped in from Gowanus Bay, an icy reminder that one of New York's worst winters was reluctant to make its departure.

Nine weeks had gone by since Frankie Yale had sworn vengeance on Denny Meehan. That was far too much time to let pass without having dispatched the White Hand gang's leader to another world, as the Black Hand boss had vowed to do.

Some of Frankie's lieutenants were getting restless, but he didn't become aware of that until his little brother, Anthony, jogged his memory.

'Hey, Frankie,' Anthony said through widely spaced teeth that produced a whistle when he spoke. 'What do you think if we have a little meeting to figure out that thing which has been bothering . . .?'

'What thing?' Frankie interrupted, glaring at his ugly-faced brother. Frankie abhorred that habit of Tony's – talking about 'that thing' as if other people could read his mind and know what he meant.

'I'm talking about Denny Meehan.' Tony laughed to ease the tension he'd created by raising the subject. Figuring out a fitting finale for the White Hand chieftain's lease on mortality was something that had been grating on Frankie day and night since Crazy Benny's leaded corpse had been fished out of the Lower Bay.

'You got some ideas, smart brother?' Frankie demanded gruffly. He began swiveling impatiently in the desk chair.

'Don't get mad, Frankie,' Tony whined. Ever since they were kids, Frankie, the handsome son of the Domenico Ioele family, was Tony's unrelentingly tyrannical adversary. Frankie had always poked fun at Tony's gap-toothed mouth and his crooked, hooked nose, and Tony, who was three years younger and still three inches shorter than Frankie, simply took the abuse. He was too frightened of Frankie's strength to fight back with fists or words.

Yet Frankie harbored an undemonstrated respect for his smaller brother because of his value in the organisation. Frankie counted on Tony as the sounding board for the gang, who seemed inclined to confide their complaints to him.

So Frankie's upbraiding of Tony for bringing up 'that thing', was more theatrical than real, but that was Frankie's style.

Of course, his question wasn't answered when he wanted to know if Tony had any ideas. Tony had never been allowed to think for himself. Yet Tony's suggestion that they hold a meeting was deeply significant to Frankie.

Since Tony never had an idea in his life, the thought obviously had come from some of the boys in the mob.

'So they're getting restless, eh?' he asked Tony with a demanding stare. 'They want me to move, is that it?'

'Yeah ... yeah, Frankie ... that's kinda what the picture is like ... you know what I mean?' Tony stammered, relieved that his brother had not made it hotter for him.

For several seconds, Frankie glared at Tony as he kept swiveling in his chair. Then he stopped abruptly and leaned forward, his face creased as though in pain, elbows resting on the desk, and hands clasped tightly together.

Tony recognised the pose. Frankie always struck it when he was on the verge of some monumental pronouncement.

'I want you, little brother, to get your ass out of here,' Yale began slowly, each word forced through tightly drawn lips. 'I

29

want you to go get hold of Two-Knife and have him come see me right away.'

Tony was out of the door as though he'd been fired from a rifle. He responded with swift and unswerving obedience to every command from Frankie, for Tony wanted nothing more out of life than to be his brother's loyal lackey. The fear Frankie instilled in Tony early on had made his demeaning subservience a part of his nature.

Twenty minutes passed. At 2:45 p.m. Willie Altierri walked into Yale's office and stood stiffly in front of Frankie's desk. Willie curled his lips in a half-smile.

'Don't give me that shit-eatin' grin, Willie,' Yale said sharply. 'Wait till you hear what we're gonna do. Go over there and sit down.'

Yale pointed to the chair beside his desk. Two-Knife walked over and settled himself squarely on the hard wooden seat. He crossed his legs and lit a cigarette with a trembling hand. Altierri always shook like a vibrator in Yale's presence. Even though he was a killer without peer. Two-Knife was terrified of Frankie, although not for the same reasons that had made Frankie's younger brother so slavishly submissive to him. To Willie, Frankie Yale represented power – the ugliest kind of power, which could dispatch other exterminators upon him if he ever made a mistake or pulled a double-cross.

Two-Knife exercised extreme care to stay on Frankie's good side. Much as he relished carving a victim into eternity, Willie had an awesome fear of his own death.

Altierri blew a puff of smoke up to the ceiling and turned to Yale, who was scribbling names on a piece of note paper. When he finished, he pushed the sheet toward Willie and asked him to read it. The names included his own, Tony Yale, Augie 'The Wop' Pisano, Don Giuseppe Balsamo, the *caporegime* in the Red Hook sector's Little Italy, known affectionately as 'Battista', after John the Baptist, and Balsamo's personal bodyguards, Vincenzo Mangano and Johnny 'Silk Stocking' Guistra.

'What time you want the meeting, Frankie?' Altierri's eyes lit up. Without being told, Two-Knife could feel in his bones that Yale was marshaling the troops for a hit on Denny Meehan.

Frankie was in the habit of making out a list such as this when he wanted to hold a council of his top lieutenants on important business. And the killing of the Irish gang's top dog was the only matter of any importance that could warrant convening that particular group of leaders.

As a rule, it was Altierri's job to round up the men when Frankie wanted them for a meeting. Yale never had to tell Altierri where the gathering would be held. Without exception, all such high-echelon Black Hand get-togethers took place in the Adonis Club overlooking Gowanus Bay on Twentieth Street. The Adonis was run by Fury Argolia – when he wasn't engaged in the more violent pursuits of his underworld calling.

Meeting there, the gang could also participate in the ultimate pleasantry of stuffing their stomachs with some of the finest Sicilian gastronomic delights this side of Palermo. Many an Italian family from as far away as the Bronx and even the eastern fork of Long Island preferred to book a wedding reception at the Adonis rather than the Astor because of the mouth-watering cuisine whipped up by Argolia's master chefs.

Two-Knife had just one question for Yale.

'What time you want them?' he asked.

'If they wanna eat, tell them to be there at eight,' Frankie replied with a flamboyant gesture. 'Fury's getting up a good spread. But the meeting is ten sharp, you tell them.'

Yale suddenly shot a look through the partly opened door. He had heard a stealthy movement on the stair landing outside the office.

'What the hell you doing there sneaking around corners?' he roared. 'Come in here so Willie can tell you to your face what you're supposed to know, ya creep!'

Tony Yale flew into the room and bounded over to Altierri who, knees crossed, was ditching his cigarette in the ashtray. Thoroughly cowed, Tony mumbled to Two-Knife, 'What's for me . . . tell me.'

Willie told him, then rose from the chair and left the room without another word. Tony shadowed him down the stairs.

The Adonis Club's wooden and shaky-legged tables were so antiquated that even the red-and-white checkered table-cloths

31

couldn't hide their condition. The chairs had cane seats and backs so badly shredded that matrons at banquets invariably got their silk gowns shorn on the rough edges. The walls and ceilings were decorated with murals that combined religious figures and scenes of Mount Vesuvius and the Coliseum. The murals were executed in 1912 by an immigrant Florentine artist who gorged himself on Fury Argolia's food and drink while he painted and was paid nothing. He had been in hock to the Black Hand's loan sharks, who had wanted to kill him until Fury Argolia interceded with a merciful plan to have 'Michelangelo', as the artist was cynically nicknamed, work his debt off with paint and brush at the Adonis Club.

Argolia never expected a Sistine Chapel, but the Florentine came perilously close to giving the waterfront social club such a pseudo-appearance.

If the atmosphere inside the club left something to be desired, the outside was worse. The buildings along the rest of the block were prime candidates for a slum-clearance program; the grimy façade of the Adonis itself was no invitation to good dining. Worse still was the rotten-egg aroma that wafted from the shore at every low tide on Gowanus Bay.

It was 8:10 p.m. on 15 March when Frankie Yale arrived at the Adonis Club in his black limousine, chauffeured by his brother Tony. Riding with Frankie in the back seat was Willie Altierri.

A second car, a maroon Pierce Arrow, bearing Don Giuseppe Balsamo and his two bodyguards, Mangano and Guistra, pulled alongside the curb right behind Yale's limo.

'Hey, *compare*!' Yale greeted Balsamo as he stepped out of the car, throwing his arms affectionately around the beefy Red Hook gangland boss. 'How's the family? How's my little godchild?'

Yale had become Balsamo's infant daughter's godfather the previous summer. By then the menace of the White Hand gang's retaliation upon the Black Hand's newly acquired territories had become reality. Balsamo's continued control of the Little Italy sector in Red Hook was a vital factor in the impending war with Denny Meehan and his army of killers.

Yale had looked upon Balsamo as a weak link in the organisation. He felt that while Don Giuseppe still maintained control over his area, he was losing some of his power in the territory. Perhaps, Frankie thought, at the age of forty-eight Don Giuseppe was becoming complacent.

But Balsamo's past record as a boss in the Black Hand was exemplary, and Yale felt there was no reason Don Giuseppe couldn't regain all of his old power in Red Hook. But something had to be done to reinvigorate Balsamo – to give him a greater sense of 'belonging' in the Black Hand family.

So when Don Giuseppe's wife, Nancy, who was forty-five years old and a grandmother seven times, brought home their ninth child, a daughter named Gina, Frankie Yale decided to infuse the spirit he thought Balsamo needed by offering to be little Gina's godfather.

Yale's ploy worked wonders. In the eight months since the christening, Balsamo's sector accounted for three 'accidental' deaths of White Hand mobsters. They were all killed in identical fashion: by the booms of cranes that crushed their skulls while they were standing on the Gowanus docks extracting tribute from the pier operators.

Followed by his entourage, Frankie Yale strolled into the Adonis Club, his arm still around Balsamo. A familiar voice greeted them:

'Good evening, gentlemen, we have prepared a banquet to satisfy a king.'

Fury Argolia laughed as he mouthed the words, perhaps because he had sensed how trite they were. Yet the six-foot-long smorgasbord table on which the Italian feast had been spread was anything but laughable.

'*Mamma mia!*' Yale enthused as he gazed at the table. 'This is unbelievable.'

The table groaned under the weight of forty platters of food, including seven selections of salad, a seemingly endless variety of antipasto, lasagne, baked clams, calamari, veal rollatini, and many other choice preparations. A side table had been loaded with more than a dozen bottles of fine Italian wine.

'Eat up, boys,' Yale said. 'Eat good. We got lots of time to talk business.'

They gorged themselves on the epicurean spread for two hours. Then the meeting was convened.

33

Frankie Yale stood up. The room became quiet.

'What we are here for is to decide how we are going to get rid of Denny Meehan,' he said somberly. 'Now let me hear from you the ideas . . .'

'What ideas you got, boss?' asked Balsamo.

The question caught Frankie by surprise. But he had a reply.

'I was figuring maybe we hit the mick bastard when he's leaving his favourite hangout, the Strand Dance Hall,' Yale offered.

'He's gonna be protected by his bodyguards when he goes to the Strand,' Balsamo suggested. 'Besides, we should try to do it without witnesses.'

'I agree! I agree!' Augie the Wop called out. 'We make it a nice private execution. It will have the same effect because those dirty micks will know that it was us who gave it to Denny.'

Yale scowled at the lieutenants who had poured water on his plan. The silence in the room was heavy. Frankie probably knew that his idea was precipitate, but he wasn't about to admit it. Doing the number on Denny at the Strand was, in fact, something that had come off the top of his head. The fact was that while he had had more than two months to mastermind the execution, he wasn't yet able to make up his mind as to just where Meehan should be gunned down.

Finally, he snickered in amusement and broke the silence.

'All right, you wiseasses, if you wanna do it private tell me how you're gonna pull it off,' he challenged. 'Do you wanna invite him to come over to one of your houses or something like that . . .?'

'Better than that, Frankie,' Altierri snapped, jumping out of his chair. 'We're gonna burn him in his own house.'

'You crazy?' Yale pounced on Two-Knife.

'Listen, Frankie,' Altierri cut in, his enthusiasm increasing visibly. 'It's gonna be a setup. One of his own boys will help us –'

'Madonn'!' Yale exclaimed. He took in Altierri with a level, measured gaze. 'Now I know you're loco. What you say, Willie, we gonna get an Irisher to help us?' He shook his head in disgust.

'Yeah, that's right,' Altierri persisted, undaunted by Yale's put-down. 'Let me tell you why, okay?'

34

Yale was still shaking his head. 'Speak – but make it fast. We don't have time to listen to such shit.'

'It ain't shit, Frankie,' Two-Knife protested. 'Because . . . you know that Patrick Foley – well, he's . . . in my pocket.'

Now the words came out of Altierri's mouth hesitantly and in a whisper. He looked apprehensively at Yale and the others because he sensed how suspicious they had suddenly become. How could he have a White Hander 'in his pocket'?

'Lemme explain,' Altierri said defensively. 'You see . . . Foley . . . well, he's . . . been dating my sister.'

The statement hit the gathering like a shot.

'You better make this real good, Willie,' Augie the Wop murmured under his breath.

'I'm telling ya the truth,' Altierri stammered nervously. He forced a smile. 'It's a real hot romance. I didn't know about it until last Christmas when he came over to the house. I almost shit when I saw him there. Then I found out he was going with Sally for a whole year. Foley wants to marry her . . .'

'And Denny Meehan wants to give the bride away, right Willie?' Yale interrupted hoarsely, his glare now more intense.

The sarcasm irritated Altierri. His thin lips pressed together in an angry line. 'Goddamn you, Frankie, what the fuck am I to do if my sister goes with Foley? I got no control over that. But what I'm trying to tell you is I had a talk with Foley and he told me he was fed up with Meehan and some of the other boys. He wants to call it quits. He swore to me that he was going legit . . .'

'Did he kiss you, Willie?' Balsamo wanted to know.

'I don't get you, Don Giuseppe,' Altierri said, puzzled.

'Because,' Balsamo said slowly, 'you shouldn't let nobody jerk you off without kissing you.'

'All right, let's cut the friggin' crap!' Yale snapped, pounding his fist on the table. 'We don't forgive Willie for letting his sister hook up with a mick, but if that's gonna help get Meehan in a setup, I wanna hear how.'

Turning to Altierri with a benevolent smile, he demanded, 'Draw us a picture, Willie.'

Altierri sighed, relieved. 'I told you I talked to Foley. He filled me in on the layout of Denny Meehan's flat on Warren Street.

Believe me, I pumped him plenty and I got a pretty good picture of the place. Denny and his wife live on the second floor in the back. What makes this a real trap is they got a window which looks out into the hall. What better do you want? Somebody goes to the window when Denny's in bed and puts him to sleep permanent.'

'You kill his wife, too?' Balsamo wanted to know, his interest now aroused.

'We don't have to,' Altierri replied casually. 'But if she's gonna happen to see what's happening . . . well, what you gonna do? Too bad, that's all. So Denny has a wife with him when he goes to heaven . . .'

'I like it, Willie,' Yale said, nodding his head. 'Very good. Smart boy. We have a drink and make a toast to your beautiful mind. You are a genius.'

As Yale poured red wine into everyone's glass, Altierri turned to him to solicit more praise. 'You don't think I'm crazy anymore, eh, Frankie?'

'A genius, I called you, a genius you are, Willie,' Yale said as he lifted his glass for the salute to Two-Knife. 'Here's to Willie, *viva* Willie!'

Everyone joined in the toast, which was followed by several moments of banter – mostly questions about Anita and Foley: how they met, and how Altierri's sister managed to keep the boyfriend a secret from Willie for so long. Yale put an end to the small talk soon enough. He was itching to get on with the plot to execute Denny.

'What boys go on this job?' Yale asked. 'Any volunteers?'

Sure, Frankie,' Balsamo said quickly. He turned to Johnny 'Silk Stocking' Guistra, who was seated next to him, and wound a fat arm around the slender bodyguard whose nickname came from the unique way he dispatched his victims into their next life. Guistra didn't believe in stabbing or shooting a condemned man, because he had no tolerance for the sight of blood. He believed strangulation was a potent yet pleasant way to put people out of the way. And the tool of his trade was a silk stocking.

'It's soft and pleasing to the touch,' he'd say. 'I wrap the stocking around the neck and I whisper, "Bye, bye, sleep tight".

I never got one complaint from any customer. It work every time.'

Being selected by his boss to be one of the hit men pleased Guistra, who turned to Balsamo and smiled, '*Grazie*, Don Giuseppe, I will not let you down.'

'Who else you say, Frankie?' Balsamo prodded Yale.

'I been thinking,' Yale replied. 'You are very generous to offer Johnny and I appreciate. But this ain't a silk-stocking job if we go by what Willie said. If Denny Meehan gets it through the hallway window, we need a gun. But that doesn't mean we don't use Johnny. He goes, but only to show the way and make sure there's no fuckup.'

Yale leaned back in his chair, and gazed at the murals on the ceiling.

'Hey, whatever happened to Michelangelo?' he asked, lowering his head and looking purposefully at Fury Argolia.

'Couple of years ago he went to Cleveland,' Argolia replied. 'I don't know if he's still there. Why?'

'I like that you mentioned Cleveland,' Yale smiled. 'That is where my thoughts are now . . .'

'Hey, Frankie!' Augie Pisano blurted as he caught onto what Yale was driving at.

'You *capish*, eh, Augie?' Yale said, pleased at his lieutenant's alertness.

'What an idea, Frankie,' Pisano chortled. 'Two of the best hit men in the business – Ralphie DeSarno and Giovanni Sciacca! Oh, you are using your head, Signore Yale!'

That was Frankie Yale's cue. He stood up and bowed slowly from the waist. The gathering clapped enthusiastically.

'Please,' Yale smiled, extending the palms of his hands, 'no more applause.' Then he sat down and asked everyone to pay close attention to what he had to say.

'I wanna have a real good laugh on Denny Meehan when this comes off,' Yale began, his face lighting up at the thought of what he was planning. 'We burn him April first and what a laugh we all gonna have on that Irish son of a bitch.' Yale smacked his lips as if savoring a tasty morsel of pasta. 'I'm gonna send him an April Fool's card. And you know what I'm writing to him?'

Yale looked around impatiently for an answer. There was none.

'It's going to say on the card, "*Buona sera, signore*",' Yale said, bellowing with laughter. The others joined in.

When the snickering subsided, Pisano said, 'Frankie, that mick bastard don't understand Italian.'

'That's my little joke, Augie,' Yale parried with a distinct edge of pleasure in his voice. 'His wife reads Italian. She translates for him. But he don't know even then what the fuck the message is all about – until after he go to bed. Then he find out because, for sure, it's gonna be for him, Good night, mister . . .'

Shortly before six o'clock on the evening of 31 March, Willie Altierri and Augie Pisano posted themselves near Gate 16 in Grand Central Station to await the arrival of the Spirit of St Louis, one of the era's crack cross-country trains. They had checked at the information desk and were told the train bringing DeSarno and Sciacca from Cleveland was on time.

At exactly 6:10 p.m. the passengers began emerging from the gate – the two killers among them. Altierri didn't know DeSarno and Sciacca, but Pisano did: he had performed a contract killing in 1917 in Columbus with them.

Pisano nudged Altierri. 'There they are,' he said just as DeSarno and Sciacca spotted him. They greeted each other with warm handshakes.

Pisano introduced Two-Knife, and the Brooklyn mobsters escorted their Cleveland brothers out of the marble terminal to a black Packard sedan parked on Vanderbilt Avenue with the motor running. Frenchy Carlino was in the driver's seat. Yale had assigned Frenchy to chauffeur the assassins to Warren Street when they paid their visit to Denny Meehan.

But the exact hour for Meehan's execution was still unsettled. The timetable couldn't be plotted until Denny and his wife had departed the Strand Dance Hall, their nightly hangout. A pair of spotters had been staked out near the Strand to phone Yale the instant Meehan and his wife left; another two henchmen had been planted on Warren Street to report when the couple arrived home.

The messages were relayed to Frankie via Fury Argolia's private office number at the Adonis Club. Yale ordered this arrangement, because he wanted DeSarno and Sciacca brought to the club for final pre-execution briefing. And he wanted to show the hired guns good fellowship; Argolia had been prevailed upon to have another banquet table of his finest food and drink prepared.

It was mostly chitchat during the period given over for eating. Then the sudden switch in Frankie's mood dictated the change in the tenor of the conversation.

One of the means by which Yale had ascended to the leadership of the Black Hand gang had been the demonstration of his ability to keep iron-fisted control over his men. He fought, bullied, even killed his way to the top. And he retained his grip on the leadership because he never let down the post of the tough guy, the man in charge.

Thus, when DeSarno and Sciacca had been feted and were filled with Fury's epicurean enticements, Frankie Yale quickly transformed the hail-fellow-well-met atmosphere into one of deadly seriousness.

'I want to see your pieces,' Yale demanded of the Cleveland sharpshooters. 'I gotta make sure they're in shape.'

He tapped his finger on the table, indicating that he wanted DeSarno and Sciacca to put their guns there.

'What is this, some kind of gag?' Sciacca questioned, instinctively suspicious.

'No gag, fella,' Yale narrowed his eyes. 'This is very serious to me. I pay you ten thousand apiece for this job and I gotta make sure your equipment is working. So, if I am not satisfied what you gonna deliver, I send you home and get somebody else to wipe out that mick. Get it?'

Sciacca turned to DeSarno with a questioning gaze. Nodding that it was all right to show their guns, DeSarno slipped his hand inside his jacket and removed a .45-caliber Colt revolver with a maroon grip. He placed it on the table, warning sarcastically, 'Be careful, Frankie, it's got bullets in it. Don't hurt yourself.'

'Thanks,' said Yale coldly, 'you just save my life.' He snatched the gun, emptied the bullets from the revolving cylinder, pointed the barrel at the ceiling, and squeezed the trigger. He smiled when he heard the click. Then he pumped the trigger a dozen times more.

'It's in good shape,' Yale proclaimed, returning the bullets to the chamber and handing the weapon to DeSarno. Then he performed the same ritual with Sciacca's piece.

'Now I'm happy,' Yale smiled benevolently. 'You boys pass my test. You are ready. Only thing now is we gotta wait and see when Denny Meehan will be ready for his bye-bye.'

At 2:30 a.m. the phone in Argolia's office jangled. Chootch Gianfredo was calling from his observation post near the dance hall.

'He just left here,' the lookout told Fury, who'd been waiting impatiently for the call. Argolia went to the corner table that Yale and the others were occupying and relayed the message.

'Good,' Yale rubbed his hands. He turned to the assassins. 'Get your coats on.'

DeSarno, Sciacca, Pisano, and Carlino hopped out of their chairs, walked briskly to the hatcheck room, slipped into their garments and returned to the table. Yale pulled his watch from his vest pocket and muttered, 'Any second now we should get the call . . .'

No sooner had he spoken than the phone in Argolia's office rang again.

'They just went into the house,' reported Nick 'Glass Eye' Pelicano, who was staking out Warren Street.

'Anybody go in with them? Argolia asked.

'Naw, they were dropped off in front of the house and the guy who brought them – I think it was Eddie McCarthy – drove away,' said Pelicano, who had worn a glass orb in his left eye since he'd lost it in the ring when he was boxing as a middleweight in the amateurs.

'How's the street look?' Argolia wanted to know.

'Clean,' was the reply. 'Only thing moving is the gutter rats and they ain't paying attention to nuttin'. They're busy eating out the garbage cans.'

Argolia hurried from his office.

'Frankie!' he shouted even before he had passed the door, 'Okay! Okay! Send 'em!'

Yale turned to the four executioners. 'You heard him,' he snapped gruffly, 'what're you waiting for?'

They rushed in quick, urgent steps toward the door. But before they were out of the club, Yale jumped to his feet and yelled almost as an afterthought, 'Give Denny my best regards!'

It was nearly 3:30 in the morning of 1 April when Frenchy Carlino turned into Warren Street and eased the Packard to a stop in front of Meehan's residence, a three-story, six-family red brick apartment building that was one of the few habitable dwellings in a neighborhood of encroaching decay and rot.

With the riches that gang leaders like the Meehans were ripping off from their illicit ventures, they could easily have afforded the most luxurious living accommodations. Yet a good many of the moneyed mobsters then – and later – seemed content to remain in the decrepit environments that had spawned them, to raise families in the same filth and squalor that not only bred rancor against society but also debased men into the enemies of that society.

DeSarno and Sciacca leaped from the car and hurried through the door of the apartment house with disciplined precision. They were already halfway up the stairs to the first floor before Augie the Wop had made it into the building.

The Cleveland hit men waited for Pisano to catch up at the floor of the stairs leading to the second floor. They had their guns out.

'Don't wait for nuthin' after we drill him,' Sciacca whispered. 'We fly like birds because this whole fuckin' apartment house is gonna wake up when the cannons go off.'

He turned and led the way up the last few steps on tiptoe. At the top of the landing was a long hallway, just as Willie Altierri had said. They walked slowly and silently on a wooden floor whose boards were so old and warped that they no longer creaked.

Finally, in the dim light of a small bulb burning at the end of the hall, they saw a window – again as Two-Knife had said. They approached with extreme caution, Sciacca leading the way. When he finally reached the window, he saw a light shining through a white sheer curtain. He wheeled around to DeSarno and Pisano.

41

'Hey, this is easy,' he said under his breath. 'I can see Denny in bed with his wife. It looks like he's getting ready to mount her . . .'

Sciacca crouched near the windowsill so that DeSarno and Pisano could see. The shade hadn't been pulled down all the way, so they had a clear line of vision through the lower panes of the window.

As the trio peered into the room, they could see Denny fondling his wife's breasts as he lay beside her.

'Now! Now!' whispered Pisano. 'Shoot him now before that fuckin' Irishman gives me a hard-on!'

Sciacca turned to DeSarno. 'I can handle this,' he said in a firm but barely audible voice. He leveled the gun until the barrel almost touched the window, sighted, and fired. Two shots rang out. The roar in the hallway was deafening.

'I got him!' Sciacca said triumphantly. 'Maybe her, too. Let's get the hell out!'

The three men raced through the hall and bounded down the stairs. They sprinted out of the building, and as they leaped into the getaway car, Frenchy Carlino floored the gas pedal. The car roared off like a shot. No one had seen them.

The two shots and Peggy Meehan's cries awakened the entire apartment house. The neighbors rushed to the Meehans' flat. They found Peggy clutching her abdomen, a widening crimson spot on her nightgown.

Peggy had been hit by the second bullet fired at Denny, which she stopped when she instinctively threw herself over her husband to protect him. But her gesture was in vain. Sciacca's bullet had plowed into Meehan's neck. Yet, it might not have killed him except for a change in the course of the bullet's progress. The Kings County medical examiner disclosed this freakish turn after he had performed the autopsy on Denny's body.

When the slug passed through the neck, it hit the collar-bone. That caused the .45-caliber slug to ricochet upwards into Denny's brain cavity.

Peggy was still in critical condition in Cumberland Hospital when her husband's funeral was held. The crowd at Denny's last rites at the Murphy Funeral Home in downtown Brooklyn was gargantuan. No fewer than nine hundred mourners turned out for the final tribute. The cortege to the cemetery was an incredible spectacle: six cars overflowed with floral wreaths, twenty limousines carried Denny's relatives and the hierarchy of the White Hand organisation, and more than two hundred cars of assorted commiserators followed.

Denny Meehan's departure left the door open for his most trusted lieutenant, William 'Wild Bill' Lovett, to take over the leadership of the White Hand gang. There were no challengers to the sandy-haired, five-foot-eight, 150-pound Lovett, who'd been regarded as the Irish mob's roughest, toughest, and smartest member since he joined their ranks at the end of World War I.

He came into the gang after he returned to the States as a war hero who had won the Distinguished Service Cross after fighting at the Meuse, one of the last offensives before Germany's surrender. Lovett quickly established himself as an irascible, hard-nosed, and hard-headed upstart. In the two short years that he had served in Denny Meehan's troops, Lovett had gotten into no fewer than thirty-five scrapes with the law.

He'd been arrested for assault thirty-four of those times because he couldn't tolerate a victim's refusal to pay tribute for 'protection'.

Meehan had often said, 'If that fuckin' Wild Bill could settle down, he'd be our best enforcer.'

The police had dubbed Lovett a psychopath 'with an extremely dangerous tendency to do harm'.

That assessment was irrefutably confirmed on 16 January 1920 – the day Prohibition began. Wild Bill had gone into Guerney's Saloon on Fourth Avenue, between Fifteenth and Sixteenth Streets, and asked for a shot of Dewar's scotch. The bartender, Amelio Rolfi, said that Guerney's was no longer serving drinks because of the new law.

'I don't give a shit about the law,' Lovett roared. 'You got a bottle there behind the bar and I want a slug.'

The bartender stood his ground. Lovett pulled a .38-caliber automatic from a hip holster and, in full view of the thirty patrons who were guzzling the new beer with its one-half-of-one-percent alcoholic content, he triggered three bullets into the man who had refused to serve him.

Lovett never stood trial. In fact, he wasn't even indicted for the killing. After his arrest, precipitated by the statements of only two of the thirty patrons in the bar that evening, Lovell beat the rap. The two witnesses subpoenaed to appear before the grand jury had both been killed in auto accidents. That Lovett was behind both deaths, the police had no doubt. But they were in no possible position to prove it.

The murder case against Wild Bill Lovett went out the window – as had all the other charges against him.

Now with Denny Meehan rubbed out, Lovett ascended the heights. He was in command of the White Hand gang.

The day after Meehan's funeral, 4 April, he called a meeting of the gang in a warehouse on Pier 7 on the Gowanus docks.

'I swear to you men,' he said with all of the emotion he could summon, 'we are going to get back at those ginzo bastards.' Then he shook his head.

'I don't get this,' he said with a puzzled face, 'how the hell is it that Pat Foley isn't here?'

'Maybe he got drunk again,' quipped Jimmy Naher, one of the White Hand's dock enforcers.

There was a crescendo of laughter, but it died out quickly when Lovett, his face severe, said, 'Somebody better go and find out where Foley is.'

Jack 'Needles' Ferry and Frank 'Ash Can' Smitty volunteered for the search.

'Well, get going!' Lovett roared.

Twenty minutes later, after most of the White Hands had left, Ferry and Smitty returned to the warehouse, supporting the seemingly limp form of Patrick Foley between them.

'Just as Jimmy called it,' Smitty said to Lovett, 'Pat's stewed to the gills.'

Lovett walked over and looked at Foley's face. He glanced at Pat's eyes, which were closed.

'This son of a bitch is faking it,' Lovett declared.

He slapped Foley's face three times. Foley's eyes opened wide, reflecting the pain he felt. That betrayed his actual condition.

'This bastard isn't drunk,' Lovett cried out, 'he's putting it on. I don't even smell liquor on his breath.'

Lovett turned to Foley.

'You dirty double-crossing bastard,' he snarled. 'Do you think you can fool me, you scumbag? You're not drunk. I don't smell any alcohol on your breath. You're putting on an act for a reason. Now, come out with it – you set up Denny, didn't you?'

Suddenly Foley was wide awake.

'Bill, you're crazy,' he protested. 'How can you think of such a thing?'

Lovett grabbed Foley by the lapels of his jacket and shook him.

'Listen, you punk,' Lovett screamed, 'I know you're the Judas. I know all about your romance with Willie Altierri's sister!'

Foley extricated himself from Lovett's grip and slid to the floor. A moment later he struggled to his knees.

'Bill, you got to believe me,' he pleaded. 'I swear to you on everything that's holy I had nothing to do with Denny's killing.'

'I don't believe you,' Lovett growled. 'But I'm going to give you a chance to get away. If you can make it, you're a free man. Now, haul your ass out – fast!'

Foley fled through the warehouse and bolted out the door. He must have believed he was on his way to freedom as he raced down the pier toward the street. Then he spotted Pug McCarthy, one of the White Hand's executioners. His bouncy steps leadened and he froze.

'Easy, Pug,' Foley pleaded as he faced the menacing twin barrels of McCarthy's .12-gauge shotgun. 'Bill just told me to take off. I'm in the clear . . .'

There was a deafening explosion. The pellets ripped into Foley's face so that even the medical examiner couldn't rely on the victim's dental records to help in the identification of the body. The only way they were able to figure out that the corpse was Foley's was from the tattoo of a swan that had been etched on his right calf when he was in the navy during World War I.

For Frankie Yale, the superbly planned execution of Denny Meehan had only one flaw. The April Fool's postcard he had sent to the White Hand leader apparently had been delayed in the mail. It didn't get into the postal carrier's bag until late in the morning of 1 April.

By then, word was out that Denny Meehan had been killed. So when the postman, Benvenuto Itaglia, reached Denny's apartment, he was very aware that Meehan was dead. Itaglia looked at the postcard, read its message, *'Buona sera, signore'* and decided not to deliver it.

Itaglia was very superstitious about bringing greetings to any house where there was a death. He decided to do what he always did in such cases – destroy the postcard.

And that left Frankie Yale completely clear with the authorities. Had the postcard been delivered, the history of the five-year Ginzo-Mick War might have been far different. And far shorter.

His hatred for Denny Meehan was so passionate that Frankie Yale had written the April Fool's card himself. And if it had been delivered to Meehan's mailbox after his murder, police could have easily identified Yale's handwriting, since he was suspected of setting up the killing.

But when Benvenuto Itaglia destroyed Yale's postcard, he obliterated the only evidence against Frankie Yale. So the murder of Denny Meehan was fated to remain one of New York's biggest underworld mysteries in the years that followed.

Chapter 4

Ambush of Sagaman's Hall

When Wild Bill Lovett was crowned overlord of the White Hand gang's empire on the Gowanus dock that early April day in 1920, the roaring twenties had just begun their riotous, raucous ascendancy.

Yet his predecessor, Denny Meehan, had not even begun to hone the mob's greedy claws for a piece of the action in the lucrative new racket foaled by the Volstead Act, which for the fourteen years of its loosely enforced existence was more popularly known as Prohibition.

There are historians of that underworld era who are convinced Meehan was so thick-headed and deficient in imagination that, had he lived, the Irish mobsters probably never would have ventured into the Klondike spawned by the bootleg booze business; they might have been content to keep their franchises on the waterfront extortion, loan-shark, and hijacking rackets, while letting others in the underworld mine the rich nuggets bubbling up from the sea of illegal hootch that was inundating America.

Not since the abolition of slavery in the middle of the nineteenth century had any issue been so widely debated, so bitterly contested, or pursued with so much determination and idealism as Prohibition. The ban against liquor became the law of the land on 16 January 1920.

In the ten weeks between the beginning of Prohibition and the demise of Denny Meehan, the man who did Denny in had already demonstrated the alertness and innovativeness that a mob leader must possess to stay up front. No sooner had the last drink been served in Brooklyn on 16 January than Frankie Yale, inordinately endowed with the sense of when to retool for change, led his Black Hand troops almost overnight into bootlegging.

Although Prohibition hit the whole of America with stunning force, some citizens, alert to the forthcoming ban, had prepared for it. In Brooklyn, as elsewhere, many liquor lovers – and opportunists – readied themselves for the cut-off of supplies by building their own distilleries.

Stills sprang up in cellars of private homes, in warehouses, in garages. But the distillation of hootch was a time-consuming, often risky venture. Some underworld groups of no particular significance in Brooklyn undertook the manufacture of illicit booze for sale to speakeasies and private consumers, but Frankie Yale disdained the idea. Aware of the bother and dangers of operating a still, Frankie preferred to leave the brewing to others and stick to a sophisticated trouble-free bootlegging operation. That was why he decided the Black Hand would only peddle booze.

To start, Frankie sent out about thirty members of his mob in the roles of 'salesmen' to solicit business from the hundreds of saloons condemned by the new law to sell drinks containing no more than one-half of one percent alcohol – which meant only the weakest-tasting. Every hair tonic had a higher alcohol content in those days.

The orders poured in. And Yale, flushed by the initial success of his sales force, searched for a source that could supply him with the large quantities of alky being demanded in his territory. He found a willing supplier in Detroit: the Purple Gang. The Michigan mob had begun the manufacture of hootch on a grand scale and was marketing a whiskey that was generally regarded as the best illicit booze produced in the United States. Connoisseurs of that era who sampled the product say the legitimate pre-Prohibition whiskey was virtually indistinguishable from the contents of the bottles shipped by the Purple Gang with their fraudulent labels: Old Granddad.

Yale's coup with the Michigan mob and his ability to supply Brooklyn's speakeasies with that hootch was the envy of Wild Bill Lovett, who, unlike his predecessor, had a full awareness of the great potential in bootlegging.

Despite the late start, Lovett was able to establish a quick, big market of his own in bootlegging. Many of the old gin mills in South Brooklyn were operated by sons of the auld sod. Though many of them already had begun to receive bootleg hootch from Yale's Black Hand supplier, when Wild Bill Lovett's emissaries finally came around and solicited their business, large numbers of them agreed to switch their business to the White Hand suppliers.

Even though the Irish innkeepers were sympathetic to Lovett and his brigade of Irishmen, the hootch the White Hand began to deliver to the bars couldn't maintain the bond. Scores of saloons stopped buying Lovett's booze and went back to the Black Hand's suppliers.

It was easy to understand: the White Hand's bootleg was of the local variety, brewed in cellars, warehouses, and garages. It had none of the body, bouquet or potency of the product trucked from Detroit. The drastic loss of clientele grated Lovett until mid-November, when he finally struck upon a course of action destined to have extensive ramifications on the White Hand gang's simmering feud with the Black Hand.

Thursday night, 18 November 1920. Ten men arrived separately at Prospect Hall on 17th Street and gathered in one of the meeting rooms that Lovett had reserved for the occasion. They were Richard 'Pegleg' Lonergan, Danny and Petey Bean, Pug McCarthy, Ash Can Smitty, Jack 'Needles' Ferry, Charleston Eddie McFarland, Aaron Harms, and Irish Eyes Duggan. The tenth man was Wild Bill.

'I called you here tonight to tell you about bootlegging,' Lovett rasped. 'I have been hearing that we should make our own liquor because the stuff we're buying is so lousy. But let me tell you that isn't the way to make a profit. And we can't get anywhere selling the bathtub booze we're pushing now . . .'

Lovett looked at his 'sales managers' who'd been supervising the White Hand's booze peddlers, studying their faces for reaction. What he saw pleased him. 'I can see you agree with me,' he smiled. 'Now let me tell you what I want to do . . .'

His next words had the effect of a bombshell.

'We're going to sell the stuff that the fuckin' ginzo Yale has been supplying to the speaks.'

There was a stunned silence. Then Lovett detected a derisive murmur.

'All right, I know what you're thinking – that we can't buy the Purple's booze because they won't deal with us,' Wild Bill speculated. The Detroit mob was predominantly Jewish and they'd sooner pour their Old Granddad into Lake Michigan than sell it to the micks.

'But who's talking about buying it?' Lovett asked with a meaningful grin. Then some of his 'salesmen' began smiling. They had gotten the drift of Wild Bill's pitch.

'All I'm saying is we're gonna get involved in something we're old hands at doing,' he went on. 'We're going to hijack the wops' liquor, just like we do the stuff that's going and coming from the docks.'

A wild spontaneous burst of applause and rousing cheers welcomed Lovett's plans.

'Good,' Wild Bill said, pleased at the quick endorsement. 'We start the hits with the next delivery.'

'You mean tonight?' Charleston Eddie asked, pointing to the clock on the meeting hall wall. All were aware that the truck delivering the Black Hand's liquor always rolled into Yale's garage on Fourth Avenue and Second Street.

It was now 11:30 p.m., just about the time the shipments arrived. Yale had instructed Detroit never to make deliveries before 11:30 p.m. or after 12:10 a.m. Frankie considered that forty-minute period the safest for hauling the illegal cargo into the garage. Any other time might attract the cop on the beat.

Frankie knew that patrolmen who pounded the pavement in

that sector invariably abandoned their posts at 11:30 and shuffled to the Fifth Avenue police station in slow time so they'd get there just a minute or so before midnight. That enabled them to go off duty just as soon as the lieutenant had read their orders to the 12:00-to-8:00 a.m. shift and turned them out. And since it took the flatfoot on the lobster shift about ten minutes to reach the post on Fourth Avenue, the time span between 11:30 and 12:10 was the safest to open the garage doors and let the truck with its cargo in.

Lovett gave McFarland a quick answer.

'No, not tonight,' he said flatly. 'We have to do a little planning on how we're going to pull the caper. Next week is plenty soon enough.'

Shortly before 11:00 p.m. the following Thursday – Thanksgiving – a gray LaSalle sedan pulled out of a small garage on Baltic Street and cruised north. In the car were four men wearing dark lumber jackets and armed with enough artillery to equip a regiment.

Lovett had a desk and phone in that garage, which was a storage depot for the domestically brewed bootleg hootch and the kegs of beer being supplied by Arthur 'Dutch Schultz' Flegenheimer up in the Bronx for distribution in Brooklyn's speakeasies.

Ten minutes before the LaSalle bearing Petey Bean, Charleston Eddie, Ash Can Smitty, and Needles Ferry left the garage, Lovett had received a call from Irish Eyes Duggan, who was in a speakeasy phone booth on Manhattan's West Street where he and Aaron Harms had been staked out in their car near the West Street Ferry to spot the truck from Detroit.

There was no George Washington Bridge, no Lincoln Tunnel, nor such other gateways to or from the west as the New York State Thruway or the Verrazzanno-Narrows Bridge then. Construction had just begun on the Holland Tunnel, and it was seven years from completion.

While a number of ferry lines were carrying cars, trucks, and commuters across the Hudson in 1920, the principal crossing – because it was the most convenient – for the traffic of the Lincoln Highway was the boats that trudged between Jersey City and

Wall Street. So there was no doubt that the truck from Detroit would come by that ferry route.

The truck had no signs to alert Duggan and Harms that it was loaded with the Purple Gang's liquor. The Michigan license plates were a dead giveaway.

After he phoned Lovett, Duggan hurried out to the car, got in beside Harms, who was behind the wheel, and said, 'Bill wants us to be sure and stay on their asses.'

Harms caught up with the truck on Canal Street in less than two minutes. He tailed it over the Manhattan Bridge onto Flatbush Avenue in Brooklyn, then stalked it until it turned into Fourth Avenue.

Duggan's and Harms's roles as bloodhounds came to an end as the gray LaSalle bearing Petey Bean, Charleston Eddie, Ash Can Smitty, and Needles Ferry pulled out from the curb and made a wide sweeping turn just after the truck had passed the stopped car. In a matter of seconds, the car cut in front of the truck, forcing the driver to jam on the brakes to avoid a collision.

Petey Bean and Charleston Eddie leaped out of the sedan with sawed-off shotguns pointed menacingly at the cab of the truck.

'Out! Get the fuck out!' screamed Eddie.

The driver and his helper scampered out of the cab meek as mice.

'Scram!' commanded Eddie. 'Get your asses on the run!'

The two men sped up Fourth Avenue.

'Get in there and start driving!' Eddie commanded. Bean climbed into the cab and gave the gas pedal a heavy foot. The truck roared off. He steered it around the corner into Smith Street, then turned into Baltic and drove the rig into the White Hand's garage. It was a minute before midnight.

It was a considerable haul: $30,000 worth of Prohibition Era Old Granddad. Charleston Eddie was ecstatic as the gang unloaded the cases from the truck.

'Jesus, Bill, what a hell of an idea you had,' he bubbled. 'This is the goddamnedest way I see to beat buying the shit we've been scrounging around for here in Brooklyn.'

Eddie had already cracked open one of the bottles and taken a swig.

'This is great stuff, maybe better than what Old Granddad himself used to make before Prohibition,' he raved.

Lovett yanked the bottle out of Charleston's hands and sampled its contents himself.

'By Christ, this is fantastic!' he echoed with a racking cough. 'This fuckin' booze can burn a guy's throat.'

When the truck had been emptied, Lovett directed Needles Ferry and Ash Can Smitty to 'dump it'. According to a prearranged plan, Ferry and Smitty were to drive the rig to Fourth Avenue and Second Street and abandon it at the curb in front of Yale's garage. That was Lovett's idea – the ultimate 'kick in the ass to the ginzo bastard'.

Lovett had it all plotted in his mind. He was as much aware as Yale of the foot patrolmen's habits of goofing off on their last half-hour of duty, and that it took the cop on the next shift some ten minutes to reach his beat after he was turned out at the station house.

Lovett also reasoned that the hijacked truck's driver and helper would head straight to Frankie Yale's garage after they'd been bushwhacked by Charleston Eddie and Petey Bean. And after the bad news about the heist had been broken to Yale, there'd be no reason to stick around the garage. Lovett had plotted it ingeniously.

As Charleston and Petey rolled along Fourth Avenue in the empty truck, they kept a sharp eye riveted on the gray LaSalle cruising some fifty feet ahead of them. Irish Eyes Duggan and Aaron Harms, in the car, were the scouting party. Harms was in the back seat, and his job was to flick a flashlight on through the rear window to let Charleston and Petey know that there were no lights or activity at the garage and it was okay to carry out Wild Bill's little joke. But if there was no signal from the rear window of the car, Peter was to drive on past the garage and discard the truck wherever it was convenient.

As the LaSalle approached the garage, a light from the rear window flashed on.

'The coast is clear,' Eddie said to Bean. 'Let's dump it.'

Petey gave the steering wheel a slight jerk to the right and braked the truck to a stop directly in front of the garage entrance.

'Scram, Petey,' Charleston rasped as he jumped out of the cab and ran to get into the LaSalle. As Bean followed Charleston into the car, Duggan hit the accelerator so hard that the car lurched forward to an instant then went dead.

'The fuckin' car stalled!' Irish Eyes screamed in a rage.

'What the hell's wrong with you, you asshole?' Charleston thundered. 'Don't you even know how to drive?'

Duggan flicked the ignition key and the motor coughed to a hesitant start.

'Easy does it,' yelled Eddie. 'Less choke! Less choke!'

Duggan threw the car into first gear, and this time the car responded to his urging. They were on their way back to tell Bill Lovett that their mission was accomplished.

'Don't tell me nuthin'. I seen it,' Frankie Yale bellowed at Augie Pisano the next morning. The gang chieftain was now in the burnout stage of his hour-long rage. Sixty minutes ago he had arrived at the garage and seen the empty truck out front, and his fury had hit heights never before witnessed by his associates. He hurled every epithet in the book, and then some Yale originals, at his rival.

His lieutenants grieved with Frankie over the lost liquor, but their anguish over the humiliation inflicted on them by the White Handers was far greater.

'Parked the fuckin' truck outside here,' Yale said for the fifteenth time, his voice now reduced to a mere roar. 'Well, I'm gonna fix them micks good. I know what I gotta do.'

He grabbed the phone on his desk and leaned back in his swivel chair. Suddenly he was calm again. His mood was almost mellow as he lifted the receiver and placed it against his ear, waiting for the operator. Several seconds went by.

'Come on, what the hell ya waiting for?' he snapped edgily. 'The goddamn telephone people,' he complained, 'they charge you an arm and a leg and they don't give you no service.'

Augie the Wop was sitting in the chair beside Yale's desk. Two-Knife Altierri was standing with his back to the window overlooking the alley, cleaning his nails with one of his knives. Don Giuseppe Balsamo, who only came to Frankie's office in dire emergencies, was ensconced in the plush maroon cut-velvet armchair in a corner of the office. The expensive, ornate chair was totally out of place amid the plain, scratched wooden furniture. It had played a dominant role in the décor of Frankie's living room until his father-in-law had suffered a heart attack and died while sitting in it. Frankie's wife was superstitious, and she had him remove it from the house. Rather than leave it on the sidewalk for the junkman, Frankie toted the chair to the garage and installed it in his office.

At first he derived sadistic satisfaction out of using the chair as a prop to unnerve his boys. When one of them had sat in it a while, Yale would say, 'Hey, how you like that chair? Comfortable?'

Nothing but compliments for the chair. Then after a few minutes Yale would say, 'You remember my father-in-law, eh? Well, the poor fella, he died in that chair.'

Some of the Black Hand's toughest cutthroats squirmed, fidgeted, and looked around for any excuse to evacuate the chair.

'Oh, you back from lunch so soon?' Frankie said sarcastically when the operator finally came on the line and asked for the number.

'I wanna talk to somebody in Chicago,' Yale continued, 'but I want to ask you which is quicker, if I take the train or if I use the phone?'

Yale generated a crescendo of laughter in his office, but only silence came through the receiver. He gave the operator the number and waited with characteristic impatience for the two minutes or so it took to route the call. Finally he said quietly, 'This is Frankie Yale in Brooklyn. Is the big guy there?'

Another wait. Then, 'Hello, Al, it's good to hear your voice. How's your mama and the rest of the family?' Yale's voice was mellow, undeniably humble. He was talking with an old friend from earlier Brooklyn days who had followed Horace Greeley's advice and gone west, and who was now well on his way to becoming the nation's most feared underworld boss.

To what did he owe the pleasure of this call from Frankie Yale, Big Al wanted to know. Frankie told him in the briefest terms, what had happened the night before. Yale was aware that

Scarface Al was a man of few words and demanded that others follow his example. He had no patience for windy explanations.

Yale got to the point. He wanted to know if Capone could spare a couple of executioners from their busy Chicago practices to perform a little extracurricular work in Brooklyn.

No sweat, Big Al told his old buddy. He'd put two of his best triggermen aboard the next Twentieth Century Limited leaving Chicago. These were, he said, two Sicilians from Cicero named Albert Anselmi and John Scalise. These Sicilians never played out-of-town engagements for anything less than $15,000 apiece.

'But, good brother,' Yale protested in his mildest, most polite voice. 'Cleveland charged only ten big ones for the *compito* on Danny Mee—'

Capone cut off Yale in midsentence. Frankie listened for several seconds, and then began laughing. It was forced laughter, but he had to show the Big Guy that he enjoyed his humour.

'Okay, good friend Al,' Yale said, 'you are justified to ask for that. I will pay it.'

Yale hung up and pushed the phone away in disgust.

'How you like that?' he asked.

'Why he putting such a big bite?' Augie the Wop asked.

'Because,' Yale replied, shaking his head resignedly, 'Al say the train fare from Chicago cost more than from Cleveland.'

When Al Capone told Frankie Yale he'd put Anselmi and Scalise on the next train to New York, that was merely a figure of speech. Underworld contract killings never come off that quickly. It takes skilful and time-consuming conniving to plot the successful rubout of a rival gangster, mainly because the intended victim is constantly alert to the dangers of assassination. Consequently, he takes precautions to protect himself.

So a number of long-distance calls between Brooklyn and Chicago followed in the days after Yale's first talk with Capone. The prickly details of the demanding assignment had to be ironed out.

Yale had decided he wanted to hurt Wild Bill Lovett in the worst of ways. But the most severe punishment the White Hand leader could suffer would not be his own death, Frankie decided.

'We gotta hurt his people,' Yale said on the phone to Scalise. 'I know just how to do it.' Frankie proceeded to tell Scalise about the forthcoming Valentine's Day dance that the White Handers were to hold in Brooklyn's Sagaman's Hall.

'I have in mind an ambush,' Frankie suggested. 'What do you think?'

Scalise wanted to know who Yale wanted killed.

'Anybody!' Yale shouted. 'Shoot crazy! Hit the crowd! You don't have to aim. Just shoot. Make a big score!'

Scalise got the message. He told Frankie that he and Anselmi would show up at Frankie's garage at seven o'clock on the night of 14 February.

'I'll send my boys to meet you at Grand Central,' Yale offered.

No need for that, Scalise replied. When he and Anselmi go on a job, they make their own way.

And at precisely the hour promised, Scalise and Anselmi walked into the garage. They introduced themselves to Yale and then Scalise asked, 'Who is the wheelman?' Yale pointed to Frenchy Carlino. 'The best driver in the whole world,' he said with a wink.

'Yeah,' smiled Anselmi, 'if he's that good how come he ain't working in Chicago?'

When laughter abated, Scalise turned to Carlino.

'What you driving?'

'Nineteen-twenty LaSalle,' Carlino replied.

'Not bad,' Scalise said. 'You got it ready?'

Carlino assured the Chicago gunmen that the car had just been tuned up, that it had a full tank of gas, and was raring to go.

'Good,' Anselmi grinned. 'If the wheels don't move, you don't move. And that could be very bad . . .'

Thirty-six members of the White Hand gang were whooping it up in Sagaman's Hall. Thirty-three of them had their wives with them; the other three had brought their best girls.

Frankie briefed the killers on what had to be done.

'You see,' he said with a frown, 'when you go in there you gotta make sure you get them at the tables, when they are sitting . . .'

57

'Hey, Frankie,' Scalise interrupted. 'You trying to tell us our business? We know what we gotta do. We don't need no instructions. *Capeesh* ?'

Yale was taken aback.

'Listen, John,' he said, stiffening, 'you are in strange territory here, and all I am trying to do is help you. Remember, you came here to do the job for me . . .'

'All right, wise guy, what you want to say?' Scalise demanded gruffly.

'I want you to shoot in the left side of the dance hall because that's where all the big-shot micks sit, get me?'

'All right, Frankie, you wanna give me the floor plan?' Scalise asked with a disdainful stare.

Yale sensed that he was up against a breed of underworld killer who wasn't about to take orders from him. But at the same time he held to a confidence that since Scalise and Anselmi had been sent by Al Capone, they could be depended on to do the job.

'Okay,' Yale finally yielded, 'this is gonna be your show.'

Forty minutes later, Scalise and Anselmi were driven by Frenchy Carlino to the corner of Schermerhorn and Smith Streets.

'There's the hall,' Carlino rasped. 'Remember, up the stairs on your right to the balcony. And don't forget – come out fast because I'm gonna drive my ass off if I don't see you after I hear the shots.'

Scalise and Anselmi left the car without a word and walked into Sagaman's Hall. The party was in full swing. Hardly anyone noticed the two Chicago mobsters, dressed in light-brown overcoats, dark fedoras, spats, and brown leather gloves. The gloves came off as Scalise and Anselmi climbed the flight of stairs to the swinging doors . . . which opened on the empty balcony. The gathering that night was modest in comparison to the crowds that jammed the hall on other festive occasions: this was a special affair, limited to the White Hand gang. And they had all been seated on the main ballroom floor.

Scalise and Anselmi pushed past the swinging doors and entered the darkened balcony. There they had an unobstructed view of the celebrants. For a moment, they stood at the edge of the balcony rail, unnoticed in the darkness, and surveyed the activity. The orchestra had just finished playing an Irish jig and the revelers had gone back to their tables.

Anselmi nudged Scalise.

'The left side, isn't that what Yale wanted?' he muttered.

'What the hell's the difference?' Scalise shrugged. 'This is a snap whatever side you wanna hit. But if Yale wants the left side, then let's make him happy.'

The two killers whipped out the nickel-plated revolvers they were carrying in holsters under their coats and took aim at the crowd of men and women sitting at the tables. An instant later, a steady fire began to pour a deadly fusillade of .45-caliber bullets into the crowd.

Women's screams pierced the haze of cigarette and cigar smoke and the steady bark of the bullets. Both men and women instinctively dove under tables. Others stood or sat, too paralysed either by surprise or fear to seek cover. Still others fought and clawed their way through the panic-stricken crowd for the emergency exits and the front entrance.

Scalise and Anselmi reached for the second revolvers they carried as backup when the supply of bullets was exhausted in the weapons they had first used.

Then the triggermen raced down the balcony stairs and out the main entrance almost before the last echoes of gunfire had faded.

Carlino had opened the doors of the LaSalle sedan the instant his ears picked up the first explosions inside the hall. Before the last of the bullets had been spewed into the crowd, Frenchy moved the car directly to the front entrance.

Their coat tails flapping behind them, Scalise and Anselmi sprinted across the sidewalk and leaped into the car. Carlino didn't even wait for them to close the doors before gunning the engine. The car bolted forward, and the whining squeal of tires was louder than the roar of the eight cylinders as Frenchy turned the corner from Schermerhorn into Smith Street. He kept the gas pedal floored until he was assured by Scalise, who was in the back seat peering through the rear window, that no one was following them.

* * *

At Sagaman's Hall, pandemonium reigned. The crescendo of wails and cries was deafening. Blood was splattered everywhere on the left side of the ballroom: on tables, chairs, the floor, and even the wall.

It looked like a battlefield. Hands, faces, bodies, legs were covered with blotches and streaks of crimson as though it had been poured on them from buckets. A dozen men and women were sprawled on the floor, some writhing in agony, others lying absolutely still. Others knelt beside the fallen ministering to their wounds or comforting them until they could be removed to a hospital.

Several frantic calls had been made to the police, but Irish Eyes Duggan had the coolest head. He phoned Kings County Hospital and pleaded for help.

'Send all the ambulances and doctors you got!' he said urgently. 'Send nurses! This is a major disaster. Everybody's been shot. They're dying! Please, send them right away!'

The sound of Duggan's voice convinced the night superintendent to dispatch two ambulances to Sagaman's Hall. Minutes later, when the police phoned in their request for medical assistance and officially confirmed the full extent of the disaster, two more ambulances appeared at the hall.

The four doctors aboard those ambulances that responded were hard put attending to everyone. They worked first on the most critically wounded. Then they pressed some of the White Handers and their women into service, directing them to tie tourniquets around victims' arms or legs to stem the flow of blood until the medics could attend them.

There were three who were beyond assistance.

Kevin 'Smiley' Donovan was obviously a dead duck. There was no need even to feel for a pulse. He had caught at least three slugs on what had once been his forehead. The .45s did a good job of proving to some of his life-long kibitzers that Smiley really did have a brain.

Jimmy 'Two Dice' O'Toole had been sitting with his back to the gunmen. Several bullets aerated his skull just above the neck, and the doctor who looked at him turned to one of the fifteen policemen now in the hall and said, 'He goes to the morgue.'

Mary Reilly was the third and final passenger for the meat wagon. Richard 'Pegleg' Lonergan's sweetheart, she was known as 'Stout-Hearted Mary' because she had raised seven younger brothers and sisters after their parents were drowned in a 1916 boating accident off Sheepshead Bay. But Mary's heart wasn't stout enough to withstand the impact of the .45 bullet that passed through it, exited from her back, and did an encore number on the forearm of Fred McInerney who'd been seated at the same table.

Tears trickled down Pegleg's cheeks as he knelt beside Mary's lifeless body.

'I'll get them for you, Mary, so help me, I'll get them . . .' he choked through trembling lips.

Other men, hardened by their professional calling to regard violence and bloodletting as a routine phenomenon of their day-to-day lives, wept unashamedly.

Not everyone had stuck around to mourn the dead and give solace to the wounded. Wild Bill Lovett, who'd been sitting at the same table as Pegleg and Mary, miraculously escaped the bullets, and sent Ash Can Smitty, Pug McCarthy, and several other boys in pursuit of the killers.

In trying to pick up the cold trail, Ash Can and McCarthy drove past Frankie's garage on Fourth Avenue on the chance that they might pick up some trace of the getaway car or its occupants. But the garage was closed tight and all the lights were out.

Frankie Yale hadn't doubted for a moment that he and his gang would be suspected immediately of pulling the ambush at Sagaman's Hall. So, as Carlino drove away with Scalise and Anselmi on their mission, Frankie, Augie the Wop, Two-Knife Altierri, and a dozen other ranking Black Handers all went to a wedding. It was an iron-clad alibi.

The reception was at the Adonis Club. While weekday weddings were a rarity, that particular one was held on a Monday night because the bride and groom had chosen to be married on Valentine's Day.

Yale and his boys were strangers to the newlyweds, their families, and the guests, but Fury had two large tables in an out-of-the-way corner of the club for the mobsters. This was standard practice for every reception at the Adonis. Any banquet Argolia booked was arranged with the understanding that the two corner tables were reserved for 'some very special customers of mine'. Fury also assured whoever was paying for the reception that there'd be no intrusion by his special guests on the party that booked the hall.

Yale and his pals didn't occupy the tables at every banquet – only when they had to have an alibi. When five detectives walked into the Adonis a few minutes after eleven o'clock that night and spotted Yale and his boys at the corner tables, they knew they had wasted their time coming over from Sagaman's Hall to question the Black Hand leader and his underlings about the shooting.

'Hiya, Frankie,' one of the detectives greeted. 'No need to ask where you and your boys were tonight, is there?'

Yale looked up and feigned surprise. He quickly pointed a finger at the plates around the table littered with scraps of meat, pasta and salad. 'Hey, are you kidding?' he asked, cocking an eyebrow at the detectives. 'Can't you see what we got here? You think we just sat down for dinner . . .?'

'Yeah, I know what you're saying, Frankie,' the detective said derisively. 'And I suppose every person at this reception will vouch that you and your boys were here since long before ten o'clock tonight, isn't that right?'

Another puzzled look crossed Frankie's face.

'Why, what happened at ten o'clock which makes you come to me?' Yale asked innocently.

'You wouldn't know anything about the ambush at Sagaman's Hall, Frankie, would you?' the detective asked.

Yale turned suddenly and looked at Pisano, who was sitting across from him.

'Augie, did you hear anything about that?' Frankie asked with an extra touch of curiosity in his voice.

'How could I?' Pisano said defensively. 'Ain't I been here all the time? You didn't see me talk with nobody, didja?'

Yale turned back to the detective. 'You see, we didn't hear nuthin'.'

'That's what we figured,' the detective said resignedly. 'But we're only doing our job, you understand that, don't you, Frankie?'

'Yeah, sure, sure, of course I understand,' Yale said condescendingly. 'But tell me something – what's this about ambush at Sagaman's? What's happened?'

'Frankie,' the detective growled, 'I don't know who your hit men were, but you can tell them when they report back to you that they made a very high score.'

'Hey, don't say I got hit men,' Yale protested. 'I am a legitimate businessman. You know what I am. An undertaker.'

The detective turned to the other sleuths. 'Come on, let's get out of here,' he said sharply. 'I can't stand the stink.'

As the lawmen started to leave, Frankie shouted, 'Hey, you forget to tell me the score. What was it?'

The detective walked back to the table. His gait was deliberately slow. He approached Yale, looked down at him for a long moment, then took the left lapel of Frankie's suit between his thumb and forefinger.

Frankie smiled sardonically as he craned his neck to look up at him. When he spotted the fire in the sleuth's eyes, he wiped the grin off his face.

Running his fingers up and down the lapel he'd taken hold of, the detective drew in a long slow breath, as though trying to restrain his anger.

'Frankie, if you didn't know twelve people were shot, then I'm letting you know it now. And you might also be interested to know that three of them are dead. That's murder, Frankie, and I want to assure you that I and these men who are with me are going to work night and day to break this case.'

The detective gave a slight tug on Frankie's lapel and took his hand away. He had a last word to offer.

'Three murders, Frankie,' he said, 'but you're going to get a break when we nail you. Because you can only fry once in the chair.'

Yale and his lieutenants kept absolutely silent as they waited for the detectives to disappear out the door. No sooner had they gone than there was an explosion of laughter.

'Didja hear that?' Frankie asked, his voice almost cracking. 'Twelve hits! Twelve hits! And three bull's eyes! *Magnifico!* I gotta call Big Al and tell him we're gonna send his boys a bonus.'

Yale summoned Argolia to the table.

'Fury,' he said ecstatically, 'how many tables over there for the wedding party?'

'Fourteen,' the reply came.

'Okay, and you got more here, right?' Frankie said. 'Put a bottle of *vino* on every table. It's on me. And go tell the bride and groom I'm gonna drink a toast to their health and happiness.'

Augie the Wop began applauding Frankie, and everyone at the two tables joined in. Yale all at once called out to Argolia, who had begun instructing the waiters to get the wine.

'Angelo,' Frankie said loud enough to be heard for several tables around, 'maybe I can get to kiss the bride, too, eh . . .?'

By then the injured at Sagaman's Hall had all been removed to the hospital and the three bodies had been photographed by police and taken to the morgue. Detectives were still milling through the crowded hall interrogating witnesses for possible leads.

The cops were no more likely to get information from the White Handers than they could hope to develop leads by questioning Yale and his Black Hands. Even if someone in the hall had been able to identify the gunmen, he wouldn't tell the police. The micks and the ginzos had their own code of laws, and it was incompatible with those adopted by the Founding Fathers in the Constitution.

Wild Bill Lovett and gang didn't need the police or any court of law to arrest, prosecute, convict, and execute the perpetrators of the bloody outrage visited on Sagaman's Hall. They had their own methods for striking back. The police knew that. The Black Hand knew that. In fact, even the public that read of the ambush chronicled in big, bold, black headlines in the next day's newspapers knew that.

The only question in anyone's mind was when the White Handers would mete out their punishment to the Black Handers.

Chapter 4

The Godfather Is Thinking of Retirement – But Not Just Yet

A steamy hot afternoon in August 1920.

Children playing stickball near the foot of downtown Brooklyn's Hamilton Avenue were distracted from their game by the arrival of Patrolmen Arthur McConnel and James 'Red' McNulty. The cops were hauling five teenaged boys into the nearby 76th Precinct police station.

'Get your asses inside!' the kids heard McNulty yell.

The redheaded cop swung his nightstick and landed well-aimed blows to the butts of the teens.

The kids were suspected of a shoplifting spree at Cheap, Cheap Sissler's Dry Goods Store on Union Street the day before. As McConel and McNulty lined up the young suspects before the booking desk, manned by Sergeant Joseph Malveesy, one of them, fourteen-year-old Frankie 'Squat' Savino, protested:

'We didn't rob nuthin', I swear.'

Suddenly young Frankie moaned. Patrolman McNulty had swung his nightstick on the kid's behind again with the admonition, 'Shut up, you lying little bastard!' Then he and McConnel turned to Malveesy and informed him of the purported shoplifting.

'Take them into the interrogation room and question them,' the desk sergeant directed the officers.

Once the teenaged 'hoods' were inside the interrogation room, Patrolman McConnel took over the questions.

'All right, you!' he shouted at Nick Delesperanzo, 'where the hell were you yesterday at about three-thirty in the afternoon?'

'I was home ... I was doing ... my homework,' the terrified Nick responded. 'I'm not kidding, sir. You could check if you want to, sir ...'

Before the youngster could finish the sentence, he was clobbered anew by McConnel.

'Shut up you little sniveller,' the fifty-eight-year-old cop roared.

'And the same goes for you, snot-nose!' the policeman addressed Frankie DeMaio, who had tried to put a word in edgewise.

'I want you brats to shut up and listen to what we're gonna ask,' McConnel ranted.

He turned to Nick Delesperanzo:

'By the way, Nickie, don't think we won't check your story out.'

McConnel refocused his attention on young Delesperanzo and scowled, 'You lying sonofabitch, you don't even go to school no more – so why the fuck you giving me this horseshit line?'

'I don't really understand what this is all about,' protested Nick Delesperanzo. 'You ain't told us nothing about what we were supposed to have done ...'

Feeling that McConnel was being too abusive with the teenaged suspects, Officer McNulty broke in.

'Someone pointed you guys out this morning and said that you did some shoplifting in Cheap, Cheap's store.' The redheaded cop then reached into his pants pocket and pulled out a slip of paper with a list of stolen merchandise reported by the store's owner, Nathan Sissler.

'Two dozen shirts, ten pairs of socks,' he started to read. 'And fourteen pairs of women's silk stockings . . .'

McNulty went down the roster of purported stolen items, then tossed the paper on the desk next to where the suspects were seated.

'Look at the list, boys,' he commanded. 'You see it? All of you, you see it.'

Nick and Frankie glanced at the paper; both looked up at the cop. An air of innocence permeated the faces of the street-wise two.

'I swear it wasn't us who stole that stuff,' Delesperanzo squealed meekly.

'Yeah,' piped up young DeMaio, the tallest of the five prisoners. 'Maybe some kids who look like us did it. Don't blame us . . .'

'I'm not the one who's blaming you,' growled McNulty. 'I'm just going by what a witness told us. He saw you fellas stealing the merchandise yesterday and fingered you. That says he saw your clique in action stealing the stuff, and he told the owner, Nat Sissler, about it –'

All at once the door of the interrogation room opened and the precinct commander, Captain Michael Conners, walked in.

'Excuse me, boys,' he said in a firm voice, 'could I talk with you for a minute?'

The two patrolmen nodded. They had no choice.

'Bring these young men out of the room to the booking area,' Conners commanded.

'Sure, sure, Cap,' said McNulty. He turned to McConnel and whispered, 'What the fuck's goin' on here . . .?'

'Beats the shit outta me,' McConnel responded. 'Why the hell don't we take these little bastards out there and find out what all this jazz is all about?'

In mere seconds McNulty and McConnel knew what 'this jazz' was all about. They knew when they spotted the familiar figure with the regal-like stance: the Black Hand's godfather – Don Giuseppe 'Battista' Balsamo.

The awesome Mafia overlord stood at the side of the booking desk, which was now manned by Sergeant Edward Mahar. As the young suspects stumbled into the main booking room, Balsamo, oblivious to the presence of the stationhouse's commander, turned to the desk sergeant and gave his rubbery face a playful tug.

'Be nice to my kids, sarge,' Balsamo said softly. 'Let them go home.'

'Gee, Don Giuseppe, I have no control over that – that's up to Captain Conners,' Mahar pleaded. It was then that the sergeant spotted his commanding officer coming out of the interrogation room with the two arresting officers and their quarry of suspects.

'Signore Balsamo,' the sergeant said with a sigh of relief, 'there is the captain – he surely has authority to release your little friends . . .'

'*Grazie*,' Balsamo smiled. 'Now I know what I must do.'

Captain Conners and Battista Balsamo were no strangers to each other. Conners had been alerted ahead of time by one of the cops dispatched by Mahar, and he knew exactly how to handle the sticky situation.

'Mr Balsamo,' Conners said as he went to the godfather and extended his hand. 'Do you mean to tell me that these boys are your nephews? . . . I don't believe it. How come they have different last names than you, sir . . .?'

Balsamo quickly straightened out the genealogical misplacements. 'The two DeMaio boys are my sister Rosalie's sons and the two Delesperanzo kids belong to my sister Catherine and Salvatore Labiase . . .' Balsamo then gave the captain a rundown on Frankie Savino which convinced Captain Conners that the next move was up to him – and it had to be a diplomatic one.

'I see what you're saying, Mr Balsamo,' the captain returned. 'It's clear to me that your interest in these young men is unmistakable – and genuine.'

'That's exactly as I thought you'd see it, my *capitano*,' Balsamo responded. 'So what you propose to do . . .?'

'Well, I'm thinking –' Conners started to say when Balsamo interrupted.

'Hey, Mike, for Chris' sake, old friend,' Balsamo came back, 'let them go. If you book these kids of mine, they're gonna have police records – and that could be very bad. It could ruin their lives . . . So let them go . . . for my sake, good Mike . . .'

Captain Conners winked at Balsamo: 'To tell you the truth, Mr Balsamo, I don't think we have enough evidence in hand to hold your kids any longer. So I am returning them into your custody since you are so closely related to them.'

The captain signaled to his officers and commanded: 'Release his nephews to Mr Balsamo. There cannot be any charge against them.'

As the five teenagers scurried out of the police station, their benefactor lingered to chat with the police commander.

'You're a nice guy, Mike,' Godfather Balsamo praised the captain. 'I like you because you're understanding. I always say it's very important to get along with police because you can always get more cooperation with people when you are nice . . .'

As Balsamo started to leave the police station he said:

'My *capitano*, it's very important to get along with the public . . . And I admire you for the way you conducted yourself today. And I want to say one last word to you – *Stata Bono Capitano*.'

'What does that mean?' the puzzled police captain wanted to know.

'It means stay well . . . This is how you say in Sicilian.'

A broad smile creased the Irish cop's face.

'You, too, Mr Balsamo.' The relieved Conners shook Don Giuseppe's hand.

Balsamo made his way out of the stationhouse and towards the young men he had just bailed out.

He felt good that he had conned the precinct commander into reprieving the youngsters. He crossed the wide stretch of Hamilton Avenue and came face to face with the five young renegades he'd just sprung from the police station. He had fire in his eyes as he stared at them. The youngsters stood in silent respect.

'What's the matter with you kids,' he almost shouted. 'Are you stupid? Why the hell you pull stunt like that when you gonna get caught. Don't you know no better? Eh? Answer me!'

Frankie Savino volunteered the response: 'Don Giuseppe, I want to tell you for all of us that we are thankful to you for getting us off the hook –.'

Balsamo looked into the face of the young man speaking to him, then into the faces of the others. 'Just let me tell you something,' he scolded. 'Don't ever get caught doing something wrong with anyone or anything in your own neighborhood.'

Balsamo looked around at his audience.

'You know why?' he demanded.

None of them spoke.

'Because people in our neighborhood might recognise you. Some know your names. Others might know your faces . . . Bad, very bad.'

Then, with a sweeping swing of his hand that passed over the heads of the just-emancipated teenagers like a wand, Battista Balsamo counselled, 'I would rather see you boys become doctors, lawyers, engineers – any profession that'll bring joy to your parents' hearts.'

The boys disappeared into the neighborhood. Balsamo strolled towards the Union Street markets area where pushcarts were lined along the curb in front of flourishing markets dispensing meats, fruit, and vegetables.

The pushcarts were lined up one after another on Union from Hicks Street past Columbia Street and then to a spill-over on Van Brunt Street. Hordes of people – mostly women – mulled about the pushcarts.

Battista Balsamo was one of the biggest entrepreneurs in that market. With two brothers and their four nephews, the Balsamo combine had corners on virtually the entire shopping center. Among them the Balsamo clan operated ten stores that sold a vast assortment of produce, meat, and fish – especially fish.

The Balsamos had the fish business truly locked up. They ran ten stores that specialised in catches that ranged from calamari, octopus, porgy, snails and lobsters to whiting, codfish, crabs, mackerel, bluefish, and tuna.

Battista held sway over the fish business. And every pushcart peddler and every store owner in the neighborhood paid *commorra* (protection money) to him to operate in that marketplace. The going rate was $10 for a space at the curb for a pushcart, $30 a week for the stores.

As Giuseppe Balsamo strolled along Union and Columbia, he was the focus of total attention. Children and grown-ups alike sidled up to him and greeted the godfather.

Balsamo loved that sort of attention – summer, fall, winter, spring – anytime he could get it. But he was especially enthralled at the large response he received that particular day in August 1920.

It was, of course, not Balsamo's favorite season of the year. He felt most at home on his turf during the dead of winter. He especially liked wearing camel's-haired Chesterfield-cut coats that were best worn in the worst of December's weather. Such a coat also provided concealment for the gun he always carried with him, a .32-caliber five-shot double-action nickel-plated break-open revolver manufactured by Empire State Arms Co. It was Balsamo's favorite piece, accurate up to a distance of forty feet. For what more could he ask?

The velvet-collared coat he wore over his shoulders served the Don well. It gave an edge over a potential opponent, for he could either draw the .32 tucked in his waistband or, if he had to ditch the firearm before a frisk, he could let the weapon slip out of his right hand and fall to the ground almost unseen.

It would be nothing more than a pistol lying on the cold cement pavement. Of course, a witness might hear a clank or two when the gun hit the deck. But no one could ever prove Giuseppe unloaded it there, so Balsamo could never be arrested or convicted of violating New York's recently enacted Sullivan Law, which forbade all citizens to bear arms without a permit.

A few days after Balsamo had sprung the five teenagers, he made his way along Columbia Street to check on the pushcart business when he sighted a familiar figure. He was Vince Mangano.

'Hey, Vince! Vince!' Balsamo shouted at the top of his lungs.

Mangano turned in surprise. 'Don Giuseppe,' he shouted.

'How good to see you,' Mangano pointed his finger in the direction of Paolo's Sicilian Restaurant around the corner on Union Street, indicating they should have their rendezvous there.

Battista reached the restaurant first. Paolo Mancini, owner of Paolo's, made a fuss over him and seated him at a large round table with chairs made of twisted wrought-iron backs shaped like hearts. Paolo placed Balsamo with his back to the wall – as he always had – and asked who else he expected to join him for lunch.

'Any minute,' Balsamo responded, 'my good friend Vincenzo Mangano will join me.'

At five-foot-five, with a rapidly receding hairline, Mancini was noted for his delicious chi-chi beans crushed and matted together like a fillet. Deep fried, they made a delectable sandwich.

Mancini also could whip up his so-called *vestedi* sandwiches which comprised ricotta cheese and chopped lungs, a mouth-watering delicacy. For the record, Paolo's was strictly a Palermitano cuisine that served many customers what they believed were the best Sicilian meals in all of New York State.

The main door to the street suddenly opened and Vince Mangano walked in. He didn't wait for the head captain to greet him, but simply looked around for Godfather Balsamo, spotted him, and walked to the table unescorted.

Battista rose to his feet when Mangano arrived and the two men greeted each other with the customary kiss on the cheek.

'*Seta, seta* [sit, sit],' Balsamo invited. 'I got to talk to you.'

'All right, all right,' responded Mangano and he sat next to the godfather at the table.

'It's very important I talk to you,' Balsamo said.

'I'm honored that you want to talk to me,' Mangano returned. 'I am most anxious to hear what you have to say . . .'

Balsamo inhaled deeply.

'You see, good friend, I am forty-nine years old and I feel I am getting old and tired.' Then he interrupted himself.

'Hey, Vincenzo, we haven't ordered yet,' Battista turned and clicked his fingers to the nearest waiter.

'We want to eat,' Balsamo said. 'No menu. Just tell Paul we want something special.'

The waiter understood and headed straight to Paul Marinaci, the head waiter who would be sure that the godfather's wish turned out to be Paolo's command.

Even as Paul rushed into the kitchen to place the order, Balsamo turned to Mangano and continued his spiel as though it hadn't been interrupted.

'You see, *paisano*,' the godfather said slowly, 'someone has to take over the day-to-day operations. I am getting very tired and I want to see some younger blood running what we have going . . .'

Mangano looked stunned.

'Don Giuseppe, what are you telling me . . . that you don't want to be the boss no more? Are you kidding . . .?

'I think I hear you say you want to live retired life,' Mangano said. 'Why, boss, you are so young yet . . .?'

'I may be young, but I don't kid about this thing,' Balsamo came back. 'I have had a long life in this thing and I want to give up my interest in the easy money.

'Twenty years is a long time in this business. I think it's about time to call it quits and maybe just keep the fish store going . . .'

Mangano frowned at Balsamo.

'Why are you telling me all this?' he asked.

Don Giuseppe reached out and put a hand on the outstretched palm of Mangano's right hand.

'Vincenzo,' the Godfather said in a solemn voice, 'I want you to take over this operation for me . . .'

Astonishment came over Mangano's face.

'You really mean what you say?' he asked in a trembling voice.

'If I did not intend to retire, I would not have brought you here to tell you all this,' Battista snapped. 'Of course I mean what I say . . . But I no go tomorrow. What I say to you is that one of these days – could be next month, next year, I don't know . . . But I am tired. So that is why I wanna have this talk with you. I want you to know where you stand . . .'

Mangano shook his head. 'I don't believe what you are telling me, Don Giuseppe. I have not been honored so much in all my life. I am overwhelmed . . .'

'I appreciate how you feel,' Balsamo said as the waiter came to the table with the salad.

'I want you to come with me tomorrow night. We will meet under the clock at nine o'clock and go to eat at Cafiero's Restaurant around the corner.'

73

But Balsamo had a condition in arranging for the succession of leadership that would go to Vincenzo Mangano.

'You bring your brother Phillipo with you tomorrow night, *capish*?' the godfather ordered.

'Why, Don Giuseppe?' Mangano asked surprised.

'Because the two of you make a great team,' Battista replied. 'I think of you and Phillipo, who I think has a big set of steel balls, can't miss when you work together. The two of you gonna make some team.

'You, Vince, are very, very smart. And Phillipo . . . well I told you how tough I think he is . . . You two, together, cannot miss to be the big boss that our thing needs here . . .'

Balsamo loved any man who used his brain and had the highest respect for him. But he also appreciated a man with muscle – only, of course, as a last resort after all else had failed to convince a recalcitrant antagonist.

This had been Don Giuseppe's credo since his earliest days as the godfather of the Black Hand. And even in very recent times, such underworld bosses as Charles 'Lucky' Luciano and Joe 'The Boss' Masseria, who had been nurtured by Balsamo, had been counselled to follow the golden rule he preached about maintaining power and control over subordinates.

Balsamo was no ordinary mob kingpin. He had a special magnetism that drew the respect not only of the Mafiosi under his command but that of all the people with whom he made contact. Don Giuseppe spoke three languages: his native Italian, English, and Spanish. That stood him in good stead in the neighborhood when he'd sit in the shade on a hot summer's day outside his tenement and welcome the residents to his side. They were, most of them, either Italian or Puerto Rican immigrants, many newly arrived.

They could neither read nor write the language of their adopted country. When they received letters written in English, they knew that they could have an immediate translation simply by going to Don Giuseppe for this favor. He was all too willing to perform it.

So grateful were many of these immigrants that they treated Balsamo as though he were royalty. Some even kissed his hand out of gratitude for the favors he performed for them.

Away from his residence, strutting along the sidewalk of Union Street for a rendezvous under the clock with his enforcers, Don Giuseppe set the standard for the way an early twentieth century mob boss should look. And in the weeks and months leading up to his decision to pass the reins of leadership to Vincenzo Mangano, Battista envisioned how his hand-picked successor would look in his Chesterfield. Satisfied, Don Giuseppe was then convinced Mangano was perfectly suited to be his successor.

Before he entered retirement, Balsamo also envisioned still another leadership role – one that had not been previously played. He decided someone should serve as 'peacemaker'. This Black Hander would have the specific mission of stepping in when disputes arose in the ranks and mediating the differences before violent means were taken to settle the conflict.

In the wisdom that came with his long experience as head of the original Black Hand gang, Balsamo wanted to avoid the needless rubouts that grew out of an 'uncivil act' committed by one card-carrying Mafioso against another. In the past, the animosity often led to the murder of a rival. Don Giuseppe felt such killings were a total waste of worthy members who could better serve the Black Hand alive than dead.

The appointment of 'The Prince of Peace' went to James 'Jimmy' Crissali, a trusted, loyal member of Balsamo's water-front enforcers. Quick-witted and cool-headed, his qualities made him an excellent choice to be the first mob *consigliere* of Kings County – indeed, the first anywhere.

In time, *consiglieres* would be appointed in Mafia families all over New York and then in every part of the country where the Black Hand operated.

This is how Battista Balsamo planned to bring his many years of rule over the Black Hand to an end. He was itching to sit back and relax and watch his successors carry on the 'good works' he had started and developed for the Black Hand. But he simply couldn't abdicate the throne immediately.

At this stage the Black Hand was in the opening round of its war with the White Hand for domination of the rackets in Brooklyn and parts of Manhattan. Much blood had been spilled already; yet much, much more would flow in the months and years ahead in the great struggle for gangland supremacy.

A quarter century had passed since the time Don Giuseppe Balsamo introduced Sicilian mobsterism as a deadly art form to the United States.

The year was 1895 and Giuseppe Balsamo, then a vibrant twenty-four, landed in New York after an Atlantic crossing in steerage from Palermo and was processed through Ellis Island with the hundreds of emigrants arriving daily.

Because he had a high ranking in the Mafia in Sicily, Giuseppe was catapulted almost immediately into a significant role of leadership in what then was a fledgling branch of Black Handers seeking to plant their roots in the United States for the purpose of exacting tribute from their fellow Italian immigrants.

Balsamo soon came to be known as Don Giuseppe and his counsel was sought by other Mafiosi in areas other than downtown Brooklyn, where Battista had set up his operation.

One of those who wanted Balsamo's guidance was Giuseppi Morello, a tough, ruthless Black Hand leader in East Harlem. Morello was being challenged for a piece of the action in his territory by an upstart Mafioso, Benedetto Madonia, who was seeking to expand his realm as boss of a gang that was into counterfeiting and operating on Manhattan's Lower East Side and looking to take over Morello's turf and use it as a clearing house for his funny money. He planned to enlist Italian shopkeepers, under the threat of bodily harm or even death, to dispense the bogus bills to their customers – and trade off their legitimate tender to Morello for a profit of twenty-five cents to the dollar.

Morello was supported in his leadership of the East Harlem Black Hand by his equally menacing brother-in-law Ignazio 'Lupo the Wolf' Sietta. But neither knew how to handle the challenge they now faced from Madonia.

'What do you think, Don Giuseppe?' Morello asked on that Sunday evening of 12 April 1903, when he and Sietta had journeyed to Balsamo's headquarters in Brooklyn. The Harlem mobster was begging advice on how to handle the threat from the upstart counterfeiter.

'This is no good to let happen for you,' Don Giuseppe counselled. 'Before you wink, you will have Treasury Department agents in your neighborhood and they will make things very hot for your other business . . .'

'What do you say we do, my good friend?' Morello wanted to know.

Battista made a slicing motion with his hand across his own throat.

Morello turned to his brother-in-law with raised eyebrows. Lupo the Wolf smiled and nodded his head knowingly.

Battista Balsamo's message had gotten over loud and clear.

'Thank you very much for your advice,' Morello turned back to Balsamo. 'I appreciate . . .'

Two days later, the afternoon of 14 April, a Tuesday, New York City police had one of the turn of the century's most baffling slayings to investigate, soon labeled by big black newspaper headlines as 'The Barrel Murder Case'.

The unidentified man was clearly the victim of a horrific mutilation. His corpse was stuffed into a barrel of sawdust and only his head and neck stuck out above the wood shavings. The face was covered with so much blood and grime that it was impossible to distinguish the features.

Yet the eyes were chillingly visible. They were wide open, froze in a gruesome death stare. Even more gruesome was that the victim's penis had been cut off and shoved into his mouth!

As Dr Albert T. Weston, the city's chief medical examiner, reported after an autopsy at the morgue, the man was stabbed and sliced no fewer than thirteen times. His throat was slashed from ear to ear, which in itself was enough to cause instant death, for the jugular was severed completely. But his killer or killers went on to insure his death by inflicting deep stab wounds on the face, neck, and upper torso.

The case went unsolved and without any visible progress towards solution for twenty days – until it was placed in the hands of NYPD Lieutenant Joseph Petrosino, the department's specialist in organised crime matters. He knew immediately that there was only one way to solve the crime: get the victim identified, then hope that a motive for the killing might surface, from which may come a focus on the probable killer.

Petrosino wasn't aware of the one factor that had handicapped the other detectives in those long and unrewarding days of their probe. The body had lain on a mortuary slab on ice with the face still muddied with blood and grit. No one had cleaned it off to enable the sleuths to get an accurate view of the victim's features.

Petrosino's first order of business was in going to the morgue and viewing the corpse. When he saw the condition of the face, he asked the medical examiner to clean it. Once this was done, the lieutenant called a police photographer to take a picture of it.

As soon as the negative was developed, Petrosino hurried to Police Headquarters at 240 Centre Street in Manhattan and directed the photo lab to make thirty prints. He had them distributed to every detective under his command, which covered seven precinct homicide squads in Manhattan. The admonition to each of his sleuths was:

'Hit the pavement and show this picture around. We've got to get an I.D. on this man who was found murdered in a barrel. Send all your findings to my office after you've cleared it with your sergeants. This is imperative. Act on this at once.'

Another investigation relating to this murder was underway at the same time – unbeknown to the NYPD and Lieutenant Petrosino. Treasury Department Agent William Flynn and a team of his investigators had been on the trail of a gang of counterfeiters who were pushing their phony money in various sections of New York City.

Flynn had one leg up on Petrosino in his search for the killer of the murdered man in the barrel only because the federal officer had a lead on the known operator of the counterfeiting ring. He also knew where the suspect met with the pushers of his funny money.

So Flynn and his men made it a part of their routine to eat lunch and dinner in The Star of Italy Café on Elizabeth Street on Manhattan's Lower East Side. They became fairly regular customers in the hope that they'd pick up bits and pieces of information about the counterfeiters.

After a while Flynn and his Treasury Department agents just about gave up hope that the man they suspected of being the counterfeit's ring leader would ever show up at The Star of Italy. Twenty days had passed during the stakeout and the federal sleuths still hadn't seen the suspect they were out to collar.

But on the twenty-second day they had a picture of the man they'd been hunting. It was brought to them by Lieutenant Petrosino and a team of his sleuths who had come with the photo of the murdered man in the barrel. Once the blood and grime had been washed from his face and its photo taken, police went to their files, matched the features with their rogue's gallery of prisoners and wanted men, and established that no one could fit the portrait of the wanted counterfeiting boss more than one particular picture from the rogue's gallery.

How did Petrosino make contact with Flynn, the Treasury agent?

Through some simple reasoning. When the lieutenant read the victim's rap sheet and saw his involvement in counterfeiting, he knew that Treasury must have had some awareness about the dead man, now positively identified as Benedetto Madonia.

At this gathering of city and federal investigators came a meeting of minds and a decision of how to proceed in solving the murder. Flynn told Petrosino that the slain counterfeiter had a brother-in-law in Sing Sing doing a three-year stretch.

'Go and see Giuseppe DiPrimo,' Flynn advised. 'I'll bet he can give you a lead. We also know him as "Benny the Convict".'

Petrosino, who could never be mistaken in a crowd for anyone else because he always wore a black derby, even when behind his desk, journeyed to Ossining, some sixty miles up the Hudson, and had a chat with DiPrimo.

Early in the conversation Petrosino showed DiPrimo the full-faced photo of Madonia taken on the mortuary slab and asked, 'Do you know this man?'

DiPrimo's eyes opened wide in recognition.

'Yeah . . . yeah . . .' he replied hesitantly, 'that . . . that's my brother-in-law . . . that's Benedetto Madonia . . .'

Benny the Convict looked up bewildered.

'What did he do . . . and why does he look so sick in this

picture?' the Mafia hood rasped. 'You know . . . he's married to my sister who lives in Buffalo . . .'

'No kidding? I didn't know that,' Petrosino said. Then in the next breath: 'And why was he in New York City last 14 April? What business did he have there?'

DiPrimo froze for a second or two. The question seemed to stun him. Then he seemed to pull himself together:

'I sent him to New York to see Giuseppi Morello to get something that belongs to me . . .'

From all that Petrosino knew about Morello's East Harlem operations, coupled with what he had learned from Flynn about Madonia's workings as a high-flying counterfeiter, the response from Benny the Convict made no sense at all.

Madonia was trying to muscle in on Morello's territory by recruiting storekeepers to make their shops clearing houses for his bogus greenery. What dealings could the brother-in-law of the murdered counterfeiter from another part of town have with the leader of the turf Madonia was trying to muscle in on?

'Hey, you make no sense,' Petrosino barked. 'Your brother-in-law was looking to boot Madonia the hell out of Harlem. So I can't believe there was anything that Morello could have which belonged to you . . .'

DiPrimo was nonplussed. He shook his head and quickly changed the subject. Taking a closer look at the photo of his brother-in-law, he asked, 'Tell me something . . . Why does Benedetto look sick in this picture . . . Is he sick?'

Petrosino felt now was the time to hit Benny the Convict with the whole load of bricks. Perhaps the shock of hearing that Madonia was dead would stir him into a confession that might finger the killer or killers.

'Your brother-in-law,' the lieutenant said slowly, each word measured for effect, 'is no longer with us . . . he is *morto* . . .'

DiPrimo paled. His eyes became glassy. His lips suddenly began trembling.

'You know something, you no good son-of-a-bitch, you *boutan*! I want you should pick up your fuckin' ass and get out of here. I'm not talking to you no more . . .'

DiPrimo jumped to his feet and shouted to the jail guard standing outside the small lawyer conference room in which he was holed up with Petrosino. 'Hey, screw, get me the fuck back to my cell. I don't want to talk to this bum no more.'

As the guard opened the door and began leading him away, DiPrimo shouted over his shoulder to Petrosino:

'Hey, I will take care of this when I get out of this fuckin' hole. It'll be on my own terms, you hear? On my own terms!'

Lieutenant Petrosino left Sing Sing with those words echoing in his ears. He had no more of a lead to Madonia's killer or killers after his talk with DiPrimo than he had before he encountered him.

Where to go from here?

On the New York Central commuter train ride back to Grand Central Terminal, Petrosino decided to launch a bold frontal attack on the Mafiosi in an ultimate push to solve Madonia's gruesome murder.

He called the homicide squad commanders to his office and passed out a typewritten list of fifteen names, all belonging to members of Morello's gang.

'Have your men round up these guys and bring them to headquarters,' he ordered. 'We're gonna give them a going-over so we can get to the bottom of who knocked off Madonia.'

By 4:30 p.m. – four hours after detectives were dispatched on the mission – fifteen snivelling Mafiosi from Morello's ranks were bunched together in a small ninth-floor interrogation room of the NYPD's headquarters building. Petrosino and a team of detectives took them one at a time to another interrogation room next door and grilled them endlessly. The room's lights had been doused and only the bulb from a goose-necked desk lamp shone directly on the face of the man being bombarded with rapid-fire questions:

'Where were you on that Tuesday when Madonia was killed, eh?'

'You know something, we know you love your leader . . . You have given Giuseppi Morello a blood oath . . . You would do anything he says to do – even kill, just like that! Didja?'

'Okay, you fuck, if you walk and tell us who did it, we'll go real easy on you . . .'

On and on the questioning droned. But the mobsters' lips were sealed. True to the oath of *omerta*, silence prevailed through all fifteen grillings.

Finally, frustrated, Petrosino sat at his desk and pencilled eight of the fifteen names on a pad. He tore the sheet out and handed it to Sergeant Michael Kearns.

'Hey, Mike,' he said sharply. 'Throw these guys in the lockup. I want them to cool their heels. Maybe then we can get some answers from them . . . The others you can let go. I don't think they can help us none.'

Giuseppi Morello, Ignazio 'Lupo the Wolf' Sietta, Pepino Fontana, Gaetano 'The Bull' Petto, Vito Cascio, Tony 'Horns' Genoa, Giuseppe Favarro, and Vito Lo Baido, whose alias was 'Deaf Vito' because of his hearing loss since birth, were tossed into the slammer.

Only one of the top-ranked members of Morello's gang eluded the dragnet Petrosino put out for the roundup. He was Don Vito Ferro, who was the overlord of all Mafia activities in Manhattan and ruled in much the same way as Balsamo did in Brooklyn – although on a much smaller scale since he was underboss to Don Giuseppe.

He may not have been clairvoyant, yet one could say that Ferro may have had a sixth sense. Perhaps he had gotten word from one of the cops on his pad about the impending roundup of Morello's gang – even that he was a target for arrest – and did the only thing that made sense. He high-tailed it to Brooklyn for an audience with Balsamo.

'What shall I do, Don Giuseppe?'

Balsamo could sense the man had lost his cool. He was playing scared cards. When a Mafiosi leader – indeed anyone in the ranks down to the lowliest bootlicker – exhibits fear, indeed even apprehension, about being taken up in a police sweep, then it's best to have the guy hit the road.

'My advice to you, *signore*,' the godfather said firmly, 'is to get out of town.'

Ferro tensed, hearing himself addressed as '*signore*'. It was an unmistakable signal: a man of Balsamo's high estate would never address a Mafioso of lesser rank by that title. Unless he was being kissed off.

As Balsamo spoke the next sentence, Ferro knew for certain that he had indeed been written out of New York City's Mafia.

'I want you should go right away to New Orleans,' Don Giuseppe said. 'It will be nice and cool for you to be with Nick Favia. He is just beginning to set up an operation there, and I know he will appreciate to get help from a *paisan* with such knowledge and experience you can offer . . .'

Don Vito Ferro went into his fadeout from the New York scene shortly afterwards, and the Mafiosi he left behind went on to live another day. None of the nine 'suspects' Lieutenant Petrosino held against their wills ever helped put a finger on the killer or killers.

Research had disclosed that there was only one torpedo who did the number on Benedetto Madonia: Gaetano The Bull Petto, one of the nine incarcerated gangsters who'd been under Lieutenant Petrosino's nose for the whole month that the nine mobsters were held in custody.

Ironically, a few days after the nine were released, Petrosino developed evidence that Petto was the killer. When he sent his bulls out to arrest The Bull, a funny thing happened.

They took into custody Giovanni Pecoraro, a spitting image of Gaetano Petto. By now, The Bull was into the wind, because no sooner had Morello's boys gotten drift that Petrosino's marauders were to come down hard on Petto, the big guy called him in for a talk.

'I want you to get your ass the hell out of town right now!' Morello directed. Petto shuffled off to Buffalo without a moment's delay and joined the Mafia family of the late Benedetto Madonia.

Why would Madonia's family welcome a member of the down-state family who put Madonia in a barrel with his throat slit and his penis between his lips like a cigar?

Because that's what life in the Mafia was like at the turn of the century – and what it is like today: they always kill a brother who gets out of line!

Now that Madonia was laid to rest, all was forgiven. He had

paid for his incursion on Morello's perlieus, and the message was on display for all to savor:

Don't try anything like this because this is what's gonna happen to you.

So The Bull, a fugitive on the run from a murder rap, joined the underworld fraternity in New York's second-largest city, 750 miles northwest, hard by the roar of one of nature's mightiest beauties, Niagara Falls.

Back in the big town, Petto's double, Giovanni Pecoraro, languished in the slammer only so long as it took him to convince a sitting judge in Manhattan Magistrate's Court that he was not Gaetano Petto.

The case was thrown out and Pecoraro was free to continue his pursuits as a member of the Morello mob.

Ironically, while Morello had wanted nothing to do with counterfeit currency in 1902 when Madonia tried to plant his funny money roots in East Harlem, the time came when Don Giuseppi decided that it wasn't such a bad idea.

He and Ignazio Sietta made a deal with Madonia's successor in the counterfeit operation and were given the distributorship in their territory. They set up candy stores, groceries, meat markets, furniture and hardware stores, restaurants, saloons, in addition to a string of other retailers, to launder their dirty money.

It worked well for about eight years – until 1913. Then Treasury agents moved in and arrested Morello and Sietta. They were convicted and sent to the federal penitentiary in Atlanta to do ten years.

Meanwhile, Don Vito Ferro performed so well in New Orleans that his expertise enabled the Mafia to expand rapidly into one of the nation's most effective and productive regions for organised crime. Unlike the landlocked cities in which the Mafia operated, the Louisiana capital had a waterfront, and it was becoming one of the country's busiest ports. As they would soon do in Brooklyn, the Black Handers were edging into the shipping lanes with their lucrative protection rackets over cargo loading and unloading operations.

Ferro played a large part in putting New Orleans on the Mafia's map as one of its biggest income-bearing territories. The

Sicilian Mafia summoned him to Palermo and gave him a significant post in the hierarchy there. The year was 1908.

He remained as a top don in Palermo for twenty-five years – until dictator Benito Mussolini ordered a crackdown on the Mafia.

With Mussolini's commandment, Mafiosi from all parts of the country were seized, placed in cages, and carted through the streets to be stoned by a cheering populace which had all too long suffered paying tribute to the killer-leeches.

The legend handed down through the years about Ferro is that he admitted to only one killing in his entire career as a Black Hander. That rubout took place at the Piazza Marina in Palermo on the night of 12 March 1909.

That was the night Lieutenant Joseph Petrosino, who had journeyed to Sicily to pursue evidence on the New York Mafiosi's ties with the bosses in Palermo, wandered into the marina to question a would-be informer.

The lieutenant was shot to death in what became one of the century's most electrifying murder cases. His assassination was widely viewed as a warning to law enforcement authorities to lay off the Mafia.

Joseph Petrosino was the first lawman to die trying to bring down the Mafia.

He was not the last.

Chapter 6

Shootout at Stauch's Dance Hall

In February 1920 Frankie Yale had no idea Battista Balsamo was planning to retire and turn the leadership over to Vincenzo Mangano and his brother Phillipo. All Frankie knew was that he had to protect his flanks against the almost certain retaliation from the White Hand after the Sagaman's Hall number he did on Wild Bill Lovett and his gang.

After a respectable interlude for mourning their dead and laying them to rest, the White Hand gang was summoned to a conclave called by Wild Bill Lovett. They met in the warehouse office of Caledonia Shipping Lines at 25 Bridge Street, hard by the limestone base tower of the Brooklyn Bridge. The agenda consisted of a single topic: how to effectively pay back the Black Hand for the outrage at Sagaman's Hall.

Twenty-five of the Irish Mafia's most notorious enforcers pilgrimaged to the ramshackle warehouse that Saturday afternoon, 21 February. A noxious, musty odor of manure hung heavy in the bleak, sparsely furnished office at the northeast corner of the building. The stench, so thick the men could barely breathe, was wafting into the office from the warehouse itself, where some six hundred bales of bulk potassium fertiliser had been stored for the weekend. The shipment, from Galveston, Texas, had been unloaded from the freighter *Miguel Sorcos* the day before and was to be trucked Monday to a feed and grain distributor in upstate Tonawanda.

'Couldn't you find another place to talk with us?' complained crosseyed Jimmy 'The Bug' Callaghan, contorting his face in disgust. Jimmy's expression made his deformity seem more pronounced: his pupils now appeared to be looking at each other across the bridge of his nose. But if anyone was inclined to mock Callaghan's somewhat comical appearance, it would not be done in his presence. The blond-haired Callaghan was a small, frail-looking man, but his violent temper more than compensated for his lack of size.

Lovett himself was sick of the stink, and he sensed that the others were as annoyed as Jimmy the Bug about having to meet in such unpleasant surroundings. Wild Bill had no idea things would turn out the way they had when he made arrangements a few days earlier to muster his troops in Caledonia's warehouse.

But he had no other choice. He didn't want all those men showing up at the Baltic Street Garage on a Saturday afternoon – or any afternoon: a rally of that size would surely tip off the Black Hand that something big was going on. And though no one had to alert Frankie Yale to guard against retaliation by Wild Bill and his minions for the bloodletting at Sagaman's Hall, a gathering of so many Irish mobsters would be like sending a telegram to their rivals that Lovett and his band were preparing to strike back.

A meeting hall or restaurant was just as inappropriate, for the gang could be spotted almost as readily there. It had to be some place more secluded. The search narrowed to the Caledonia's warehouse after Needles Ferry and Charleston Eddie discovered that no one would be working on that Gowanus waterfront pier over the weekend. Wild Bill had asked Ferry and Eddie, while on their extortion collection rounds, to check pier superintendents for such a spot. Frank McCarthy, the Caledonia Lines' pier boss, told the boys that his company's facility at 25 Bridge Street would be available. McCarthy had failed to tell Ferry and Eddie about the fertiliser shipment that would be stored in the warehouse over the weekend.

'How stupid can you guys be?' Lovett scolded Needles and Charleston before the meeting got underway, 'What are you trying to pull, setting us up in this horseshit place?'

'I swear to you, Bill,' Ferry pleaded. 'McCarthy never told us anything about the crap he put in here. It wasn't in the warehouse when we came here a couple days ago. He only told us that nobody was gonna be here, that we could use the office, and he gave us the key.'

Lovett shook his head disgustedly. He walked to a chair and stood on it.

'Fellas,' he said raspily, 'I can't stand this smell any more than you can. But there's no choice. So hold your breaths and listen to what I have to say. It won't take long.

'I called you here because of what happened to Jimmy O'Toole, to Kevin Donovan, and to Mary Reilly,' he said in a voice choked with emotion. 'They were killed by those dirty ginzos who didn't even have the guts to pull the job themselves. They hired out-of-town hit men to do their dirty work. That's because their own people don't have the balls to handle their problems: they've got to bring in outsiders when they want to spill our blood.'

Lovett slammed his clenched right fist into the palm of his left hand.

'We aren't like that, no sir,' he shouted, his face knotting with rage. 'At least when we have problems we take care of them ourselves!'

He let a moment pass. As he sensed that his words had sunk in, he went on: 'You better believe it that we Irishmen aren't going to let those lousy wops get away with what they did at Sagaman's Hall because –'

He was interrupted by a wave of applause, whistles, and shouts. The gathering approved of what he was saying.

'Tell us how we're going to get those lousy ginzos!' a voice sounded as the tumult died down. That call was echoed a half-dozen times by others in the room.

'Okay,' Lovett said tensely. 'I think there's one man among us who's got a right to speak his mind and tell us how he'd like to get back at those murdering Black Handers. I am speaking about Dick Lonergan.'

Wild Bill struck an emotional note which all at once precipitated another outburst. As the applause and cheers subsided, Lonergan limped his way to the chair on which Lovett stood. Wild Bill relinquished it to Pegleg. All eyes were on Lonergan. He was the sympathetic hero; one of those who died in the ambush at Sagaman's Hall was his girlfriend, Mary Reilly. And there was also what the gang knew about his early suffering wrought by the loss of his left leg.

When he was twelve years old Lonergan, while playing with friends in the Long Island Rail Road's yards on Sixty-ninth Street in the Bay Ridge section of Brooklyn, had hitched a ride aboard a freight car. He fell from his perch between an oil tanker and a lumber car and hit the ground alongside the tracks. But his left leg did not clear the rail completely.

The wheels of the lumber car passed over his leg and severed it about six inches above the ankle. His playmates summoned help and young Richard was rushed to Victory Memorial Hospital, where doctors amputated the stub below the knee. It saved his life. But Dick Lonergan was fated to live as a cripple.

In the months following the accident, the youngster was outfitted with a wooden stump which enabled him to walk – and which inevitably inspired the kids in his neighborhood to call him 'Pegleg'. The name stuck for the twenty years since that accident, although his friends seldom called him that.

Because of his physical handicap, Lonergan had never made it with the opposite sex. Girls politely turned him down for dates during his teenage years; as he grew into manhood women rejected his advances. It wasn't until he met Mary Reilly that Lonergan finally found acceptance by a woman. Their friendship grew into romance and finally into a proposal of marriage – which Mary accepted. They were to have been wed that coming June. Mary's death left Pegleg shattered beyond description. His only ambition now was to avenge her death by taking as many Black Hand lives as he could. He had already told Lovett that any plan to retaliate against the Italians must include him.

'If you don't pick me,' Pegleg had said to Wild Bill, 'I'll take things into my own hands. I'm gonna even the score whether you decide to cut me in for the hit or not.'

With Lonergan's passion for revenge so intense, Lovett knew he'd be a damned fool not to put the man in the lineup of annihilators dispatched against the Black Hand. After all, Lonergan had approached Lovett the previous Wednesday with the scheme of how to strike back at the Italians. He had laid it on the table for Wild Bill after they'd returned from Mary's funeral. Lovett had been astounded not only by the uniqueness of Lonergan's plan but by the infinite thought and attention to detail that had gone into it. Lovett decided then and there that Pegleg himself should be granted the privilege of getting up before the gang and giving the rendition of his brilliant blueprint for death.

Pegleg shifted restlessly as he stood on the chair now, his balance seemingly precarious as he tapped his wooden leg around on the seat searching for a comfortable stance. When he finally found a position that pleased him, he glanced at the faces staring up at him. Searching eyes peered from beneath the wide-brimmed hats, pinched lips drew together in anticipation of what he was about to say. Pegleg drew in a long nervous breath.

'I hear,' Lonergan began at last, the words coming softly and slowly, 'the wops are going to hold a victory celebration for the score they made on us. It's gonna be next Saturday night at Stauch's Dance Hall on Surf Avenue. I say that's when we should rap them, really lay it into 'em.'

It was a sweet plan. Lonergan proposed that he and three cohorts pose as the four-piece orchestra hired to play the affair. Pegleg and the other three executioners would present themselves at the door as a string ensemble. But instead of Stradivariuses or Cremonas, their violin cases would hold sawed-off shotguns, .45-caliber automatics, and yes, even a tommy gun or two.

'How are you gonna play music when Frankie Yale's boys see they got one orchestra there already?' hulking Eddie Lynch, the enforcer for the gang's loan sharking operations, challenged from the back of the room. 'They'll stuff you in your own violin cases before you get past the door.'

Lonergan smiled wryly at his detractor. 'That's where you come in, Eddie,' he quickly responded, pulling a piece of paper from his pocket and handing it to Jimmy the Bug, who was standing directly in front of Pegleg. 'Pass it back to Eddie,' Lonergan said. A hand reached out and the paper was relayed to Lynch. As he read the writing, Eddie's round nervous face screwed up with frowning suspicion.

'What the hell is this?' he growled.

'That's the names and addresses of the musicians,' Lonergan said firmly. 'What you and some of the other boys are gonna do is stop them from showing up –' Pegleg took another deep breath. 'No rough stuff, you understand. Just make sure they stay home awhile. And when me and the other violinists are finished with our numbers, you can let them go to Stauch's. They'll be needed then to play a funeral march.'

A sudden shifting of feet accompanied by an undercurrent of murmurs was a signal to Pegleg that the gang was duly impressed with the scenario so far. The smile on Wild Bill Lovett's face and some others inspired Lonergan to unveil the rest of the plot with even greater enthusiasm.

It was a simple plan, much less complicated than Pegleg had led the gang to believe at the outset. Their initial impression was that the 'orchestra' would mount the stage before breaking out its 'pieces' and begin playing the cadenza of hot lead.

'What are you guys gonna do after you shoot up the place, walk through the crowd of ginzos saying "Excuse me, please," and go out the front door?' Joe 'The Boozer' Bean yelled derisively.

'No, no, no!' Lonergan shouted.

'You got it all wrong, Joe,' Lovett interrupted Pegleg's response to Bean, the brother of Petey and Danny. 'Dick didn't say they'd shoot from the stage, although maybe he left that impression. The way it's really gonna be, Dick and whoever goes on this one will jump out of the car on Surf Avenue, walk into Stauch's right through the main doors, and start blasting.'

'Hey, that's real great,' rasped Ernie 'Skinny' Shea, one of the White Hands' waterfront extortion collectors. Our guys'll be in and outta the joint before them Sicilian scum know what hit 'em!'

But the plan didn't sit right with Shea's sidekick in shakedowns, Wally 'The Squint' Walsh.

'Why don't you just go in with the rods showing?' he asked in his gravelly voice, his eyelids shuttered. 'What the hell for do you need to get fancy with violin cases and all that shit?'

'Because,' Lovett said slowly, his patience running out fast at the thickheads who apparently hadn't listened closely when Pegleg was covering that ground. 'You see, Wally, there are gonna be maybe one or two wops at the door who'll be watching who goes in. So if our guys hop out of the car with their artillery showing, they'll be wiped out before they even put their feet on the sidewalk.'

Charleston Eddie then raised a very good point when he asked how Lonergan expected even to reach the door of the dance hall without being recognised.

'I know what you're saying,' Pegleg grinned in spite of the oblique reference to his wooden leg. But he was prepared with an answer. 'That's all gonna be taken care of,' he assured them. 'Bill's gonna buy me one of them new artificial legs. You can wear a shoe with it and it looks like the real thing. I was measured this morning for one, and it'll be ready for me first thing Tuesday.'

The boys began clapping for Lonergan. And buoyed by the seeming acceptance of his plan, Pegleg began doing a jig on the chair.

With no further questions, Lonergan asked for three volunteers to accompany him on his mission. Nearly every hand in the warehouse office was flung in the air.

'No good,' Lovett said. 'We gotta make this fair.' He took off his gray fedora and placed the crown in the palm of his left hand. Then, urging Lonergan off the chair, Wild Bill stepped up so everyone could see what he was doing. He stuffed his hand into his coat and pulled out a fistful of white marbles, which he began dropping into the hat. 'One, two, three . . .'

The count went to fourteen and his hand was empty. Lovett then pulled another handful of white marbles and continued dropping them, one at time, into his chapeau. '. . . twenty, twenty-one'. He stopped and returned the remaining marbles to his pocket. Then he went to his pocket and pulled out three black marbles. 'One, two, three,' he counted as he let them fall into the hat.

Then, holding the fedora above everyone's head, Lovett ordered, 'Everybody come and take a marble. The ones who pick the blacks go with Dick on this job . . .'

The luck of the draw went to Irish Eyes Duggan, Danny Bean, and Charleston Eddie McFarland, who were cheered lustily and pounded on their backs by their less fortunate brethren.

'Don't worry you guys who lost out,' Lovett consoled his boys. 'There is still gonna be action for a lot of you men. I'm sending at least another six of you as a backup, just in case Dick and his "orchestra" don't read their music too good.'

The concerto for murder was scheduled to be played at Stauch's one week hence. Curtain time was eight o'clock on Saturday, 26 February, by which point some fifty-five members of the Black Hand gang would have been seated at the tables around the dance floor with their wives or dates, and when some of the crowd might very well indeed begin wondering why the orchestra had not yet taken the stage and struck up the strains of 'Santa Lucia', Frankie Yale's favourite number. The gang's 'entertainment committee' had planned it that way because they wanted Frankie and his missus to lead the dancing. It was their way of paying homage to Yale for his brilliant direction of the Sagaman's Hall ambush.

Not in his wildest dreams did Pegleg Lonergan imagine that things would go the way they did when he and his sidekicks in slaughter went to Stauch's Dance Hall. As confident as he'd been in presenting his plan, first to Wild Bill Lovett, then to the White Hand's rank and file, all sorts of anxieties burned inside him.

Pegleg's overriding concern was the very apprehension advanced by Charleston Eddie. Since Tuesday morning when the artificial leg was strapped on, Lonergan had spent hour after hour trying to master a walk that would look natural. But as Saturday night approached, he hadn't mastered that miserable artificial limb. While for the first time since the accident he wore trousers with both legs down to his ankles and two shoes, he still hadn't managed to walk without a limp. Yet the improvement was so dramatic that Lovett assured Pegleg no Black Hand lookout could ever recognise him.

At six o'clock on Saturday night the men appointed for the hit rallied in the White Hand's garage on Baltic Street. Wild Bill Lovett personally checked each of the weapons packed into the violin cases to be toted to the Coney Island dance hall by Pegleg Lonergan, Irish Eyes Duggan, Danny Bean, and Charleston Eddie.

Lovett also checked each of the revolvers, automatics, and shotguns the backup team was taking to the scene. Picked for that assignment were Joey Bean, Ernie Shea, Wally Walsh, Eddie Lynch and Jack 'Squareface' Finnegan. Their driver was Ernie 'The Scarecrow' Monaghan. Danny Bean's brother, Petey, had been singled out for the honor of driving the black Chevrolet sedan that would carry the team of hit men to the hall.

'All right, you guys,' Lovett said after he had satisfied himself that his executioners were prepared to move out. 'Go get 'em!'

A whoop and cry exploded from the gathering, but Lovett quickly muffled it.

'Nobody's celebrating yet!' he scolded his boys. 'You do the job first and then we'll have something to cheer. Now get the hell out and get it done!'

Lonergan led the way out, followed by Charleston Eddie and Danny and Petey Bean, with Duggan trailing behind them. The backup team then left the garage and got into the second car, a black 1919 Packard sedan. The two cars roared off toward Coney Island.

A powdery snow began falling just as the White Handers started towards their destination.

'Shit!' Petey Bean shouted as he spotted the small white flakes buffeting the windshield. 'I hope this goddam snow doesn't screw us up.'

'Take it easy, Petey,' Lonergan pampered the hot-headed wheelman. 'It's all gonna be over and done with before the streets even get slippery.'

Had it been the middle of July, a half-million persons or more would have been wandering around Coney Island's beaches, boardwalks, and amusement grounds. But on that windswept, snowy night of 26 February, the only visible activity in America's famed bathing and amusement resort was in Stauch's Dance Hall, where fifty-five celebrants had gathered for their revelry. Elsewhere, the streets were deserted.

As Petey Bean cruised along Surf Avenue he kept a sharp eye out for any movement outside Stauch's which might indicate that too many lookouts were guarding the hall. But as he drew nearer, Petey blurted, 'There ain't nobody at the doors! Jesus, this is gonna be a snap!'

As a matter of fact, Frankie Yale and his bunch had been lulled into believing a report that had been planted for their benefit that afternoon. Lovett had sent Needles Ferry to O'Brien's Saloon, one of South Brooklyn's hotbeds of scuttlebutt, to drop a word or two, 'inadvertently, of course', that the White Hand was planning to sack one of the waterfront warehouses that night. Figuring that such shenanigans would command considerable manpower, Yale reasoned it would be highly unlikely that Lovett would divert any of his boys for an escapade in Coney Island.

So only one guard, Joe 'Rackets' Capolla, had been conscripted for sentry duty at the doors. But, as fate ordained it, not even Joe was at the doors as Petey Bean pulled the Chevy to a stop in front of the dance hall.

Capolla wasn't at his post because he had come down with a sudden case of diarrhea. And without calling for a replacement, he left to answer that peevishly demanding call of nature. The men's room was a mere five steps from the entrance, which may have been why Joe didn't ask for a stand-in. At any rate, his presence in the men's room was registered by one Antonio Sisiliato, who himself was straddling one of the thrones when Capolla barged in, his trousers at half-mast even before he had reached the john. Had Joe not managed to expedite the evacuation of his loose bowels as quickly as he had, history might have recorded a different ending for the chapter in the war between the ginzos and the micks. Certainly it would have been a different outcome for Joe Capolla. For he came back the very instant Pegleg Lonergan and his three henchmen burst through the main outside doors and into the entrance foyer of the dance palace.

Capolla made an heroic effort in the face of the awesome artillery that by now had been drawn from the violin cases and suddenly levelled at him. Joe lived just long enough to hurl his body against the double swinging doors of the main hall and cry, 'Look out . . .!'

His words were drowned by the deafening blast of bullets that almost sliced his torso in two.

He didn't fall as quickly as one might be expected to after the heart and pulse had stopped functioning. Instead he stood erect, like a statue, for the longest time, framed by the swinging doors which had caught him in a vicelike hold. All the while blood from his back, chest, and stomach cascaded out of him like Niagara, and formed a large pool on the floor.

When Capolla's massive body finally toppled and hit the floor, it was with a sickening splash that spattered his gore over his assassins. Lonergan and his team of killers merely stepped over Joe's dying bulk and surged into the hall, guns blazing.

The revelers – the cream of the Black Hand's crop of aristocratic extortionists, loan sharks, bootleggers, hijackers, and hit men – catapulted from their chairs and dove under the tables for protection. Many of them gallantly dragged their wives and sweethearts with them.

But whoever had escorted Anna Balestro to the dance that night was rated a poor score for chivalry. Anna, the buxom, angel-faced sister of Albert Balestro, a funeral director who fronted for Frankie Yale in his chain of parlors, was struck by a .45-caliber slug on the left side of her head. The bullet tore through her brain. Her body, toppled from the chair in which she'd been sitting, crunched on the floor with thunderous impact. After all, she weighed two hundred and forty pounds.

Lonergan, Charleston Eddie, Danny Bean, and Irish Eyes Duggan sprayed their lead at random into the crowd, making it a simple case of pot luck for those who stopped the bullets and for the more fortunate ones who didn't.

Giovanni Capone (no relation to Scarface Al) was one of the unlucky ones. Giovanni, who worked as a tombstone engraver when he wasn't busy breaking into warehouses for the Black Hand, was struck with a charge of buckshot exploding from the muzzle of the sawed-off shotgun wielded by Irish Eyes. Though the whole front of his face was blown away, Capone was heard blurting profanities in a voice that carried for several long minutes. Witnesses swear Giovanni's words were leaping out of his neck, for he had neither lips nor mouth through which his voice could have come.

Another of Yale's more valuable underlings, Giuseppe 'Momo' Municharo, a soldier in the protection rackets, also had the misfortune of catching a volley from Duggan's shotgun. A gaping hole was opened in his abdomen, giving the stricken crowd a cutaway view of Momo's intestines, which were still bulging with the spaghetti á la Milanese that he'd feasted on before coming to the dance.

The piercing screams and cries of the women, and many of the men as well, were like a replay of a sound track from the earlier carnage visited by the Black Hand on the Irishmen at Sagaman's Hall.

Several of the more alert Italian mobsters had managed to unlimber their guns from their holsters and fire back at the four assassins. But the shots were pegged so carefully in order to avoid hitting their own people that they missed their intended targets as well. Only after Lonergan was satisfied that enough blood had been spilled and had commanded his accomplices to retreat from the hall were the beleaguered Black Handers offered a clear field of fire.

Then one of Yale's boys made a quick score. Augie the Wop Pisano earned a notch on his automatic when he drilled a .45 bullet into the fleeing Danny Bean. It caught Danny in the back of the head. He crumpled in a heap on the vestibule floor, inches from the outer doors – and from Joe Capolla's corpse. Another second and he'd have been breathing the fresh, snow-filled, sea-scented air of Coney Island.

Pegleg, Charleston Eddie, and Duggan made it out of the hall unscathed and leaped into the getaway car.

'Roll it, roll it!' screamed Pegleg.

'Where's Danny?' cried Petey Bean, frantically searching the dance hall entrance for a sign of his brother.

'They hit him, Petey,' Duggan said crisply. 'He ain't gonna be comin' out. You'd better step on it before we all get it.'

Suddenly the Packard with the backup team roared alongside the Chevrolet.

'Hey, what the hell you waiting for?' Eddie Lynch shouted from the window. 'It's over, get your ass going, Petey!'

Then, turning to Ernie the Scarecrow, who was at the wheel beside him, Lynch barked, 'Fuck 'em. We ain't waiting. Step on it!'

The Packard roared along Surf Avenue like a frontrunner in the Indianapolis 500. But it wasn't alone for much of its flight. For, at Lonergan's urging – he had put the barrel of his gun against the driver's head – Petey Bean at last pulled away from the dance hall. And not a second too soon. Just as the car began skidding around the corner into Stillwell Avenue on a pavement made slippery by the falling snow, the crackle of gunfire was heard. The Italians were shooting from the windows and steps of the dance hall. But the bullets flying at the fleeing vehicle went wide of their mark and the White Handers got safely out of range.

But Petey Bean didn't remain behind the wheel for long. He was too absorbed by the concern for his brother's uncertain fate.

'What did they do, shoot him?' his voice choked.

'Yeah, yeah,' Pegleg replied. 'He was too goddamn slow running out. They dropped him right inside the door.'

'Why the fuck didn't you carry him out?' Bean screamed, all at once breaking into convulsive sobs.

'No way we coulda done that, Petey,' Charleston Eddie said from the back seat. 'I saw what happened. They got him in the back of the head . . .'

Bean began weeping so hard that when the speeding car almost mounted the sidewalk as Petey was making a turn, Lonergan decided it was time for a change of drivers.

'Stop the fuckin' car!' he bellowed. 'I ain't gonna let you drive no more.'

Lonergan turned his head as the car stopped. 'Get your ass behind the wheel,' he said to Charleston Eddie. The doors were flung open and the change of drivers quickly took place. The ride the rest of the way back to the Baltic Street Garage was smooth.

'A hell of a score!' cried Pegleg as he limped into Wild Bill Lovett's office. 'We really gave it to them.'

'Yeah, I kinda figured you boys would,' Lovett said softly. 'But you lost one, didn't ya?'

The information had come from the backup team, which had watched the White Hand assassins fleeing the dance hall and had beaten them back to the garage. Wally Walsh had told Lovett that only three of the gang came out of Stauch's.

No one had to identify the casualty for Wild Bill after Pegleg, Charleston Eddie, and Irish Eyes Duggan walked into the office trailed by a sobbing Petey Bean.

'Okay, okay,' Lovett said awkwardly, giving the bereaved Petey a sidelong glance. 'It hurts me very much that they knocked out Danny, but that's the kind of chances we're all taking in this friggin' business.'

Lovett took a deep breath. 'Now give it to me straight and no bullshit. I want to know what the score was.'

'High – very high,' Duggan replied in a self-contained voice. 'We left a whole lot of them bleeding like pigs . . .'

'Yeah,' interrupted Charleston Eddie with a sudden burst of enthusiasm, 'we really tore them apart. They had nobody at the door and we got in with no trouble. But then guess who we saw?'

Eddie looked at Lovett, anticipating that he'd ask 'who?' Instead the White Hand's chieftain snarled, 'Cut out the fuckin' questions and give me straight answers on the rundown!'

'Okay, okay, Bill,' Eddie cowered. 'It was Rackets Capolla. You shoulda seen the look on his face when we hit him. You shoulda seen him standing up after we blasted him in the gut . . .'

Duggan and Lonergan described the rest of the massacre to Lovett, but Lovett's reaction was subdued. He was pleased, but he didn't want to stage a celebration because Petey Bean was there. Danny Bean didn't mean a hell of a lot to Wild Bill Lovett – Danny was just another hand as far as he was concerned – yet in Petey Bean's presence Lovett felt he should display a modicum of sorrow for the man who was left behind.

By 8:15 p.m. Surf Avenue was suddenly alive with traffic. Ambulances and police cars streamed toward Stauch's Dance Hall, where nine people had caught the bullets and shotgun pellets in flight and were in need of medical attention.

Remarkably, unlike the Sagaman's Hall ambush, none of the six men and three women wounded by the gunfire was seriously injured; their wounds were uniformly minor ones. Fury Argolia, the restaurateur, had caught a slug in his right shoulder, but the bullet merely tore through the flesh without touching the bone.

Others were either grazed by bullets or hit with the spray of the shotguns at such great distances that the pellets merely pierced their skins. All nine of the wounded were extremely lucky. They were taken to Coney Island Hospital for emergency treatment, but not one of them was kept overnight as a patient. They were sent home after their wounds were patched.

Rackets Capolla, Anna Balestro, Giovanni Capone, and Momo Municharo were morgue cases. They were given exquisite funerals. That was the least Frankie Yale could do for them. In fact, he charged the families only half price for the send-offs.

The fifth fatality of the shootout, Danny Bean, went to his requiem in a plain pine coffin because his gang boss, Wild Bill Lovett, didn't have Frankie Yale's connections with the undertaking industry. The White Hand always had to pay going retail rates for its funerals.

But the tears and euologising for Danny Bean were no less profound than the sobs and exaltations for Anna Balestro and the three Black Hand banditi who were laid out in their stately brass-handled mahogany caskets.

Emotions at the Italian funerals ran much higher, not only because their toll at Stauch's was so much greater than the casualties the Irish had suffered, but also because one of their dead, Anna Balestro, was an innocent victim. Her death had been as unwarranted and cold-blooded as Mary Reilly's. And it aroused as much outrage in Frankie Yale as Mary's killing had stirred in Wild Bill Lovett.

While standing at Anna's graveside beside her brother, Albert, Frankie wept unashamedly. With tears running down his cheeks, he whispered to Albert, 'So help me, God, I'm gonna make those Irish sons of bitches pay through their noses for taking this girl's life . . .'

Frankie put the palm of his right hand slowly up to his face, covering his lips. Then, just as slowly, he moved the hand outward, blowing a kiss.

It was a meaningful sign that had originated with the code of the so-called *omerta* traditions established during the rise of the Mafia in Sicily more than a century before.

It was the kiss of death.

Chapter 7

Charleston Eddie's Last Sunday Matinee Flick

In calculating the revenge he would take against the White Hand, Frankie Yale decided that it would be foolhardy to strike back pell-mell with another ambush or mass shooting. There'd been two bloodbaths in less than a month, one against each side, and what had really been achieved? The score was dead even: three White Handers and three Black Handers had been wiped out, along with one woman from each of the 'families'.

'So what's gonna happen if we hit 'em back?' Yale asked some of the boys who dropped into his office after Anna Balestro's funeral. 'Sure, we knock off a few more miserable micks. But then what happen? They come back at us again, maybe even waste our wives or girls. I don't like it. They ain't playing percentages.'

'What you got in mind?' Augie the Wop put in. 'You think we should maybe not do nuthin' for what they done, eh, Frankie?'

Augie didn't intend to sound sarcastic, but the question was pregnant with derision.

The blood rising in his face, Yale jumped to his feet and brought his fist down on the desk. 'Those big balls on you,' he bellowed, 'You better take them to wherever you got 'em and get your old ones back. If you don't I'm gonna break 'em down to size.'

Pisano paled. He turned warily and stared at Yale's *compare*, Don Giuseppe Balsamo, who was reposing in the maroon velvet armchair, the one Frankie's father-in-law had liked so much until he died in it. Augie was seeking some support from the man who was his good friend. But Don Giuseppe had his gaze fixed on the floor in front of his feet, scrupulously avoiding Pisano's eyes. Sparing people from Frankie Yale's wrath was not one of Balsamo's commitments to his Mafia fiefdom.

'Awright, Frankie, for chrissake, lay off him,' Fury Argolia pleaded. 'He didn't mean to insult you.'

Fury, his right arm in a black cloth sling to facilitate the healing of the bullet hole in his shoulder, was one of the select few Black Handers who could speak up to Yale and not incur his wrath. Frankie respected the fiery Argolia, because he measured a few cuts above all the others in intelligence. He was also an amiable departure from the conventional Black Hander whose only calling was gangsterism. Argolia didn't have to be a mobster, because his career as a successful restaurateur preceded his entry into the rackets. His friendship with Yale and some of the boys in the mob had evolved years before when they began patronising Fury's eating establishment. Gradually that association aroused his interest in the Black Hand's activities and ultimately brought about his involvement with them.

In the early years, when the Italian gang was a loosely knit organisation and had yet to be molded by Frankie Yale into a unified force with solid direction and purpose, Fury's role was that of confidant and 'advisor'. After the Black Hand broke into the big time and cut itself into the White Hand's protection rackets on the waterfront and other areas, Argolia became a 'high counsellor' for the gang, directing a branch in which he had firsthand expertise – the shakedown of retail merchants for protection.

Argolia considered the time and effort he invested in the Black Hand organisation something akin to civic duty, much the way law-abiding citizens served on school committees and join neighborhood associations of the Elks, the Kiwanis, and the Knights of Columbus.

There was a brief moment of scowling silence after Fury had interrupted Frankie's tirade against Augie the Wop. Then Yale sat down and snorted in amusement at Argolia's intercession on Pisano's behalf.

Frankie's lips curled gradually into a smile. 'Fury, you are smart,' he said slowly. 'You and I are old friends. Did you understand me when I said there been two big killings in a month and four of theirs and four of ours are gone? Do I make sense to you?'

'Sure you do, Frankie,' Argolia said. 'You want to end the mass murders, but that doesn't mean what they did to us on Saturday night is forgiven . . .'

'Exactly!' Yale burst in, turning to Augie the Wop with a penetrating stare. 'Why the hell ain't you smart like him, eh? See how Fury understands me?' Then with a level, measured gaze at Battista Balsamo, Frankie asked in a reverent tone, 'What do you think, *compare*? Do I make sense or don't I?'

Balsamo shifted uneasily in the chair.

'Frankie, I got no bones to pick with you,' Don Giuseppe said with a polite smile. 'You know I go all the time with what you say. If you think we should not waste them by the numbers . . . well, you're the boss, my good friend . . . And Augie didn't mean no insult . . .'

Balsamo gestured toward Pisano who sat stiffly in the chair beside Yale's desk. Augie the Wop's dark heavy eyebrows slanted in a hard frown, almost obscuring his small brown eyes. He was almost relieved that Fury and Don Giuseppe had taken the pressure off by placating Yale.

'Yeah,' Frankie snorted, 'I see now you people understand me and see things like I see them.'

Yale leaned forward and rested his elbows on the desk.

'Listen to me,' he said in a low but intense tone. 'You gotta look at it from how things gone for us. Look, we went big-time little more than three years ago, right? So what we did was cut ourselves in for a big hunk of everything those micks had going for them. They operating for years, right? And we come in and become big men right away . . .'

Yale pounded his fist on the desk again.

'We did it with muscle,' he said sharply. 'We showed 'em we weren't scared to move in their territory. We took over and we come a long way . . .'

Frankie methodically went over the Black Hand's achievements: the infiltration of the waterfront that snagged more than a score of shipping firms and pier operators under the Italian gang's terrifying thumb; the commanding lead taken over the White Hand in the first thirteen months of bootlegging since the Volstead Act became law and ushered in the era of Prohibition; the burgeoning control over South Brooklyn's small businessmen who'd been terrorised into paying weekly protection tribute to Fury Argolia's enforcers; the many other activities such as hijacking and warehouse rip-offs that were directing thousands of dollars weekly into the Black Hand's coffers.

'So what do the drunken micks do?' Yale went on. 'They try to stand up to us. They wanna teach us lesson and they waste Crazy Benny. But we don't stand still for that. We get back at them . . . boy, how we get back!'

Yale rocked back in his chair, laughing hard.

'We take one out ourselves. But what a score . . . we . . . we . . .'

Yale could hardly contain himself now. His voice was so choked up by laughter that he was unable to speak.

'We take out their number-one guy,' chortled Two-Knife Willie, who was standing in his usual place by the window. For a change he wasn't cleaning his fingernails with the knife in his hand. He was running the blade up and down a day's stubble of beard on his right cheek, making a shaving sound. As he spoke, Altierri lowered the knife from his face and made a quick, slicing gesture across his throat.

'So Denny Meehan makes the score even, eh, Frankie?' Altierri's thin lips twitched.

'More – more than that,' Yale said, still chuckling. 'Meehan makes like five Crazy Bennys. When you want the big man, they gotta sit up and take notice.'

105

'But then they come back and steal our booze,' Fury observed with his usual objectivity. 'So we pull the Sagaman's thing and you got three of them gone and how many more laid up . . .'

Argolia's voice trailed off, then he turned to Yale, his face suddenly somber, and nodded his head in agreement.

'But they don't stand still,' Fury continued. 'They pay us back quick . . .'

'Right, right, right!' Yale snapped, his voice triumphant. 'That's my whole point! It's tit for tat. And what I'm saying is that ain't the way to play with them micks. Don't forget – they been around a long time and they know the score. They know how to play the game . . .'

Yale suddenly turned to the window and pointed a finger in a direction which he meant to indicate Chicago.

'Look at Johnny Torrio and Capone,' Yale said gravely. 'They got their own Irish bastards up against them. And you know Johnny and Al ain't no dumdums. They're smart. Yeah, they're smart and they know what to do. But they got that Dion O'Bannion and his bunch, and they can't get nowhere yet. It takes time. Sooner or later they gonna put the micks down, but you can't do a thing like that in twenty-four hours.'

'And if you're smart, you don't pull no more ambushes for a big score, right, Frankie?' piped Augie the Wop, now at last finding his voice after Yale's scathing denunciation.

'Smart boy,' Yale complimented, pleased that he had finally gotten through to the numb-skulled Pisano. 'I forgive you, Augie, because I know sometimes your brain sleeps while you are awake.'

The office exploded with laughter, but Yale quickly called for quiet.

'I got one thing I want to say,' he rasped, his eyes opening wide. 'We are gonna even the score for what those goddam Irishers did. But it's gonna be done nice and easy . . .'

Yale narrowed his eyes and made his mouth a tight slit as he glared across the room at the plaque on the wall bearing the two broken knife handles hanging in memory of the number Altierri had done on Greaseball Pignatore, the squealer.

'We know who the ones are who shot us up in Coney, don't we, eh?' Yale asked meaningfully.

'Sure, Frankie,' Argolia said, putting his hand up to his shoulder. 'I know who hit me . . . that sonofabitch Charleston Eddie . . .' Fury drew in a deep breath. 'And I also know he was the one who got Anna,' he said slowly. 'I know that because he was the only one who had a revolver. The others all had big artillery.'

'Okay!' Yale shouted. 'And we also know Irish Eyes Duggan, Pegleg Lonergan, and Danny Bean was there. Well, we don't have to worry none about Bean. He ain't gonna bother us no more. It's those other three we get. And I say we're gonna wipe 'em out!'

Yale crashed his fist on the desk once more.

'One at a time!' he screamed. 'Ya hear me? I said one at a time! But we're gonna get 'em all!'

Yale's performance earned him a round of applause. But it was a short round, for Frankie was all business.

'Listen to me,' he said heavily. 'The one I got in mind for the first hit is that *bastardo* who wasted Anna. The same one who got Fury. That sonofabitch Charleston Eddie . . .'

'What you figure on doing?' Don Giuseppe cut in. 'Do you want one of my boys to take care of him?'

'I appreciate your offer,' Yale smiled, 'you are a good friend in time of need. But I don't think it's so smart to use our people. I don't want it so those fuckers can blame us. This number we're gonna do on Charleston is special. It's gotta be different . . .'

To this day Brooklyn homicide detectives still carry the case of Charleston Eddie McFarland in their 'active-unsolved' files. And while it remains one of the borough's most puzzling killings, not even the most optimistic sleuths can muster the slightest bit of hope that they'll ever stamp the case 'closed'. If and when they transfer the yellowed reports and crumbling documents in McFarland's case folder to the 'inactive' file, it will be done without having officially identified the killer.

For all practical purposes, Eddie's killer, as he has been identified to the authors, could never be arrested, prosecuted, and convicted for the crime – nearly seventy years after the fact.

The police had exactly a dozen years to catch up with Charleston Eddie's slayer. But because they lacked clues to his identity then, Edward 'Honey Boy' Fletcher remained a free man, to practice his special skills for the Purple Gang until 1933. Then his fearsome leadership of the Detroit mob, after a long apprenticeship as one of its most gifted executioners, ended abruptly by a severe affliction of lead poisoning. Honey Boy did not recover, and his secret of what happened that Sunday afternoon 19 March 1921 in Para's Court Theater in Brooklyn went with him to his grave.

It was one of the neatest, smoothest rubouts ever pulled off by any mob. And it was masterminded by Frankie Yale.

The orchestration for Charleston Eddie's extermination was one of Frankie's virtuoso performances. It was executed with such cunning and finesse that even the most vigilant White Handers, who'd never for a moment put Yale and his band of cut throats beyond suspicion, could not find the remotest evidence that Yale or his gang had anything to do with McFarland's bloody sendoff.

How could Yale or the Black Hand be suspected when the evidence uncovered at Para's Court Theater that Sunday afternoon conclusively indicated that Charleston Eddie was killed by one of his girlfriends, apparently during a lovers' quarrel?

Yale knew that Eddie had a lovely, blue-eyed blonde sweetheart, Joan Finnegan. And since he'd begun squiring the colleen around some nine months before, Charleston had become a creature of habit in at least one aspect of his romance with her. Every Sunday afternoon, Eddie unfailingly took Joan to the neighborhood movie house, Para's Court Theater on Court Street, at the fringe of the Gowanus docks.

The source of Frankie's knowledge about this was Willie Altierri, who'd been delegated by Yale to study Charleston's routines and report where Eddie could best be ambushed. Yale gave Two-Knife the assignment late on that Saturday night after the wounded and dead had been carted away from Stauch's Dance Hall, and when Yale had been apprised of the carnage and had been told who killed Anna Balestro.

Yale was astonished by Altierri's quick results. In less than twenty-four hours Two-Knife had compiled a complete dossier on Eddie's daily routines. Willie discovered that among Charleston's regular hangouts were the White Hand's garage, McGuire's and O'Brien's saloons, and Mahar's Pool Hall on Fourth Avenue. However, none of these places lent themselves to the kind of inconspicuous death Frankie wanted to visit upon Eddie. Certainly it would be reckless to make a hit at the mick's garage, and the saloons and pool hall would be no better because there'd be too many witnesses.

'Hey, tell me something, Willie,' Yale asked suspiciously. 'How come you only been a shadow for one day and you know so much about Charleston and this broad he takes every Sunday to the movies? How in the hell can you know that, eh?'

Altierri smiled gloatingly. 'Because I happen to know Sally Lomenzo pretty good, that's how,' he responded ambiguously – and with just a bit too much arrogance to suit Frankie.

'Willie, you stop playing fuckin' guessing games with me,' Yale snapped at the edge of annoyance. 'How did you know about the show . . . who is this cunt Sally, speak up?'

Willie sat cold and controlled in the chair in front of Yale's desk. It was a rare moment when he had the shots to make the boss hang on tenterhooks. Two-Knife was a prankster at heart and his greatest pleasure was holding people in suspense when he was telling them something. But Willie was well aware that Yale had a limited capacity for taunting jests. Looking up he saw that Frankie was rapidly running of patience.

'See, Frankie,' Two-Knife put his hand on his groin and made a jerking up-and-down motion. 'Sally can't live without this big Sicilian sausage I got between my legs, understand? Three, maybe four times a week she's gotta have it all the way up, otherwise she goes outta her damn mind. So, me, I keep her happy . . .'

'Awright, so you're humpin' her,' Frankie broke in sharply. 'I don't wanna know nothing about your fuckin' sex life, *stupido*! All I ask you is who the broad is? What's she gotta do with what you tell me that Charleston Eddie takes his girl every Sunday to Para's Court? Now you wanna tell me, Willie, or do I gotta chop your ass up?'

'Hold on, Frankie, that's what I'm trying to do,' Altierri leaned forward with a wide grin. 'She's the cashier at the theater . . . So

109

when I'm tailing Eddie and the broad and I seen them stop at the booth to buy tickets, I got to thinking . . .'

'Thinking what, Willie?' Yale asked, his curiosity suddenly aroused.

'When I see how they both stood outside the booth and bullshitted with Sally, I said to myself, hey, Willie, my girl's gotta know these people. Maybe they been coming there regular or whatever. So after they go in, I slip up to the booth and Sally gets real surprised and excited. She says it's too early for her to leave. She think I came to take her out for a lay. But I says to her I wanna rundown on them two who just went in. Well, whaddaya think she tells me? She doesn't know Charleston too good, only from him bringing the skirt to the show. But the broad, she tells me she's Joan Finnegan and she knows her from the neighborhood. And then Sally says that they been coming to the show like Siamese twins every Sunday afternoon for near a year . . .'

'Hey, Willie, you are a real smart boy, you know that?' Yale said gleefully.

'Wait, Frankie, that ain't all,' Altierri interrupted. 'You're gonna be proud of me for what else I found out. Charleston and the broad always sit in the next-to-last row in the center aisle . . .'

'How do you know that?' Yale demanded.

'I seen them,' Altierri answered. 'I went in and seen them sitting there.'

'But what makes you so sure they always sit there?' Yale pressed.

'Because that's what Sally said . . .'

'Willie!' Frank broke in with annoyance. 'How can your broad know where they sit when she's in the goddam booth outside the theater?'

'Hey, Frankie,' Altierri roared back with a toothy grin, 'can you stay locked up in a fuckin' ticket booth for twelve hours without going inside to take a piss . . .?'

Frankie Yale decided it would be more prudent to again import an out-of-town torpedo for the hit. But Altierri tried to talk him out of it.

'Frankie, for chrissake, you got me,' he shouted. 'I'm the best blade man in the business, goddammit! Why don't you let me stick him?'

Yale shook his head. 'No good, Willie,' frowned Frankie, 'that broad of yours is one people too many who would know you went into the theater . . .'

'But, Frankie, listen to me. Nobody can make Sally say nothing against me. I trust her . . .'

'Yeah, Willie,' smiled Yale, 'I know you trust her. But me, I don't trust nobody. So forget it. I know what I gotta do . . .'

Once again, Yale phoned Al Capone, who was already aware of the setback the Black Hand had suffered at Stauch's Dance Hall. The shooting had made page-one headlines even in Chicago, despite the fact that by then the city's newspapers had a torrent of blood and guts dripping from their columns chronicling their own violent underworld wars and rubouts.

Yale gave Capone a rundown on what he wanted done. Al responded quickly that he had 'just the right man' for the job.

'Who you gonna send?' Yale asked.

'Somebody who can throw a knife twenty-five feet and not miss what he's throwing at,' Capone answered.

'We don't need nobody to throw twenty-five feet,' Yale said. 'This is a setup in a movie house.'

'Then, good brother, don't worry,' Capone assured Yale. 'The guy I have in mind will finish off Charleston Eddie one, two, three. I will send him to you and you won't be disappointed.'

But before proffering the Detroit slasher he had in mind for Frankie's special assignment, Big Al indulged briefly in some long-distance levity that confounded Yale.

'You must be kidding, brother Al,' Yale choked. 'You can't be serious that you tell me to give the job to Frank Galluch – are you?'

Capone roared with laughter. Galluch was the thug who administered Capone's facial scars during a falling out between the two in the earlier Brooklyn years. That Galluch was still among the living in that year of 1921 can be attributed to the fact that when the two-bit hit man etched Al's face, Capone was just a bloody smalltime punk himself. He commanded no power in the then loosely knit Black Hand and, consequently, Galluch was free from reprisal by an organisational directive. Capone had since gone to Chicago and risen to great power, while Galluch remained a soldier in the Brooklyn Black Hand. The years had dulled Al's thirst for vengeance. Moreover, he felt the scars were a sort of status symbol that distinguished him from other underworld figures. That's why he was able to kid Yale about using Galluch to take care of Charleston Eddie.

When Capone finally informed Yale that Edward 'Honey Boy' Fletcher was to be McFarland's executioner, Frankie asked whether the Michigan stabber could be depended on to perform well.

'Frankie, would I send you a boy to do a man's job, I'm asking you?' Capone said in a hurt tone. 'If you ask me to help out a friend like you, what else can I do but offer you the best in the business. Let me put question to you, pal: when I sent Anselmi and Scalise to help out, did you call me to complain about their work?'

Of course not, Yale assured Capone. It was a thoroughly proficient performance. But just the same, Frankie asked Al in his most respectful voice whether he could just briefly describe Honey Boy's qualifications – simply to put Yale's mind at ease.

'Frankie, I'm very busy,' Capone said bluntly. 'All I'm gonna do is ask you one more question. Who do you know who can stick blade through somebody's eye from twenty-five feet and never touch the lashes, like I told you this guy can do, eh?'

Frankie said he never heard about anyone who could do that.

'Yes, you have, Frankie,' Capone rasped with sarcasm. 'Because I just told you about such a fella. You will see him next week. And please, good friend, don't forget the pay is fifteen big ones. *Buon giorno, signore.*'

No mobster in any part of the country was held in greater esteem as a fashion plate than Frankie Yale. He had the flashiest, most expensive wardrobe in the underworld. But on that Saturday night of 19 March, Frankie met an equal in the man who arrived from Detroit to produce the next day's short-running hit at Para's Court: 'Charleston Eddie's Last Sunday Matinee Flick.'

Frankie Yale, Willie Altierri, Battista Balsamo, and Augie

Pisano did double takes when Honey Boy Fletcher was escorted by Tony Yale into the Fourth Avenue garage office. Frankie's little brother had met the Purple Gang's agent of post birth control at Grand Central and conveyed him to Brooklyn in Yale's personal sedan.

Fletcher made his spectacular entrance in a dark-gray Chesterfield overcoat, pearl-gray spats worn over black patent leather shoes, a wide-brimmed gray Stetson fedora, and a snazzy double-breasted mauve suit whose ample lapels were fashioned from a glistening pale purple satin. But what stunned everyone most of all was the four-carat diamond stickpin adorning Honey Boy's wide, thickly knotted yellow silk tie.

It took Yale a few long moments to recover from the shock of the Beau Brummel standing in front of him. Finally he leaped to his feet, walked around the desk, hand extended, and greeted the visitor warmly. After brief amenities, Honey Boy was introduced to the others. Then Yale got down to the briefing. When he had finished dealing the setup, Frankie asked if Fletcher had any questions.

The executioner shrugged. 'Just one thing bothers me. You didn't mention what picture is playing. That's very important . . .'

Yale straightened in his chair and gazed at Fletcher, bewildered. The others were also stunned by the question.

'Why is that so important?' Frankie hacked.

Fletcher grinned all at once. He bent over Yale's desk and almost laughed. 'Because, Frankie, I don't want to be bored by a lousy movie if I already seen it . . .'

As it turned out, the feature film that Sunday was *The Return of Tarzan*, starring Gene Polar and Karla Schramm.

'Shit!' the Detroit cut-up grunted the next afternoon as Willie Two-Knife steered the black Chevrolet coupe around the corner of DeGraw Street and pulled up to a sedate stop on Court Street, some twenty feet from the movie house.

'What's wrong?' Altierri asked.

'I saw that picture in Detroit two months ago,' he replied. But then Honey Boy glanced at the bottom of the marquee and smiled. 'Oh, that's nice, they got a Charlie Chaplin short. I'm pretty sure I didn't see that one.'

Altierri pulled out his watch from his vest pocket and glanced at the time. It was 3:15 p.m.

'In five or ten minutes he should be passing by,' Two-Knife said in a whisper. He turned to Honey Boy and began laughing.

'What's funny?' Fletcher asked.

'You sure don't look like the dapper Dan you was last night,' Altierri teased. Fletcher was wearing his 'working clothes': a red-and-black checkered lumber jacket, black slacks, and plain black leather shoes.

As they sat waiting for Charleston Eddie and Joan Finnegan to arrive, Altierri and Fletcher discussed how they performed their respective killings with their knives.

'One, that's all I ever need,' the Purple Gang exterminator replied. 'As long as I have a good solid blade, you can be sure you're going to do the job right. Why do you ask, Willie, because you're a two-blader?'

'Well, I kinda like to feel secure, you know what I mean?' Willie said. 'When I stick a guy, I want to jam it into him. And most of the goddam time the blades bust on me. I got too much wrist action. That's why I always carry a spare, so I can be sure I finish the job –'

Suddenly his words cut off.

'Hey,' he said with a start, screwing his head for a clearer glimpse in the rear-view mirror. 'Charleston and the broad are coming.'

Two-Knife pulled his knit longshoreman's cap down to his eyebrows and threw up his right hand to shield his face as Charleston Eddie and Joan Finnegan neared the car.

'Take a good look, Honey Boy,' Altierri said firmly. 'That's your man . . .'

'Yeah, I see him,' Fletcher said easily. 'It's a shame, isn't it?'

'What's a shame?' Willie asked, lowering his hand from his face after Eddie and the girl strolled past the car without noticing the occupants.

'He's a fine broth of a lad,' Fletcher said sadly. 'Don't you feel the least bit sorry that he's going to be wasted?'

'Naw, not me,' Two-Knife growled. 'After what he done to us at Stauch's, he shoulda been wiped out a long time ago . . .'

Altierri turned and looked sharply at Fletcher.

'Hey, you ain't gonna back out because you're goin' soft, are you, babe?' Willie demanded.

Fletcher yanked the handle and opened the door. Putting one foot on the sidewalk, he glanced at Altierri and winked.

'Of course, I'm going soft, Willie,' Honey Boy quipped. 'I'm going for the softest part of Charleston Eddie's body . . .'

Slamming the door shut, Fletcher strode briskly to the theater box office, bought a ticket, and disappeared inside.

An usher walked over to Honey Boy and offered to light his path to a seat.

'No thanks,' Fletcher said politely as he stood beside the shoulder-high retaining wall behind the last row of orchestra seats. 'I prefer to stand here a while.' He looked up at the screen. The Charlie Chaplin short was on. The usher moved away and Honey Boy squinted in search of Charleston Eddie and his girlfriend. When his eyes had adjusted to the darkness, he had no difficulty spotting his quarry in the exact place Yale had said McFarland would be sitting: the next-to-last row of the center orchestra section. Most of the seats in the back four rows – the smoking section – were empty.

Fletcher eased himself into the last row. It was unoccupied except for the usher who was sitting in the end seat on the right. Honey Boy made his way to a seat about three removed from the one Charleston Eddie was occupying in the row in front. He didn't want to make his presence obvious by sitting directly behind McFarland. Joan was on Eddie's right, nestling in his embrace. Charleston's right arm was wrapped around Joan's shoulders.

With one eye on his target, Honey Boy settled back watching the Charlie Chaplin two-reeler flickering on the screen. He had no idea how long it would take before he could finish off Charleston Eddie. Certainly he couldn't be killed while Joan was beside him. But Fletcher had every confidence that if young Miss Finnegan was anything at all like the broads he'd taken to the movies, sooner or later she'd be heading for the powder room. Then he'd have a clear field to operate.

A half-hour passed. Honey Boy began to get edgy. All of a sudden Joan extricated herself from Eddie's embrace.

Fletcher sensed the time had come for the pilgrimage to the ladies' room. Sure enough, he heard her whisper, 'I'll be right back, sweetheart . . .'

Before Joan was halfway out of her seat, Fletcher was up from his. He stealthily shifted over to the seat directly behind McFarland. As Joan disappeared up the darkened aisle, Honey Boy looked to the right where the usher had been sitting. He wasn't there: he had gotten up to guide a couple to their seats down front. The other seats in the back rows were still unoccupied.

Honey Boy reached into his waistband and pulled out his shiv, a butcher knife with a twelve-inch blade that'd been honed to razor sharpness.

With a swift, practiced motion, he looped his left arm around Charleston Eddie's chest and steadied him with an iron grip for the kill. Then he quickly arced the knife across the front of Eddie's neck. It sliced deeply into McFarland's throat. Blood gushed like a geyser. Honey Boy had severed Eddie's jugular vein and with that single sweeping slice had also succeeded in penetrating the voice box. Eddie was unable to utter an outcry, which certainly would have commanded some attention in a theater whose audience was sitting watching the film.

There wasn't any question in his mind that he had finished off Charleston Eddie with that one slash. But that wasn't Honey Boy's style. He was a perfectionist, a killer who delighted in leaving his victims beyond all possible reclamation. So, for good measure, he plunged the knife into Charleston Eddie's chest. But once wasn't enough. He pulled out the bloodied knife and repeated the procedure like a skilled surgeon.

Both times Honey Boy's penetrations were flawless. As the autopsy revealed, he made two clean cuts in the victim's heart.

Honey Boy coolly removed a woman's handkerchief from his pocket, wiped the blood from the knife, and tossed the handkerchief on the floor at Charleston Eddie's feet.

That created the 'evidence' for the motive dreamed up by Frankie Yale: that McFarland's death wasn't gangland revenge but merely the culmination of a lovers' quarrel.

Fletcher slipped the knife into his waistband, rose from his seat, and walked out of the theater. He got into the car beside Willie. Sighing deeply, Honey Boy murmured, 'Get going.'

Altierri pulled away from the curb and headed for Yale's garage. As they passed the theater, Two-Knife asked, 'How did it go?'

'Like a charm,' Honey Boy grunted. 'But it took too goddamn long.'

'Why's that,' Altierri wanted to know.

'I thought that cunt'd never go and take her piss,' Fletcher grumbled. Then after a moment, 'But it really came off beautiful . . .'

Joan returned from the ladies' room and went to her seat beside Eddie. She sat down and said softly, 'Hi, I'm here.' Eddie didn't reply. Joan turned to him and asked, 'Eddie, are you going deaf?'

The movements on the screen were reflected in McFarland's glassy eyes. Joan surmised that her beau was too deeply engrossed in the movie to answer her. But just then Joan moved her foot on the floor and it slid on something slippery.

'Hey, honey,' she complained softly, 'someone must have spilled soda on the floor.'

Still no response from Eddie.

'All right,' Joan said annoyed, 'if you can't take your eyes away from the picture for a second and pay attention to me, I won't bother you.'

Joan wheeled around to the usher who had returned to his seat in the back of the theater and asked him to shine his flashlight on the floor to see why it was wet and slippery. He came over and aimed a circle of light at the spot she indicated.

Joan burst into a piercing scream.

The slime that she had felt underfoot was a bright red liquid that was dripping from Charleston Eddie's neck and chest.

Seconds later the screen went dark and the house lights came on. People in the orchestra section in the front swiveled around sharply to see what was going on. Women screamed shrilly at the sight of Charleston Eddie, upright and unmoving in his seat, his eyes wide open, the expression on his face frozen, and the front of his light-tan suit, white shirt, and light-blue tie a wet crimson mass.

Joan Finnegan was hysterical. Her head hung limply over the backrest beside Eddie, her body heaved convulsively. Her eyes stared up at the balcony ceiling. 'Oh God, Eddie,' she wailed over and over. Then finally, 'Why did this happen to you . . . who did this . . . oh, Eddie . . .'

Within minutes two uniformed patrolmen entered the theater and hurried to the row where Eddie's body was postured so grotesquely in his seat. One of the officers edged into the row and approached Joan, who was still sobbing convulsively.

'Come on, miss,' he said quietly, taking her arm. 'You must leave here.'

Joan lifted her head and turned to look at Charleston Eddie's face, which by now was white as a sheet. The blood had drained out of his head and the flow from the monstrous slash across the front of his neck had ceased.

She screamed again. The policeman put an arm around her back and coaxed her out of the seat. Slowly she rose to her feet, but her legs gave out. By then the cop had his hands on Joan's waist, and he managed to support her. Then he slowly eased her out into the aisle.

He led her to the lobby and into the manager's office as other patrolmen and detectives swarmed into the theater.

'I don't know who did it,' Joan wailed as detectives questioned her. 'I didn't see anyone . . .'

She sobbed out the events exactly as they had occurred: she had left Eddie vibrantly alive in his seat, and when he returned from the ladies' room she found him bleeding and lifeless.

A detective walked into the manager's office with the bloodstained ladies' handkerchief that was on the floor next to the body. He dangled it by a small corner pinched between his thumb and forefinger.

'We found your handkerchief, young lady,' he said solemnly. 'You didn't go to the powder room without it, did you?'

Joan was stunned. She stared sharply at the handkerchief.

'That isn't mine,' she said.

The detective looked up surprised. 'You mean to tell me this belongs to another girlfriend?'

'I don't know anything about another girlfriend,' Joan snapped, her voice still choked. 'I tell you it isn't my handkerchief and there was no one else with Eddie and me . . .'

Joan's answers failed to clear her of suspicion. The detectives whisked her to the Union Street Precinct for more intensive questioning. Meanwhile, police instituted an inch-by-inch search of the movie house for the death weapon. It was an exercise in futility, for the knife that had snuffed out Charleston Eddie's life was being toted back to Detroit by Honey Boy Fletcher.

Although Joan Finnegan was grilled until midnight and for many additional hours on succeeding days, her story, much as the cops found it hard to swallow, remained unvaryingly the same. While they didn't believe that Joan was the actual killer, the law enforcement officers on the case felt she at least knew who the slayer was or at the very least, had more information than she was giving.

The medical examiner's findings, based upon the autopsy, finally helped relieve the pressure on Joan. The sizable depth of the neck wound and the twin punctures in Eddie's chest, which sustained three rib fractures, indicated to the M.E. that 'a person of unusual strength' had to have wielded the knife. That characterisation didn't fit the five-foot-two, 110-pound blonde whom the cops questioned.

Authorities began to turn to other avenues in search of Charleston Eddie's killer. But every trail hit a dead end. In time, the homicide detectives, committed to investigate numerous other murder cases, invested less and less time and effort in trying to solve the biggest murder mystery that ever played Para's Court Theater.

Chapter 8

Furman Street Finale

'Frankie,' the voice on the other end of the telephone said. 'Guess what happen?'

'Hey, Willie, don't play no fuckin' games with me,' Yale shot back, recognising Two-Knife's voice. 'Just come straight, what happen?'

'Somebody killed Giovanni Desso,' Willie said nervously. 'Who the hell would want to knock him off, Frankie?'

Yale flew into a range. 'What!' he bellowed. 'Where'd this happen?' He pounded his fist on the table so hard that the place settings for dinner his wife had laid down so carefully were sent scattering.

'Who do this?' Frankie demanded furiously. 'Tell me what you know! Speak up!'

'Frankie,' Altierri stammered. 'I don't know more than what I am telling you right now. All I found out was that they shot Giovanni near the piers –'

'Near what piers?' Yale screamed.

'By Third Avenue and Twenty-first Street.'

'That where he works?'

'Yeah, I think so, Frankie.'

'Okay, okay?' Yale returned. 'Listen to me, Willie, I'm gonna ask you to do somethin', understand?'

'Sure, sure, Frankie, anything you say.'

'I want you tomorrow to get hold of Don Giuseppe and tell him to meet me at my café,' Frankie ordered. 'Tell him be there by eight o'clock. Tomorrow night, catch?'

Altierri assured Yale he'd have the godfather there.

Two weeks earlier Yale had closed a deal to take over the Sunrise Café on Fourteenth Avenue and Sixty-fifth Street in the Borough Park section of Brooklyn, in the immediate vicinity of two of the Irish mob's most successful speakeasies, and had retained Giovanni Desso's brother, Antonio, as the manager. Antonio had been first a bouncer, then a bartender at Fury Argolia's Adonis Club. Fury was reluctant to let Antonio leave his job behind the mahogany, but could hardly refuse Yale the favor.

Frankie needed a sharp, aggressive, and personable individual like Antonio to run his new establishment. Desso, a Mediterranean version of Toots Shor, didn't let Yale down. In the first two weeks of Antonio's management Sunrise business increased by leaps and bounds. It became the swingingest spot in Borough Park – much to the dismay of Wild Bill Lovett and the White Hand gang. Evidently the Sunrise's success under Yale's ownership and Antonio Desso's management caused business at the rival emporiums to take a nosedive. Although Lovett was not directly involved in operating those speakeasies, he and his gang felt the crunch of the Sunrise's competition in declining liquor orders. In effect, the drop had cut into the mob's profits.

Wild Bill Lovett called a meeting early in the afternoon of 18 June 1921, to ask his lieutenants for the view on dealing with the crisis.

Ash Can Smitty proposed a solution whose crudeness corresponded to his personality. 'We should toss a stick of dynamite into the joint,' he said in all seriousness.

Pug McCarthy asked Ash Can whether his intention was to bomb the Sunrise while customers were in the café or after hours, when innocent patrons would not be killed or maimed.

'What's the difference,' Smitty snapped with characteristic insensitivity. 'If they want to do their drinking in that ginzo's speak, let 'em learn.'

Needles Ferry had a better idea. 'Why don't we put a torch to it?' he proposed. 'All we need is a can of gasoline and a match.'

Lovett didn't go for either idea. 'If we do that,' he said reasonably, 'how long do you think it'll be before those *gimbrones* do the same thing to our places? We don't want to start that kind of war. All we want is to get people to stop going there and come back to our speaks.'

'The only reason Yale is doing the business he's doing is because he's got that smartass Tony Desso working for him,' Needles Ferry put in. He was tackling the real issue: that without Desso the Sunrise would be just another run-of-the-mill Prohibition Era saloon. But so long as Tony was managing the café, the crowds would flock there.

Lovett began to smile. 'You've hit it right on the head,' he said, pleased with Needles's observation. 'Without Desso that speak'll be a shithouse. He's the reason the crowds are going there.'

'Hold it!' Pegleg Lonergan interrupted. 'I heard Fury Argolia is having a *shit* hemorrhage because Frankie took Desso away from him. Half the people who used to go to the Adonis are boozing it up at the Sunrise now. But Fury ain't about to tangle assholes with Yale, you know that. The slob's just gonna have to suffer through it. Fury let him take Desso away and he isn't gonna ask for him back. Even if he did, that fuckin' Yale would never let him go. Frankie's cleaning up there and all that loot's going into his pocket. It's like his funeral parlor. His boys don't get a nickel out of that friggin' opera–'

Suddenly Lovett flung his hands above his head, interrupting Pegleg. Wild Bill's face lit up with a glow. Lonergan had just given him an idea.

He jumped onto one of the liquor cases stored in the White Hand's garage to make himself seen and heard by everyone there, and trumpeted the thought that had just occurred to him: 'All we've got to do is get rid of Tony Desso. It's simple as that. Then Yale's café business got nowhere to go but downhill. What do you think?'

A chorus of approving shouts broke out. 'Great idea, Bill,' cried Needles Ferry.

'What a brainstorm!' Pug McCarthy echoed hoarsely.

'Tony Desso is dead!' yelled Irish Eyes Duggan.

It was common practice for both the White Hand and the Black Hand chieftains to delegate each gang member the task of keeping tabs on one or more rival mobsters. The assignments involved ferreting out information on where the man lived, worked, and played; what his day-to-day routines were, where he might be expected to be found at any given time. This was a salient aspect of underworld strategy, because no one could foresee when it might become suddenly exigent to foreclose on someone's existence.

The man delegated to compile the dossier on Tony Desso was Harry 'The Fart' O'Toole, who didn't come by his nickname accidentally. Harry, it seems, was wild about baked beans. He would eat them morning, noon, and night, and in between. The consequence of that penchant for the vegetable possessing the property of infinite expansion once it enters the stomach was a continual emission of intestinal gases. Many were audible, but without exception they were perceptible to the olfactory nerves of those in his presence. That is why on that Saturday afternoon, Harry the Fart was standing in isolation in a corner of the Baltic Street garage. He was never permitted to mingle with the boys in close quarters.

'Who did I ask to watch Tony Desso?' Lovett asked from his perch on the liquor case.

'Me,' O'Toole piped up, moving towards the gathering.

'Just stay where the hell you are!' Irish Eyes bellowed.

'Do your friggin' talking from there. You take one more step and I'll boot you in that dribblin' asshole of yours!'

Harry froze. He stared at Lovett and hunched his shoulders.

'That's okay, Harry,' Wild Bill said. 'You stay where you are and speak up real loud. Go ahead . . .'

'Well, I know Tony always goes to Pier Twenty-One on Sundays,' O'Toole said, letting out some air. 'It's because I think he goes to see his brother who works there.'

'Who's his brother?' Lovett asked.

'Beats the shit outta me,' Harry the Fart replied with a shrug. 'I wouldn't know him if I fell over him.'

'What time does he go there?' Wild Bill wanted to know.

'Between two-thirty and three usually,' O'Toole replied, letting another one go, to the amusement of the gathering. 'He stays about a half hour, then he walks out to Third Avenue and takes the El to work. Up until a couple weeks ago, he used to go to Fury Argolia's place. But since then, I guess you know where he's been goin' –'

'How the hell does he get from Third Avenue to Fourteenth Avenue?' Lovett interrupted, peeved. 'You're not gonna tell me he walks, are you?'

'He takes the fuckin' trolley, for chrissake, Bill,' Harry the Fart rasped. 'How did the hell you *think* he gets there?'

Snickering surfaced in the group gathered around Lovett. No one spoke to Wild Bill in that tone. But O'Toole could get away with it because everyone had long since been convinced that his intake of baked beans had softened his brain.

'Where's Pier Twenty-One, around Twenty-first Street?' asked Lovett, smiling benevolently at the gang's outcast.

'Yeah, that's exactly where it's at,' Harry the Fart replied, releasing one of his best blasts of the afternoon.

'Okay,' Wild Bill muttered, turning to Pug McCarthy and Needles Ferry. 'You guys got the job. Do it right. That's all I have to say.'

Hardly anyone heard the crackle of exploding bullets that following Sunday afternoon at the deserted intersection of Third Avenue and Twenty-first Street. Only a few saw the man who had walked out of the warehouse on Pier 21 with a jaunty gait and headed for the underground MBT train station stairs. He was only a few feet away from the first step when the air was rent for an instant with the unnerving bark of gunfire.

Four of an undetermined number of bullets found their marks: one in the middle of the forehead, another in the neck, and the third and fourth in the middle of the chest.

The assassins were gone even before the victim crumpled to the sidewalk, so certain were they of having hit their target.

Less than a minute after the police arrived on the scene they called the mortuary wagon.

The men who fired the bullets erred in only one detail, which wasn't discovered until after the body had been removed to the morgue and members of the Desso family were summoned to make the tearful identification.

The man whom Pug McCarthy and Needles Ferry leveled was not Antonio Desso, but his younger, look-alike brother, Giovanni, the dockworker.

'This fuckin' crime has to be the worst thing ever pulled!' Frankie Yale cried the next morning from behind his garage office desk on Fourth Avenue. 'We're gonna get those mick sons of bitches if it's the last thing we do!'

The assemblage of Yale's fifteen top soldiers was a mere observance of form. Frankie wanted to let the boys know that something was being done about Giovanni Desso's killing – and being done quickly.

Two-Knife Altierri was already on the urgent mission that Yale had ordered the night before.

Two-Knife tracked down the godfather a few minutes before noon in Caffiero's Restaurant at the corner of President and Columbia Streets, where he could be found any lunchtime cramming the empty areas of his stomach that had not been filled by the four fried eggs and hot Italian sausages his wife served him for breakfast every morning at nine. Don Giuseppe couldn't face the beginning of any afternoon before refueling on one of the delicious pasta dishes for which Caffiero's was noted. On this particular day it was a plate of spaghetti al la marinara and a side dish of a half-dozen meatballs.

'Hey, Willie!' Balsamo hacked through a mouthful of food as he spotted the messenger entering the restaurant. 'Come here and sit down with me.'

Balsamo had no idea that Two-Knife was bringing him a message from Frankie Yale. As Altierri sat, Don Giuseppe called one of the waiters over. 'Nicko, my friend,' he said to the white-aproned cup-bearer, 'bring this fella here the same thing I am eating.' Then, turning back to Altierri, Balsamo smiled. 'You like spaghetti, no?'

'*Si, si,*' Willie answered. 'I'll join you because I'm hungry. But that is not why I came to see you . . .'

Balsamo whipped his head around and gave the waiter a sharp stare. It appeared he was hovering over the table as though trying to catch a drift of the conversation.

'Hey, Nick,' the godfather scowled, 'you hear what I ask you to get my friend? What the hell you waiting for?'

The waiter pivoted on his heels and scampered toward the kitchen.

Balsamo looked at Altierri with a curious scowl. 'What you say, Willie? You come here to tell me something?'

'Yeah, Don Giuseppe,' Two-Knife said grimly. 'Frankie wants for you to see him tonight at the Sunrise . . .'

Altierri briefed Balsamo on what had happened the previous afternoon. Don Giuseppe was staggered by the news. He hadn't heard about Giovanni Desso's killing because he'd been home until only a few minutes ago, and then had come straight to Caffiero's for lunch.

Back at the garage, Yale was chasing the gang out of the street. He wanted them to put their ears to the ground and pick up any sound that might offer a clue to the killer or killers of poor Giovanni.

'I give you till tonight, no later than seven, to tell me who do this terrible thing to this poor boy,' Yale ordered. Frankie was genuinely grieved by Desso's death. It was a rubout that defied logic. Why would anyone want to visit harm on Giovanni, who was one of the most peace-loving denizens of the docks? He only played a small role in Black Hand activities on Pier 15, where he was a checker. Because he was big and muscular, Giovanni sidelined as a persuader for the waterfront loan sharks when dockworkers fell behind in their payments. Though the last thing he wanted was to use force, Giovanni had on occasion broken some fingers and an arm or two in his zeal to keep creditors' accounts current.

But deep inside, Giovanni had deplored violence. He was always quick to show contrition those times when he forgot his own strength and cracked somebody's bones. Desso would trip over himself in his eagerness to apologise. He'd say, 'Cheez, I dunno how that happen. I'm so sorry. But you got nothin' to worry 'bout. It no happen no more – because next time you gonna pay on time, right?' Giovanni was all heart.

A few minutes before eight o'clock that Monday night, Don Giuseppe Balsamo entered the Sunrise Café flanked by Vincenzo Mangano, who was to be his successor when he went into retirement, and Silk Stocking Guistra, his bodyguards. They checked their coats and made their way past the bar. Balsamo spotted Yale sitting at a table at the back of the dining room. He turned to his guardians. 'Vincenzo, Giovanni, you stay here and have a drink. I want to talk to Frankie alone.'

Yale was in a somber mood as Don Giuseppe hunched in the chair beside the Mafia chieftain. Frankie's greeting was muffled, 'Hiya, *compare*.' Then he was strictly business.

'You hear what happen to Giovanni Desso, eh?' Yale asked in a low, choked voice.

Balsamo nodded sadly. 'Willie told me,' he said.

Yale put his hand on Don Giuseppe's thick forearm and squeezed it hard. 'My good friend, when I ask Willie last night to have you come here, that's because I depend on you for big favor. Up to few minutes ago, I was no sure what I would ask you to do for me. Then our good friend, Frenchy Carlino, come to me, right here at this table. He sit where you are sitting. And you know what he say to me? He say, "Frankie, I find out why they kill Giovanni Desso." I am surprised. I want to know why. So I ask him. You know his answer? He say they kill Giovanni by mistake. They no intend to kill him. You know who they want to kill . . .?' Frankie's voice rose.

Balsamo leaned forward anxious for the answer.

Shaking Don Giuseppe's arm with uncontrolled fury, Yale half-screamed, 'They wanted to kill his brother! You hear! Antonio Desso, my manager!'

'Why they want to do that?' asked Don Giuseppe, trying not to let his face show the pain he was feeling in his arm from Yale's viselike grip.

'Why?' Frankie said. 'You ask why they want to kill Antonio?

Because if they kill him they kill my fuckin' business . . .' Yale took a deep breath and exhaled with a loud 'ehhhhhh'.

'And that means one thing they want to do,' he rasped. 'They wanna hurt me!' He removed his hand from Balsamo's arm and closed the fingers into a fist. Then he drove the fist into his left palm.

Balsamo jiggled his head in a commiserating gesture. 'Frankie, he asked slowly, 'do you have idea who shot Giovanni?'

Yale tightened his lips, then let out a long breath.

'You betcha I know.' He turned away with a scornful look. 'It was Pug McCarthy and Irish Eyes Duggan. And you know how Frenchy find out it's them?'

Balsamo lifted his shoulders. He had no idea how Pug and Irish Eyes had been fingered as Desso's destroyers.

'Frenchy find a dockworker by name of Benito Fusco who work with Giovanni on the pier,' Yale explained. 'Benito sneak away from job Sunday afternoon and go across the street to that Anselmo's speak on Third Avenue. After couple drinks, he start to go back to job. But just when he open door, he hear shots. Benito duck behind door because he get scared. He think they are shooting at him. Then he see Giovanni fall down and he know they are no shoot at him . . .'

Yale swallowed and contorted his lips in a mean arc. 'Benito not only hear bullets and see men shoot Giovanni,' Frankie said slowly. He finished his sentence, at first separating each word from the next by a long pause, 'but . . . he . . . hear . . . one . . . say . . . to . . . the . . . other . . . man . . . "Hurry up, Pug, we gotta get outta here."'

A vicious smile spread on Frankie's face, 'Do you know who Pug mean?' he asked, waiting for Balsamo to respond.

'You kidding?' Don Giuseppe wheezed. 'Sure I know. It be Pug McCarthy, the Irish cuntface.' The Black Hand always referred to blond-haired, fair-skinned, pretty-boy type Hibernians as cuntfaces. So many of the Italians had dark hair, swarthy complexions, and rough-hewn countenances that their vanity prompted them to associate these features with masculinity. Anyone who didn't have what they called 'manly character' in his face – especially an Irishman – was referred to as a cuntface.

'Something else I'm gonna tell you, Don Giuseppe,' Yale said, hoarsely sure of himself. 'The mother who was with Pug McCarthy was that *fongool* Irish Eyes Duggan.'

'You sure?' Balsamo asked.

'Sure I'm sure,' Yale shot back. 'I get phone call from Glass Eye this afternoon. You know what he say? He say he see Pug and Irish Eyes drive to McGuire's speak just before four o'clock on Sunday. That's only a few minutes after Desso got hit. Glass Eye say they got out of car in big hurry and go inside. That mean nothing to me when I hear it from him. But when Frenchy tell me tonight about what Benito told him, I put two and two together.'

Holding his hands out, palms up, like the Pope, Yale raised his eyes to the ceiling. 'I thank God I got smart boys who find out things like this,' he said, now closing his eyes and clasping his hands prayerfully against his chest. A second later, he made his cross and murmured, 'Amen.'

Yale's motive in summoning Balsamo that night was to ask a big favor. He wanted Don Giuseppe to avenge Giovanni Desso's murder with his own men.

By the time he had dispatched Willie Altierri to tell Balsamo that Yale wanted to see him at the Sunrise, Frankie had no idea who had killed his manager's brother, but was fully confident that his boys would find out before too long. What Yale wanted first and foremost was assurance that once the killers had been identified their exterminations would be not only swift but something very special. Or, as Yale put it that night to Balsamo: 'I want Wild Bill Lovett and the whole fuckin' mick gang to remember this number.'

Balsamo studied Yale's face somewhat skeptically. Then all at once his own face lit up. 'Hey, Frankie, I understand what you are asking.' He broke into a wide grin.

'You know, eh?' Frankie smiled back.

'You want to use my family, right, *compare*?' Don Giuseppe said, inhaling with such pride that his chest expanded over the table. This was a moment he had been waiting for. He was deeply honored, for never before had Yale asked Balsamo for that kind of a favor. Until then, Balsamo's executioners were limited in their work. Their services had been confined to Little Italy, Don Giuseppe's home base from where he supervised the Mafia activities. Don Giuseppe let Yale and other overlords of the realm tend to the day-to-day bashing of heads – or even the killings that were necessary to keep the operation on an even keel.

The boys Yale wanted for the job, the three Mormillo brothers, possessed uncommon skills. Their specialty was camouflaging murder so adroitly that it looked like nothing but an unfortunate accident. Their forte was crushing the skulls of rival extortionists who ventured too close to Red Hook's docks. The Mormillos had developed the technique to a science. All three happened to be crane operators. Not only were they crackerjacks in loading and unloading ships, they had also become perfectionists with the booms of their cranes.

By mid-1921 the number of White Hand extortionists who'd met those unfortunate mishaps on the Red Hook docks was up to five. And with that record, Balsamo was eminently suited now to do for Yale what he had never done before, provide his own personal assassins for the number that had to be performed on Desso's killers.

Long ago, Yale and Balsamo had a meeting of the minds. It was on an adage Frankie first advanced: 'Every Irishman you kill, you got that many less to bust your balls.'

'You took the words out of my mouth,' Don Giuseppe had agreed.

Pietro 'Shotgun' Mormillo, Dominick 'The Gee' Mormillo and 'Bloody' Nino Mormillo never begrudged their leader the credit, praise, and gratitude that heaped on the godfather for their achievements. How could they take umbrage at old Don Giuseppe? They had grown up at his feet.

The Mormillos and Balsamos lived next door to each other on Columbia Street. More often than not the three little boys would be at Balsamo's house. He would put them to bed, telling them stories about life in Favarote – how, for example, the barefoot man whose feet hurt from working all day in the fields waited on the dirt road at night until a rich landowner came by, then hit the landowner on the head and took the shoes off his feet.

There were many such stories, all revolving around the Maffia in Sicily, which was bound by close ties of fellowship and capable of any crime. Balsamo's favourite story was the history of the Maffia. Night after night the boys importuned Don Giuseppe to tell the story again.

'Once upon a time,' Battista Balsamo would recite, 'there were in Sicily many *latifondie* [great landed estates]. Then after that *skongeel* from France who call himself Napoleon invade Sicily, there was great trouble. Everybody come and rob the *latifondie*. So the people who own the *latifondie*, they hire nice Sicilians. You know, regular people. And they say to them, "You protect my *latifondie*, soon there is no more trouble." And that's what they do.

'So, children, after while the people who tell owners of *latifondie* what to do become known as Maffia. They are wonderful people. They tell others who they work for on *latifondie*, who work for them, how much they make, and they take no shit from nobody.

'Now lotsa those people who help owners of *latifondie* have come here to Brooklyn – and to Manhattan. And they are doing the same thing here they do in Sicily.'

Listening in rapt attention, the Mormillo boys always applauded Don Giuseppe after he finished the story. Don Giuseppe Balsamo, brother of the Mormillo brothers' mother, was the boys' uncle.

Exactly one week after Giovanni Desso was wasted, Shotgun, The Gee, and Bloody Nino Mormillo made their way to the corner of Fourth Avenue and Sackett Street, where, they were told, Augie The Wop Pisano would pick them up.

It was a Sunday, 26 June. By 1:30 p.m. the Mormillo brothers stood on the street corner waiting. Minutes later a black Buick sedan pulled to a stop at the curb. The brothers recognised the driver, Augie Pisano.

'Get in!' he called to them. They drove a short distance to Union Street, turned the corner, went halfway down the block, and stopped in front of Antonio's Fish Market, which was always closed on Sundays. But this Sunday, owner Antonio

Fugetta was there, because he had some important straightening out to do.

'You fellas come with me,' Pisano said, and led the way to the door of Antonio's market. Augie tapped three times on the glass pane. A second later the lock was turned from the inside and Antonio opened the door, and stepped back to admit the four men. Then he closed the door, locked it, and led them to the back of the store. He yanked on the door lever of a large walk-in ice box used to store fish, entered, and a moment later walked out holding a .12-gauge shotgun and two .45-caliber automatics. Without a word he handed the shotgun to the Mormillo whose nickname was derived from that weapon. He gave Dominick the Gee and his brother Bloody Nino the automatics. Then Antonio turned to Augie the Wop, smiled blandly, and said, 'That's it. They are all ready. I clean each piece and load it. They gonna work very good.'

Augie nodded and gave Antonio a wink. Then he patted him on the shoulder. Finally, he looked at the Mormillo brothers and snapped, 'Come on. We go to the car. Just be careful nobody see you with that artillery. You wait. I take a look outside first.'

He opened the door, stuck his head out, and glanced up and down the street. The coast was clear. 'Now!' he said urgently and led the way back to the car. They drove to Atlantic Avenue, then headed west toward Furman Street.

An hour earlier, Frankie Yale had phoned Don Giuseppe Balsamo and alerted him that Pug McCarthy and Irish Eyes Duggan's numbers were up. He had gotten word from Nick Glass Eye Pelicano that the two Irish mobsters had driven together to McGuire's Saloon on Furman Street in a 1919 gray Ford Coupe. Everything had been arranged in advance: where the Mormillo brothers would meet Pisano and where they would pick up the weapons. 'Send your nephews to meet Augie,' Yale told Balsamo.

As the Buick came with a hundred feet of McGuire's Augie began slamming his hand against the steering wheel. 'That's the car,' he shouted excitedly, pointing to the gray Ford coupe parked outside the saloon. Pisano swerved sharply into the curb and braked the car to a stop directly behind another parked vehicle about four car lengths in back of the Ford.

'We wait,' he whispered. 'Sooner or later they gotta come out.' He glanced at his watch. It was 1:45. Time passed slowly for Augie and the three assassins. Twenty minutes, thirty minutes went by. Pisano stared at his watch again. 'Shit,' he grunted, 'fifteen after two and those humps are still boozin' it up.'

Maybe it's better that way,' said Shotgun, who was sitting beside Augie. He reached down and stroked the shotgun propped between his knees. 'They will not feel the pain so much if they are drunk.'

Pisano rapped the steering wheel again. 'There they are,' he said excitedly. 'Get ready!'

Augie gave McCarthy and Duggan no more than the time they needed to get into their car and start south on Furman Street – towards the direction of the docks. Irish Eyes was driving. Pisano eased the Buick away from the curb and tailed the Ford, leaving only a few car lengths between himself and his target. As McCarthy and Duggan neared the dock area, where they obviously intended to make a U-turn and come back on narrow two-way Furman street, Augie floored the gas pedal. The Buick roared forward and in a few seconds had narrowed the gap on the Ford. Just then, Duggan slowed down at the East River bulkhead, directly in front of the Gowanus Stevedoring Company's warehouse on Pier 2, and began making his turn.

The Buick was on top of its target. Augie hit the brakes, and before the car had come to a skidding stop, the Mormillo brothers had leaped out. The screech of brakes and the squeal of tires unnerved Duggan. He jammed on the brakes instinctively to avoid what looked like a certain collision.

Whatever other thoughts Irish Eyes – or Pug, for that matter – might have had right then, they were not able to share with anyone. The simultaneous blasts from the shotgun and the two automatics reverberated along the waterfront like one resounding clap of thunder. Irish Eyes and Pug pitched forward. Duggan didn't have far to go. The steering wheel prevented his bloodied head from falling far. It slammed against the wheel with a sickening thud, but Irish Eyes probably never felt the pain because the first blast had ripped open the side of his head: more than likely, all his sensibilities had been numbed by then.

McCarthy toppled forward with such force that his head smashed through the windshield. Even if seat belts had been around in 1921, Pug's life couldn't have been spared. The blood spurting from his nose, mouth, and around his ears wasn't from the slivers of broken windshield glass that stuck in Pug's head like a porcupine's long sharp spine; it was from the shotgun pellets and bullets that riddled his pretty face. It left a crazy zigzag pattern of red over the Ford's hood.

As quickly as they had rendered their deadly threnody of lead, the three executioners flung their weapons over the bulkhead into the water and embarked on the second phase of their assignment. Bloody Nino yanked open the door on the driver's side, and with a quick, effortless motion pushed Irish Eyes Duggan's limp corpse toward McCarthy's unmoving form. Then Nino began to turn the steering wheel to the right. But his hand slipped on the blood that had dripped from Duggan's head. He wiped his hands dry by running them over Irish Eyes' suit sleeve. Then he finished turning the steering wheel. The Ford was now pointed toward the bulkhead.

Nino slammed the door and called out, 'Come on, heave it!' Shotgun and Dominick the Gee put their shoulders to the back of the car and began pushing mightily. Bloody Nino steadied the steering wheel as the car was rolled toward the water's edge.

When the front wheels were within a foot of the bulkhead, Bloody Nino released his grip on the steering wheel, jumped away, and scurried back to add his own weight in pushing the car and its lifeless occupants toward a watery grave.

For an instant it seemed they might not succeed in forcing the car over the bulkhead. Just as the front wheels dropped over the edge, there was a grinding crunch. The chassis had caught on the lip of the protective waterfront wall!

'Shit!' screamed Dominick. 'Push hard! Push hard!'

With a mighty combined effort the brothers thrust themselves against the back of the car and managed to push it into the water with one final lunge. It went in nose first, like a plane in a dive. A splash, and the whole car disappeared under the murky surface.

The Mormillo brothers waited at the top of the bulkhead only long enough to watch the brief rolling circle of waves ripple from the vortex of the whirlpool caused by the car's plunge to the riverbed.

'Bubbles,' Dominick the Gee smiled. 'Beautiful bubbles. Look at 'em coming up . . .'

They hurried back to the waiting Buick; Augie the Wop made a flying start on the getaway up Furman Street. But before they'd gone more than a block they heard the disturbing wail of a siren. Ahead of them speeding in their direction was a police car!

'Cops!' cried Shotgun. 'What the fuck we gonna do?'

'How the hell they come so soon?' Dominick the Gee croaked from the back seat.

'I ain't got nowhere to turn,' Augie the Wop trembled. 'They fuckin' got us trapped.'

'Stop the car – we make a run for it,' Bloody Nino cried. 'That's our only chance.'

Augie swerved into the curb and jammed on the brakes. The frightened killers were just opening the doors when the police cruiser, which had been roaring toward them with undiminished speed, swept right past and raced onward toward the waterfront.

'Wheeew!' Augie let out a long sigh of relief. 'I thought we were dead.' He pulled the car away from the curb and continued the journey along Furman. As they turned the corners into Fulton Street, another siren was heard. A second police car was speeding in the direction of Pier 2.

The gunfire on the waterfront had triggered a call to police from someone in the neighborhood, and the bluecoats were hurrying there to investigate. Pisano was nervous about the second police car. Only when it sped past did he feel easier. 'Those friggin' cops sure scared the shit outta me,' he snorted as he drove along Fulton towards the Adonis Club, where the gang always rendezvoused for its 'alibi' get-togethers. Augie wanted to be sure no one was following. He glanced into the rearview mirror. When he saw no cars – especially no police cars – behind, he began humming his favourite Sicilian tune, 'Gela Luna Menzu Mare . . .'

The eight patrolmen who made the scene in the two police cruisers were stumped when they went in search of evidence to corroborate the report of gunfire. They found no bodies, not even a trace of blood to indicate anyone had been wounded. But then they approached the spot where Pug and Irish Eyes had been blasted in their car. The officers caught sight of the spent cartridges strewn on the street: eight .45-caliber copper casings and four empty .12-gauge shells. Then the cops saw the skid marks of the Buick, and, finally, noticed tire tracks in the sand leading to the end of the pier. They walked to the bulkhead and peered into the water. They couldn't see the car, but suddenly they perceived a few small air bubbles breaking on the surface. They watched more closely as several more suspicious bubbles rose to the surface.

Patrolman Robert Alongi turned to the other policemen. 'I'm going to phone the precinct for grappling hooks and a tow truck,' he said. 'I think something's down there . . .'

A half hour later, poking into the water with a fifteen-foot grappling hook, one of the patrolmen hit something hard about ten feet below the surface. 'Hold it!' he shouted. 'I've got something here!'

The sergeant in charge of the detail hurried over. 'What did you hit?' he asked in an anxious voice.

'I'm not sure,' the cop answered, 'but it sure as hell is something big.' He ran the pole over a smooth surface, off which the pole then slid and plunged freely for some five feet, imbedding itself in the silt on the river bottom. The cop turned to the sergeant. 'No doubt about it,' he said confidently. 'There's something there in the water.'

'Okay,' the sergeant said loudly, 'I want a volunteer. I want somebody to swim down there and see if he can figure out what that thing is.'

Patrolman Alongi came over. 'Want me to go down, Sarge?' he offered. 'I'm a good swimmer.'

Alongi removed his uniform, shoes, socks, and undershirt, leaving on only his shorts. He walked to the bulkhead and dove into the water, making certain he entered where the pole had indicated enough clearance to the river bottom without hitting the submerged object.

He remained underwater some thirty seconds. When he surfaced, he maneuvered himself into a position that brought him over the roof of the car. Then he stood up in water that was just at his waist.

'What is it?' the sergeant asked urgently.

'A car,' Alongi responded. 'And if you want to know what's in the car,' he went on. 'I think you'll find a body . . .'

Alongi had swum around the car and stuck his hand into the open window on the driver's side. He had felt a body, all right. Irish Eyes Duggan's body, which was next to the steering wheel. But he didn't yet know that another corpse was in the front seat beside Duggan's bullet-ridden hulk.

'Give me the hook and I'll put it on the rear bumper,' Alongi said. The sergeant and another patrolman handed Alongi the hook which was attached to a chain on the tow truck hoist. Alongi lowered it into the water, then jumped off the roof and disappeared below the surface once again. Seconds later, he resurfaced. 'Okay,' he said, 'start hauling her out.'

It took about twenty minutes to pull the gray Ford out of the water and beach it on its wheels on the street beside the bulkhead. But even before the car had been set down, the policemen had seen the bodies of the two shot-up White Hand gangsters in the front seat. Pug McCarthy's head was still protruding through the broken windshield. In addition to the torn and hanging flesh of Pug's face, a huge sliver of glass was sticking out of his right eye. The cops were nauseated.

Don Giuseppe Balsamo had conducted himself admirably in this special engagement for Frankie Yale. As the toasts were given at Fury Argolia's restaurant that afternoon, Frankie was mindful of the extraordinary services that Shotgun, Dominick the Gee, and Bloody Nino Mormillo had rendered in avenging the mistaken-identity murder of Giovanni Desso.

'I will have more work for you boys,' Yale said gleefully as he drank to the brothers' good health and long life. 'You make me so happy today.' Then, looking at Balsamo with an endearing smile, he said, 'You, *compare*, must be very proud of your nephews, eh?'

Balsamo's chest swelled with elation. 'Of course, of course,' he trilled. 'I always say my nephews are the best there is . . .'

* * *

The elimination of Irish Eyes Duggan and Pug McCarthy represented the fourteen and fifteenth rubouts in the war between the White Hand and Black Hand gangs. And it had been only eighteen months after the conflict between the Irish and Italian mobs had begun.

Of the fourteen victims, the Black Hand had lost five, the White Hand nine of its members. The Italians were very definitely winning the war.

Chapter 9

A Botched Job

Nearly eight months had passed since Irish Eyes Duggan and Pug McCarthy were blasted out of sight. The White Hand had yet to pay back Frankie Yale and his Black Hand *gimbrones* for that dastardly defilement of Celtic manhood. The shooting war that had raged almost uninterruptedly since the Irish mobsters mobilised against the Italian's infiltration of the rackets had passed into a period of uncomfortable ceasefire. Not one murder, not even a shooting, stabbing, or bludgeoning in that time.

Did that mean the conflict was over? Had Lovett lost his lust for revenge? Or was he simply waging a war of nerves against Frankie Yale?

Lovett had a different reason for keeping his gang's guns holstered. If Frankie Yale and his band of cutthroats began to sense a reluctance by Lovett and his predators to even the score after the ignominious Duggan-McCarthy episode, that was exactly what the Irish gang leader wanted them to think.

Lovett had neither lost his lust for revenge nor wavered in his determination to square accounts for the Italians. That he hadn't struck back in the many months following the Furman Street shooting was a tactical ploy on Wild Bill's part. He wanted Yale and the Black Hand to think exactly what they were thinking now in early February of 1922 – that the White Hand wouldn't hit back. The Italians were falling into the very trap Lovett had set for them: they became complacent and, consequently, let down their guard.

That state of mind was never more apparent than on the early evening of Tuesday 7 February. The farthest thought from Frankie Yale's head was the White Handers and the awareness that his life might be in immediate peril. Frankie had other, happier reflections to occupy him as he sat in his Sunrise Café and nourished himself on a succulent steak. Sharing his repast were Gino Ballati and Miguel Dimessico, two heavyweight Black Hand operatives from the Bay Ridge section.

Ballati, a rangey six-footer weighing in the neighborhood of 185 pounds and with a parrot's beak for a nose, was in charge of loan shark activities at the mammoth Brooklyn Army Terminal. Dimessico, five-feet-seven, was built like a gorilla. He weighed at least 260 pounds, which had no small influence in the reputation he enjoyed as one of Brooklyn's most feared enforcers. His jowls hung like misplaced mammary glands and his deep-socketed, dark eyes were given a particularly menacing look by the thick black eyebrows that hung over them like awnings.

The Army Terminal, which had been the point of embarkation and debarkation of troops during World War I, had become by the 1920s one of the military's chief depots on the Eastern Seaboard for the shipment of material to U.S. troops stationed in Panama, Hawaii, the Philippines, and other overseas installations. Although the army was in charge of the base, the ship loadings were handled by longshoremen. And that was the basis for the Black Hand's operations in that section of Brooklyn's sprawling waterfront. Dockworkers always seemed to be in need of loans. Money was always readily advanced by the hawk-faced Ballati, whose usurious rates were the same as those imposed by the Black Hand shylocks on the other Brooklyn piers: one dollar a week interest on every five dollars loaned.

When payments fell behind at the army installation, Miguel Dimessico stepped in. He was a hell of a persuader for prompt payment, and untold numbers of borrowers became believers in this principle after encounters with Miguel. His favourite tactic was to grab a delinquent debtor and squeeze him in a bear hug.

This invariably convinced the man who owed the money that it was better to repay the loan than to feed his family that week.

On rate occasions Ballati and Dimessico performed another service for the Black Hand: protecting the person of Frankie Yale. The assignment didn't come often because Yale's main bodyguards were his star wheelman, Frenchy Carlino, and his faithful right hand, Augie Pisano.

On that particular February evening, however, Carlino and Pisano had been given the night off because what Yale was planning didn't seem, to him, to require the 'first team'.

Down in Lower Manhattan, his good *paisan*, Joe 'The Boss' Masseria, was throwing a bash in Duane Hall at 115 Park Row, on the corner of Duane Street. Masseria had invited Frankie to the festivities. And since Joe was one of the people who had nudged Yale in his rise to the leadership of Brooklyn's Black Hand, Frankie wouldn't even think of missing Masseria's party.

Masseria had succeeded Ignazio Sietta, known as 'Lupo the Wolf', after an unfortunate accident deprived Ignazio of bodily functions. That happened when Sietta tried to intervene in a street-corner brawl between two of his lieutenants, Benedict Frizolli and Frank 'The Greaseball' Persico. Frizolli, who had been harassing The Greaseball with a knife, lost his temper when Lupo the Wolf stepped in. The Wolf bled to death on the sidewalk from the punctures Benedict pierced in his stomach.

February had come in like a lamb, but that night hail, sleet, and gale winds lashed New York in a savage storm. Frankie Yale was determined to make it to Joe Masseria's shindig regardless of the weather.

He had dressed for the occasion in his Beau Brummel best: a dark-gray double-breasted suit, a white shirt, a blue polka dot tie. He donned light-gray spats over his black patent leather shoes. At the coat check he claimed a gray Chesterfield, and charcoal-gray fedora.

He sat beside Gino Ballati in the back seat of the Cadillac and Miguel took the wheel. Within fifteen minutes they were crossing the Brooklyn Bridge into Manhattan. As he turned into Park

Row, Dimessico suddenly shouted, 'Hey, look who the hell's on that corner!'

'Who?' asked Yale, craning his neck from the back seat.

'Wild Bill Lovett!' Dimessico replied, alarmed. 'What the fuck's he doing here?'

Yale jerked his head around and caught an eyeful of his rival standing on the corner of Chambers Street, hard by the Municipal Building. 'Beats the shit outta me,' he grumbled. 'I don't got no idea why he's here.'

'The guy's gotta be crazy to be in Joe Masseria's territory,' rasped Ballati.

'Sure, sure,' Yale said nervously, peering out the window to make certain it was really Wild Bill. 'That's him, all right,' Frankie said in a low, worried voice.

'What you want me to do?' asked Dimessico.

'Just go to the dance,' Yale said. 'That crazy Irishman sure as shit ain't gonna pull nothin' down here. Masseria's boys will hang him by his balls if he tries anything.'

Dimessico pulled the Cadillac into the parking space on Duane Street some hundred feet from the corner of Park Row. The three got out of the car. They trudged through the slush toward the ballroom entrance, holding grimly to the brims of their hats against the buffeting winds that drove the hail and sleet into their faces like sprays of buckshot.

As they rounded the corner and approached the front doors of Duane Hall the hail and sleet were joined by .38-caliber dumdum bullets which had not been forecast by the weather bureau.

Dimessico caught two of the flattened missiles in the back of his head. The impact pitched him against the brick wall beside the front doors of the dance hall as if he'd been kicked by a horse. His 260 pounds bounced off the wall as though made of rubber. He plummeted into the slush, face down. He lay absolutely still.

Ballati and Yale also went down. But their dives were voluntary – an instinct for self-preservation rather than direct hits by the bullets. Frankie rolled himself over and over on his Chesterfield until he reached cover under the running board of a parked car. Ballati creeped and crawled toward a stone stoop that promised him protection. But Gino just couldn't creep and crawl fast enough on the slippery sidewalk. He was zinged in the left shoulder and cried out in pain. Yet he managed to reach shelter alongside the stone stoop. From there he would see where the gunfire was coming from.

'Frankie!' he shouted. 'They're shooting from the window across the street. On the second floor . . . I can't use my rod . . . I been hit . . .'

Yale wanted to shoot back himself. But he was hugging the ground so tightly that he couldn't open his coat to get his gun out. Sooner or later, Frankie reasoned, Masseria's boys will be coming out to investigate the gunfire and they'll settle accounts with the guys shooting from up there.

But Masseria's men never heard the shots. The dance was underway by then, and the blare of the sixteen-piece band drowned out the disturbing explosions that might have filtered into the hall.

Thus Yale and Ballati were compelled to remain pinned down in the sleet and snow and driving wind until, at least, the pelting of lead had ceased. And when it had, Yale figured that was it. The gunmen surely weren't going to hang around any longer in Joe Masseria's territory.

Frankie scrambled to his feet and bolted for the front doors of the dance hall. He got his hand on the knob, but before he managed to open the door two more explosions rang out in quick succession. The first dumdum put a perfect hole in the wooden door just to the right of Frankie's head. The second slug tunnelled its way into Frankie's back and penetrated his right lung.

Yale screamed in agony and collapsed on the stoop. As he slithered down, he turned the knob fully and the weight of his body caught against the door forced it open. His cries brought help.

Gouverneur Hospital was built like a fortress. Even into the early 1980s in its state of decay, long after the city gave it up as a place to treat the sick and wounded, it retained the appearance of an impregnable citadel that could withstand the onslaught of an attack by invading forces. While its appearance was even more imposing in 1922, the police were not altogether confident that Wild Bill Lovett and the White Hand gang could not penetrate its bulwarks and finish off the job they had started on Frankie Yale. A half dozen patrolmen were posted at the hospital's entrances to guard against such an invasion.

Yale's wife, Maria, his mother, Rosalie, and little brother Tony sat in the waiting room while Frankie underwent four hours of surgery performed by a team of four doctors. In the end, they succeeded not only in removing the flat-headed bullet from Yale's lung, but effectively patched up the damage in the lobe of his lower bronchial tube.

Two days later Yale's superb physical condition and will to survive had brought him back to the world of the living in such great shape that the detectives who'd been waiting for an opportunity to talk to him were finally given the green light by the doctors.

'Who did this to you, Frankie?' Detective Sergeant Luigi Alongi asked. The police department figured that an Italian detective – he was Patrolman Robert Alongi's brother – would have a much better chance of getting information out of Yale than an Irish cop.

Frankie waved his right forefinger at Alongi.

'What the fuck made you become a cop?' Yale swallowed. 'Didn't nobody tell you guineas ain't supposed to be cops?'

Alongi smiled uneasily. 'Frankie, look what I'm trying to do,' he said. 'I want to help you avoid getting killed when you get out of the hospital. Whoever shot at you the other day is going to try it again. The next time could be the last. What do you say? You want to tell me who it was shot you?'

'Hey, Luigi,' Yale spluttered, 'whoever did this to me is sweatin' it out right now. He's wonderin' what's gonna happen to him when I get outta the hospital. Do you think I should louse him up by sending you out to take him, eh?'

Alongi was totally frustrated. He was unable to extract any information from Yale about who fired the dumdum bullets that night. Yet there was no question in the minds of police investigators that the lead had been drilled by members of Yale's rival underworld faction. Though they had no clues as to which

White Handers were the assassins, the lawmen rounded up a quartet of Irish mobsters and brought them to a Gouverneur Hospital lineup beside Yale's bed.

The cops picked Wild Bill Lovett, Pegleg Lonergan, Garry Barry, a longtime sidekick of the late Denny Meehan, and Joey Bean, brother of the late Danny and the very much alive Petey Bean. In fact, Garry Barry and Joey Bean were the gunslingers who had opened fire from the tenement window on Yale and his bodyguards outside the dance hall. Pegleg Lonergan had gathered the information that Yale was going to Masseria's party, and Lovett, of course, ordered the hit and was at the scene to make certain it was executed. When Lovett, Lonergan, Barry, and Bean were hustled into Frankie's hospital room, the look of fear on their faces was unmistakable. What inside information did the police have to nail them as the assassins, they were asking themselves.

In fact, the detectives were only guessing when they picked on these four. Lovett was a natural since he was the leader. Lonergan was singled out because he had considerable stature in the gang since originating and executing the Stauch's Dance Hall massacre, he was now generally regarded as the man most likely to succeed Wild Bill Lovett, if he should ever lose his capacity to lead the mob. As for Joey Bean and Garry Barry, there was no reason for picking on them except that they happened to have been in the White Hand garage when the detectives went looking for prospective suspects.

The scene in Frankie's hospital room would have made an excellent script for a Broadway comedy. Yale's dialogue was hilarious.

'Hey, you cops crazy or somethin'?' he scowled. 'Why you bring my friend Bill Lovett here? You mean you think he want to hurt me, eh? *Maddon*, your brain is going soft . . .'

Frankie turned an icy smile on Lovett. 'Hey, Bill, why don't you tell these here flatfeet how much good pals you and me are to each other? Eh, why don't you do that?'

His words dripped with sarcasm, and everyone in the room, detectives and White Handers alike, recognised it.

'Sure, Bill, tell us about it,' Sergeant Alongi prodded. 'Swear on Saint Patrick that you had nothing to do with the business of shooting up Frankie and his boys. Why don't you do that?'

This wop cop, Lovett thought. *I'd like to cut his tongue out for mentioning St Patrick*. Different words came out of his mouth. 'Frankie's telling it to you straight,' Wild Bill said in a tone as phony as Yale's. 'There are no hard feelings between us. I would never do anything to hurt a hair on Frankie's head . . .'

Wild Bill looked at Yale, whose head was propped on two pillows, and forced a smile. 'Ain't that right, Frankie?'

'All the way, pal,' Yale coughed, suddenly clutching his side. The right lung was hurting him. 'We love each other like brothers,' he gasped.

A doctor standing at the door moved in and told Alongi to end the interview. 'Mr Yale is a very sick man,' he said. Alongi nodded. He and the other detectives had sensed the hopelessness of trying to get Yale to finger his assailants. They escorted Lovett and the others out of Frankie's hospital room and released him to the street.

'Don't come back to visit your friend,' Alongi warned. 'You do and I'll lock your asses up!'

Chapter 10

Robbing Hood a Robin Hood

It was 1 March before Frankie Yale was discharged from the hospital. He was sent home to convalesce.

And Frankie knew that the twelve miles from Manhattan's South Street to 1605 Fourteenth Avenue were pitted with countless perils that could cause an immediate relapse. So Frenchy Carlino and Augie the Wop had come to escort him home.

Frankie shook hands with the doctors and nurses at the hospital, handing each of them a sealed envelope, twelve in all. He felt that the four doctors who saved his life deserved the century notes he put in each of their envelopes, and the nurses had been so good to him that twenty dollars apiece was the very least he could do to show his appreciation.

'I come back again –' Frankie stopped in midsentence when he realised what he was saying. '– I mean, I come and visit you sometime, eh?' he corrected with a laugh.

Besides Carlino and Pisano a few of Joe Masseria's boys were there as bodyguards also. Joe the Boss wanted Yale to have safe conduct at least until he crossed the Brooklyn Bridge. Masseria didn't want any more shots pegged at Yale in Lower Manhattan.

Joe the Boss considered it bad form to have alien gangs shooting each other in his territory. There were enough killings going on in the hostilities his mob was having with young Turks like Salvatore Maranzano, Joe Profaci, Thomas 'Three Fingers Brown' Luchese, Joseph 'Joe Bananas' Bonanno, and Stefano Magaddino, among others.

Masseria envied Yale because he had no such problems with his own people in Brooklyn. The Black Hand there was unified under Frankie and solidified by the fatherly guidance of Don Giuseppe Balsamo. Upstarts who might have wanted to set up their own 'family' enterprises in the Brooklyn underworld would be signing their own death warrants – and they knew it.

Masseria's problem was that Manhattan was cut up into territories with regional bosses running the show in each one. While they were all Sicilians, they were not all from the same parts of Sicily. And Joe the Boss had a blind spot with that. Anybody who didn't come from Palermo was 'low class'. So guys like Magaddino, Luchese, and Maranzano, whom fate had decreed to be born in Castellammare del Golfo, were treated like inferiors by Masseria. From time to time the boys who worked for Joe the Boss found themselves busting heads or shooting up perfectly legitimate Sicilian mobsters simply because they didn't come from Palermo.

With the protection Frankie had that day, the ride from the hospital was safe and sound. One of his first acts on his return was to attend mass at St Rosalia's Church, just two blocks north of his home. He wanted to let God know that he appreciated the new lease He had given him on life. He also wanted to ask the Lord to make reservations in the world beyond for the men who had committed that unspeakable crime on Park Row.

'After you do this to me,' Yale was saying out loud as he knelt in the first-row pew, 'what You think I should do, eh?'

'Get even! Get even!' answered Augie the Wop, who was on his knees on Frankie's right. Frenchy Carlino, who was on Yale's left, knew better than to answer the boss. Carlino had been to church with Frankie before, Pisano had not.

'Shut up!' Yale turned to Augie the Wop. 'I'm not talking to you.'

As Frankie finished his communion with The Higher Power, he crossed himself. 'And I wanna thank you for giving me okay to fix up that *fongool* Lovett and his Irish *disgraziato* ...' Catching himself, Frankie said, 'Hey, God, You forgive me because I use bad language in church. But I no have to tell you how bad I feel, eh?'

Just as he was about to rise from the pew, he felt a hand on his shoulder. Someone in the second row had walked behind the three kneeling men without their hearing him and startled them. Instinctively, Augie the Wop whipped out his .45-caliber automatic, wheeled, and pointed the barrel into a length of black cloth. It was the vestment that Father John Costa was wearing. The gun in his ribs prompted Father Costa to murmur a trembling litany.

'*Che posto e questo? Che cosa e questo?* Hey, Frankie, what's the matter with this fellow? I don't do anything to him ...'

Pisano was as startled as the priest. He scrambled off his knees, put the gun back in its holster, cupped Father Costa's right hand in his, and began kissing it.

'Oh, *padre*, forgive me,' he begged. 'I didn't know it was you.'

'Hey!' Yale shouted angrily at Augie. 'You crazy or something? Why you do that for to the good *padre*, eh?'

'Shhh,' the priest interrupted Yale. 'Don't scold the poor man. Don't you hear him say he's sorry. It's all right. I'm not sore ...'

Then, smiling, the priest said, 'Frankie, I am glad to see you here tonight. I said many prayers for you to get well.' He took a deep breath. 'Frankie, I want to have a little talk with you after you have finished your prayers.'

'Oh, I finish,' Yale said, standing up. 'What you want to talk about?'

The priest was burdened by a crisis in the neighborhood.

'You know, Frankie,' Costa said, 'there is a coal strike.'

'Sure, Father, I know,' Yale replied. 'When I got home today I almost freeze my ass off. Excuse me. I mean I freeze. You understand, eh,' Yale smiled sheepishly.

'Yes, Frankie, I understand,' the priest said. 'And that is why I came here to talk about it ...'

Costa knew that Frankie had considerable influence with important persons in the Brooklyn community and elsewhere. Couldn't he do anything about helping the poor people who weren't receiving coal deliveries?

'They are freezing in their homes,' Father Costa pleaded. 'Only tonight, Frankie, I visited a family on Sixty-sixth Street and Twelfth Avenue. The sight was pitiful. The children were sleeping with their coats and shoes on to keep them warm. Even the thick wool blankets they cover themselves with don't help them to keep warm. It's terrible.'

Frankie put his arm around Father Costa and wrapped him in a warm, affectionate embrace.

'Hey, Father,' Yale said. 'I feel like I wanna cry when I hear how terrible the people suffer because they got no coal. All I gonna say to you is tell them I'm gonna take care very soon. They ain't gonna freeze no more.'

'God bless you,' intoned Father Costa.

'Think nothing of it,' Yale replied with a smile. 'Anytime you need anything for the poor people all you gotta do is let me know. It's my pleasure to help the unfortunate children of God . . .'

If anyone knew how to strike a responsive chord in Frankie Yale, it was Father Costa. The pastor of St Rosalia's had begun striking responsive chords in Frankie just about a year before.

Costa had a dream then. He wanted to build a church. The idea was not unique in Brooklyn, because every priest who conducted services in a storefront or rented hall dreamed of building a St Peter's West in Brooklyn. That's how Brooklyn came to be called 'the Borough of Churches'.

In the search for financial backing to make his vision a reality, Father Costa conducted many fund-raising drives. The parishioners gave generously, some as much as a tenth of their weekly salaries. But when the donations were added up, there wasn't even enough, figuratively speaking, to pay the fee for the city building permit. The parishioners were all poor. Many worked on the docks. Others ran small businesses in the neighborhood. Yet all of them, without exception, were paying tribute in one form or another to Frankie Yale and his hoods.

On the docks, those who borrowed from the loan sharks paid outlandish interest rates that condemned them to perpetual hock. The Italian longshoremen who kept their heads above water and didn't seek advances from the shylocks also paid: it was the weekly graft collected by the underworld for getting them their jobs on the waterfront. The little storeowners who barely eked out a living wage were also made to bear the Black Hand's burden of weekly 'protection'. Missed instalments seldom occurred because that meant instant cancellation of the insurance policy, which was inevitably followed by an ash can through the window or other severe damage to the establishment – or worse, to the owner.

It was shortly after the funerals of Rackets Capolla, Giovanni Capone, Momo Municharo, and Anna Balestro, the victims of the Stauch's Dance Hall shootings, that Father Costa cornered Yale and had a heart-to-heart talk with him about the tragic consequences of continued underworld warfare.

'Where is this going to lead, Frankie?' the priest had asked. 'Four people dead, so many hurt. When is this going to stop? Did you ever think you might be next?'

'Hey, Father,' Frankie interrupted. 'We got one of theirs . . .'

Costa shook his head. 'It makes me sad, Frankie,' he had said mournfully. 'You are lucky to be rich. You make so much money and what do you do with it? You use it to buy guns and bullets to shoot people. You think that's right?'

'What you think I should do when people wanna hurt me, eh, Father?' Frankie asked. 'Should I let them hurt me?'

'You should pray, Frankie. Come to our little church on Sunday and pray . . .'

'You kiddin' me or somethin', Father?' Yale asked. 'What should I pray for, eh?'

'Well, this Sunday the entire parish will be praying for something that we want very, very much,' the priest had said meaningfully.

'What's that?' Yale's curiosity had been aroused.

'A new church,' Costa replied, looking deeply into Frankie's eyes. 'We are going to pray that somehow we can raise the money and build a new church.'

Yale knew a bite when it was put on him. This was a bite. But he rather liked the idea. The more he thought about it, the more he liked it. *Hey*, he said to himself, *maybe if I help to build this church God will be more on my side. He will protect me from all this trouble that fuckin' Lovett is making for me.*

Not long afterward, Yale made his first contribution to Father Costa. Pretty soon the foundation was poured for the new church.

'You no kid me, the foundation cost twenty thousand, that so, Father?' Yale had asked as he stood on the construction site with Costa.

That was the truth, the priest assured Yale and now there was the iron and steel that had to be installed for the frame. That would take, oh, perhaps fifty thousand. After the iron and steel, there were the bricks and stone, then came the interior – plastering, woodwork, marble, tile, then ...

It worked. Frankie Yale gave and gave and gave. His generosity seemed limitless. And when the church was finally dedicated and Frankie Yale entered the new building with his wife and two young daughters the parishioners greeted him as though he were Pope Benedict XV. They all but washed his feet with showers of praises for having made St Rosalia's Church a splendid reality.

The fact that the church happened to bear the name of Frankie's youngest daughter was purely coincidental. Father Costa just happened to like the name. But if the parishioners suspected that the church was not named after the saint canonised in Rome but little Rosalia Ioele (the real name of mobster Frankie Yale), well, they could face one reality: it took Rosalia's daddy's money to make that church possible.

They could have also asked themselves where Rosalia's daddy got the money. Who knew better than they? The money came from them, the poor slobs who were paying the Black Hand through their noses for protection, for employment, for everything.

For those immigrants who had toiled and experienced the corrupt life of the *latifondie* in Sicily, Brooklyn was nothing more than a transplanted *latifondie*. They had fled Sicily to get away from the Maffia's clutches, but the Maffia had reached four thousand miles across the sea to keep them under its thumb in the home of the brave and the land of the free.

No church anywhere had ever been built with as much stolen money as St Rosalia's. That it was built at all was because of a priest's timely approach to a robbing hood with an appeal that turned him into Robin Hood who gave the people something in return for the hundreds of thousands of dollars he had extorted from them.

Frankie sprang into action the morning after Father Costa urged him to help out the people caught in the grip of the coal strike. He ordered all his trucks engaged in delivering Prohibition hootch to the speakeasies to cease operations at once. He called a meeting of the forty drivers of those trucks.

'Hey,' he said to them, 'I got job for you that got nothing to do with bringing liquor to the speaks. This is something special I want . . .'

He told the drivers that their trucks would be used to haul coal to the families whose bins were empty because of the strike. He directed the men to drive to Linden, New Jersey, and bring back truckloads of coal for those unfortunate, freezing Italian families in Brooklyn.

By the next day coal had been delivered to the homes of virtually every St Rosalia parishioner. The furnaces were fired up once again. There was wide rejoicing among the poor Italians who had suffered so interminably through the long coal strike.

Frankie Yale was their *eroe* once more. Scores of black-shawled women tugging their children by the hand pilgrimaged to St Rosalia's and lit candles to Frankie Yale for what he had done.

Frankie couldn't see the glow of those candles from the Sunrise Café, but his face had a luminosity that night. He was listening to some phenomenal tidings carried by Two-Knife Altierri, who happened to have been at the right place at the right time to eavesdrop on a conversation.

The place was Spilleti's speakeasy on Court Street in downtown Brooklyn, and the conversation Willie happened to overhear at the bar was between two brothers who were New

York Police Department cops: Patrolman Robert Alongi, who had discovered the submerged car with the corpses of Irish Eyes Duggan and Pug McCarthy, and Sergeant Luigi Alongi, who had tried to get Frankie Yale to put the finger on the Duane Hall assassins.

The Alongis spoke in whispers, but Willie's sharp ears picked up just enough of what Luigi was saying to make him raise his antennae.

Luigi was telling Robert about the evidence the cops found in that second-floor apartment from which the gunmen fired their shots at Ballati, Dimessico, and Yale.

'I swear to you,' Altierri related to Yale. 'I heard the cops say they found a four-leaf clover drawn on the wall in the empty apartment. The cop from Manhattan said it was done with green crayon . . .'

'So what the hell you tellin' me that I don't already know,' Yale said at the beginning. 'We know it was that cock-suckin' Lovett and his cock-suckin' Irishmen who shot us up . . .'

Yale pounded the table with his fist. 'But what we don't know is who did the fuckin' shootin'.'

Altierri smiled. 'Yeah, but Frankie, that's what I'm trying to tell ya. I know one of them –'

'Who?' demanded Yale, his voice loud enough to be heard several tables away.

'Joey Bean,' Altierri said flatly.

'How you know that?' Yale's voice rose again, his interest almost feverish.

'I heard the cop from New York tell his brother that when they picked up Lovett and the other guys to bring them to the hospital to show them to you, they gave them a toss first,' Two-Knife explained. 'And what do you think they found in Joey Bean's pocket?'

As Altierri paused, he drew a sharp reprimand from Yale.

'Willie, no fuckin' guessing games,' he growled. 'Just tell me what they found.'

'A green crayon, Frankie, that's what they found!'

That was when Yale's face lit up. He looked at the ceiling and murmured, 'I know whose side You on, God. Thank you very much for bringing this information to me. I will not let You down . . .'

Chapter 11

Always Kill a Brother for Revenge

It is axiomatic in some sectors of the underworld community that revenge is sweeter when it is not taken against the person who committed the harm. While he may justly deserve the extreme punishment of death for his outrages, the theory is that it is better instead to take the life of someone near and dear to him, such as a son or a brother.

Joey Bean certainly earned the mark of death for his part in killing Miguel Dimessico and seriously wounding Gino Ballati and Frankie Yale. But that wasn't the punishment decreed by Frankie Yale when he held a council of his top lieutenants on the afternoon of 22 March 1922.

The meeting, which Battista Balsamo had condoned the day before when Yale had pilgrimaged to see his *compare*, was so important to Frankie that he even invited Joe the Boss to attend. Masseria, however, had other business that day and sent an emissary, Victorio 'The Professor' Pascalle, to represent him. Among the others at the caucus in Frankie's Sunrise Café were Balsamo and his two bodyguards, Vincenzo Mangano and Silk Stocking Guistra, Two-Knife Altierri, Augie the Wop, Tony Yale, Fury Argolia, Chootch Gianfredo, and Glass Eye Pelicano.

'What I call you for,' Frankie said as he opened the meeting, 'is to decide how to get back at Lovett and his fuckin' crowd for what they done to us at Joe Masseria's dance. I'm only gonna say one thing: we gotta get 'em and get 'em good, understand?'

Although Yale had already decided on the plan of attack, he wanted his boys to get the impression that this was a democratic organisation in which they all had a voice in policy making. Frankie didn't have to remind the gathering who one of the two gunmen was. Word of what Altierri had overheard in Spilleti's speakeasy had already circulated among the mob. Everyone was aware that Joey Bean had been fingered by Sergeant Alongi as one of the gunmen. The green crayon was the prime piece of evidence linking Joey with the second-floor apartment from which the shot had been fired.

'So we go after Joey Bean and rip him up,' suggested Fury Argolia.

'Yeah, that's what we gotta do,' Altierri jumped in. 'And nobody but me is gonna get this job. I wanna take care of him myself.'

Willie whipped his two knives from their holders and held them aloft. Their shiny, razor-sharp steel blades glistened in the shafts of sunlight filtering through the window near the large circular table where they sat.

'I bet you think I wanna cut Joe up with these here shivs, eh?' Willie taunted. 'Well, if that's what you think, you're fulla shit.' He began to laugh viciously. Then he slipped the knives back into the leather sheaths strapped to his body. Everyone's eyes were on Willie. He was up to something, but no one knew what.

Altierri didn't disappoint his audience. He put his hand inside his jacket, reached to the back of his pants waist band, and pulled out his hand. Everyone gasped. Willie was gripping a large meat cleaver.

Raising it over his shoulder, he brought it down with a swift, practiced swing towards the middle of Glass Eye's head. Fortunately, Two-Knife was on Pelicano's blind side. Nick would have had to change his underwear had he seen the cleaver descending upon his dome.

As it was, Altierri's demonstration terrified all the onlookers.

'Hey, what you do, you crazy or somethin'?' Yale thundered, jumping to his feet.

Willie, of course, broke his swing a few short inches from Glass Eye's hairline. But had he not been able to control its descent there'd have been one less Black Hand that afternoon.

Two-Knife then thrust the meat axe at arm's length over the table and let the gathering appraise its glistening steel blade.

'This is what I call my special comb,' Altierri said with a tight smile. 'With it I'm gonna part Joey Bean's hair better than his barber.'

'Hey, that's pretty good,' chuckled Augie the Wop. 'You gonna turn him into two-headed fella, right?'

Everyone laughed. Others added their own punch lines, which made the next few minutes of the meeting amusing. But Yale finally had his fill of the levity that had taken over what was to him a deadly serious matter.

'Okay, you guys,' he snapped, 'you make the jokes after the score is even, you hear what I say?' He glanced around the table. All smiles vanished.

Of course, he wasn't addressing himself to Victorio Pascalle, who was there representing Joey the Boss. Pascalle had not taken part in the levity. In fact, he hadn't said a word yet. But the moment for him to address the gathering was at hand.

Pascalle had been sent to propose the way his leader, Masseria, thought the situation should be handled. Joe had discussed the idea on the phone with Yale. Frankie liked it, so he asked Joe to come over and tell the boys about it. Joe sent Victorio to speak for him.

In truth, the scheme was really dreamed up by Pascalle, which was one of the reasons he was nicknamed 'The Professor'.

'All right,' Yale said, 'I want you to listen to idea my good friend Joe Masseria come up with for us. I'm gonna let Victorio tell you all about it.'

Turning to Pascalle, Yale said, 'Go ahead, Professor, you speak.'

Pascalle was a suave, dapper figure with none of the coarseness that characterised the majority of the Italians who toiled for the various gangs. Victorio was descended from an aristocratic family in Milan. His father was a professor of languages at the University of Milan. His mother had blood ties with Massimo d'Azeglio, who had been prime minister of Piedmont during the nineteenth century. Just before the outbreak of World War I, Victorio, then a freshman at the University of Milan, received orders to report for active duty in the Italian army. He didn't answer the call because he abhorred military service. He sneaked off to Naples and got a job as a seaman aboard a freighter sailing for New York.

As soon as the vessel docked on an East River pier in lower Manhattan, Pascalle jumped ship and high-tailed it into the city's melting pot. He got a job as a porter in Angelo Provinzano's Gay Times saloon on Forsythe Street. The saloon was a gathering place for the gang that would eventually be headed by Joe 'The Boss' Masseria.

Not long after he took over the organisation, Masseria went to the Gay Times one afternoon for a drink. While seated at his table, Joe scratched out some figures on the tablecloth, which represented some of the take from loan sharking and extortion that his boys had turned in that afternoon, and tried to add them up. Joe, who could count up to twenty without any trouble because he had ten fingers and ten toes, ran into problems when the sum was higher.

Joe tried a few ways to tote up the figures he'd scribbled down, but they didn't add up. In exasperation, he yanked the cloth off the table and threw it on the floor.

Pascalle came over and gently replaced the white linen sheet on the table. Then he spotted the numbers Masseria had written on the cloth. He glanced at them only briefly and shook his head. That disturbed Joe the Boss.

'Whatsa matta?' Masseria growled with a sharp look. 'You tryin' to tell me somethin'?'

'Of course, I can see why you are angry,' Pascalle said in a British accent so high-bred that it astounded Masseria. 'Your addition,' said the porter, 'is not correct.' For a moment, Masseria thought this was a put-on.

'Hey,' he said severely to Pascalle, 'you think you can add up these numbers, wise guy?'

Of course, Victorio could – and did.

That was Pascalle's last day pushing a mop. Masseria dragged him to the gang's headquarters, an old garage on Delancey Street, and installed him behind a desk as the mob's bookkeeper.

Over the eight years since Pascalle had been elevated to that position, he had earned increasing respect and admiration from Masseria. While Joe the Boss usually had no tolerance of Sicilians who were not from Palermo, his attitude toward Victorio was completely different. Coming from Milan, which is not in Sicily, and possessing an impeccable family background, the college-educated former porter gained Masseria's total trust and confidence – so much so that Pascalle became a sort of 'prime minister' for the gang. When it was necessary to negotiate with rival gangs in disputes over territorial rights or other controversies, Victorio would accompany Joe the Boss to meetings with their chieftains and high commands. More often than not Pascalle's diplomacy generated peaceful solutions to the problems and greatly reduced the number of internal wars that had been bloodying the sidewalks of lower Manhattan almost daily.

There were times when Pascalle's skills in achieving peaceful settlements fell short of their lofty aims. On those occasions, Masseria took off the silk gloves and unleashed the torpedoes.

Masseria's strategy in violence, however, was not always to strike the enemy with his own troops. The genius of Joe's college-bred 'prime minister' devised such infinite variations on extermination that conventional methods of gangland executions seemed obsolete by comparison. No better example of The Professor's advanced techniques for murder can be cited than the one he put forth that afternoon of 22 March at the Brooklyn Black Hand's conclave.

'Gentlemen,' Pascalle smiled with an air of nobility, 'before I get to the heart of the matter that is uppermost on your minds, I want to remind you of a famous saying by a famous man . . .'

Augie the Wop looked at Willie Altierri and whispered, 'You think Joe Masseria send this guy to jerk us off or somethin'?'

'The saying goes, "Heat not a furnace for your foe so hot that it do singe thy self",' the Professor spouted in his noble diction.

Don Giuseppe's jaw dropped. He turned to Frankie and refrained from commenting only because Frankie was smiling proudly at Masseria's emissary. Yale had heard about the Professor but had neither seen nor turned an ear on him in action.

'Bravo!' Yale applauded. 'What you say I agree with.'

Fury tapped Yale on the shoulder. 'You understand what he say?' Argolia asked, incredulous.

'Sure, sure I *capisco*,' Frankie said. 'What's the matter, Fury,' he chided, 'you don't understand good English? Continue, please, Professor. What you say so far is very good . . .'

Thank you, *Signore* Ioele,' Pascalle said politely. 'As I was about to ask, who can tell me the name of the person who wrote that saying?'

Pascalle gazed into blank faces. Finally, Chootch Gianfredo, who had been thrown out of grammar school after his third bout with the fourth grade, volunteered to answer: 'I know, I know!'

A smile crossed The Professor's face. 'Fine, tell us who said it.'

'George Washington,' Chootch said confidently.

The others looked at each other and then turned stony-faced to Victorio, waiting to hear whether Gianfredo had passed the test.

Pascalle shook his head. 'No, I'm afraid that isn't right,' he said crisply.

'Eh, I figure Chootch is too stupid to know who said that,' Johnny Silk Stocking rasped. Then, turning to The Professor, he added, 'Hey Victorio, why don't you tell us who said that. Nobody here gonna figure that one out . . .'

'Oh, yes,' Pascalle said softly, looking at Yale, who was smiling smugly. 'Mr Ioele, I'm sure, can tell us who the author of that saying was.'

'Frankie's gonna cut this guy's balls off,' Augie the Wop said under his breath to Tony Yale.

'Of course,' Frankie said, sucking in a deep breath. 'I'm sure the one who say that was Shakasp . . . Shakeupspeer . . . yea, Shookupsepeer is the one who say that, right?'

'Very, very good, *Signore* Ioele,' The Professor said approvingly. 'You are one hundred percent correct. It was indeed William Shakespeare.'

Frankie had been tutored in advance by Pascalle. The whole bit was a bit of a setup. And it was The Professor's job to dress the stage for the masterful plan he had thought out for getting revenge against Joey Bean.

'I realise that Shakespeare's language may be a bit archaic today and that some of you may not have divined the precise message he was trying to put across,' Pascalle said.

'You can say that again,' Augie the Wop piped up.

'Yeah,' Willie Two-Knife added, 'what does that mean . . .?'

'Now, I'll tell you,' The Professor said. 'Translated into everyday English, what Shakespeare was saying is that you must never make it so hot for anyone because you yourself may get burned.'

'*Madonn*',' rasped Altierri, 'you trying to say we don't hit Joey Bean because we gotta be afraid we get his back?'

'No, that's not it at all,' The Professor answered. 'There is a way, and I am going to tell you about it after I quote one other very important figure.'

'Hey, Tony,' Johnny Silk Stocking whispered to Yale's brother. 'You think Frankie brought this guy here for laughs?'

'The saying is "You never hurt the one you hate".'

Pascalle saw the stunned looks on all the faces – except Yale's, who knew what was coming. 'What you do,' he started again, 'is hurt someone your enemy loves.'

'Who, his mother?' Augie the Wop cracked.

The Professor shook his head. 'No, that's the whole point,' he said, descending a few steps from his scholarly pedestal. 'We want her to suffer, too, I'm sure you all agree with that.'

'You ain't shittin',' Two-Knife said, slamming his hand on the table. 'Maybe if I cut her in the gut she'll suffer, eh?'

'No, gentlemen, that isn't my message to you,' Pascalle said quickly.

'Hey, Professor,' interrupted Mangano, 'is what you telling us coming from Joe Masseria, no bullshit?'

'Absolutely none,' Pascalle said. 'The words I am conveying to you are directly out of Mr Masseria's mouth.'

'Funny he don't talk like you do,' Mangano commented sharply.

'Hey, hey!' Frankie Yale broke in. 'Will you fuckin' guys clam up and listen to what this man's tryin' to tell ya, eh?'

In the silence that ensued, Pascalle proceeded to outline the plan – the plan to kill not Joey Bean, but his brother Petey!

When The Professor finished explaining the details, the gang were ecstatic.

'Hey, Victorio,' Chootch shouted ebulliently, 'who the hell dream up that? It's terrific.'

'The author of this plot is my boss, Mr Masseria,' The Professor said loyally. 'And I am certain that he will be delighted to hear that it meets with your approval.'

'How long did it take Joe to figure this out?' asked Augie the Wop in a reverent tone.

'Not long,' Pascalle replied. 'Mr Masseria, you see, is a great admirer of Dante and he is fascinated by the poet's descriptions of the terrible tortures visited on the treacherous souls who were committed to purgatory. Mr Masseria has been won over to the idea of making people suffer for the wrongs they visit on others. He does not believe in killing them because that does not allow them to agonise for their acts.'

Yale, who'd been prepared for the punch line, slid his chair back and stood up. 'What The Professor say to you is, if Petey Bean gets it, then Joey is gonna be living in hell without bein' dead. And his *boutan* mama, too.' Then turning to Pascalle, 'Ain't that right, eh?'

'I am amazed at how you grasp things so quickly, Mr Ioele,' The Professor said, bowing grandly from the waist.

The day of Petey Bean's death was set for 8 August. Why it had taken Victorio Pascalle some five months to set Petey up for the kill is understandable in the light of the intricate plot for murder that The Professor had woven.

At 4:45 on that Sunday, the last threads of the rare tapestry of death designed by Pascalle were woven into place. It had been a miserable midsummer day, with the temperature peaking at 97 degrees and the humidity steaming to an unbearable 82 percent. Shortly after one o'clock, thick ominous rain clouds suddenly swept over the New York sky, casting a weird nocturnal darkness over the city.

A couple of miles to the south of South Brooklyn, more than half an estimated 750,000 bathers at Coney Island surged first for the bathhouses, then for the trains of the BMT Rapid Transit System and trolley cars in a mad dash for home before the heavens burst open.

Shortly before 3:00 p.m., the skies erupted with blinding flashes of lightning and deafening thunderclaps. On both sides of Baltic Street in the block between Nevins and Bond Streets, which was lined with flat-roofed four-and-five story brownstones with ornate filigree-edged facades and small two-step stoops jutting out of every doorway, scores of dwellers sat out of the sidewalks or simply hung over their windowsills futilely seeking relief from the oppressive heat. They were not panicked into flight by the clouds, lightning and thunder because they had but a few feet to scat for refuge.

A young woman, pretty, shapely, blonde, wearing a figure-hugging one-piece red silk tassled dress whose flared, pleated skirt fell just above the knees, sat next to an elderly fat woman in a black dress that came down below her calves on one of the stoops. The fat woman was crocheting and making small talk with the younger woman, who was nodding politely but not really paying attention. She was more concerned about the imminent downpour, which might very well ruin her plans for that evening.

Kathy Culkin was waiting for her husband, Daniel, who was due home from Coney Island around 4:30 p.m. He was not one of the bathers, but a rookie patrolman stationed at the Coney Island precinct. Unlike most city cops, Culkin was not on rotation duty but doing a straight 8 a.m.-to-4 p.m. tour, because of the demand for extra daytime patrols to control the crowds at Coney during the summer.

Because Monday was always his day off, Dan and Kathy had fallen into the routine of going out Sunday nights. At least that's how it had been since Dan graduated from the police academy in June and was assigned to duty in Coney Island. Kathy was dressed as she was that Sunday afternoon because Dan was taking her dancing at the Roseland Ballroom in Times Square.

Kathy glanced up at the lightning and murmured a silent

prayer for it not to rain, when suddenly a man's voice said, 'Hi-ya, Kathy, you said you wanted to see me?'

She glanced down from the stoop and saw a freckle-faced, medium-sized man, about five-feet-nine and 160 pounds, light-brown hair parted in the middle, combed back, and pasted down with pomade. His lips curled in a careless smile, ogling her lecherously. Kathy was stunned. Her first impulse was to wonder if Dan was playing a prank on her. Had he sent a friend to flirt with her for laughs? For an instant she thought Dan might be hiding behind one of the other stoops up toward Nevins Street. She turned her head, searching for a sign of her husband, who always walked home from that direction because it was the shortest way from the Pacific Street stop on the Sea Beach express line.

She saw nothing of Dan and turned back, half scowling at the man who'd spoken to her. He was dressed in white summer-weight linen trousers, a white silk sport shirt open at the collar, and a blue flannel double-breasted captain's blazer with gold buttons. He had his right foot planted on the first step of the stoop, the other on the sidewalk. She also noticed that he was wearing pointed black-and-white oxfords.

The old woman looked up momentarily when the stranger uttered his remarks to Kathy, but then went back to her knitting, pretending she was paying no mind to what was going on.

Still not certain that someone wasn't pulling her leg, Kathy stammered softly, 'Who are you?'

All at once the man's face grew grim. He frowned in puzzlement. 'You kiddin' or somethin'?' he asked, annoyed.

'What do you mean?' Kathy came back, now more bewildered than before.

The man jammed his hand into the right patch pocket of his jacket and pulled out a small piece of ladies' pink stationery. He unfolded it and thrust it at Kathy.

'Read it, baby, and tell me you didn't send me that note.'

As he spoke, he lowered his eyes and stared at Kathy's crossed legs. She sensed what he was leering at, and quickly pulled her skirt as far as it would go over her knees.

With considerable apprehension, she reached out, took the note from the stranger's hand, and began to read the message which had been written in blue ink:

Dear Petey,

I heard so much about you that I am most anxious to meet you. I live at 325 Baltic Street. If you want to take me out, I'll be sitting on the stoop around four o'clock this afternoon waiting for you. You'll know me when you see me because I have blonde hair and a shape I know you'll like.

Until then,
Kathy

The horror in Kathy Culkin's face surfaced before she was half way into the first sentence. By the time she had read the entire note, she was livid. She hurled the note at the man. He tried to catch it, but the gusting winds that had been building up for some time whipped the paper up and deposited it in the gutter in front of the house next door.

'You must be insane to come here and bother me,' Kathy snapped angrily. The old woman stopped knitting, put her work on her lap, and looked darkly at the man.

His lips rapidly tightening into a snarl, the man regarded Kathy with insistent eyes.

'You must be a really crazy dame to pull crap like this on me,' he said loudly. 'Who the hell do you think you are, anyway?'

Kathy bounded to her feet. She shook a scolding finger at the man and screamed, 'If you don't get out of here and leave me alone, I'm going to tell my husband.'

Before Kathy could complete the sentence, the man took his foot off the stoop, stood erect on the sidewalk, and interrupted her tirade by shouting. 'I think you're a pig. I wouldn't take you out on a bet. You stink!'

The old woman grabbed her knitting needle and stabbed the air in front of the man's face. 'You'd better get out of here and leave Kathy alone before I put this in your eye,' she sputtered in a thick brogue.

The man turned to the old woman. 'You try and do anything like that I'll stick the fuckin' needle up your fat ass,' he snarled.

Kathy burst into tears.

'You're not going to get away with this,' she sobbed. 'My husband is a policeman; I'm going to tell him.'

By now the man was at the end of his patience. People up and down the street were looking at him. He decided there was nothing to be gained in arguing with the woman anymore. The note, addressed to Petey Bean and delivered to him by a little boy a half hour earlier while he was boozing it up in McGuire's saloon, must have been a practical joke.

Petey started to walk away. But after a few faltering steps, he felt like having the last word. He turned and shouted at Kathy, 'You can go and take a hot shit for yourself, you fuckin' cunt!'

The profane parting he fired at Kathy seemed to puncture the clouds. No sooner had he spoken them than the rains that had been expected all afternoon exploded from the skies in a sudden deluge.

Petey Bean, thinking of his sharply creased white linen trousers, his spanking new captain's jacket, and his spotlessly clean white-and-black oxfords, sailed into the nearest hallway for refuge. It was the hallway next door to the one at 325 Baltic.

The downpour drove Kathy and the old woman into their hall, as it did everyone else who'd been loitering on the stoops and sidewalks or elbow-propping on the window ledges. The block was suddenly deserted as the rain slashed down with relentless fury. In a few quick seconds the middle of the street was transformed into a river.

It was 4:35 p.m. when the figure of a man in tan cotton slacks and tan sleeveless sport shirt battled through the wall of rain as he made his way at a trot along Baltic. He had been caught by the cloudburst as he was scurrying along a stretch of Nevins Street alongside an open construction site. He had nowhere to duck for shelter, and was so drenched that there was no point in seeking cover. He wasn't far from home, he reasoned, and a welcome change into dry clothes.

If Petey Bean, huddled inside the vestibule peering out through the open door, took notice of the man as he went by, there couldn't have been any reason to give him much thought, except to wonder what kind of a nut would be out in weather like that.

From his place in the doorway, Petey could not see where the man was going; and when the man turned and climbed the stoop of No. 325 next door, Bean had no way of observing that move unless he stuck his head outside. But that would have gotten him wet, and Petey had no intention of mussing his hairdo or his wardrobe. He was willing to wait out the rain until midnight if necessary.

The rain had eased up by 4:50 p.m., when residents of the block, who wouldn't have ventured out of their houses without good reason, streamed into the street and formed a large cluster around the human form lying in the gutter. The water on the street, coursing its way down a slight incline towards the sewer catch basin at the corner, rippled upon the body and broke in small waves in the puddle that had formed against the corpse.

The precautions Petey Bean had taken to keep his best Sunday outfit clean and dry were so much wasted effort, for now his clothes were ruined in the water and mud of the street. But it didn't make much difference to Petey at that point; he was quite dead.

Petey had made three mistakes that afternoon. The first was falling for the invitation delivered by the little boy who came into the saloon looking for him. His second mistake was reaming out Kathy Culkin when she spurned his advances. His third – and most grievous – was taking refuge in the hallway of the house next to Kath's.

It was Dan Culkin who'd passed by where Petey was huddled at the height of the downpour. He had entered the hallway of No. 325 and Kathy, standing with the old woman just inside the door, quickly related the horrendous experience she had just undergone and burst into tears. The old woman affirmed her story. Culkin, outraged, asked which way the man had gone. Kathy said she saw him going into the house next door to escape the rain.

Culkin flew. He had no trouble locating Petey. And then, Petey Bean was lying dead in the gutter with off-duty Patrolman Culkin standing over the body and the neighbors rapidly forming a crowd.

When Patrolman Charles Brophy of the Butler Street Precinct reached the scene, Culkin identified himself as a policeman and flashed his shield.

'What happened?' Brophy asked.

Culkin related how Bean had treated Kathy, and how he found Petey in the hall and tried to make an off-duty arrest.

'Just as I grabbed his arm to bring him to the station house,' Culkin said, 'he jumped me and tried to slug me with a blackjack he pulled from his back pocket. He swung at me and I ducked. But he still caught me over here.' Culkin rubbed the right side of his head. 'Then I let him have it with a couple of punches. I think I hit him twice and he went down. His head hit the curb and he didn't move. I tried to help him up but there was no way I could lift him. Then I took his pulse and couldn't feel any. I'm pretty sure he's dead.' Culkin shook his head sadly. 'I sure didn't mean to kill him. I didn't hit him hard at all. It's just that – well, I think he slipped on the wet sidewalk and fell. That's what I think really happened . . .'

An ambulance physician from nearby Holy Family Hospital confirmed Culkin's diagnosis. Petey Bean was indeed dead, and his body was carted to the Kings County Morgue for autopsy.

Dan and Kathy Culkin were taken to the Butler Street stationhouse and questioned by detectives. Their detailed statements of their separate involvements with the victim satisfied the sleuths. It seemed like a case of justifiable homicide, but it wasn't up to the detectives to make that decision. The facts would have to be handed over to the Kings County District Attorney, who would then present them to a grand jury for a final judgment. Dan and Kathy, meanwhile, were allowed to return home.

The next day, after the medical examiner's preliminary report was delivered to the police, detectives went to Culkin's house and arrested him for homicide. The pathological examination revealed that the frontal bone of Petey Bean's skull had been broken. The medical examiner believed the fracture was not the result of Bean's head hitting the sidewalk but was caused by a blow from a heavy weapon, such as a blackjack. Culkin vehemently denied that he had struck his wife's molester with the blackjack, but the detectives didn't believe him.

After being mugged and fingerprinted, Culkin was booked and taken in handcuffs to the Magistrate's Court in downtown Brooklyn for arraignment. The judge ordered him held in $1,500 bail. When Kathy couldn't find a bondsman to post her husband's bail, Culkin was remanded to the Raymond Street jail. He spent the night there, but was released the next morning after his parents put up the security.

About two weeks later the District Attorney's office brought the facts of the case before the grand jury. Culkin and his wife testified about the events of that Sunday afternoon. The grand jury also listened to other testimony, and ultimately returned a no-true bill, which means that Culkin, in effect, had not committed a crime.

What saved the young policeman from standing trial for murder was the testimony of an assistant medical examiner, Dr M. E. Martin, who told the grand jury that although Petey Bean had suffered a fractured skull, that was not the contributing cause of his death. Bean, the doctor swore, had died of a cerebral hemorrhage – brought on by acute alcoholism!

While Dan Culkin beat the rap that could have sent him to prison until his hair turned gray, he didn't escape the test of innocence at his police department trial to determine his fitness to return to duty. The guidelines of department trials are stiffer, and the cop on the carpet cannot take refuge in his constitutional rights which the courts are compelled to tolerate.

The rookie's testimony about the events of that Sunday afternoon didn't satisfy the trial commissioner, despite the medical examiner's findings. What Patrolman Culkin didn't explain was *how* the White Hand gangster's skull had been fractured. He could have explained it easily but he didn't dare.

The facts, as the authors have pieced them together, show that Petey Bean had indeed tried to defend himself against the off-duty policeman. But indications are that he was not resisting arrest; he was repelling Culkin's attack – an attack that Petey

Bean had no reason to doubt was designed not just to lay him low but to kill him.

Culkin could easily have explained the frontal bone fracture to Petey Bean's head. He could have gotten himself off the hook at his police department trial by saying, 'Yes, I believe I caused it because when Bean swung at me with the bill, I took it out of his hands and hit him. That's what caused the fracture.'

But on the advice of his attorney, Culkin denied that he struck Bean with the blackjack. For had he done otherwise, he would have spoken contrary to his sworn testimony before the Kings County grand jury.

And then he would have been subjected to prosecution for perjury.

There's no question the death of Petey Bean stands as a classic example of the gangland tenet that it is better to take the life of someone near and dear to an enemy, than the enemy itself.

Chapter 12

Mistaken Identity

Wild Bill Lovett lit a cigarette and made a deep sucking sound as he dragged the first puff into his lungs. As he exhaled, he leaned hard on the battered desk in the gang's garage on Baltic Street, folded the newspaper he'd been reading, and slammed it on the desk.

'I don't believe it, no fuckin' way I believe that cop killed Petey because he insulted his wife,' Lovett raged. 'There's gotta be more to it than that . . .'

The story in *The Brooklyn Eagle* recounted the details of Patrolman Daniel Culkin's dismissal from the police department despite his earlier exoneration by the grand jury of culpability in Bean's killing.

'Even the fuckin' cops didn't buy the story,' Lovett shouted. 'They fired him! That's gotta tell us something, don't it?'

He looked around at the fifteen of his boys who were sitting in a semicircle of chairs around the front of Lovett's desk. Wild Bill wanted someone to say something.

'You think this was a setup, right Bill?' Pegleg Lonergan asked tightly.

Lovett curled the fingers of his right hand into a fist and shook it at Lonergan. The gesture was not meant to display anger at Pegleg but, rather, the exasperation Wild Bill felt over the incongruous, even inexplicable, circumstances surrounding Petey Bean's death.

'You know this whole thing stinks and I don't have to spell it out for you,' Lovett's voice rose. 'You know goddamn well that fuckin' cop was lying . . .'

Joey Bean, the last of the three Bean brothers, leaned forward and narrowed his eyes. 'Petey never carried a blackjack in his whole life,' Joey said slowly. 'The only thing he ever had on him was a gun. But he didn't have no gun on him when he went to meet the broad. I know that because I was with him in McGuire's. When the kid came in and gave Petey the note and he read it, he took the piece outta his pocket and gave it to me to hold. So he was clean when he went to see the cunt . . .'

'That's exactly what I'm getting at,' Wild Bill snarled. 'There's a fuckin' coverup somewhere. Somebody's lyin'. And there's no fucking doubt the cop is the one that ain't tellin' the truth . . .'

'You think it was the cop's blackjack?' Aaron Harms suggested.

Lovett shook his head. 'Naw, he was too smart for that,' Wild Bill said sourly. 'I read in the paper that they checked the cop's locker at that stationhouse and found his gun and blackjack there. Besides, the one Culkin used on Petey wasn't the kind the police use. It was longer and bigger.'

'How do you think they got an Irish cop to pull a stunt like this?' Ash Can Smitty wanted to know.

'What makes you think an Irishman can't be bought, stupid?' Eddie Lynch growled. 'You saw how they got to one of our own, didn't you?'

Lynch referred to the late and lamented Patrick Foley, Sally Altierri's boyfriend, who had given her brother, Two-Knife Willie, the layout of Denny Meehan's flat which enabled the Black Hand to usher in a change of leadership of the White Hand.

'Think we should burn Culkin?' Lonergan asked Lovett.

Wild Bill shook his fist again. 'That doesn't solve the problem,' he said hoarsely. 'We wipe out the cop, but how does that even the score with Yale and the ginzos? They don't give a shit what happens to that prick. That just somebody they got to do their dirty work for them. No, what we gotta do is get one of them . . .'

'Hey, I know who we should waste,' cried Wally 'The Squint'

Walsh. 'What about what I told you the other day that I had heard, eh, Bill?'

Lovett's eyes narrowed as he started at The Squint, whose eyes were hidden behind his tightly drawn lids. 'Wally, you sonofabitch. I completely forgot what you told me. Hey, I must be losin' my fuckin' mind. Yeah . . .'

Lovett finally unclenched his fist and clapped his hands. Then he slapped the desk with both hands. 'Wally! For chrissakes. Hey, tell everybody what you told me, okay?'

Walsh had run into Joan Finnegan a few days before. She was still trying to shake the trauma brought on by her horrendous experience in Para's Court Theater, where she and Charleston Eddie Mcfarland attended their last Sunday matinee flick. What passed between Walsh and Joan in their casual meeting was mostly idle gossip, but there was one thing the girl told Wally that hit him like a lightning bolt.

'She said to me that the broad who works in the cashier's booth – her name is Sally Lomenzo – she was working at the place when Eddie got his throat sliced –'

'How does she figure in this shit?' interrupted Ash Can Smitty.

'Hey, just wait until the fuck he finishes, will ya!' thundered Lovett.

'I'm getting to it right now,' The Squint smiled. 'That Sally's had the hots for our old pal and buddy, that bastard Two-Knife Altierri, the greatest guinea alive . . .'

Wally took a deep breath and tried to open his eyes. But dim as it was in the garage, the light was too glaring for him. He made a face, reflecting how much it pained him to unscrew his eyelids.

'I put some things together,' Wally went on, feeling more at ease now that he was back squinting. 'I figured that if that wop cashier is going with the ginzo, she's gotta be the one who tipped Willie off about Eddie and Joan going to the nickelodeon every Sunday.'

'Hey, Wally,' interrupted Needles Ferry with a horse laugh. 'If you'd open your fuckin' eyes you'd see the Court ain't no nickelodeon. They are fuckin' chargin' twenty cents –'

'Oh, why don't you shut your ass and let Wally finish tellin' us the goddamn story,' Lonergan broke in angrily. 'Here we are talkin' serious and you're horse shittin' around. Shut your fuckin' mouth, Needles.'

'Come on, Wally,' Lovett said eagerly. 'Tell 'em how you got it pegged.'

'Okay,' Walsh responded, taking in a deep breath. 'I checked around and found out that Willie's been saddlin' that Sally for a long time – yeah, going back long before they gave it to Eddie that Sunday. So, I figure who would know that Eddie and Joan been going to the show every Sunday – except Two-Knife. He gets his information from Sally. After that, it's a setup.'

'You mean you think Two-Knife did the number on Charleston?' Aaron Harms asked with a gleam in his eyes.

'Nobody else *but*, baby,' Wally said, his chest swelling with pride that filled him. He was the first of the gang to link Altierri to McFarland's murder. Tenuous as it was, it was enough to sate the thirst of the White Hand, revenge-bent as they were now to burn someone in the Black Hand for the murder of Petey Bean as well as Charleston Eddie.

'You mean you're gonna hit Willie Altierri?' asked Ernie 'Skinny' Shea with unrestrained glee.

Lovett broke into a broad smile that reflected his satisfaction that a target for the killing had been selected and his sanction of the hit.

'Any objections?' he asked in a smug tone.

'Yeah!' yelled Joey Bean.

Everyone jumped.

Lovell stared menacingly at Bean. 'What did you say?' he scowled.

'Only this, Bill,' Bean came back in a hard but respectful voice. 'I don't say okay unless I'm in on the job. You just don't forget – I gotta even two scores. One for what they done to Danny and the other for Petey . . .'

Lovett grinned with relief. 'Why, Joey,' he said in a soothing, placating voice. 'Nobody here would think of not lettin' you go out on this one. In fact, I'm even gonna give you the honor of pickin' the boys you want to work with you, whaddaya think of that?'

Bean lifted his heavy, muscular frame from the chair, walked over to the desk, and shook Lovett's hand.

'Thanks, Bill,' Joey said appreciatively. 'You won't be sorry for this, no sir. I'm gonna see to it that we do a real splashy number on that greasy two-knife ginzo . . .'

A fall day. Bright sunshine. Cloudless skies. Too beautiful and too warm for 28 October. The time: 2:30 p.m.

A black 1921 Lincoln touring car turned the corner of Third Place and cruised along Court Street, slowing gently to a stop at the curb in front of Veronica's Fruit & Vegetable Market. Eddie Lynch, driver of the lumbering four-door vehicle, put the car in neutral and turned to the two men in the back seat.

'He should be coming by any minute,' Lynch said.

'Any minute, my ass,' rasped Joey Bean. 'He's in the fuckin' place already. I see him up on the chair gettin' his shine . . .'

'You sure it's him?' asked Jimmy The Bug Callaghan, his eyes crossing sharply over the bridge of his nose.

'Whaddaya want me to tell ya, that you're too fuckin' cock-eyed to know the difference?' Bean growled. 'I know Altierri when I see him. I don't even have to see him. I can *smell* that wop a mile away.'

'Okay,' Lynch snapped. He put one foot on the brake, the other on the clutch, and threw the car into first gear. 'I'll start tear-assin' as soon as you guys finish him off. Now, go get 'im.'

The gold lettering on the large plate-glass window next door to Veronica's advertised 'Carmine's Bootblack'. It was run by Carmine Balsamo, a nephew of Don Giuseppe. Carmine's only connection with the *Union Sicilione*, the Black Hand, the Mafia, or whatever other name the Italian underworld in Brooklyn was called in those days, was through his mother, Maria, Don Giuseppe's sister.

Carmine earned a very good living in his bootblack shop, because he had three chairs to give shines and because he also cleaned spats and blocked hats. But most of all because he was related to Godfather Battista Balsamo and, by extension, to the Black Hand overlord Frankie Yale, godfather to Battista's daughter, Gina.

Cognisant of that kinship to Don Giuseppe Balsamo and to Frankie Yale, the big and small of the Brooklyn underworld came to Carmine's Bootblack to have their shoes shined, spats cleaned, and hats blocked. Carmine had the market cornered for these services in South Brooklyn. The only reason the Federal Government didn't go after Carmine was that Uncle Sam wasn't so strict about monopolies in those days.

The local cops had a definite interest in Carmine, yet were never able to generate the evidence they needed to prove a case against him. Three times in less than two years before that sunny October afternoon, bootblack shops had opened in the neighborhood, only to go out of the business before the grand opening sign could be taken down.

Joey Bean and Jimmy The Bug Callaghan grabbed the sawed-off shotguns from the floor of the car, jumped out, and ran to Carmine's Bootblack. Carmine spotted the muzzle of the shotgun in Bean's hands. He didn't see the weapon Callaghan was wielding because he didn't even bother to look at Callaghan. He dropped the shoe brush he had been using to polish a pair of black shoes and crash-dived to the floor.

The customer up in the chair whose feet were in the black shoes was astonished to see the bootblack behaving so erratically.

'Hey, Carmine,' he called, his lips twisted in a mean-looking smile, 'Whatsa matter with you, eh?'

'Jump!' Carmine shouted as he scrambled frantically toward the back of the shop. 'Jump!'

Suddenly the customer with the blond hair neatly combed back from his narrow forehead caught a movement on the street outside. His cold blue eyes opened in horror. 'No! No!' he yelped.

Too late. The searing volley of lead from the twin barrels of the sawed-off shotguns creamed the big plate-glass window; the impact of the fusillade, aimed straight at the head, literally lifted the man's body out of the chair. It came down, bent at the waist, and fell head-first to the floor, knowing a bottle of black liquid shoe polish off the bottom of the footstand.

Before the shoe polish and the blood gushing from the victim's splintered head had begun blending into a hideous black-red mixture on the floor, the two assailants, driven by Eddie Lynch, were roaring past the store for a clean getaway.

As a crowd gathered outside Carmine's Bootblack and police inside the store questioned Balsamo about the brazen daylight gangland hit, a young man bulled his way through the lines of the curious on the sidewalk, screaming, 'Let me through . . . I gotta see . . .'

He finally reached the door, but a patrolman put his hands out and held the young man back. 'You can't come in here,' the cop said.

'I gotta go in,' the youth choked, tears in his eyes. 'Because I gotta see my father . . .'

'Who are you?' the policeman asked.

'Vincenzo Gibaldi.'

'Oh,' the patrolman said, lowering his eyes. 'I'm very sorry, son . . . I'm very sorry . . .'

Carmine Balsamo spotted the young man at the door. 'Excuse me, please,' he said to the policemen questioning him. 'I gotta talk to this young fella.'

Balsamo went to the door. He took the young man into his arms. Tears were streaming down Balsamo's cheeks. 'Vincenzo,' cried Balsamo. 'They kill your papa . . . oh, Vincenzo, Vincenzo . . .'

Carmine comforted the eighteen-year-old son of the smalltime bootlegger Antonio Gibaldi. Other than that slight illegality, Antonio Gibaldi's pursuits in life were always on the up and up. He was a devoted family man, the beloved father of six children, the oldest of whom was Vincenzo, who was sobbing inconsolably in Carmine Balsamo's embrace.

And Antonio Gibaldi bore a striking resemblance to Willie Two-Knife Altierri. So striking was the resemblance that on the Saturday afternoon of 28 October 1922, Joey Bean and Jimmy the Bug Callaghan mistook Antonio Gibaldi for Two-Knife.

Chapter 13

One for My Father

'You shoulda seen the way we blew his head off,' Joey Bean trumpeted as he strutted into the White Hand's garage. His cockiness was out of character for him, but that afternoon, after the satisfaction he felt at the score against the Black Hand ginzos, he felt he could swagger a little.

'Yeah,' chirped Jimmy The Bug, 'a direct hit. We splashed his brains all over the wall. They're gonna need one of those vacuum cleaners to put all of him in the coffin.'

Wild Bill Lovett was ecstatic. 'Great, great!' he shouted. He jumped out of his chair and rushed to shake Joey's and Jimmy's hands.

'Hey, how about me?' Eddie Lynch said in a hurt voice. 'Don't I get no credit?' He turned to Bean and Callaghan. 'Why don't you bastards tell Bill about the clean getaway, why don't ya?'

The shotgun killers looked at each other and smiled. They turned to Lynch and give him the finger. Everybody laughed. Everybody was happy. Wild Bill broke out a bottle of Canadian Club from a case smuggled from Ontario for the boss's private use, and poured drinks for everyone.

A little past five o'clock the celebrations ended abruptly. Ash Can Smitty tore into the garage and asked in a panicky voice, 'What the fuck went wrong?'

'Whaddaya mean what went wrong?' Lovett slurred. 'Whaddaya talkin' about?'

Smitty unfolded the late edition of *The Brooklyn Eagle* he was carrying under his arm and flattened it on Lovett's desk.

The eight-column banner headline read:

BOOTLEGGER BLASTED IN BOOTBLACK SHOP

'Hey,' Lovett gasped. 'Willie Altierri ain't no bootlegger. Where the hell did they get that from?' He snatched the newspaper and began reading the story. Bean, Callaghan, and Lynch moved behind Lovett and leaned over his shoulders trying to see what distortion in the story could have resulted in Altierri being labelled a bootlegger in the headline.

Lovett's face grew grim and dark, then took on increasing shades of red as anger began to boil in him. He slammed the newspaper on the desk and scrambled to his feet. He reeled slightly from the liquor he'd been gulping, but his mind was alert to the horrendous goof-up his boys had committed.

'You stupid fuckin' assholes!' he bellowed. 'You know who you killed, don't you?' He wheeled around, stuck his nose almost into Bean's face, and screamed, 'You killed a fuckin' small-time ginzo bootlegger. How can you be so goddam dumb? Where in the hell were you lookin', eh?'

Lovett landed a quick open-hand on Bean's face, then caught Callaghan on the return with a swift backhand rap on the cheek. The assassins cowered and jumped away as Lovett unsuccessfully aimed two more slaps at them.

'Bill, for chrissakes,' Callaghan cried in a trembling voice. 'The guy was a fuckin' double for Two-Knife . . .'

'Yeah,' squeaked Bean. 'You shoulda seen him. A spittin' image of Willie. No shit, Bill.'

'Oh, shut your asses, I don't wanna hear no more of your shit,' Lovett growled in disgust. He wobbled back to the desk and sank heavily into the chair. 'Get the fuck outta here! Scram!' he yelled at Bean and Callaghan. 'I hope Yale puts fuckin' bullets in your heads. You deserve it.'

Joey and Jimmy scampered out the door as Wild Bill turned to Lynch. 'Where the hell were you?' he demanded gruffly. 'Can't you tell the difference between a shit like Gibaldi and Willie Two-Knife . . .'

'I was in the car,' Lynch said defensively. 'What can I tell ya? Joey and Jimmy spotted him and they seemed so goddam sure it was Two-Knife . . .'

'Shut up,' snarled Lovett. 'I don't wanna hear no more.'

He grabbed the bottle and poured himself another drink.

At times undertakers have been able to perform wax wonders on the physiognomies of victims who have been demolished by savage force. Faithful restoration of the face in such cases will inevitably generate high praise for the mortician from the deceased's family and friends. For there is hardly anything as precious as a final opportunity to view the remains of a dearly departed and see him as he looked in life.

Pasquale Sessio always prided himself on the perfection he achieved in his art at his Sessio Funeral Home at the corner of Carroll Street and Fifth Avenue. The families of Little Italy always went to Sessio for their funerals because of his skill in sculpting faces for their journey to the divine abode. Pasquale was called *Il Ristabilirere* (The Restorer). Regardless of age, no one looked old and wrinkled, once laid out in one of Sessio's caskets. Nor did Pasquale let anyone's face carry a scar or even a scratch to the grave.

But Michelangelo himself could not have reshaped Antonio Gibaldi's features. When Joey Bean and Jimmy the Bug described to Lovett how extensively they had obliterated their target's head, they weren't stretching the truth.

So it was a sealed coffin for Antonio. And for his wake, which lasted three days and two nights, the big and small of the Italian underworld pilgrimaged to Sessio's to pay their respects to the grieving family.

No one suffered more anguish than young Vincenzo Gibaldi, who held vigil beside his father's bier every moment that Sessio's doors were open to the procession of mourners. Kneeling in front of the casket, as long as an hour at a stretch, tears trickling down his cheeks, hands twisting rosary beads, lips moving tremblingly in silent prayer, Vincenzo invariably uttered his own closing, loudly enough to be heard throughout the mortuary, 'We'll see them, Papa ...'

That was his vow that his father's murder would be requited. A chorus of voices in Italian and English resounded each time the son swore vengeance on the killers.

'*Dateglieli*, Vincenzo!'

'Give it to them, Vincenzo!'

On the morning following his father's interment in Cypress Hills Cemetery, Vincenzo Gibaldi strode into a Fulton Street sporting goods store, bought a Daisy repeating air rifle and a large supply of BB's, then went to his backyard for serious target practice. Until that day, Vincenzo had never held a gun in his hands.

He returned frequently to the store for new supplies of shot. He drilled himself continually with the air rifle, seeking perfection in marksmanship. Before long, he could line a dozen empty cans on top of the fence and pick them off one at a time in sequence, hitting each with just one shot.

Barely a year had passed since William Barclay Masterson, better known as Bat, had died at his rolltop desk in the office of *The Morning Telegraph* in Manhattan. Masterson had spent the last year of his life as a sports-writer, far from Dodge City where he had once maintained law and order with his blazing six-shooter. Vincenzo Gibaldi had not forgotten what he read in Masterson's obituary. The legendary Kansas sheriff, who had twenty-seven notches in his gun, had a theory that a man needed three qualities to make the grade as a killer with a gun:

Courage, skill in handling the weapon, and above all, steadiness – the quickness and cool to make the first shot count every time.

These became Vincenzo's aims as he practiced like a man possessed to achieve excellence with his Daisy.

By 15 April 1923, just after his nineteenth birthday, Vincenzo Gibaldi began making inquiries among his father's friends about buying a revolver. He felt ready to fulfil the vow he'd made over his father's casket.

He was directed to a Greek seaman on the Gowanus waterfront who offered Vincenzo a piece stolen from a shipment of the Remington Firearms Company being loaded aboard a freighter bound for Rio de Janeiro. It was a .38-caliber revolver.

'How much?' Gibaldi asked.

'Fifty dollars,' the Hellenic thief wanted.

'Too much,' Vincenzo protested. 'I don't have that kind of money.'

'How much you got?' the seaman asked with a smile.

'Thirty dollars,' Vincenzo said, pulling the money out of his pocket and offering it to the Greek.

'I take,' he said. He grabbed the money with one hand and handed the gun over with the other.

Vincenzo Gibaldi was in business.

Two nights later Gibaldi borrowed his brother Frank's car, a maroon Chevrolet roadster, as he had done on some ten prior occasions in the past two weeks, and drove to a sporting goods store in downtown Brooklyn's main shopping district. He bought a box of .38-caliber bullets and proceeded to a destination on Furman Street that had been the object of his intense study and surveillance during the preceding two weeks.

As Vincenzo parked at the curb, he couldn't help smiling to himself. There, right down the block, was the black LaSalle that he'd been tailing almost nightly from its present location to a destination some eighteen miles distant in Teaneck, New Jersey.

Vincenzo pulled his father's gold watch and chain out of his vest pocket. He held the timepiece near the window. The light from the street lamp illuminated the face. It was 9:15 p.m. *Any minute now*, he told himself.

Before returning the watch to his pocket, Vincenzo ran his fingers over the case and murmured, 'We'll see them, Papa . . . tonight we'll see them . . .'

Then Vincenzo spotted the object of his pursuit. He came out of McGuire's saloon, got behind the wheel of the LaSalle, and drove south to the waterfront. He made a U-turn at precisely the place that Irish Eyes Duggan and Pug McCarthy had made their turnaround that Sunday afternoon of 26 June 1922, when they were ambushed by the three Mormillo brothers. The LaSalle then turned north on Furman and headed for Flatbush Avenue. Vincenzo didn't have to fall in behind. He knew damn well what route the LaSalle would be taking. Only after the big sedan had lumbered past him on the return trip to Furman did Gibaldi finally start up his car, drive to the end of the street, and make his U-turn in front of the Gowanus Stevedoring warehouse.

By the time Vincenzo reached the approach to the Manhattan Bridge, he had the LaSalle in his sights again. When the car came off the bridge and headed west on Canal Street, Vincenzo fell in behind at a discreet two hundred feet. He didn't want the driver to suspect he was being followed.

The LaSalle coursed crosstown on Canal, turned north on Hudson Street, west on Fourteenth, then north again on Tenth Avenue, which became Amsterdam Avenue at 72nd Street. A left turn brought the LaSalle to the ferry slip at the foot of 125th on the Hudson. The ferry crossing the river to Fort Lee on the Jersey side was already in the slip. An attendant signalled the LaSalle to drive down the ramp and board the ferry in the left-hand lane. Vincenzo, who was directly behind, was signalled to drive into the right-hand lane.

When he braked his car to a stop at the bow of the ferry behind the protective chain, Vincenzo was on the right side of the LaSalle.

Out of the corner of his eye, Gibaldi saw the driver in the next car turn his head briefly and glance at him. Gibaldi pretended not to be aware of the other man's movements. After all, there was no way the man driving the LaSalle could know who Vincenzo Gibaldi was.

When the ferry docked in Fort Lee, Gibaldi was once again on the LaSalle's tail. Because Vincenzo had followed the LaSalle about ten times in the past two weeks over that very same route, there was no reason that night for the driver to suspect the car that had been beside him in the ferry stall was tailing him.

On those prior occasions, Vincenzo had followed the LaSalle to its destination: the spacious concrete driveway of an impressive Colonial-style dwelling situated about a hundred feet off the road. Each time in the past, Vincenzo drove right by the house in his brother's maroon roadster. At most, the man behind the wheel of the LaSalle may have surmised that the car behind was driven by a late commuter like himself and headed for a destination beyond his own house.

But on that Tuesday night, 17 April, the headlights that shone behind the LaSalle didn't fade out of his rearview mirror when the LaSalle's driver turned into the driveway.

The man behind the LaSalle's wheel certainly had registered the presence of the other car as he turned off the ignition and stepped out into the driveway.

He stared apprehensively at the man getting out of the maroon roadster. Even in the darkness, Vincenzo Gibaldi saw the disquieted look on the other man's face. That look pleased Vincenzo; the man knew now what was about to happen.

Gibaldi whipped out the .38 revolver that he'd bought from the Greek seaman. He had loaded the gun with the bullets he purchased that night while waiting for his quarry to leave McGuire's. Now all he had to do was cock the trigger.

The click of the hammer shot terror through the man standing alongside the LaSalle. 'What do you want?' he asked in a choked voice.

There was no response. In the glare of the Chevy's headlights Vincenzo saw the man's face tighten in fear. Now, with precision cultivated by following Bat Masterson's admonition to make the first shot count every time, he squeezed the trigger.

The bullet plowed into the man's chest. His body hurled backward. Before he hit the ground two more bullets struck him. The first spun his body around. He collapsed in a heap on the driveway as Vincenzo fired the last three bullets into him.

Gibaldi quickly reloaded his revolver and fired six more slugs into the victim, aiming for different parts of the body: the stomach, the middle of the chest, and between the eyes. Working calmly and coolly, he emptied the spent cartridges from his gun once again and slipped six more bullets into the chamber. Then he fired that round, reloaded and triggered off six more shots – making it a total of twenty-four.

Not a single bullet missed its target.

Certain that he had performed the execution in a manner that would have met with Masterson's approval, Vincenzo got into

Don Giuseppe—"Battista"—Balsamo, the first
godfather

The Clock on Columbia Street

Frankie Yale in 1918

William "Wild Bill" Lovett, leader of the White
Hand gang

The Adonis Club, meeting place of the Black
Hand gang. Inserts: Richard "Pegleg"
Lonergan (L); "Needles" Ferry (R)

John Scalise (L) and Albert Anselmi (R),
triggermen of the ambush of Sagaman's Hall

Frankie Yale's death, July 1, 1928

Vincenzo Gibaldi, who became "Machine Gun
McGurn," and his wife, Louise Rolfe

Al Capone

St. Valentine's Day massacre 1929

his car, backed out of the driveway, and roared off towards the Hudson River ferry crossing in Fort Lee.

The racketing roar of gunfire had awakened Edna Callaghan from a sound sleep. She threw on a housecoat and ran to the front door to investigate. The night was clear and a full moon cast all the illumination Edna needed to spot the crumpled body on the driveway alongside the LaSalle.

She screamed hysterically at the sight of her husband of just four months lying dead.

All the pleasures and joys of suburban life which Jimmy The Bug had dreamed about with his bride became reality right after the wedding, when they moved into the palatial $75,000 Colonial-style house in Teaneck. That night, 17 April, all their visions of a happy lifetime together were shattered.

Vincenzo Gibaldi left no clue that might enable Jersey authorities to link him with the killing.

Vincenzo had not only partly avenged his father's killing that night, but he was also free to pursue other human targets he was aiming to get for the grievous error the White Hand made that afternoon in Carmine's bootblack shop.

Chapter 14

Two More for Papa

As much of a mystery as the shooting of Jimmy the Bug Callaghan was to the Bergen County police, there was something about the crime that was even more puzzling than the mere lack of clues.

It was the Indian-head nickel that had been pressed into The Bug's right hand. Detectives from the Bergen County prosecutor's office had no doubt that the five-cent piece was put into the victim's hand after he had been raked to death by the two dozen bullets. There was no way in the world Callaghan could have held the nickel in his hand after he faced his executioner's fire, for the impact of the first bullet or two would have unflexed The Bug's fist if, in fact, he'd been holding the coin, and it would have fallen out of his hand. So the nickel had to have been placed there after Callaghan collapsed on the driveway. But why? Was it the killer's calling card, so to speak? What significance, if any, did it have in The Bug's rubout?

Authorities were to get no more of a clue to that mystery than they were to turn up a lead on the assassin himself.

In South Brooklyn, they didn't have to conduct an investigation to figure out what the Indian-head nickel signified. Frankie Yale came up with the answer even before he had finished reading the story about Callaghan's murder the following morning in the *New York American*.

'Hey,' he turned sharply to Fury Argolia, 'that young kid of Antonio Gibaldi, what's his name, you know?'

'Which one?' Fury said. 'He got two or three boys, no?'

'No, no, no,' Yale said quickly. 'The one who cry all the time at Antonio's funeral . . . you know, the boy who say, "We'll see them, Papa." You know who I mean . . .'

'Yeah, I remember him, Frankie,' Argolia said brightly. 'He was the one crying all the time while he pray at casket, right?'

'That's him,' Yale said. 'You remember name?'

'No, Frankie, I no remember,' replied Argolia. 'Why you ask, my good friend?'

'Because he is the one who waste Jimmy the Bug,' Yale chuckled. 'I figure that out by reading the newspaper. You see how smart I am?'

'How you figure it, Frankie?' Argolia asked, taking a sip of his coffee. They were having an early breakfast at the Foltis-Fisher self-service cafeteria on DeKalb Avenue. Yale had asked Fury to meet him there because, among other things, he wanted to plan a red-carpet reception for the forthcoming visit of a dignitary from Chicago: an old and dear friend named Alphonse 'Scarface' Capone.

Whenever things were quiet in the war between the ginzos and micks, Yale liked to meet his people in public places. 'I like to see the little people,' Frankie would say. Seeing the little people, as he called them, gave Yale the opportunity to study different businesses the little people patronised, to see what made the businesses tick. By getting those personal, first-hand glimpses into various retailing opportunities, Yale was able to dream up ways to extend his rackets into those lucrative fields.

On that Wednesday morning, 18 April 1923, Frankie was putting together an extortion package he was planning to open before a full-fledged meeting of the Black Hand. Yale went to Foltis-Fisher's for breakfast because he had decided the time was ripe to move in on downtown Brooklyn's big cafeterias and restaurants. Visions of great new riches danced before his eyes.

'We can sell them protection and laundry service,' Frankie had explained to Fury during their breakfast. He pointed to the aprons worn by the help, the towels they were using to wipe dishes and silverware, and to the great need Foltis-Fisher, as well as Bickford's and other Brooklyn cafeterias, had for this indispensable service.

By all means, protection was a must for those eating places. Frankie pointed to the delivery truck standing at the curb. Crates of lettuce, hundred-pound bags of potatoes, and fifty-pound bags of onions had been unloaded and placed in a sidewalk elevator in front of the store. The foodstuffs were being lowered to the basement for storage as Yale directed Argolia's attention to the activity on the sidewalk.

'If somethin' happen to all that food, it would be very bad, eh?' Frankie said to Fury. 'That's why these restaurants need protection, you understand?'

Yale had started out with the idea of selling only protection to the cafeterias. The laundry idea had germinated after the call from Chicago the previous evening, when Capone let it be known he was coming to Brooklyn to visit his parents and family. While on the phone, Capone gave Frankie a quick rundown on things in Chicago.

Things were going very well. The boys in Chicago had spread out into lucrative new rackets. The restaurant laundry service was one of those profitable sidelines. Al didn't have to draw pictures for Yale. It was so simple that Frankie was angry with himself for not having thought of it before.

'All you do,' Capone said to Yale, 'is get yourself a laundry.'

'How much that cost?' Frankie asked.

'No, no,' Capone scolded. 'What'sa the matter, Frankie? Where's your head? You don't buy laundry – you take over. You become partner, *capeesh*? You walk into boss of laundry and show him how he need you to make bigger profit . . .' Capone began to laugh. 'Can anybody refuse such nice offer, eh, Frankie?' Big Al asked.

What else could Yale do but laugh then, too?

It took only until the next morning to set the wheels in motion for a brand-new racketeering venture for Brooklyn's Black Hand gang.

Before he met Fury, Yale had dispatched Two-Knife Altierri, Frenchy Carlino, and Augie the Wop on a visit to Santo

Grimaldi, owner of the Beach Street Laundry, a medium-sized operation which supplied aprons, towels, and other linens to restaurants, meat markets, grocery stores, and other businesses. Two-Knife was to convince Grimaldi that he was running his business all wrong and there could be no way to avoid bankruptcy without the Black Hand's help.

Yale had no doubt Grimaldi would be more than willing to accept the generous offer from Altierri, Carlino and Pisano. After all, it was just a matter of lining up new customers for Beach Street's laundry services. The fact that Foltis-Fisher and Bickford's and other cafeterias and restaurants were getting their linens from other laundry services was a minor detail.

'After you convince them they need our insurance for their protection,' Yale said to Argolia, 'then everything fall in place, you understand?'

'By and by we sell them meat and vegetables too, eh?' Argolia laughed.

'I always say you very smart fella, Fury,' Yale squeezed Argolia's arm. 'You catch on right away. That's why I like you so much, *paisan*.'

Then Yale spotted the *New York American*'s headline as a customer at a nearby table held up the newspaper he was reading:

BROOKLYN MOBSTER SLAIN IN JERSEY

Yale went to the sidewalk newsstand outside the cafeteria, bought a copy of the *American*, and brought it back to the table.

What made Yale so certain that Antonio Gibaldi's son had killed Callaghan was the knowledge of what was found clutched in the South Brooklyn bootlegger's hand after he was blasted in the bootblack shop: three Indian-head nickels. That was the money to pay Carmine Balsamo for the shine he was giving Antonio. But death came so instantaneously to Gibaldi that his reflexes stopped all at once. The hand holding the coins remained closed – frozen by the rigor mortis that almost certainly took hold of the body. The nickels were still in his clenched fist when the medical examiner's men scraped Gibaldi into the litter and moved his remains to the morgue.

Yale was delighted by Jimmy the Bug's killing, which he hadn't ordered, but almost immediately began to wonder about the White Hand gang's retaliation.

Yale didn't mind if the White Hand blamed him and his mob for the latest killing; it was such a splendid rubout that Frankie would just as soon take credit for it. And, in fact, he wanted to seek out and congratulate the young man who, he was convinced, had performed that assassination in a very professional manner.

After they had finished breakfast, Frankie and Fury walked over to Court Street,

'Watcha say, good friend,' Yale said to Argolia as they approached Carmine's Bootblack, 'me and you need shine, right?'

They walked into the shop and hoisted themselves up on the high chairs. Carmine strode out from the back and greeted them with a deep bow.

'*Buon giorno, Signore Ioele, buon giorno, Signore Argolia,*' Balsamo said humbly.

There was no charge for the shines. 'I have such great respect for you *Signore* Ioele and *Signore* Argolia that you embarrass me if you offer money,' Carmine said.

When Frankie and Fury left Balsamo's place, they also knew which of Antonio Gibaldi's sons had made the vow over the casket to avenge his father's death. Yale left instructions for Carmine Balsamo to send word immediately to Vincenzo Gibaldi that Frankie wanted to see him at the garage.

Shortly after three o'clock that afternoon, a handsome teenager who looked deceptively taller than his five-foot-ten height and heavier than his 165 pounds, walked into the Black Hand's headquarters. Glass Eye Pelicano was posted as a lookout inside the entrance.

'What you want?' Nick Glass Eye asked.

'I want to see Frankie Yale,' the youth responded, a smile creasing his round face.

Pelicano looked closely at the short crop of light brown hair and his antennae went up.

'You Irish?' he demanded, reaching for his holster.

The visitor looked startled. 'No,' he said sharply. 'I'm Italian . . .'

'What's your name?' Pelicano snapped.

'Vincenzo Gibaldi,' the answer came.

'Oh,' Glass Eye said hoarsely, 'you Antonio's kid, eh?'

'That's right,' Vincenzo replied smartly.

'Come with me, young fella,' Pelicano said, taking young Gibaldi by the arm and leading him up the stairs. 'Frankie wait for you . . .'

As Vincenzo was ushered before Yale's desk, Frankie rose from his chair and put out his hand in greeting.

'Welcome, Vincenzo,' Frankie said. He came from behind the desk, took the visitor by the arm, and introduced him to Altierri, Pisano, Carlino, Argolia, Don Giuseppe Balsamo, and his bodyguards, Vincenzo Mangano and Johnny Silk Stocking Guistra.

'Take a chair and sit down,' Yale said after Gibaldi had shaken hands with everyone. Frankie went back to the desk. He studied the young man's face for a long moment, then smiled and shook his head.

'Vincenzo, you have big balls,' he said. 'I like the way you work. The job you done on The Bug was *magnifico*.'

Gibaldi paled. His eyes opened wide. He felt terror-stricken.

'How did you find out . . . who told you . . . am I going to be arrested?' Vincenzo stammered.

'Relax, young fella,' Yale soothed. 'You got nothing to worry about. You pulled perfect job. Nobody gonna pin the rubout on you, believe me. The cops don't know shit about who killed . . .'

'How do *you* know?' Gibaldi interrupted, his fright somewhat lessened.

Yale winked. 'Ahhhh,' he sighed gloatingly, 'it's my business to know these things. I find out anything I gotta know about . . .'

Vincenzo shook his head in amazement. 'You sure scared me, Mr Yale,' he said, letting out a deep breath.

'Hey, hey!' Frankie yelled. 'Don't give me that Mr Yale shit. The name is Frankie. Understand?'

Gibaldi smiled. 'Okay . . . Frankie,' he said a bit hesitantly as he tried to adjust to the change.

'That's better, Vincenzo,' Yale came back, grinning.

Then Frankie got down to the bottom line of why he had called Vincenzo in. A proposition: Yale wanted the nineteen-year-old Gibaldi to join the Black Hand as an assassin.

'Frankie,' the young man said quickly. 'I'm not ready for that. I have some unfinished business in Brooklyn. Let me take care of what I have to do and then we can talk again . . .'

Yale was stunned. 'What unfinished business you got?' he blurted.

Gibaldi smiled. 'You mean you don't have any idea?' he asked in a tone that implied volumes.

'Okay,' Yale rasped. 'So you got unfinished business. I let you finish. But I want you work for me.'

'All right, Frankie, I'll work for you,' Vincenzo said. 'But don't give me anything to do until I get through with what I have to do first. That suit you?'

'Sure, sure, it suit me fine,' Yale returned, dragging on his cigarette and blowing a curl of smoke toward the ceiling. 'By the way . . .' he looked at Gibaldi with a measured glance, 'who is next on your list, Vincenzo?'

Gibaldi's face crinkled, darkened by a grim expression.

'Frankie,' the young killer said slowly, 'when it happens you are going to be the first one to know. That okay with you?'

Yale nodded. 'Yeah, it's okay with me.'

When Frankie Yale gave Vincenzo Gibaldi tacit approval to conduct one-man reprisals against his father's killers, the Black Hand leader had no idea as to what lengths the slain man's son intended to go with his vendetta against the White Hand. Frankie knew that only two men had wielded the shotguns that killed Antonio Gibaldi. He also knew who the assassins were, since Carmine Balsamo had identified Joey Bean and Jimmy the Bug Callaghan to his uncle, Battista Balsamo, who in turn told Frankie Yale.

With Callaghan dead, Yale reasoned that Vincenzo's next target would be Bean. But Frankie was wrong. Not in his wildest imagination could he have guessed who Gibaldi's next victim was.

* * *

Nine o'clock. Saturday night. 12 May 1923.

Wild Bill Lovett had been in his flat on Front Street only a few minutes. He had come back to dress for a night on the town. Some of the boys were picking him up at ten and were to drive him to Buckley's, a waterfront nightspot at Tilary and Bridge Streets, one of the White Hand's favourite spas for booze and broads. That was for openers. Afterward, they would head for another of the many Brooklyn Irish drink-and-dance joints patronised by the clan.

That was a routine Lovett followed almost every Saturday night – and it was a ritual that Vincenzo Gibaldi had become very much aware of after a few weeks of surveillance.

Vincenzo had done a thorough job of staking out Lovett. He had also made a complete study of the layout of Wild Bill's digs and found it would be no problem scaling the vertical ladder which dangled from the fire escape to the alley alongside the three-story tenement, then climbing to the third floor and surprising Lovett in his boudoir.

And that was precisely what Gibaldi did. He caught Wild Bill, fearless winner of the Distinguished Service Cross, dauntless leader of the White Hand gang, with his pants down!

Wild Bill was standing in front of the dresser mirror in his shorts, combing his hair, when Vincenzo Gibaldi sneaked up the fire escape and approached the window of Lovett's bedroom. Crouched on one knee, he peeked into the room. Lovett was trying to make his part as straight and perfect as he could. Several times he combed out his hair and started over. The sight of the big White Hand chieftain fussing over his mane amused Gibaldi. But not for long.

He raised the loaded .38-caliber revolver in his hand and brought the sight up to his eye. Through the closed window, he aimed the barrel carefully at the center of Lovett's chest.

He squeezed the trigger. The bullet tore into Wild Bill's right breast and spun him around. Vincenzo heard Lovett cry out in pain and shout 'Mother fucker!' Before Gibaldi could hit his mark with the second bullet, Lovett threw himself on the floor and began crawling frantically for his gun, which was in the shoulder holster draped around the bedpost.

Vincenzo was furious with himself. Bat Masterson never would have approved.

Gibaldi was suddenly unnerved. He fired two quick shots at the figure on the floor struggling to reach his gun. The bullets were triggered almost blindly, yet somehow each slug caught a piece of Lovett's anatomy; one went through Wild Bill's right shoulder, the other found its way into his left thigh.

But the next three bullets missed their intended target completely, plowed into the wall and gouged out chunks of plaster.

Vincenzo couldn't reload on this job the way he'd done in Teaneck. Front Street didn't have the isolation of the suburbs; neighbors were certain to hear the shots and would soon come out of their apartments to see what was happening. And the cops wouldn't be far behind.

Tucking the gun into his pants waistband, Vincenzo gave himself a couple of more seconds at the window – just enough time to pull an Indian-head nickel out of his pocket and toss it into the room through the bullet-shattered window pane. His aim was dead-on. The coin landed on Lovett's crouched body, bounced off, then, incredibly rolled on its edge toward Bill's right hand and flattened on the floor just inches away from his fingers.

Vincenzo Gibaldi scrambled down the fire escape and made his getaway through the alley without being spotted.

Not a minute later, tenants in the house emptied out of their apartments and surged to the door of Lovett's flat. Neighbors in nearby tenements poured out into the street and asked each other whether that was gunfire they heard and wondered from where it came and at whom it was directed.

John and Ralph Flanagan, two brothers who lived in the apartment next to Lovett's, tried the knob but the key was in the lock. They put their shoulders to the door and forced it open. They went in and found Wild Bill moaning in agony.

'Call an ambulance,' he pleaded weakly. 'I'm hurt very bad . . .'

The Flanagans lifted Lovett off the floor and put him on the bed. John picked up the receiver of Lovett's phone in the living room and asked the operator to connect him with Cumberland Hospital.

'Man shot,' Flanagan said. 'He's in bad shape. Send an ambulance right away . . .' He gave the victim's name and address.

In less than ten minutes police cruisers with sirens wailing pulled to screeching stops in front of Lovett's house. Uniformed policemen and detectives jumped out of the cars and dashed upstairs.

'Who did this to you, Bill?' asked Patrolman Eugene O'Brien, one of the first cops in the apartment. O'Brien knew Lovett because the Baltic Street garage was on his regular beat.

'Hey, Gene,' he gasped, 'you make out you don't know me, okay. I like you a lot. I'll do anything for you. But if you think I know who did this to me, you're crazy. The fuckin' shots came through the window. I didn't see a friggin' thing. And that's no shit. It's the fuckin' truth . . .'

Lovett was taken to Cumberland and immediate surgery. The shoulder and leg wounds weren't critical. But the .38 slug which entered the right breast had lodged in what surgeons termed the *maxilla intercostalis internus*. It took four hours in the operating room to remove that slug.

Lovett remained on the critical list and wasn't allowed visitors for two days. On the third day, he began a remarkable recovery.

His first two callers were Pegleg Lonergan and his attractive, voluptuous sister, Anna. For six years – ever since Wild Bill returned from the service – Anna had been trying to win Lovett's affection. But Bill had no interest in falling for Anna because it would mean marriage. He wanted his freedom, to carouse with broads who were content to be – and to be known as – Bill Lovett's pieces of ass.

But now, in his hospital room, Wild Bill was struck by Anna Lonergan's compassion and concern for him. She sat beside his bed and ran her fingers gently, lovingly through his sandy hair. In an emotion-choked voice she whispered, 'Bill, I love you . . . I've always loved you . . . If anything happens to you I'll die . . .'

Lovett took Anna's hand in his and held it. His grip was weak, but Anna felt the tenderness and warmth he was trying to convey.

'Anna,' he said, his voice barely a whisper, 'I know how you care for me and . . .'

195

His words faded away. He shut his eyes. He still pressed Anna's hand. Then he looked at Anna again. 'Sweetheart,' he said weakly, 'when I get well . . . the first thing when I get outta here is I'm gonna ask you to marry me . . .'

'Oh, Bill,' Anna broke into tears. She put her head beside Lovett's on the pillow and kissed him on the cheek.

'Bill,' she sobbed, 'I love you. I love you so very much . . .'

'I love you, too, Anna,' he said softly. 'I really love you . . .'

Two weeks later, on 25 May, Bill Lovett was discharged from the hospital. He was met by Eddie Lynch, Ernie the Scarecrow Monaghan, and Pegleg Lonergan. Anna Lonergan was there, too.

Instead of taking Lovett to his flat in Front Street, Eddie Lynch drove to Lonergan's family home on Myrtle Avenue.

'Hey, what're you doin'? Lovett asked in astonishment.

Anna, who was sitting beside Wild Bill in the back seat, whispered, 'Bill, we're taking you to my house because . . . well, Bill, I want to nurse you back to health. You don't mind, do you . . .'

There was no objection from Lovett.

Frankie Yale couldn't believe the headlines in the *Sunday News* and the *Sunday American* which thundered the news of the attempt on Wild Bill's life.

'Who the fuck pulled that stunt?' Frankie screamed on the phone to Fury Argolia. 'You got any idea?'

'Maybe one of his own people,' suggested Fury.

'No fuckin' way,' Yale stormed back. 'This is something I got idea about. I want you to call Don Giuseppe and ask him check on the friggin' kid, what hell's his name . . .?'

'You mean Vincenzo?' Argolia said.

'Yeah, yeah,' Frankie blurted. 'Get the goddamn kid to come see me tomorrow, ya hear?'

Argolia heard. The next day Vincenzo Gibaldi showed up at Yale's garage.

'You know anything about what happen to Bill Lovett on Saturday?' Yale asked testily.

'What do you mean, do I know?' Gibaldi smiled. 'Know what? What happened to Lovett?'

'Hey, don't play no funny games with me,' Yale snapped. 'If you know, say so. If you don't know, tell me you don't.'

'All I have to say, Frankie,' Gibaldi came back in a flat voice, 'is that whoever shot up Bill Lovett sure did a lousy job.'

'You ain't shittin' he did,' Yale growled. 'And I wanna tell you somethin'. Whoever did it, his ass is gonna be in lotsa trouble. Because now the fuckin' micks gonna be comin' after us.'

Yale pounded the desk with his fist repeatedly.

'The whole crazy thing is our people don't have nothing to do with this here shootin'. I never gave no contract on Lovett. But you think those fuckin' Irish are gonna believe it?'

Yale exhaled a long, low *wheeeeeew*.

'Awright, Vincenzo, get your ass outa here,' Frankie commanded.

Young Gibaldi got up from the chair and walked out. As he hit the street, Vincenzo smiled to himself. He really believed he had hoodwinked Frankie Yale.

Vincenzo Gibaldi's next target would be his last for a while in Brooklyn. He was going to settle accounts with Joey Bean, then put the artillery in temporary storage.

Gibaldi's vendetta against the last of the three Bean brothers had taken on new purpose and direction. Although he wanted to study Joey's habits thoroughly and make the score at the right time and right place, Vincenzo now had to move quickly. In a few days he would be leaving town.

Lovett was still in the hospital when his gang decided to strike back at the Black Hand. Of course, they thought they were the ones who tried to kill him. The plan was drawn up by Pegleg Lonergan, who had taken command of the White Hand while Lovett was laid up.

Lonergan had received word that Two-Knife Willie Altierri was playing poker at a rooming house on Brooklyn's Eighteenth Street near Fifth Avenue with four subordinates in the Italian underworld the night of 18 May.

The card game was already underway when the White Hand assassins made their way into the tenement and tiptoed to the basement flat occupied by Ignazio Amadeo. Voices betting on cards for straights, full houses, and other winning combinations came from behind the closed door. They listened closely until convinced Altierri was one of the players; Willie's name had been uttered several times as the game progressed.

They broke open the door and barged in with guns drawn. Four of the cardplayers didn't recognise the raiders. But Altierri recognised Eddie Lynch and Joey Bean immediately.

'Willie!' Bean shouted, 'you scumbag motherfuckin' whore. I finally got you where I want you. But I ain't gonna kill you yet. I wanna watch you squirm and sweat. When I kill a guinea, I gotta make sure the grease in him oozes outta his fuckin' body. And that's what I'm waitin' to see you do – sweat your fuckin' ass off . . .'

Altierri had his two knives strapped to his body, but he couldn't get to them in time. He sat like a zombie as Lynch, Bean, and their two confederates covered him with their guns.

Willie sensed the micks were aiming to delay the execution as long as they could to prolong his fear of dying. Out of the corner of his eye he noticed the open window that faced an alley. It was no more than eight or nine feet from his seat at the card table.

It was very chancy, Willie told himself. He'd be gunned down before he reached the window.

But suddenly Ignazio Amadeo must have cracked under the pressure. He leaped to his feet and screamed at Joey Bean. 'Hey, why don't you stop the horseshit and get outta here. You guys come here to break balls or somethin' . . .?'

It was his farewell address. Amadeo was suddenly exposed to the business end of Bean's .38. The bullet caught the blustery Italian in the chest and he went down, glassy-eyed, open-mouthed, and limp. Perfectly acceptable form for one who'd taken a piece of hot lead in the heart.

And in the brief seconds that he commanded Bean and Lynch's attention, Willie Altierri leaped from his chair and dove head-first out the window.

Before the micks got around to poking their heads and hardware out of the window for a bead on Two-Knife's back, Willie was out of sight.

The White Handers spared the other cardplayers' lives, but not without making them age. They fired a volley of shots over the Italians' heads which sent them thrashing and squirming across the floor, futilely seeking cover. Bean and Lynch roared with laughter.

'Lousy gutless guineas,' rasped Joey. He swaggered to the table where some two hundred dollars of gambling money was spread out. He scooped it up and stuffed it into his pocket. Then he turned, spat in the direction of the frightened men cowering on the floor, and walked out with his confederates.

Two nights later, Vincenzo Gibaldi began to move in on Joey Bean. Not because of the latest outrage Bean had committed, but because Vincenzo's time in Brooklyn was quickly running out.

When Capone came to town to visit his family, Frankie Yale took him to Fury Argolia's Adonis Club. Capone was feted royally. Scarface Al was intrigued by Frankie's accounts of an ambitious triggerman named Vincenzo Gibaldi, only nineteen and with two big notches in his gun.

Capone found it hard to believe that Gibaldi did solo numbers on such formidable underworld terrors as Jimmy the Bug and Wild Bill.

'I can use boy like him in Chicago,' Capone said to Yale. 'Maybe you let me have, eh?'

'Anything for good friend like you, Big Al,' Yale agreed. Frankie didn't really feel he was giving too much away. He had taken a liking to Vincenzo for the job he'd done on Jimmy the Bug. But Yale's sentiments had changed quickly after Vincenzo's abortive attempt on Lovett's life. Frankie didn't want people in his organisation acting impulsively and on their own.

Yale sent for Gibaldi and introduced him to Capone.

'I pay you three hundred a week,' Al offered Vincenzo. That was more money than Gibaldi had seen in his whole life.

'I'll take it,' Vincenzo responded instantly.

Capone gave his newly hired gun five days to get to Chicago and start working for him. It was enough time to go after Joey Bean.

* * *

It was 9:30 p.m. on 20 May when the maroon Chevrolet roadster cruised along Dean Street and came to a smooth stop in front of a four-story tenement just off the corner of Fifth Avenue.

The corner building was where Joey Bean lived with his wife, Eleanor. Their apartment was on the second floor. As Vincenzo reasoned, it would be merely a matter of waiting for Joey to come home.

Gibaldi found a nice safe place to hide and wait for Bean: it was an alcove in the hall near Joey's apartment door. Joey would not see him there until it was too late.

Vincenzo didn't go into his niche a minute too soon, for just as he stepped into the alcove the door of Bean's apartment opened. It was Eleanor. She was in her housecoat. She was taking the garbage down to the street.

Seconds later, the door downstairs reopened and Vincenzo heard a man and woman talking.

'I'm goddam tired,' the man said.

'Well, go to sleep early, why don't you?' the woman asked.

Gibaldi peeked out and saw the woman in the housecoat. And with her was her husband, Joey Bean. Vincenzo had the hammer already cocked. He just had to wait for Bean to reach his apartment door. He was a stride behind his wife when she opened the door and walked in.

Gibaldi took one short step out of the alcove and had a clear field of fire. Six shots ripped from the barrel of his .38 in rapid succession. Bean yelped in pain. His knees buckled and he crumpled to the floor in a heap.

Bean's wife began to scream with the first shot. By the time Vincenzo had emptied his gun into Joey, she was hysterical.

Eleanor saw Gibaldi from inside the apartment and tried to go after him. But her husband's body blocked her exit.

'Give him a nice funeral, lady,' Gibaldi said to her as he stepped around Bean's hulk. He stopped at the head of the stairs, turned, and dropped his calling card on the floor. It was the Indian-head nickel that had become his trademark in murder. Then he sprinted down the stairs.

In thirty-three days Vincenzo Gibaldi avenged his father's

murder by killing the two gunmen who had taken his life and wounding their leader.

Two days later, the son of the late Antonio Gibaldi boarded a train at Grand Central and headed for Chicago.

Shortly after Vincenzo Gibaldi went to work for Capone, he became known as Machine-Gun Jack McGurn.

Chapter 15

Wild Bill Lovett, R.I.P.

Anna Lonergan wanted more than anything to be a June bride. After the way she had nursed Wild Bill Lovett back to health in her parent's bedroom, he wanted nothing more than to give Anna her wish. He agreed to a June wedding.

But Anna and Bill were compelled to postpone the wedding until some family unpleasantness had been straightened out.

Anna's father, John, who was also Pegleg Lonergan's father, was murdered. But that was one killing of an Irishman which no one could blame on Frankie Yale or the Black Hand. It was all in the family: a Lonergan family affair.

The killing was what the police at the Poplar Street Precinct described as a 'family dispute'. They also called it a 'husband-wife quarrel'. The only thing they couldn't call it was murder, because the cops would then have to get along on just their police salaries.

The Kings County District Attorney's office goofed up the case. They assigned it to Assistant District Attorney Joe Schwartz, who had just joined the staff, fresh out of New York University Law School. In fact, the ink on his L.L.B. was still wet when he hung it up in his office in Brooklyn's Criminal Courts Building.

Somebody forgot to tell Schwartz what the name Lonergan meant in the Brooklyn community. By the time he was informed, the grand jury had listened to the evidence Joel had presented to them and returned a murder indictment against John's wife, Mary Lonergan. Schwartz didn't prosecute the case because, by the time the trial was held two months later, he was back working behind the counter of his father's delicatessen in Brownsville.

It was because of that indictment that the master bedroom in the Lonergan house was available for Wild Bill Lovett's convalescence: John Lonergan had traded his old accommodations for a plot in the Cypress Hills Cemetery. And after the horrendous faux pas that Joel Schwartz committed, even Warren Gamaliel Harding and all his Presidential powers couldn't keep Mary Lonergan from a lodging in the Raymond Street jail.

When the trial opened on 13 August, a 'shirt-sleeved' crowd of 29,452 packed nearby Ebbets Field to watch the Brooklyn Dodgers, dead last in the 1923 National League pennant race, take on the New York Giants who, under John McGraw, were heading toward their third flag in a row. In downtown Brooklyn, where they began selecting the jury that was to sit in judgment of Mary Lonergan, the temperature in the steaming courtroom must have been at least twenty degrees higher than in the ball park. But the spectator section didn't have a single shirt sleeve showing. Not that coming to court without a jacket was prohibited. But if these spectators removed their jackets the court officers would have had to arrest forty-eight of them on charges of carrying firearms.

Seating in the courtroom was by invitation only. And only members of the family were given seats. Members of the White Hand family.

No one paid much attention to the early phase of the trial, which involved selection of the jury. But once the panel was picked and sworn, all eyes in the spectator section turned and stared at the jurymen. The idea was to draw the jurors' attention away from the proceedings and make them aware of the stares from the forty-eight spectators, who were sweating like pigs in their jackets. Mama Lonergan could be accused of blowing up a subway train during the rush hour and the 'jury of her peers' couldn't have cared less.

All the jury wanted was to make sure the spectators did no more than stare. Once, during the second day of the trial when the prosecutor was questioning the medical examiner, things got sticky.

'Is it possible,' the DA asked, 'that the victim committed suicide?'

The witness hesitated for the longest time. Finally he replied, 'From a reasonable medical point of view, I don't think so . . .'

Just then, Ernie the Scarecrow Monaghan, seated in the first row on the side of the jury box, stuck his hand inside his jacket. Five jurors who spotted the movement bent down to tie their shoelaces. They straightened up only after they stole glances over the jury rail and saw that Ernie had taken out a handkerchief to wipe the perspiration from his face.

The most dramatic moment of the trial came on the fourth day, Thursday, when Mary Lonergan took the stand. Her testimony about how her husband mistreated her throughout their twenty-nine years of marriage, how night after night he beat and bruised her, and how wretched life with Lonergan had been for her, opened the lachrymal floodgates. There wasn't a dry eye in the jury box after that – especially when they saw the sea of handkerchiefs surface in the spectator section.

When the defendant told how she took the gun belonging to Pegleg ('My son only carried the gun to protect me from his father') and put a bullet through the old man's bean when he was about to brain her with a baseball bat, the jury lost complete control of its emotions. The judge had to call a ten-minute recess.

By this time no one could doubt the outcome of the trial. The jury almost met itself coming back from the deliberating room, that's how quickly it reached its verdict of not guilty.

Pandemonium broke out in the courtroom. No one was more pleased with the verdict than Pegleg Lonergan. The story goes that if his mother had been convicted he would have ripped off his artificial limb and beaten every juror to a pulp. Moreover, Lonergan would have had it on his conscience that an innocent woman went to prison for him, although that was only a secondary consideration to Pegleg – even if the martyr happened to be his own mother.

Everything they said about old man Lonergan was true: he was a drunk, a wife-beater, and more. He double-timed Mary by scrounging around with any floozy he could make. He was a lousy provider. He was many other bad things, too. What he got he had coming to him. But it wasn't Mary who put the bullet in his head. She only said she did to spare her son the inconvenience of arrest, prosecution, conviction, and imprisonment.

Immediately after the verdict was returned on Friday, 17 August, Anna Lonergan and Wild Bill Lovett made a mad dash to the chambers of the judge who had just presided over the murder trial. They wanted him to marry them.

With the just-sprung Mary Lonergan and Pegleg standing by as witnesses, the judge pronounced Anna and Bill man and wife.

That night, with breakneck arrangements worked out by Eddie Lynch, Aaron Harms, and some of the other boys, a double celebration was held in Patrick Mulhern Caterers on Fourth Avenue, Forty members of the White Hand, accompanied by their wives and sweethearts, turned out to toast Mary Lonergan for the way she put the blindfolds on the lady who holds the scales of justice, and to wish the newlyweds happiness and long life together.

Long before the celebrants had gotten a real bag on, Wild Bill sneaked his bride out of the place and drove upstate to a Catskill Mountain resort hotel that was to be their honeymoon retreat for the next two weeks.

There is a tale that has been told and retold over the years that purports to be a faithful account of Mr and Mrs Lovett's first conjugal romp in the hay.

The story, conceivably narrated to some of his boys by Lovett himself after returning from the honeymoon, invests Anna Lovett with the signal honor of having been as pure as St Agnes when she cuddled up to Bill on their wedding night.

In the morning, after the euphoric slumber that inevitably follows the ecstasy of physical satisfaction, Bill Lovett awakened beside his still-sleeping bride and was greeted by a sight that elevated him to a state of rapturous delight.

The sheet was stained with blood!

When Bill and Anna returned to Brooklyn, they went house-hunting. But not in Brooklyn. Anna wanted to get away from Brooklyn and New York City. She wanted Bill to get out of the rackets.

'How long do you think this can go on?' Anna would ask in impassioned pleading with her husband. 'You were almost killed once. Who knows if you'll be as lucky the next time. Bill, I love you too much. I don't want to lose you . . .'

Anna began brainwashing Bill the day she brought him home from the hospital. During the two weeks of his convalescence at the Lonergans she didn't let a day, indeed an hour, pass without saying something that she hoped would persuade Lovett to give up his crooked ways and turn to legitimate pursuits.

'You can work on the docks and make an honest living,' Anna harped away. 'Try it . . . please, won't you?'

Anna's persistence finally prevailed. The way Lovett looked at it, Anna's brother, Pegleg, was in line to succeed him as boss of the White Hand. So, by stepping down Bill wouldn't exactly be stepping out; he'd still have ties with the mob through his brother-in-law.

On Friday evening, 21 September 1923, Lovett summoned the boys together in the Baltic Street garage.

'I know what we have meant to each other, guys,' Will said in an emotion-choked voice. 'I tried very hard to run things smooth and make us all a lot of dough. And I think we did pretty good.'

'We sure did,' piped up Eddie Lynch.

'Yeah, Bill,' seconded Ernie the Scarecrow, 'we ain't never had no complaints against you. We love you like a brother . . .'

'So, that's why I called you here tonight,' Lovett said slowly. 'Because . . . well, you know I just got married to a very beautiful . . .'

A cheer went up.

'You sure got a swell wife,' Ash Can Smitty trilled with enthusiasm. 'They don't come no better than Anna . . .'

'That's exactly why I decided like I did,' Wild Bill went on, 'Anna wants me to . . . you know, kinda give somebody else a chance to run things . . . ya understand?'

Lovett hesitated. He was stammering. But his message was coming across.

'Hey, you ain't quittin' us, are ya, Bill?' Ernie the Scarecrow asked in a surprised tone.

Lovett put his head into an up and down motion – half yes, half no. 'I want you guys to know that I'm not really quitting like you might think,' he said placatingly. 'I'm just gonna step aside . . . because that's what Anna wants me to do . . .'

A murmur of astonishment rippled over the gathering.

'Hold on, hold on!' Wild Bill yelled. 'What the hell's going on here? Don't you guys understand what I'm tryin' to tell ya?'

'Yeah, that you're quittin' us,' blurted Wally the Squint Walsh.

'That's the way it sounds to me, too,' pitched in Ernie Skinny Shea.

'In a pig's ass!' growled Lovett, tightening his face in anger. 'That ain't what I said. All I want you to know is that from now on this mob's gonna be run by a guy who's every bit as capable of handling things like I been.' His determination was clear. The gang sensed that they had no alternative but to accept the change in leadership.

'Anybody that don't agree, I want him to speak up right now,' Lovett demanded.

No one said a word.

'Okay,' Lovett spoke in a louder, firmer tone. 'Now any of you got a rap against Dick Lonergan I want you to tell me personally right now – because I'm pickin' him to take my place . . .'

A roar erupted, signalling the gang's overwhelming, indeed unanimous, approval.

'Speech!' cried Ash Can Smitty.

Lonergan got up and delivered his inaugural address, promising he'd run things as smoothly and effectively as Lovett had.

'Besides,' he smiled, 'if I come across any problems I can always go to my brother-in-law for advice.' He turned to Lovett and asked, 'Right, Bill?'

'All the way, Dick,' Lovett replied with a toothy grin.

Applause and whistling rang out.

Richard Lonergan was now officially invested as Wild Bill's successor, the third reigning monarch of the infamous White Hand gang.

Bill and Anna Lovett bought a bungalow in Little Ferry, New Jersey, about twenty miles southwest of the late Jimmy the Bug Callaghan's former home in Teaneck. They settled down to what they prayed would be a quiet, untroubled existence.

Not many days afterward, Bill went to work in Jersey City's shipyard as a welder, getting two hundred and fifty dollars a week straight pay. That was a hundred over scale for welders. The superintendent of ship construction at the yard was Frank Driscoll, a former pier manager on the Gowanus waterfront who'd paid tribute to Lovett and his White Hand enforcers for many years. Driscoll volunteered the excessive salary not only because he recognised Lovett's great skill as a welder but because he also wanted to stay healthy.

By six weeks, Wild Bill had adjusted to the pattern of his new life. He was supremely happy. On the evening of Wednesday, 31 October, Bill came home from work and said to Anna that he had the urge to drive into Brooklyn and have a drink or two with some of the boys.

'Just for old times' sake,' he told his wife. Anna had no objection. After all, Bill had made a complete turnaround. He had settled down and become completely domesticated. What matter, Anna asked herself, if Bill goes back to Brooklyn once in a blue moon to bend an elbow with his old cronies?

So Bill went to Brooklyn and made his way to the Lotus Club, a speakeasy at 25 Bridge Street, one of the White Hand's more popular haunts. But he found none of the boys from the gang at the Lotus. It was midweek and the place had only a handful of customers. One of the patrons was an old friend, a longshoreman named Joe Flynn.

'Hey, Joe,' Lovett said grandly, 'I'm gonna buy you a drink.'

That's how it started. Three hours later, Wild Bill and Flynn had polished off more belts of Prohibition alky than the Surgeon General of the United States would recommend for a dozen hardy drinkers. They were out of their minds, thoroughly plastered. Flynn still had enough mobility in his legs to stagger out of the Lotus shortly before 10:30 p.m. and wobble his way to his ground-floor apartment two blocks away, where he threw himself on his bed and fell into a deep sleep.

In his stupor, Lovett couldn't make it to his bedroom. The nineteen-mile drive to Little Ferry was totally beyond his capacity. The only thing he wanted was to curl up someplace and go to sleep. And that was precisely what he did. He stumbled from the bar to a wooden bench at the back of the speakeasy, threw himself down, and tried to sleep. But the bench was too hard for his head, so he got up, stumbled his way to the bar, and found the solution to his problem: the red-and-black plaid lumberjacket that Joe Flynn had left behind on a bar stool. Lovett took the jacket back to the bench, rolled it up like a pillow, and lay down with his head cushioned and comfortable. In seconds he fell into a coma-like sleep.

At a little after eleven o'clock, John Flaherty, the bartender, found himself staring across an empty stick. He decided to close. He glanced over at Lovett stretched out on the bench, dead to the world. Flaherty decided to lock up the joint without disturbing Wild Bill, who'd never know the difference.

'Hey, Tony!' Flaherty called out. He was summoning Antonio Maglioli, the porter who was in the kitchen filling a pail with hot soapy water to mop the floor. Every Prohibition Era speakeasy, whether run by Italians, Irish, Germans, Norwegians, or any other ethnic group, had one characteristic in common: the porters were all Italians.

Tony came out of the kitchen and looked at Flaherty, who had his coat and hat on.

'Hey walyo,' Flaherty said to Tony. 'I'm going home, but I want you to do me a favor, okay?'

'Sure, sure,' Tony said obediently. 'What you want me to do?'

Flaherty pointed to the sleeping Lovett. 'Leave him alone,' the bartender said. 'That's Wild Bill Lovett. He's good for at least another ten hours where he's at. He'll still be crapped out there when you get back in the morning. So you can let him out then, okay?'

'Okay, boss,' Tony smiled, 'you go home and sleep. I take care everything. You no worry 'bout nothin', boss . . .'

Antonio Maglioli had finished mopping the floor about an hour later. He put on his coat and hat, walked over and glanced at Wild Bill Lovett, who was snoring soundly. No doubt he'd find sleeping beauty in that same state when he returned in the morning, Tony told himself. He locked the speakeasy door and started for home.

Tony lived on Fourth Avenue, two doors from the Black Hand garage. He was just passing the garage when the door opened and Willie Altierri walked out.

'Hey, Tony, how you doin'?' Two-Knife greeted the porter.

'Good, good, Willie.' Tony replied with a smile, walking over and shaking Altierri's hand.

'What's new, anything, Tony?' Altierri said, making conversation while waiting for the rest of the gang to come out of the garage.

'You wanna hear somethin' funny,' Tony chuckled. 'Guess what big shot got drunk at Lotus tonight . . . I bet you can't tell me . . .'

'Hey, Tony,' Altierri said, annoyed, 'you know I don't go near none of them fuckin' Irishers' piss places. So how the hell can I tell ya, eh?'

'Okay, okay, Willie don't get mad. I tell you awright? Itsa Wild Bill Lovett . . .'

Altierri's eyes popped open. 'He was there?' he asked, swallowing hard in disbelief. 'I thought the fucker quit and went to live in New Jersey.'

'Maybe he do,' Tony said, 'but he ain't in New Jez tonight because I close him up in Lotus just now . . .'

Altierri found that even harder to believe, even after the porter recited how Lovett had drunk himself into a stupor and fallen asleep on the bench. Willie grabbed Maglioli by the lapels of his coat and shook him.

'Hey, Tony, you no fuckin' lyin' to me, are you?' Willie almost screamed.

'No, no,' quaked the porter. 'I tell truth . . . I swear . . .'

Just then Vincenzo Mangano, Johnny Silk Stocking, and Augie the Wop walked over.

'Hey, Willie, leave the fuckin' guy alone,' Pisano shouted. 'Why the hell you botherin' him for?'

'I bother him for this,' Willie rasped. 'I wanna know if he bullshittin' me.'

Altierri repeated what Maglioli had told him about Lovett. Now everyone's interest was aroused. When the porter insisted he was telling the truth – that Lovett actually was dead asleep in the Lotus – Guistra put his hand on Maglioli's shoulder.

'Hey, Tony,' the Silk Stocking said. 'You got the key to the Lotus, right?'

'Yeah, I got,' Maglioli answered.

'Gimme,' Guistra said, letting go of the shoulder and putting the hand out for the key.

'What you gonna do?' the porter asked, sorry now that he had mentioned Lovett's plight to Altierri.

'We gonna put blanket over him,' Guistra smiled. 'We don't want him to catch cold, *capeesh* . . .'

Tony was trembling now. '*Mama mia*,' he murmured as he reached into his pocket for the key. 'You no tell nobody I give to you, eh, good Johnny?'

'Hey, Tony,' the Silk Stocking said slowly, 'you know we love you like father. Who we gonna tell, eh?'

The key changed hands.

It was 1:15 a.m. The three figures who'd stepped out of the black 1921 Packard sedan whose motor was running with Augie the Wop behind the wheel made their way into the speakeasy.

A 25-watt bulb was the only illumination in the saloon. It was hanging from a fixture on the wall over the back door leading to the kitchen. The light cast was yellowish and weak, but Altierri, Guistra, and Mangano found it more than adequate. It let them see that the sleeping body on the bench was indeed Bill Lovett's.

'Look at him,' Two-Knife said with a ghoulish laugh, 'he's gonna die and he doesn't know a fuckin' thing about it . . .'

Guistra and Mangano had their .38-caliber automatics out.

'Shoot him! Kill!' cried Altierri.

The guns blazed: fourteen shots, seven from each weapon.

211

The medical examiner's autopsy disclosed what had snuffed out Wild Bill Lovett's life was a blow that literally split his head open. That fatal injury was inflicted after Guistra and Mangano had emptied their automatics at Lovett and found that all they had done was stir him out of a sound sleep. They themselves had been drinking so heavily at Yale's garage that when they unlimbered their fourteen shots, only three hit the target, and none of those had any more punch than to stir Lovett out of a sound sleep.

Only after Lovett cursed a blue streak and tried to struggle to his feet and pull his own gun was the finishing touch administered: Two-Knife Altierri's shiny meat cleaver ended Wild Bill's protests. Altierri split open Wild Bill's scalp almost along the very line he always took great pains to shape as the part in his hair.

The police investigation into Wild Bill's murder focussed on one central character: Joe Flynn, the hard-working longshoreman who never had a brush with the law in his life. Poor Flynn underwent hours and hours of tortuous questioning, all because he happened to have had a few drinks with Lovett – and because his jacket was on the bench where Wild Bill's dead body was found.

Eventually, Flynn was absolved of complicity in the crime. After that, the rubout of Wild Bill Lovett, like so many other underworld exterminations then, became another unsolved murder in the files of the NYPD.

The send-off for Wild Bill Lovett was a classic. It was one of the biggest funerals ever. More than fifteen hundred mourners came to the interment in Cypress Hills Cemetery, where Lovett was laid to rest in his flag-draped coffin with full military honors.

Anna Lovett was inconsolable. Toward the end of the graveside service, she tried to throw herself into the six-foot excavation that was waiting to receive the casket with her husband's remains.

'I want to go with him!' she wailed as Pegleg and Eddie Lynch struggled to restrain her.

* * *

Today, nearly seventy years after his death, visitors to Cypress Hills will find no clue of Wild Bill's underworld infamies from the inscription on his headstone. For it bears the legend:

WILLIAM J. LOVETT
BORN 1892 – DIED 1923

Ironically, Wild Bill Lovett was lowered into his grave with the Distinguished Service Cross draped around his neck. His final resting place is the hallowed ground that holds the remains of thousands of America's war heroes dating back to the Revolution.

Chapter 16

The Price War

'Nino Paterno came to work this morning and told me that our *disgraziato* nephew is selling all the whiting, snails, and calamari five cents cheaper than everybody else . . .' Dominick Balsamo complained to his older brother, Don Giuseppe. The elder Balsamo had an ironclad deal with the boys who controlled the distribution – and rackets – at New York's Fulton Fish Market, where all the catches of the sea were unloaded from the fishing boats and dispersed by the land-based fish wholesalers to retail markets throughout the metropolitan area.

No fish deliveries could be made in Brooklyn unless they were sanctioned by Don Giuseppe. And the tacit understanding with all of Balsamo's retailers was that they'd stick to a pre-fixed price set by him and would not undersell the competition. If they wanted to charge a higher price for the fish, they were free to do so.

Balsamo was greatly disturbed by his young brother's report that Peter Licato, who was their sister Angela's only son, was undercutting the competition in his fish store down the block by knocking off a nickel a pound on lobster, tuna, crab, shrimp, and all the other quality seafood.

'Don't you think you should go talk to Peter?' Dominick asked his brother.

'No,' Battista answered at once. 'Talk is cheap. I fix his ass a

214

better way, so he remember this happen and he no do this pricecut shit no more.'

'What you do, my dear brother, Giuseppe?' Dominick asked.

'I send Augie the Wop and a couple other of the boys to tell the other markets to lower the price,' Balsamo decided. 'I tell the managers of the stores to knock down the cheap fish to eight cents a pound. That will fix that *disgraziato* Peter's ass real good.'

Balsamo had some apprehension about whether his plan to undercut his nephew was viable, since Peter made his profit from the higher-priced seafood. So Don Giuseppe included a special on jumbo shrimp that would undercut his nephew's counter price of 65 cents a pound to the unheard-of price of 45 cents.

Next day, some forty South Brooklyn fish markets caved in to Balsamo's directive and put squid, snails, and whiting on sale at eight cents a pound, and the shrimp at forty-five cents.

In his own retail market on Union Street, Don Giuseppe added another special: he put cherrystone clams on the board as a lead item that could catch the eye of any housewife out fishing for a bargain in seafood. He put the crustaceans on sale for twenty-five cents a dozen – a nickel under the usual price.

During the following days, other markets copied Balsamo's lead and sold stucco, baccala, porgies, and other delicacies from the deep at greatly reduced prices to go along with the already three-to-five-cent-a-pound break they were giving patrons for the line of seafood Balsamo commanded be undercut from nephew Peter Licato's bargain prices.

Within a few days, all of downtown Brooklyn's shopping housewives were feasting on the price war being waged against Licato's fish market. Not only were they able to buy the several kinds of seafood the Balsamo nephew had put on sale for less in all the other markets, but were also able to benefit day to day from the 'super specials' the various markets offered.

One day they could go to Dominick's and buy shrimp at forty cents a pound. Next day clams at Don Giuseppe's would be selling for twenty-two cents. Porgies in yet another Balsamo brother's store, Bastiano's Market, were at an all-time low of fifteen cents a pound. Flounder filets at Ignazio's were almost being given away for twelve cents a pound.

215

Peter Licato was suddenly doing a starvation business.

The specials he had offered in the first few days of his effort to undercut the competition were suddenly rotting on the showcase ice. The crowds that had swarmed to his market for the bargains had suddenly evaporated. It was only then that he went out, saw the crowds swarming to the other markets, and got the message. He had no way to profitably match the bargain-basement prices at which the other stores were selling fish.

Despite the raging price war that was bringing customers by the droves to their stores, the retail fish merchants weren't happy with all this new-found business. They sensed a trend of dwindling profits. After all, they were still paying Battista Balsamo the going rates for orders he was delivering from the Fulton Fish Market, but their net take was shrinking dramatically.

'Something has to be done,' John Palamino, one of the fish market owners, told Don Giuseppe. 'The situation is very bad . . .'

Balsamo called a meeting of the fish market owners. Thirty-five of the forty in the South Brooklyn area attended the gathering in Dominick Balsamo's gambling 'casino' at 102 Union Street, a highly profitable venture he conducted in addition to his seafood store next door.

Acting as mediator, Don Giuseppe was quick to point a finger of blame that had generated the crisis in the fish industry.

'You, my *Babo* [stupid] nephew,' he scowled at Peter Licato, 'are to blame for this situation. You are too damn greedy. Because what you did – you try to undercut our family – you make so much trouble for everybody. But I no let you get away with this . . . I no let nobody get away with this kinda shit again . . .'

An undercurrent of grumbling arose and the gathering of merchants from the thirty-five retail fish outlets turned and glared at Licato, who lowered his eyes in shame.

'One like you,' Balsamo continued to ream out his nephew, 'could never wear an overcoat like I have on all these years. You don't even have what it take to become a *cappeli storta* [crooked hat, an ordinary run-of-the-mill gangster or wise guy]. You don't know how to give respect . . .'

Balsamo continued the degrading insults to his nephew until he spotted the arrival of a familiar figure at the back of the casino, standing in the last row of the gathering.

He stopped and summoned Victor Mangano, his own hand-picked successor, to come front and center. As Mangano wended his way through the crowd to join his benefactor and mentor, Balsamo introduced another nephew, Carmine Balsamo, nick-named 'Billy the Kid', who ran one of the family retail fish markets nearby.

'He want to say somethin' to you,' Don Giuseppe told the merchants. 'Please listen to him.'

'Thank you, *zio* [uncle],' Carmine said in a reverent tone, then turned to the crowd:

'Why can't we start an association of fish merchants? You know, like the stevedoring companies have on the docks. My brother Tommy told me that the longshoremen have their union which protects them against unfair labor practices. The dock companies also have their association of shipping companies that bargain with the union when a dock strike is threatened –'

Don Giuseppe suddenly cut his nephew short. 'Carmine,' he smiled, 'I only let you speak here today because I want everybody know the idea is yours, that you talk to me other day about forming association. Now I want everybody know it is gonna happen.'

With a wide sweep of his hand Balsamo signalled Mangano to take center stage. Turning to the crowd once more, Don Giuseppe said, '*Signore* Mangano is man to form this organisa-tion my nephew speak about. Vincenzo has the brains, knowl-edge to form organisation, and the big balls to make it work. I pick Vince Mangano to run the show . . . And now please listen to what he gotta say . . .'

Mangano got to the point at once. 'What we gotta do right away is get lawyer to draw up the cooperation papers. I already take care of this matter. Is to my good friend Patsy Deconozza, who have law offices on Montague Street. He is draw up the papers.

'When they are ready, everybody will sign as charter member. The papers have what you call by-laws, which mean that anybody try to undersell anyone in organisation is gonna pay cash penalties – and they gonna be pretty big fines. I tell you you gonna get hit for five hundred dollars for first offense and one thousand for second . . .'

A sudden wave of *ooh*s and *ahh*s rose from the gathering, followed by a crescendo of applause and cheers.

'Wait, you ain't heard the whole thing,' Mangano broke into the reaction. 'There better not be a third offense, because if there is – we will run whoever break the rules out of business.'

Mangano was given a three-minute standing ovation. When the applause died down, Frank Ricotono, who owned one of the largest fish markets in South Brooklyn, wanted to know if there was to be an election of officers to run the organisation – and whether dues were to be assessed to the members.

'I answer yes to both questions,' Mangano rasped. 'I cannot tell you just yet how much dues gonna be. But I want as many of you as can make it tomorrow night to come to meeting at Orazzio's Pool Hall. We will vote for board and then decide how much dues everybody pay.'

'You want us to be at Orazzio's?' a voice in the back called out.

'I figure we first all meet under the clock. Say eight-thirty. Then we see how many head we got and go all together there. That way Orazzio can see how many we are and give us a nice setup instead of everybody coming in one at a time.'

The following night, 23 May 1924, the fish merchants began gathering on the sidewalk in front of the jewelry store on Columbia Street at about 8:15 p.m. By 8:20 about twenty-five of them had assembled under the clock. A stream of panicky calls began to pour into the 76th Precinct on Hamilton Avenue from edgy residents, who feared the gathering was an augury of an impending outbreak of gang warfare.

A half dozen detectives in two unmarked squad cars were dispatched to the scene. It was just minutes before 8:30 p.m., the time Mangano had set for the gathering.

The detectives jumped out of their cruisers prepared to deal with a desperate crisis – but then backed off and sighed with relief. They recognised the gathering was made up not of Mafiosi gangsters but a bunch of legitimate fish merchants whom the detectives knew almost to the man.

'What's going on?' Detective Michael Crowley called to Carmine Balsamo.

The godfather's nephew walked over to Crowley, shook his hands, and explained, 'We are just get together to form association of the neighborhood fish merchants. We meet here because we all go together to Orazzio's.'

'Well, that's good to know,' Crowley said. 'You had us worried. We got a bunch of calls from people in the neighborhood that there was gonna be some kind of gangland killing.'

'Hey,' Carmine Balsamo said quickly, 'do we look like we wanna kill somebody?'

'You could never get me to say that!' the detective answered. 'I guess I'll just say goodnight . . .'

Crowley signalled the other detectives. There was hardly any likelihood the fish dealers were going to rumble that night. The detectives got into their cars and drove away.

Mangano arrived at 8:35 p.m. 'Sorry I was late,' he addressed the gathering. 'I had to take my wife to the doctor for her hand. She cut it when she peel onions. She be all right.'

Mangano led the way over the two blocks to 73 Union Street where Orazzio Donofrio ran his poolroom. Orazzio ushered them to a back door in the pool hall which led down to the basement.

As he turned on the lights, he said, 'You got lotsa room here.' The basement was spacious. It had about forty folding wooden chairs. It was frequently used as an auxiliary meeting place by Frankie Yale when his garage was not suitable for certain undetected business he wanted to pull off.

The meeting lasted an hour. Vincenzo Mangano was elected president and others among the fish market owners filled the rest of the slates. Each market in the association was assessed a $500 initiation fee and membership dues of $200 quarterly.

The new association was given the title of F.I.S.H.: Federation of Italian Seafood Handlers. But membership wasn't to be limited to merchants in the South Brooklyn area where the price war had raged.

'To make this thing a success we must go outside our area and sign up the fish markets all the way to Bay Ridge' (a two-mile stretch along the perimeter of Upper New York Bay), Mangano said. That suited the charter members of F.I.S.H., because they felt that once they went back to a regulated retail schedule of prices, stores outside their area could undercut them and hurt their business.

Don Giuseppe Balsamo and Vincenzo Mangano dispatched F.I.S.H. representatives to sign up the scores of fish markets beyond the area where the charter members did business. The recruiting was a huge success. Only two merchants balked. But not for long.

Both caved in when two huge rough-looking emissaries lugging five-gallon cans of kerosene showed up one quiet, late afternoon and confronted the merchants separately. First, Tony 'Spring' Romeo and Constantine Scaffidi dropped into La Rocca's Fish Market on Fifth Avenue; a while later they went to Umberto Portonova's Fish Emporium on Smith Street.

The visitors didn't have to light the kerosene once they poured it over the inventory of edible seafood in the respective stores.

From that day on, no fish merchant ever failed again to ante up the dues he was required to pay as the price of doing business.

A redeeming feature in this newly started shakedown racket was in the results F.I.S.H. achieved. Fish dealers from Baltic Street in South Brooklyn to the perimeter of Bay Ridge all enjoyed a wonderful monopoly. They sold their fish at fixed prices set by the organisation – and they all prospered from the high prices they commanded for their mussels, scungilli, calamari, shrimp, clams, lobsters, mackerel, filet of flounder, and all the other catches of the day hauled in Don Giuseppe Balsamo's trucks from the Fulton Fish Market across the East River and delivered to the stores.

Now Balsamo had eighty more stores to peddle his fish – at greatly inflated profits – and at the same time all the retailers were also laughing all the way to the bank with the greatly enhanced profit structure wrought by the structured prices mandated by the F.I.S.H. But the godfather never thanked his *disgraziato* nephew Peter Licato for bringing about this gargantuan windfall from the price war he initiated.

Only the poor families who lived in Brooklyn and who could least afford it were once again caught in the Mafia's clutches by this latest wrinkle in racketeering.

Chapter 17

The Year of Vesuvius

The fish price war was one small episode in the saga of the underworld during the roaring twenties. Yet it was a significant chapter in terms of the widening dominance the Black Hand was attaining over the White Hand for control of the rackets. However, unlike the take-overs of so many other illegal ventures, this was a bloodless coup.

So far, it'd been 'tit-for-tat' in the hostilities between the ginzos and micks. Although the Italians were slightly ahead in the number of hits they'd made on the Irish, the difference in the score was not all that significant. But Wild Bill Lovett's assassination was to illustrate the old saw that goes: 'Revenge is like a boomerang. Although for a time it flies in the direction in which it is hurled, it takes a sudden curve, and, in returning, hits your own head the heaviest blow of all . . .'

Vesuvius may be the only feasible comparison to the volcanic eruptions and violent human destruction that followed Lovett's dispatch to the great beyond. In fact, the catastrophes of Pompeii in the years A.D. 79 and A.D. 1631 do not approach the duration of the violence and bloodshed that swept across

Brooklyn's topography in the last months of 1923 and through almost all of 1924. Death was swift and merciful in the Vesuvius disasters. Death in the greatly accelerated war between the ginzos and micks following Lovett's death was protracted, brutal, and agonising.

Nineteen Black Hand and twenty-one White Hand lives were wiped out. It was the most ruthless slaughter in underworld history, unmatched even by those which became so much a part of Chicago's legend.

'For every one of us they take, we're gonna get three of them,' Pegleg Lonergan vowed. Pegleg had called the gang together in the Baltic Street garage the morning following Lovett's funeral.

'My brother-in-law is dead,' Lonergan said in a choked voice. 'Those rotten fuckin' guineas are gonna pay with their yellow hides –'

Pegleg's words were drowned out by wild cheers.

'Let's kill every ginzo!' screamed Eddie Lynch. 'Why don't we go after the big *gimbrones* right now?'

'Yeah!' yelped The Scarecrow. 'Let's stick it up greasy Yale's ass!'

'Kill Yale!' cried Wally the Squint. 'Let's blow his fuckin' brains out!'

'Hold it!' yelled Lonergan, trying to suppress the bedlam.

'You fucks are gonna listen to what I gotta say . . .'

There was an immediate silence. Lonergan was determined to assert himself as the White Hand's new leader. The gang seemed to sense that. Pegleg knew this was his test: he had to show the boys who was boss.

'The first thing we do is knock off the dirty wop porter who fingered Bill to the guineas,' Lonergan said. 'I got the word from John Flaherty who tends bar at the Lotus. He told me what happened that night . . .'

Five days later, 4 November, Antonio Maglioli left his flat on Fourth Avenue and headed for Schermerhorn Street, to St Constantine's Greek Orthodox Church. His old friend Gerasimos Poulos's daughter, Chrysanthe, was being married that afternoon to Aristides Karamanlis.

The ceremony in the church lasted nearly two hours. Everyone threw rice at the bride and groom as they came down the steps and into the back of the rented Cadillac for the drive to the reception in Michel's Restaurant on Flatbush Avenue. The distance from the church to Michel's was roughly twenty blocks, approximately a mile. Some guests drove in their own cars; others took the trolley; many chose to walk.

Maglioli was among those who went to the reception on foot because it saved a nickel. By 4:05 p.m., he had covered fourteen blocks. As he crossed Atlantic Avenue at Flatbush, a car bore down on him. It was a black Ford sedan and it moved up Flatbush at high speed. Sunday strollers and some who were making their way to Michel's on foot saw the car turn the corner into Atlantic on two wheels. Shrieks and cries alerted Maglioli, who was directly in the path of the speeding auto.

Maglioli wheeled, saw the car bearing down on him. He tried to jump clear, but his legs didn't have the bounce. He was struck with such force that his body flipped up over the hood and flattened against it. The driver, without slowing down, swerved the car sharply to the left, then to the right. It caused the body to roll off the hood and crash to the pavement. The car never stopped.

Maglioli's mangled remains were beyond medical reclamation. His body was removed to Kings County Hospital's morgue. Police took statements from witnesses. No one could recall seeing a license number on the car. Some witnesses swore the car didn't have license plates. They were right. It didn't.

'You shoulda seen the way the fuckin' wop flew through the air,' The Scarecrow laughed. He had been in the front seat beside the driver of the Ford.

'Yeah,' bellowed Eddie Lynch, who was behind the wheel. 'He landed right on top of the hood. I thought we were gonna give him a ride all the way back here . . .'

A powdery snow had just begun falling on Monday night, 24 December, but the last-minute shoppers along Fulton Street on that Christmas Eve of 1923 seemed to welcome the white dusting. The Yule spirit was everywhere, and the snow promised a white Christmas.

No one can ever know what thoughts were coursing through the mind of Eddie 'Ducky' Callahan that night. A distant cousin of Eddie Lynch and a soldier in the White Hand army of waterfront extortionists, Ducky had gone shopping for his wife Mary's gifts. He had selected a dainty white lace slip and two pairs of silk stockings. They had been wrapped in Christmas paper and bore tags reading: *'Merry Christmas, my darling Mary. We'll have many more together.'*

The word of why Mary Callahan's husband didn't return home from his shopping trip was brought to her by detectives of the Bath Avenue Precinct on Christmas Day. Two little boys, trying out their Flexible Flyers on an embankment in the deserted Canarsie section, had spotted a strange red coloring in the snow. On closer observation they determined that the large pool of red surrounding what looked like a man's head was blood. There wasn't much left to the head, but the clump of bloodied skin and bone was attached to a man's body. The stiff right arm was clutching two gaily wrapped Christmas gifts.

Responding to a phone call from one of the parents of the boys, who had run home to report the grisly find, police went to the scene and discovered that the victim was Eddie 'Ducky' Callahan, not by looking at his face, which wasn't there, but from the A & S receipts in his pockets.

The cops had no more success solving that murder than they had finding Antonio Maglioli's killer six weeks earlier.

Dominick 'the Gent' Martano and his brother Giovanni had gotten off the boat in Brooklyn in late November, and were recruited immediately into the Black Hand because they had come with impeccable credentials from Catania. And they had their cousin's, Willie Two-Knife Altierri's, personal recommendation.

Dominick was anything but a gent. He was a cold, ruthless killer, as was his brother. The two were part of the organised conspiracy that fought the rise of Mussolini and his Grand Council of Fascism in 1923. But after Mussolini officially militarised the Fascist armed squads into his own personal army called the *Milizia Volontaris Fascista per la Sicurezza Nazionale*, the days of Fascist opponents like the Martano brothers were numbered. They fled Italy to avoid capture and execution for the numerous assassinations they committed against Fascist followers.

They'd been in Brooklyn barely a month that Christmas Eve in 1923 when Frankie Yale sent them out to do the number on Callahan. Ducky had been singled out for extermination for no other reason than that Yale wanted to even the score for Antonio Maglioli's killing. Although the porter wasn't an official member of the Black Hand, the service he performed for them in providing Altierri with information which led to Wild Bill Lovett's extermination was considered a priceless contribution. Thus Tony's hit-and-run murder, Yale decided, had to be avenged.

Frankie didn't care which White Hander was laid low in reprisal, just so long as he got the message across to Lonergan and the rest of the Irish that the Black Hand had struck back.

It was Ducky Callahan's tough luck that he happened to be spotted on Fulton Street alone and unprotected among the shoppers. Credit for the sighting went to Glass Eye Pelicano, who recognised Ducky as Ducky went into Abraham & Straus. Nick rushed to a pay booth and phoned Yale, who was hosting a Christmas party for the boys in his Sunrise Café. Frankie ordered Glass Eye to keep Ducky under surveillance until Altierri's cousins made the scene.

Why Altierri's cousins?

'I wanna try out the boys,' Frankie said to Two-Knife. 'You brag and brag how good they be. Now I wanna them show me . . .'

Dominick and Giovanni Martano could no more get to Fulton Street by themselves than they could get to the Antarctic. To them, Brooklyn was a maze. The subway was a mysterious underground railroad that they swore they'd never ride again after they had foolishly decided to try it out for kicks one day. They ended up at the last stop in Van Cortlandt Park in the Bronx, some twenty miles from South Brooklyn. Fortunately, an

Italian-speaking cop found them wandering on the platform and bailed them out of what might have turned into an Immigration and Naturalisation Service deportation. The policeman found out where they were staying and phoned Willie Altierri, who drove to the wilds of the Bronx to retrieve his cousins.

With that episode involving Dominick and Giovanni very much on his mind, Yale put his assassins in Frenchy Carlino's custody with explicit instructions.

'Don't let these here *fongool* foreigners outta your sight or we never find 'em again,' Frankie commanded as he dispatched the Sicilian hit men on their mission in downtown Brooklyn. Turning to Altierri, Yale said in a sarcastic whisper, 'Any more cousins you got like these, I want you say to them stay where the hell you come from ...'

Nick Glass Eye was standing outside A&S's main entrance when he spotted the green 1921 Ford sedan coming along Fulton. He signalled Carlino to pull over to the curb, walked over, and said, 'He hasn't come out yet. He's getting some presents wrapped. But I know he's gonna come out from those doors because he gotta go home that way.' Pelicano pointed up the street toward Flatbush Avenue.

Carlino heard a click, then another click. It came from the back seat, where Dominick The Gent and Giovanni were cuddling sawed-off shotguns in their laps. They were getting ready to aim at the department store's doors, crowds and all.

'Hey!' Frenchy snapped his head back in a hushed voice. 'You can't kill him here! Too many people! Whatsa matter with you, crazy?'

Carlino ordered the trigger-happy brothers to put their weapons on the floor and get out of the car.

'You wait at the door,' Frenchy said, 'When he comes out, you grab and bring into car ...'

Five minutes later, at 9:05 p.m., Pelicano nudged the two killers. 'There, there,' he said, pointing to a heavyset man with a black overcoat and black fedora, carrying Christmas packages under his arm.

As Callahan came out to the sidewalk, he looked up at the snow which had begun falling while he was in the store. He turned up his collar and started walking. He had taken but a few steps when the Sicilian torpedoes swooped down on him from behind and grabbed his arm.

'Hey, what the hell ya doin'?' Ducky demanded, trying to struggle free. But the Martanos had considerable experience kidnapping Mussolini Fascists on the streets of Catania, which were crowded not only with people but also donkeys and goats.

It was a breeze for them to throw Ducky into the back of the car, and pile in on top of him. Pelicano slammed the back door shut and hopped into the front beside Carlino, who drove away before anyone on the street could figure out what was happening.

'Looks like a pinch,' someone said.

'Yeah, probably a shoplifter,' another said.

A half hour later, Carlino had reached his destination in the Canarsie, designated by Yale for Ducky's bump-off. Frankie had picked that out-of-the-way site for a very sound reason.

'You dump him out there and nobody find him for few days,' he said to Frenchy. 'If you leave in South Brooklyn, we not be able celebrate Christmas. The fuckin' cops come around and bother shit outta us . . .'

So Eddie Callahan never got to give his wife the lovely gifts with the sentimental greetings.

For all of the grief and heartbreak Mary Callahan suffered that Christmas, she had one small consolation. That was the knowledge that her husband didn't go to his grave without her Christmas present to him.

Even though the O'Brien Brothers Undertakers Inc., on Sixth Avenue, told Mary that Ducky would be waked in a closed coffin, she had them dress him in the green sweater jacket that she had knit.

Pegleg Lonergan got word through the gangland grapevine that Callahan was killed by the two newcomers from Sicily.

Two nights later, 27 December, Giovanni Ignazzio Martano walked out of Pericone's Neapolitan Kitchen, a restaurant on Fifth Avenue and Fourteenth Street, sated. He had just gorged himself on a delicious meal of veal marsala and spaghetti. He took a deep breath of the fresh, clear night air.

Seconds later he lay on the sidewalk with a huge hole in the middle of his torso. A single shotgun blast fired from a dark sedan, make and year unknown, did it after the vehicle had slowed down outside the Neapolitan Kitchen.

The gunman was never identified but the wheelman was described by a witness as a 'very skinny man with a gaunt look'. To the police, that sounded very much like Ernie Skinny Shea. But the thin man came off the grill without a hair singed. He claimed he'd been to the movies that night, the Para's Court.

What picture did he see?

Ernie didn't remember because, he said, he'd slept through the whole show. But he had a ticket stub in his pocket to prove he was there – and that was the alibi that got him off. If the cops could have taken fingerprints of that stub, they'd have found layers of prints: Ernie Skinny's, Wally the Squint's (he gave the stub to Ernie), unidentified (belonging to a theater-goer who threw the ticket away after leaving Para's Court, only to have Wally pick it up from the sidewalk to provide Ernie Skinny with his out), and Evelyn Coleman's (the girl who relieved Sally Lomenzo in the cashier's booth and handed the ticket to the unidentified theater-goer).

On 8 January 1924 – twelve days after Giovanni Ignazzio Martano's demise – the White Hand completed its parlay of extermination that Mussolini's Fascist followers couldn't effect against the dreaded Martano brothers.

That evening, Dominick the Gent was walking along Fourth Avenue toward the Black Hand garage. Dominick was making terrific progress in finding his way around Brooklyn by now. He was able to walk from his rooming house to the garage, a distance of two and a half blocks, without getting lost.

He was just a few feet from the garage entrance when a maroon coupe came up from behind. The man beside the driver lowered his window and pointed a .45-caliber automatic at Martano. Martano caught five of the seven slugs triggered at him. That made him the third Italian to bite the dust in the nine weeks since Wild Bill Lovett's rubout.

After that, lower-echelon enforcers, extortionists, bootleggers, and loan sharks of both gangs were wiped out one after another. Hardly a week passed in 1924 when one or two White Handers or one or more Black Handers didn't meet violent death at the hands of rival mobsters wielding guns, knives, and meat cleavers. On the docks, baling hooks and the booms of cranes were employed as weapons of death in the epidemic of assassinations.

By the beginning of November 1924, the tally in the thirteen month war raging between the ginzos and micks had mounted to forty.

The fact that the Black Hand had lost two fewer soldiers than the White Hand was of little consolation to Frankie Yale. He knew that with the way things were going the advantage could change hands by next week, or the next day.

There was nothing anyone could do to stop the slaughter.

Then Yale was summoned to Chicago by Alphonse Capone for a favor. When Yale took the call, he couldn't believe Scarface was serious.

'Ya gotta be kiddin', Big Al,' Frankie said incredulously. 'You want I should come and make funeral arrangements – in Chicago? What for, eh?'

Don Miguel Merlo was dying of cancer. He had twenty-four, no more than forty-eight hours. Al could think of no one who could arrange the kind of splash send-off he had in mind better than Frankie Yale.

'You the only one I know can make right funeral for my good friend,' Capone said in a voice that Yale sensed was a put-on. Scarface wanted him out there for something much more important and dramatic. As an undertaker himself, Yale was well aware that he wasn't needed to arrange a funeral in Chicago. When it came to gangland obsequies, no place on earth could outdo Chicago. Capone certainly didn't have to call on Yale to arrange the ceremonies for the disposition of Miguel Merlo's remains.

Although sensing the ruse, Frankie couldn't turn a deaf ear to Al's request. The next afternoon, 8 November, Yale, accompanied by Two-Knife and Augie the Wop, boarded the Twentieth Century Limited at Grand Central.

229

Two old acquaintances, Albert Anselmi and John Scalise, the two Sicilians from Cicero who'd come east at Capone's direction to help spill some Irish blood for Yale at Sagaman's Dance Hall on Valentine's Day of 1921, met Yale and his men at the Illinois Central Railroad Station.

'*Buono sera, Signore Ioele,*' Anselmi greeted Frankie with a warm handshake.

'Hey, Albert, hey, John, how you be?' Yale said excitedly, turning to shake Scalise's hand next. Then, as they turned to greet Altierri and Pisano, Frankie wanted to know, 'How come Alphonse send big men like you to pick me up, eh?'

Scalise shook his head. 'Al wants to make sure nothing happen to you,' he said crisply. 'Things in town are little hot right now . . . you know the big troublemaking mick is giving Johnny and Al hard time . . .'

'You mean O'Bannion?' Yale asked. Dion O'Bannion, head of Chicago's White Hand gang, was battling Capone's Black Handers in much the same bloody fashion that the micks were fighting the ginzos in New York for supremacy over the underworld.

Scalise and Anselmi both nodded: yes, the problem was O'Bannion.

'Me and Giovanni want to bust that fuckin' Irishman,' Anselmi said straightforwardly. 'But Al say he got better idea . . .'

Something in the tone of Anselmi's voice suddenly told Frankie what was in Capone's mind when he called him to Chicago. It sent a chill through him.

'Come on,' Scalise said. 'Let's go. Al wait for you . . .'

Scalise and Anselmi escorted the visitors from Brooklyn out into Michigan Avenue. As they walked from the terminal, Yale spotted a Rolls-Royce parked at the curb and recognised it as Capone's bullet-proof limousine. Capone's chauffeur William 'Three Fingers' Jack White, who had been Big Al's sidekick from his Brooklyn days, was behind the wheel.

'Hey, long time no see,' White greeted Yale as he got into the back with Altierri and Pisano.

'Say hello to Willie and Augie,' Yale said, introducing his confederates.

Anselmi and Scalise rode up front on the drive to Capone's new headquarters, now situated in Cicero. For political and other pressing reasons, Scarface had been compelled to move his base of operations to the Chicago suburbs, but he and Johnny Torrio still controlled the rackets in the Windy City with an iron grip.

Yale couldn't help but wonder what sort of trouble O'Bannion and his Northside Gang were causing for Capone and Torrio. He could have asked Anselmi and Scalise, but decided to wait and hear all about it from Al himself. Besides, there was another thought on Frankie's mind.

'Hey, how is Don Miguel, eh?' he asked.

'*Morte . . . ieri sera . . .*' Scalise turned, shaking his head sadly.

Well, at least Capone hadn't lied to Frank. If Merlo had died the night before, Al had given it straight to Yale. Maybe, Frankie tried telling himself, Capone really wanted him out there just to make funeral arrangements. But he wasn't convinced.

And he was right. Just as the welcoming amenities with Capone, Torrio, and a fast-rising leader of the Chicago chapter of *Unione Sicilione*, Miguel Genna, were over, Big Al addressed Frankie:

'I ask you to come here because I want big favor.' Capone walked toward him from behind his big oak desk. He stood in front of Frankie and put his hamlike hands on Yale's shoulders.

'My good friend, I have already plan everything,' Scarface said in a slow, deliberate voice. 'You have one small job, but very important job, for Don Merlo's funeral . . .'

Capone gave Yale a beneficent smile.

'You just order the flowers . . . then go inspect them . . .' Capone said.

'Flowers?' Frankie asked tightly.

'Flowers,' Capone replied with a smile, squeezing Yale's shoulders. It was a meaningful squeeze. 'You order by phone . . . then you go and see how they look. If you no like – and you no gonna like – you let fuckin' florist know . . . *capeesh*?'

No. Al wasn't getting through to him. Yale wanted Capone to make things clear.

'Hey, Frankie,' Capone said quickly. 'Lemme ask you, who is giving me such big headaches in this town? You know?'

'O'Bannion,' Yale said quickly.

'Hey, smart boy,' Scarface rasped, patting Yale's right shoulder while still clutching Frankie's other shoulder.

'Now, do I gotta tell you what that dirty Irisher use for front, eh?' Capone asked.

Now some of the fog was clearing. Yale was beginning to smell something. But he didn't yet see the whole picture.

'They tell me O'Bannion is lousy florist,' Capone continued. 'He don't deserve to be in business . . . So after you order flowers and you don't like them, you, my good friend, put him out of business . . .'

'What!' Yale exclaimed, his voice choking. 'You call me to wipe out O'Bannion?'

'Exactly,' Capone said, taking Yale into an endearing embrace. 'You like, eh?'

Yale was stunned. 'Al, for chrissake,' Frankie rasped. 'Why you want me to do this when you got everybody . . . what I mean . . . Whatsa matter with your boys, eh?'

'Frankie, Frankie,' Capone said placatingly. 'I'm gonna give you two of my best boys, Alberto and Giovanni. You don't have to do nothing. Only talk. You talk nice. You fool Dion. And then – boom, boom – that's all . . . eh, how you like?'

Yale was still stunned. He looked around the office. Torrio was nodding his head up and down and smiling broadly, approvingly.

'I agree with Al,' Torrio said airily. 'I vote for you myself.'

'Me, too,' Genna echoed. 'We trust nobody else to arrange this funeral . . .'

'Hey,' Yale snapped, coming out of a stupor. 'You call me here for Merlo's funeral and you want me to make one for O'Bannion!' He began pacing the office, '*Madonn*', what you do to me . . . I don't like this . . .'

Frankie walked over to an armchair and sagged into it, putting his hands up to his head.

Capone nodded to Genna. 'Miguel, tell him what we plan, you want to?' Al offered.

Yale took his hands down from his head and looked about the room. Capone, Torrio, and Genna were smiling.

'Go, go, Miguel, tell him,' Capone pressed eagerly.

'Well, I gonna speak to ya,' Genna said. 'We talk about new president for our thing . . . we look all over, here in Chicago, over in Cleveland, Detroit, lotsa places. We no find one we look for. We want somebody smart, somebody strong to become number-one man . . .'

Yale's interest was suddenly aroused. In the national scheme of things, Frankie didn't hold a position as high as he thought he should in the *Unione Sicilione*. Genna, for example, commanded more influence and power because he represented the whole of Chicago, while Yale was only the boss of the *Unione*'s branch in Brooklyn. And while Brooklyn had almost the population of Chicago, it was a geographic oddball because, technically at least, it composed one-fifth of New York City. Manhattan, for example, had four representatives in the *Unione*: Joe Masseria, Joe Adonis, Frank Costello, and Charles Lucky Luciano. Each of these Italian underworld bosses controlled pieces of Manhattan and each held a rank in the *Unione* equal to Yale's. That situation had never sat right with Frankie, who felt that his control over a territory much larger than any ruled by the Manhattan gang leaders entitled him to a higher standing in the national fraternity of the Italian underworld.

But now Genna's hint that the *Unione* might make him president started the wheels spinning wildly in Yale's head. The old president, Genna's brother Amadeo, had died in October, and his successor had not yet been picked. Yale knew what great influence Miguel Genna had in the society, for together with the late Amadeo and five other brothers, all from Chicago, they comprised what amounted to the ruling hierarchy of that organisation. With Miguel and his five surviving brothers backing him, Yale reasoned he could attain that exalted place in the *Unione Sicilione* to which he had aspired all these years.

Yale gazed at Capone with a honeyed smile.

'Okay, my good brother Al,' Frankie said cheerfully. 'You got me again . . .'

It was a masterpiece of simplicity. Three men walked into the Schofield Florist Shop to look over a two-thousand-dollar floral piece one of them had ordered by phone the day before for Merlo's funeral. It was 11.55 a.m., 10 November 1924.

The tallest of the three men shook hands with Dion O'Bannion, but it was anything but a friendly handshake. He squeezed O'Bannion's hand with a viselike grip. O'Bannion, who was alone in the store, sensed trouble immediately. He tried to back away, but he couldn't. The man holding his hand wouldn't let go.

Then the two shorter men pulled guns. One shouted, 'Look out, Frankie!' The tall man released his grip on O'Bannion's hand and stepped back. Seven bullets struck Chicago's Irish gang leader: one sliced through his right cheek, another ripped through his neck, another pierced his jaw, and two went through his breast. He collapsed backward into the huge floral arrangement of white carnations and red roses that had been prepared for Miguel Merlo's funeral and the weight of his body toppled the gaudy wreath. As he lay in that tangle of flowers, the gun was pressed to his head and a sixth bullet tore into it.

The assassins ran out of the store and hopped into a blue sedan whose driver roared away.

In their routine roundup of underworld figures, Chicago police gave Frankie Yale serious consideration. But they couldn't pin the crime on him.

'I only come to Chicago to go to Miguel Merlo's funeral,' Yale insisted. 'Why should I wanna hurt O'Bannion? What he do to me, eh?'

Chicago authorities were compelled to release Yale – despite the order book in Dion O'Bannion's florist shop which showed the entry:

11/9/24 – $2,000 floral arrangement, Miguel Merlo funeral; Frank Ioele will see himself before delivery and pay, noon tomorrow.

Yale swore he didn't keep that appointment to look over the wreath, although he didn't deny ordering it for Merlo's funeral.

'Of course I call O'Bannion and tell him to make up nice piece for Don Merlo,' Yale said. 'You see how much I respect Dion . . . so how come you think I kill him, eh?'

Where was Yale when O'Bannion was killed, the cops wanted to know.

'My good friend Sam Amatuna take me to lunch,' Yale said. 'We eat big meal, good food, at Palmer House ... You check there, you see.'

Detectives checked. They saw. A waiter named Nick Delassandro, who worked Station No. 3 in the dining room, swore on his children that Yale and Amatuna had sat at one of his tables at a little before 11:30 and stayed well past 1:00 p.m.

'I served them myself,' Delassandro said. 'I even tell you what they eat and drink if you wanna know ...'

That wasn't necessary. The cops didn't want to hear what Yale or Amatuna had for lunch. They knew a coverup when they heard one, yet there was nothing they could do about it, no way to pin O'Bannion's killing on the big banana from Brooklyn, or the two suspected triggermen, John Scalise and Albert Anselmi.

Nick Delassandro's $280 indebtedness to Capone's loan sharks was cancelled. It was an act of executive clemency that Big Al felt was the least that could be done for a memory as sharp as Nick's.

Many other mobsters were put on the grill, including Johnny Torrio.

'Why should I have Dion killed?' he asked. 'I just arranged for Mr Ioele to give him $2,000 worth of floral business.'

'How can you ask me if I knocked him off?' Capone asked with a pained expression. 'My brother Frank would never forgive me after all those nice flowers Dion sent for the funeral of my beloved friend Miguel.'

The responses from all the other mobsters suspected of a capability to know off O'Bannion were about the same.

After attending Merlo's splashy funeral, Frankie Yale, Johnny Torrio and Al Capone, flanked by bodyguards, entered the undertaker's chapel where O'Bannion was laid out and sat in front of the bier.

War preparations began to take shape almost immediately after O'Bannion was laid to rest. Hymie Weiss, who took over O'Bannion's mob, quickly fitted out a half-dozen large autos with the newest of weapons that were to bring gangland slaughter to a new high: Thompson sub-machine guns capable of firing seven hundred rounds a minute. A challenge was hurled by one of O'Bannion's henchmen, Louie Alterie, a three-gun torpedo.

'Who killed my pal? Are they men? Let 'em face Louie. I'll shoot it out with them all, anywhere, anytime, even at the corner of State and Madison.'

No one took up Louie's challenge to have it out on Chicago's busiest street corner; moreover the O'Bannion gang suddenly found itself leaderless when Louie mysteriously hightailed it out of the city. He stayed away for ten years.

Seventy-four days after O'Bannion's demise, Johnny Torrio and his wife, returning from dinner in their limousine, were suddenly confronted by a big car with a man on the running board whom Torrio recognised as one of the O'Bannion mob's assassins.

'Give it the gas!' Torrio screamed to his chauffeur. He and his wife hit the floor. They were safe for the moment.

But when the limo came to a stop in front of Torrio's home at 7011 Clyde Avenue, the other car wasn't far behind. As Torrio and his wife sprinted toward the front door, a battery of guns spat flames. Torrio toppled to the sidewalk in agony. One of the gunmen bent over him and pulled the trigger once more – but the pistol was empty.

Leaving Torrio for dead, the assailants piled into their car and sped away. Torrio, his jaw broken by bullets, shotgun slugs in his body, was taken to the hospital. One of the bullets had torn through his throat and left him without a voice for months. His recovery was slow but he came through.

The call was too close for comfort. Torrio, loaded with more money than he could spend in a lifetime, decided he'd had it. He called on Al Capone and spelled out the master plan which would hand Scarface Torrio's territory and make him supreme commander of Chicago's underworld.

'I'm gonna turn things over to you,' he told Big Al. 'There's only one thing – my percentage. You can send it to me in Brooklyn. That's where I'm going. I'll be happy there. That's where my heart is and that's where I belong.'

Then, trying to narrow his pop eyes to show his meanness, Torrio warned: 'Remember, kid, if you mess things up I'll come back . . .'

And so Al Capone became the King of the Rackets. Torrio lived in Brooklyn for thirty-two years. A heart attack killed him in a New York barber shop in 1956.

A fortnight after Yale had done the favor in Chicago for Big Al, twenty-five directors of the *Unione Sicilione* met in New York City's McAlpin Hotel. Frankie was elected the national president of the *Unione Sicilione*.

With this, he reached heretofore unscaled heights of power and prestige in the American underworld. His influence extended across the nation. And that was invaluable in his long struggle with the White Hand for complete control over Brooklyn's rackets.

Chapter 18

New Heights of Power

The war ceased with puzzling suddenness at the beginning of December 1924. This was immediately after Frankie Yale had been fingered as one of Dion O'Bannion's suspected killers and then elected president of the *Unione Sicilione*.

The White Hand suddenly came to grips with grim reality: Yale and his Brooklyn mob had attained new heights of power because now they had a working relationship, officially, with Black Hand mobs in virtually every region of the United States. Pegleg Lonergan and his band looked warily at their detested rivals who now commanded the kind of strength that could annihilate the White Hand at the snap of Frankie's fingers.

So Pegleg called off the orgy of killings. The dividends in lives saved were realised immediately. For no sooner had the micks stopped their deadly ambushes against the ginzos than the ginzos halted their savage retaliations on the micks. Just like that.

To Frankie Yale, the letup in hostilities was a significant sign. He saw it as an indication of weakness, and, indeed, fear on the part of Lonergan and his boys. No question in Yale's mind that his reputation as a killer of gangland giants, coupled with his newly acquired power in the national *Unione*, had brought the

Irishmen to grips with the new reality: they were just a bunch of local hoodlums who had spent the past four years trying to stop the Black Hand infiltration into the rackets and, despite all the bloodshed and violence, had failed.

The Italians' influence and control of illicit activity had proliferated. And every gain the Black Hand made was a step back for the White Hand.

Now the future of the Irish mobsters was even bleaker. For if they couldn't destroy the Italians while they were still a local mob, what chance had they after the Brooklyn Black Hand had become part of a national syndicate and its boss, Yale, was the man on the throne?

Frankie was quick to take advantage of his new position of power – and the White Hand's apparent cessation of hostilities.

'We gonna finish off those drunken Irishmen for good now,' he told the gang at a meeting early in January 1925. 'They got no more heart for fight.'

To Augie the Wop, to Don Giuseppe Balsamo, to Johnny Silk Stocking, and to almost all the boys, it sounded as though Frankie was preparing for a final pitched battle against the White Hand.

'What I'm gonna do is make deal with Pegleg,' Yale said.

'You mean you ask him to give up?' Pisano quipped.

Yale smiled. 'Kinda, but he no gonna know that's what he be doin'.'

Yale's package for Lonergan was decorated with many olive branches and was labelled 'coexistence'. The contents were in fact small 'bombs', set to 'explode' at predetermined times in the months ahead and designed to diminish by degrees the Irish mob's hold on waterfront rackets. Frankie felt if he could excise the micks from the extortion and loansharking activities on the piers, he would effectively remove them as an underworld power in Brooklyn. The money from the illicit activities on the docks was the Irish gang's biggest source of income. Without it, Lonergan and his boys would be better off going legit because the rest of the rackets – bootlegging, hijacking, and protection – amounted to very little income. By now Yale was selling booze to at least ninety percent of the Prohibition Era speakeasies in

Brooklyn, and he had also brought the Mob into a position of unchallenged supremacy in the protection rackets perpetrated on wholesale and retail businesses.

Sometime in mid-January Fury Argolia telephoned Pegleg and informed him that Frankie was anxious to sit down and talk with him.

'Tell him to come and see me here,' Lonergan said, meaning the Baltic Street garage.

'Frankie think it better you come to my restaurant,' Argolia said slowly. 'Besides, he wanna buy you dinner . . .'

Surprisingly, Pegleg consented.

On Saturday night 17 January, Lonergan, flanked by Eddie Lynch and Ernie the Scarecrow, walked into the unfamiliar terrain of the Adonis Club. Frankie Yale, who, aware of his new power, felt he needed no bodyguards for this encounter, welcomed him warmly. He was betting his life on his belief that while he was president of the *Unione Sicilione* no White Hander would dare harm a hair on his head.

Yale and Lonergan had known each other since 1915. They had met in saloons and spoken to each other, occasionally attended dances and other social functions. But since the outbreak of the ginzo-mick war in 1920, they had nothing to say to each other. They passed one another on the street from time to time, but their eyes never met.

Now, at the Adonis, they spoke to each other like long lost brothers. With Fury providing a festive spread for the distinguished guests to feed on, Yale slowly, deliberately, and very effectively laid down his proposals for 'coexistence'.

His voice was silky and his approach soft-sell. 'Hey Dick, where we end up with all this here killin', eh? Who get hurt? The people we love. You don't know how sorry I am about Bill Lovett, but I swear to you I have nothing to do with that. I swear on my wife and my mother and my children . . .'

From a purely technical standpoint, Yale was telling the truth. The man who made the decision to execute Wild Bill was Two-Knife Altierri. Frankie wasn't consulted because he wasn't at the garage that night when Two-Knife bumped into Antonio Maglioli and learned that Lovett had drunk himself into a stupor at the Lotus Club – which isn't to say that Frankie Yale wouldn't have sanctioned what Altierri did. But at least he could now face Pegleg Lonergan and swear, truthfully, that he had nothing to do with the killing of the White Hand chief's brother-in-law.

Frankie got down to the nitty-gritty without too many preliminaries.

'I don't like all this killing,' Yale said with a scowl. 'Not necessary. You and me and our boys can make lotsa money without shooting each other . . .'

He paused. Lonergan, Lynch, and Monaghan were listening intently.

'Brooklyn is a big place,' Yale went on. 'Take the docks. I give you for instance. We fight each other for piece of the action, and for what? There be so much action there we don't have to be fightin' . . .'

Then Frankie unveiled his master plan.

According to Yale's formula, the White Hand and Black Hand would do a trade-off for control of the docks. The Italians would give up all extortion and loansharking activities on the Furman Street and Greenpoint piers, while the White Hand would abdicate all claims to the Green docks from Seventeenth to Thirty-sixth Streets.

'You got a deal,' Lonergan said, shaking Yale's hand.

The waiter poured everyone a fresh glass of chianti and they drank to a long era of peace and prosperity between the Italian and Irish gangs.

Peace prevailed for five whole months. It was June before Pegleg Lonergan suddenly awakened to the screwing he and the gang had taken from Frankie Yale. The realisation came as shipping activity on the Furman Street and Greenpoint piers declined dramatically because of a severe drop in ocean, or foreign, trade. But the end of the postwar boom didn't affect the Green docks to any great extent because the freighters using those facilities were engaged mainly in domestic, or coastal shipping, which was continuing at peak level.

'Those lousy ginzos have fucked us!' Lonergan screamed after rallying the gang to let everyone know that he was repudiating the agreement with Yale. 'They ended up gettin' the best docks because they knew ahead of time which of them was gonna be workin' when things got tight!'

Pegleg ordered the gang back to the Green docks to resume operations in extortion and shylocking as though they'd never been away.

'And if any wop son of a bitch gives you any lip, blow his fuckin' brains out!' he ordered.

That was exactly what Ernie Skinny Shea and Wally the Squint Walsh had in mind when they were confronted by Augie the Wop Pisano and Johnny Silk Stocking Guistra on one of Don Giuseppe Balsamo's piers which housed the Intercostal Shipping Lines warehouse. It was the early afternoon of Friday 19 June.

'Hey, you guys must be lost,' Pisano said to Shea and Walsh. 'You ain't supposed to be fuckin' round here. Didn't nobody tell ya about deal we made?'

'Lonergan says the deal stinks,' Walsh growled. 'So it's gonna be like it used to be.'

'I think you should take a friggin' walk before you get your stupid head handed to you,' Pisano screamed.

Walsh quickly thrust his hand into his jacket for the .45 he was carrying in his shoulder holster. But Silk Stocking was much quicker on the draw: he had his .38 automatic whipped out and levelled at Walsh before he could even get his hand on his gun.

Guistra plowed two slugs into Walsh's chest. The Squint's eyelids popped wide open for just an instant. Then they closed and his legs buckled. He collapsed to the wooden deck with a thud.

As the shots were being fired, Ernie Skinny flung his arms up high over his head.

'Take it easy, Johnny,' he quivered. 'I ain't gonna make no trouble . . .'

'You fuckin' right, you ain't,' the Silk Stocking growled. 'I oughta blow you goddam brain out, too. But if I do, then nobody's gonna go tell Lonergan what happen here. So, get your ass back to him and let him know what's gonna happen if he tries cuttin' in again.'

Shea wheeled around and scampered like a frightened rabbit to the car parked next to the bulkhead.

'Hey!' Pisano shouted after him. 'Don't go 'way yet . . .'

Shea turned and saw that Guistra had his gun trained on him.

'Come back here!' Johnny ordered. Shea slithered toward Pisano on shaky legs.

'Open the friggin' trunk,' Augie the Wop snapped. Shea ran to the back of the car and raised the lid. Then he was forced to help Pisano carry Wally the Squint's corpse and dump it into the trunk.

As he slammed the lid shut, Pisano snarled to Shea, 'You take your friend back to that one-leg Lonergan and tell him we don't want no dead or drunk micks dirtying up our nice, clean docks.'

As he drove away, Shea could hear Augie the Wop and Johnny Silk Stocking laughing uproariously.

Pegleg Lonergan almost hit the fifteen-foot-high overhang when Ernie Shea barged into the garage and gasped out the horror of what had happened.

He lit a cigarette, got up from behind the desk, and paced the garage with rapid, limping steps. Ernie, Needles Ferry, Eddie Lynch, The Scarecrow Monaghan, and Aaron Harms looked on in stony silence, waiting for Pegleg to take hold of himself.

'Wops! Guineas! *Gimbrones! Fongools!* Motherfuckin' sons of bitches!' Lonergan ranted. 'They're gonna pay for this! They're gonna bleed till their dirty black hides become white!'

He went back to his desk and sank heavily into the chair.

'That does it!' he shouted, still hysterical. Lonergan was out of his mind. 'Let's hit them anywhere! Just go out and hit anybody! We gotta shoot them down! Kill them!'

The boys went out and in quick succession knocked off three lowly Black Hand rank-and-file loansharkers, Antonio Abondando, Victor Cerullo, and Michael Donofrio. They were gunned down while making their rounds on separate stretches of the Green docks over a two-day period immediately following Wally the Squint Walsh's stunning murder.

The Black Hand struck out against the tottering White Hand mob like a buzz saw after these assassinations.

243

The bark of bullets and the flash of fire from the muzzles of revolvers, automatics, and sawed-off shotguns was awesome – and continuous. One after another, mick mobsters toppled on street corners, in alleys, in speakeasies, and along the entire stretch of South Brooklyn's waterfront.

Pegleg Lonergan and his Irish killers retaliated with a relentless spray of their own hot lead, and settled many scores with Frankie Yale's musclemen and heavy bombers. But the Black Hand held a steadfast dominance in the bloody feud.

The ginzo's supremacy was reflected in the toll of dead in the six months after the peace pact between Yale and Lonergan was broken.

By early December 1925 the wave of terror had taken the lives of twenty-six White Handers but only eight Black Handers. The overwhelming superiority of the Italian mob had now been established beyond all doubt.

By then, too, panic had taken hold in the White Hand ranks. Many of its executioners, enforcers, extortionists, bootleggers, hijackers, and other racket-orientated predators had quit the gang in fear that the next time a trigger was squeezed it might be zinging lead at them.

Despite the rapid deterioration of his criminal kingdom, Pegleg Lonergan stubbornly clung to the thin hope that he would somehow spring back to a commanding position over Brooklyn's rackets. He refused to see himself and the bedraggled remnants of his once-mighty underworld empire as it now really was: a deposed power, shorn of all its influence, strength, and ability to lock horns with the cartel structured by Frankie Yale.

Yet Lonergan persisted in spending more time in the planning of mayhem and murder against Yale's troops than in pursuing the more productive goal of recouping at least some of his lost ground in the rackets.

As a result, even those White Handers who had stuck loyally by the gang and remained allied with Lonergan rapidly became disenchanted with Pegleg's leadership.

On the afternoon of 12 December 1925, Eddie Lynch put in a call to Frankie Yale to say he wanted to see the Black Hand leader on a matter of greatest urgency. Frankie asked Eddie to drop into Fury Argolia's Adonis Club at 3:00 p.m. on 24 December.

'I talk to you there because I got important business to attend with Fury,' Yale said to Lynch.

The business was a Christmas night party that Yale was sponsoring at the Adonis. This, however, was no ordinary Yule shindig, for the guest of honor was none other than Alphonse Capone.

Capone, now the sole and undisputed ruler over all of Chicago's rackets, was coming to New York!

Chapter 19

The Adonis Club Christmas Massacre

Capone's eight-year-old son, Sonny, had developed a mastoid infection behind his left ear. The condition had become so advanced that young Capone was threatened with the loss of his hearing – if not his life. Doctors Capone consulted in Chicago said they couldn't perform the operation with any hope that they could save the boy's hearing.

His search brought him to a renowned Park Avenue eye, ear, nose, and throat specialist. Capone is said to have offered the surgeon $100,000 if he could make the boy well. The doctor refused the money. He said he would perform the surgery for his regular fee of $1,000.

Sonny Capone went under the knife in Dr Lloyd's Sanitarium on St Nicholas Place in Manhattan. The operation was a complete success. With Al Capone relieved of that tremendous burden, he accepted Frankie Yale's invitation to spend Christmas night with him and some of the boys at their annual Yule bash at Fury Argolia's restaurant.

But when Eddie Lynch dropped in that Thursday afternoon of 24 December and Frankie listened to his spiel, he was impelled to consider cancelling Capone's fete.

'You no shit me, Eddie, you really tell the truth?' Yale asked for the third time.

'Frankie,' Lynch said, his tone now almost one of exasperation, 'why the hell would I come and meet you on your grounds and give you a line of bullshit, eh? What am I gonna get out of it, can you tell me?'

'Maybe a hole in the head if you jerking me off, that's what you get, Eddie,' Yale sneered. Then, as an afterthought, added, 'I don't think you give me hand job, Eddie. I think I believe you . . .'

The tidings Lynch brought to Yale were of Pegleg Lonergan's plan to invade the Adonis Club on Christmas night and 'blast the joint apart'. Lonergan knew that the Black Hand had a bash in the Adonis every Christmas night and, traditionally, it was a stag affair that featured stripteasers and girls from some of the Broadway nightclub chorus lines who served as drinking, dining, and dancing companions for the gangsters.

'How he gonna do this?' Yale asked crisply. 'How many people he gonna use, eh?'

'Five beside himself,' Lynch said quickly, 'Wanna know who they are?' Yale nodded, and Eddie proceeded to reel off the names: Aaron Harms, Patrick 'Happy' Maloney, Joseph 'Ragtime' Howard, James 'No Heart' Hart, and Jack Needles Ferry.

'Hey, who are those other guys?' Yale asked darkly. 'Only ones I know about are Aaron and Needles. Where the other ones come from, eh?'

'New guys,' Lynch said. 'Happy, Ragtime, and No Heart used to drive the liquor trucks for us. But since we lost so many speaks because of you . . .' Lynch winked at Yale and gave him a sly smile. That pleased Frankie. Although he was well aware of how he had decimated the White Hand's grip on bootlegging as well as the other rackets, Yale had never had a White Hander concede to him that his gang was making the micks hurt.

'So what Pegleg do,' Yale asked, arching his eyebrows, 'he make truck drivers hit men?'

Eddie chuckled. 'That's the size of it, Frankie,' Lynch said. 'You got it figured . . .'

'Wait a minute,' Yale said suddenly. 'How come he don't pick you for job, eh? You pretty good hit man, no?'

247

Lynch nodded and let his face crease with a pained expression. 'Dick isn't talking to me,' he began hoarsely. 'He thinks I've gotten chicken . . .'

'You get chicken!' Yale interrupted with surprise.

'Yeah,' Lynch went on. 'Last week he sent me and Aaron out to do the number of DeAmato . . .'

'Hey, you go on that job?' Yale broke in with even more surprise. The number on James 'Filesy' DeAmato, one of Battista Balsamo's loan sharks, had turned into a debacle for Pegleg Lonergan. He had sent Lynch and Harms to drill a bullet into Filesy's head. But Lynch and Harms ran into a slight problem at the last minute. They trailed DeAmato along Hoyt Street, which was fairly deserted on Sunday nights. Filesy happened to turn around and spot the two assassins on his tail. He took off like an Olympic sprinter and rounded the corner into Fulton Street, where he settled down into a slow jog among the throngs of window shoppers.

'I told Aaron to forget about knocking off Filesy with so many people around, but he didn't listen to me,' Lynch explained to Yale. 'He said he was gonna get him anyway. So he took off by himself –'

Yale began to laugh. 'So fuckin' Harm's gun jammed, right?'

'Yeah, that's what happened,' Lynch replied with a grin.

'And Filesy kick shit out of Aaron and knock him all over Fulton Street, right?' Frank chortled.

'That's the size of it,' Eddie said with a shrug. 'So when I got back to Pegleg at the garage and he heard what happened, he reamed my ass out. He called me yellow and all kinds of shit like that. So I made up my mind that I wasn't gonna work for that sonofabitch anymore.'

'Hey, kid, you mean that?' Yale said, unable to conceal his enthusiasm.

'That's right, Frankie,' Lynch shook his head. 'And . . . well, if you got a job for me . . . I'll work for you.'

'*Madonn*'!' Yale exclaimed. 'I'm gonna have a mick working for me! Hey, wait till I tell Alphonse. He gonna shit!'

Eddie Lynch's eyes opened wide. 'Who did you say?' he asked, puzzled.

'Hey, Eddie, whatsa matter, you don't know Alphonse Capone, eh?' Frankie asked with emphasis on the name.

'I *thought* you said that,' Lynch replied. 'But how's Capone gonna hear about me joining you? You mean you're gonna call him up in Chicago to tell him that?'

'Naw, naw,' Yale said dryly. 'Alphonse is right here in Brooklyn . . . That's why I come here, to fix up Christmas party for him.'

Yale's face suddenly grew somber. 'Holy shit!' he almost groaned. 'I gotta tell Al there ain't gonna be no party for him tomorrow night. That fuckin' Lonergan . . . I gotta set a nice trap for him but I don't want Big Al to be around when the fuckin' shootin' starts.'

Yale stuck a hand out to Lynch. 'Let's shake, you fuckin' Irishman,' he said with a wide smile. 'I think I'm gonna like that you work for me.'

Lynch shook hands with Yale, and then took him by the arm and led him to a table where Fury Argolia and Augie Pisano were seated. He introduced the new member to the startled Black Hands and had Eddie sit at the table.

'You fellas treat Eddie nice,' Yale said. Then, turning to Fury, 'Hey, Angelo, what the fuck you sit there, eh? Get one of your slow-assed waiters to bring my good friend something good to eat. And give him plenty of *vino*, okay?'

Frankie then dashed into Argolia's office and put in a call to Capone's parents' home, where Al and his wife, Mae, were staying. When Scarface got on the line, Yale told him about Pegleg Lonergan's plan to shoot up the Adonis during the Christmas night party.

'Hey, you think that fuckin' one-leg shit is out to get me, eh, Frankie?' Capone roared. He was more amused than angered by the thought that he might be the target of a fading underworld chieftain like Pegleg.

'No, good Al,' Yale put in quickly. 'He don't know you gonna be at party. He just wanna waste my boys . . .'

Frankie gave Capone the details of the assassination plot brought to him by Eddie Lynch. Just as Yale expected, Scarface got a big charge out of hearing that Lynch had switched sides and was now working for the Black Hand.

'So, what I think, good Al,' Yale went on to Capone, 'is you don't come to party tomorrow night because there's gonna be a little shootin', you understand?'

There was a long silence on the other end of the line.

Finally, Capone said, 'Hey, Frankie, in *che direzione e* Adonis Club . . .?'

Frankie was puzzled. 'What you mean, Big Al?' he asked. 'You know where Angelo's restaurant is . . . but . . . but you don't tell me you gonna come if there's gonna be shootin'?'

'You fuckin' right I'm gonna be there,' Capone almost shouted. 'What the fuck you think I am, anyway?'

'But, Alphonse,' Yale said, his tone imploring, 'I don't want nothing happen to you –'

'Hey, Frankie,' Scarface countered, his voice sounding angry. 'How you think I make my way up in Chicago, uh? By hiding out from the action?'

Capone then proceeded to ream Yale out. He reminded Frankie that he had been accompanied to New York by Albert Anselmi and John Scalise, two of the Midwest's ace assassins who had prior experience in coping with Brooklyn White Handers.

'Frankie,' Capone said sharply, 'you go through with plans for party. I want you set up nice tables for everybody and be sure put lotsa decoration on walls. I want this be very good Christmas party, understand. But . . .'

Capone paused, undoubtedly for effect.

'Good Frankie, you listen to me,' Capone continued. 'I don't want you should worry too much about the lameleg and his boys. When I come over tomorrow night, I gonna be there early, maybe seven o'clock. I gonna tell you then how we gonna handle those *fongool* Irish. You hear me what I say, eh?'

Yale heard. And he proceeded with the decorations in the Adonis Club for the Christmas night party. Bright red and green crepe paper was tacked on the walls and holly wreaths were hung; mistletoe dangled from the ceiling over the entire dance floor. The boys had asked Frankie to put up plenty of that evergreen shrub on the ceiling because they didn't want to miss out on the kissing when they danced with the Broadway showgirls . . .

* * *

At seven o'clock Christmas night, Capone, flanked by Anselmi and Scalise, strutted into the Adonis. Yale was already there, and so were Don Giuseppe Balsamo, Augie the Wop, Two-Knife Altierri, Frenchy Carlino, Anthony Yale, Vincenzo Mangano, Chootch Gianfredo, Glass Eye Pelicano, and some fifty-five other Black Handers.

'Good friend Al!' Yale exclaimed as Scarface walked in with his bodyguards. Frankie shook hands with Al, then with Anselmi and Scalise.

Capone looked around the restaurant, studied the decorations and the setups at the tables, then nodded approvingly.

'Very nice, very nice,' he smiled. 'You should be interior decorator, Frankie,' Capone sparkled in approbation of Yale's preparations for the party. Then Scarface looked around the area inside the Adonis Club's foyer near the hatcheck room. His eye caught sight of a dark gray curtain draped loosely on one of the walls. He took hold of the material and gathered it up in his hands until the bare wall behind it was exposed. Capone turned to Anselmi and Scalise.

'Behind here, that's where, *capeesh*?' he said cryptically.

Albert and John nodded, all smiles.

Then Capone turned to Yale. 'Frankie, my good *paisan*. I want you to forget I am here tonight. All I want you should do is relax and have good time. I take care of door, you know what I mean, eh?'

Yale didn't need to have Capone draw diagrams for him. Many years ago, before he had gone off to start his meteoric rise as Chicago's overlord of crime, Scarface had worked at the Adonis Club as a bouncer!

By eight o'clock some sixty-five members of the Black Hand had arrived at the Adonis and the festivities were well underway with the Brooklyn Black Hand's specialty, Old Granddad, cascading into the glasses of the revelers.

At 8:10 Capone, who'd been standing at the door looking out, turned and signalled to Scalise and Anselmi. They left the bar quickly and ducked behind the dark gray curtain. Capone's signal was also picked up by Yale, who was seated at a table with Argolia, Balsamo, and Pisano. The three empty chairs at the table were held for Capone, Anselmi, and Scalise.

Capone's gesture meant that Lonergan and his henchmen had arrived and were about to enter the Adonis.

Pegleg led the way.

'Good evening,' Capone smiled, 'it is my great pleasure to welcome you . . .'

Lonergan did a double take.

Harms, Mahoney, Howard, Hart, and Ferry each came through the door.

A *mirage*, they all thought. It was just someone who looked like Al Capone, scar and all. *No,* they told themselves, *it couldn't be Al Capone. What the hell would the Chicago gangland boss be doing in Brooklyn working as a greeter in the Adonis Club? Ridiculous! That was some guy who only resembled Al Capone.*

Looking at the freckle-faced, red-haired Pegleg with a polite, almost humble gaze, Capone said, 'You and your friends can hang up your coats over there . . .' He pointed to the hatcheck room.

'We ain't here for no party,' Lonergan said gruffly. 'All we wanna do is see somebody inside . . .'

Then he gave Capone a shove. 'Excuse me, you're in the way,' he muttered as he brushed by Capone and led his gang into the main dining room. Every one of the sixty-odd Black Handers seated at the tables around the dance floor had at least one hand under the table. Every one of the hidden hands was gripping a gun. But they all had orders not to shoot – unless Capone and his sidekicks should happen to run into trouble. Otherwise, this was Capone's show all the way.

No sooner had Lonergan and his boys breezed by Capone than they whipped out revolvers and automatics and pointed them at the crowd in the dining room.

'Everybody freeze!' Lonergan yelled.

Fury Argolia, who was watching the action from behind the door of his office, had one hand on the switchplate on the wall. As soon as Lonergan had barked his command, Fury doused the lights in the dining room. As the place fell into darkness, everyone carried out the instructions given to him: dive under the table for cover.

As expected, when the lights went out, the guns in the hands of the Irish assassins blazed away. But they were in a terrible spot. The area they were standing in, just at the edge of the dining room, was still illuminated by the light of a small chandelier. That made them perfect silhouettes for the man who'd greeted them on the way in and his two confederates, who by now had come out from hiding behind the drapes.

Capone, Scalise, and Anselmi, each armed with a .45 automatic, unleashed a fusillade at Pegleg and his five henchmen.

Aaron Harms had the distinction of being the first to fall. He stopped a bullet in the back of his head and two more in his spine.

Needles Ferry and Happy Maloney, though they had also been hit from behind, were able to crawl for cover, as were Lonergan, ragtime Howard, and No Heart Hart, none of whom had caught any lead at first.

They returned the fire at Capone, Anselmi, and Scalise. But they were shooting blindly, for the Chicago killers had moved to the massive mahogany bar and were drilling their bullets from behind it. The only targets Lonergan and his boys had were the blinding flashes from the muzzles of the three automatics barking fire at them from the darkness of the bar.

'Light up! Lights up!' Capone shouted all at once from behind the bar. It was the signal to Fury to flick the dining room lights on for a second or two then turn them off again.

As the lights went on, Al, Albert and John took fresh sightings on the Irishmen and zeroed in with an accurately aimed barrage.

Happy Maloney caught four .45 slugs in the breast – in addition to the two earlier bullets that got him in the right leg. He collapsed to the floor wailing in agony.

Ragtime Howard caught only one, but it had the same effect as the four that ended Happy's life. It plowed into his forehead, tore through the centre of his brain, and opened a hole in the back of his head on the way out. Ragtime didn't utter a sound as he fell.

Three down, three to go.

Lonergan, Ferry and Hart were doomed unless they could find better cover – or, better still, make a break for the door.

No Heart opted for the door; Pegleg decided to find a safer place to hide – behind the grand piano next to the wall beside the hatcheck room.

Neither of these courses of action was open to Needles Ferry. He'd been shot in both legs by the previous volley and couldn't move.

So when Capone shouted a second time, 'Lights up!' and Fury flicked them on, Needles was a sitting duck for Capone and his sharpshooters. Before the place was plunged into darkness again, they picked him off with eighteen bullets.

As the firing squad was unleashing its salvo at Needles, No Heart Hart began his flight for freedom. Busy exterminating Ferry, the gunmen didn't spot Jimmy until he flew out of the dining room and past the blazing guns on his way to the exit.

By the time the trio turned to fire at Hart he was out the door. Even then, the killers unleashed a quick broadside after him, but the bullets merely splintered the thick wooden door. Capone ran around the bar to the door and yanked it open. He poked his head outside.

'Shit! He got away!' he roared.

Then he wheeled around. 'Lights up!' he yelled. 'Leave 'em on this time, ya hear!'

Fury snapped the lights on in the dining room once more.

There was only one remaining live Irishman in the Adonis Club: Pegleg Lonergan, whom Al had seen limp his way into hiding behind the baby grand.

Capone strutted into the dining room, his automatic pointed at the piano, and thundered a challenge to the White Hand chieftain:

'Hey, Pegleg, you *figlio puttana* [son of a bitch whore], come outta there. I wanna take ya outta your misery!'

Lonergan's response was immediate: a rapid succession of explosions from the muzzle of his automatic. But Pegleg's aim, if indeed he was aiming at all, was quite bad. The bullets peppered the wall some eight feet from where Al was standing. They wrenched a Christmas wreath from its hook and it fell to the floor.

'Your aim stinks,' Capone shouted to Lonergan, who was pinned in a small triangle formed by the keyboard side of the piano abutting the wall at a forty-five degree angle.

Scarface took careful aim and triggered three quick shots at

Pegleg. There was a cry of pain. A second later, the automatic Lonergan had been holding dropped to the floor.

Capone took slow, cautious steps toward the piano, his gun still levelled in Pegleg's direction. But Lonergan had disappeared from sight behind the baby grand by now.

As Capone reached the piano, he began to laugh loudly.

'Hey, everybody,' he cried out triumphantly, 'come and see old lame-leg.'

The Black Handers, who had been huddled under the tables, emerged like moles and gathered around the piano.

Everyone began to laugh with Capone. Pegleg Lonergan's body was draped limply over the piano stool. Capone's aim had been unerring. All three bullets he fired had struck Lonergan in the back of the head.

The shooting orgy had lasted barely two minutes. But it was the most eventful two minutes in the five-year struggle for supremacy between the ginzos and micks.

The death of Richard 'Pegleg' Lonergan and his four sidekicks that Christmas night of 1925 effectively ended that brutal, bloody, terrifying period in the history of the underworld.

At the outset, the Irish mobsters were the dominant overlord of the rackets in Brooklyn. In the end, the Italian gangsters had taken over – not only in the Borough of Churches, but in Manhattan as well, although in that latter locale the Irish were never a force to be reckoned with. And with that crushing final blow delivered by Scarface Al Capone as a favor for his good friend Frankie Yale and the Black Hand, a new era had begun.

Other trigger-happy, vicious, and ambitious men followed Frankie Yale as leaders of the *Unione Sicilione*, or the 'Syndicate', as it is most popularly referred to today. Each of those chieftains, in his own time and in his own way, helped to make the organisation a little bigger, a little stronger, a little more ubiquitous in its control of gambling, narcotics, labor racketeering, loansharking, prostitution, pornography, and even such legitimate ventures as garbage collection, hotel and restaurant supply companies, vending machine operations, and numerous other enterprises.

Yet had it not been for Frank Ioele and his gang of ginzos – with the beneficent blessing of the first godfather, Battista Balsamo – the Syndicate might never have materialised and grown into the monolithic structure that it is today: a coast-to-coast network of 'families' who control a far-flung empire.

The war the micks lost to the ginzos in that five-year struggle from 1920 to 1925 wasn't lost only by that band of Irish gangsters; it was a war that all America lost, the costliest conflict in this country's history. Because it gave rise to the most treacherous band of organised crime cutthroats any country in the world has ever encountered. Americans have suffered, and will continue to suffer, interminably, increasingly at the hands of the Mafiosi, who will rise to power after leaders like Yale and Capone have passed on and their reins of power taken by men of equal or greater will and determination to milk Americans for all they're worth.

It was then – and is now – a twentieth century conspiracy vitalised by a nineteenth century mentality that works as effectively today as it did a hundred years ago on that tiny island of the Italian boot . . .

Chapter 20

'We'll See Them Kid . . .'

Sunday, 1 July 1928.
  A bright, sunny, summery day.
  Perfect for a ladies' garden party.
  Ideal weather for a drive in a new car . . .

Two and a half years had gone by since the Black Hand had effectively eliminated the White Hand from the Brooklyn rackets. Frankie Yale had Brooklyn under such absolute control that if any young Turk in the underworld as much as made a ripple in the placid existence of his criminal domain, he was a prime candidate for a sanity test in Kings County Hospital – or its morgue.

Frankie Yale had virtually no troubles in the first half of 1928. There was one very slight irritation, but it had nothing to do with domestic affairs. For several months Alphonse Capone had been bugging Frankie for another favor. For a change it wasn't another act of extermination.

Capone wanted Yale to exert his influence in the *Unione Sicilione* to put one of Al's flunkies at the head of the Chicago chapter.

Since 1924, when Miguel Genna succeeded the late Miguel Merlo as top banana of the Chicago chapter, many changes had taken place in that city's *Unione* leadership. Genna's term in office expired very suddenly in May of 1925, when he contracted a fatal dose of lead poisoning, administered by the boys of George 'Bugs' Moran, who inherited the late Dion O'Bannion's Northside Gang.

With a push from Capone, Sam 'Samoots' Amatuna succeeded Genna. That put Sam Samoots in debt to Al, which meant that Scarface could get all the favors he wanted from the *Union Sicilione*'s Chicago cutthroats.

But after only after nine months in office, Amatuna was incapacitated while getting a hot towel in a barber shop. Bugs Moran's boys splattered Sam Samoot's brains into the barber's hot towel with a well-aimed shotgun blast.

Big Al tried to get himself another patsy for the presidency of the *Union Sicilione*'s Chicago branch: a slippery character named Tony Lombardo, whose olive oil and cheese business camouflaged his nefarious works in the underworld.

But Capone's handpicked candidate had a rival who also aspired to the *Unione*'s leadership: Joseph Aiello, a renegade in the eyes of many Italian mobsters because he had committed the unpardonable sin of forming an alliance with Moran's Irish marauders. Certainly Capone didn't want somebody consorting with the enemy to ascend to the *Unione*'s presidency.

Al appealed to Frankie Yale to exert his influence as national president to get Tony Lombardo elected. But Frankie refused to intercede: he said he wasn't going to endorse either candidate because he didn't want to get involved in 'local politics'.

Capone was infuriated. And that wasn't all that bothered Big Al about Frankie Yale at that time. There was something far more disturbing.

Scarface had a working agreement with Frankie to have his boys oversee liquor shipments landing on Long Island from bootleggers' ships and assuring them safe conduct through New York aboard trucks delivering the alky to Chicago. Yale's only responsibility was to have his boys escort the rigs from the Rockaway docks, through Queens and Brooklyn, and make sure they got safely across the Hudson River for their journey west.

There were no problems until the spring of 1927. Then the hootch going to Capone began getting waylaid. As more and more trucks vanished on their way to Chicago, Big Al, very suspicious by nature, got in touch with James Filesy DeAmato, one of Frankie's boys who had done the number on Aaron Harms on Fulton Street the night the White Hander's gun jammed. Filesy and Capone were pals from Big Al's Brooklyn days. There wasn't any favor Jimmy wouldn't do for his old buddy – including espionage.

'I want you just keep eye on Mr Ioele,' Capone said to DeAmato. 'I think maybe Frankie is giving me screwing, understand?'

Filesy understood. Three weeks passed. One night he called Capone in Cicero.

'You right, Big Al,' DeAmato whispered. 'I seen what happen tonight. Vincenzo Mangano and one of the Mormillo brothers, they grab one of your trucks on Hamilton Avenue and Smith Street and they take booze to Frankie's garage.'

That was mid-June of 1927. A fortnight later, Filesy phoned Scarface in the Chicago suburb where he was headquartered and informed the Big Guy that two of Yale's Black Handers had hijacked another of Capone's liquor-laden trucks. That night he spoke a little too loudly in the phone booth.

At 9:30 p.m. the following Monday, 7 July, Filesy was walking along Twentieth Street on his way to a nearby speakeasy. As he passed in front of No. 123, an old brownstone, a dark sedan screeched to a stop alongside the curb. Six shots exploded from the window nearest the sidewalk. Then the car barrelled away. James Filesy DeAmato, forty-one years old, was dead. The bullets that tore into him were .38s, yet the front of his face looked as though it had been shelled by a howitzer. That was because all six slugs were dumdums.

Sunday, 24 June 1928, Nearly a year had gone by since DeAmato was gunned down. Whether Scarface Al got himself another stool pigeon to keep score of the liquor shipments that Yale was hijacking isn't known. But fewer and fewer trucks were reaching Chicago, and Capone was most unhappy. Even on vacation in

Palm Island, Florida, Scarface couldn't relax thinking about all that hijacked booze. And to top it off, Frankie Yale wasn't lifting a finger to help Capone's pal Tony Lombardo, the olive oil and cheese biggie, to get elected head of the *Union Sicilione* in Chicago.

That Sunday, John Scalise, Albert Anselmi, Fred 'Killer' Burke, and Vincenzo Gibaldi, son of the slain Brooklyn bootlegger who by now had made his reputation in Chicago as a killer for Capone, summoned by the boss, dropped in to see what Big Al wanted.

Scarface entertained his guests royally for two days and nights. From sunup to sundown, they swam in the pool and soaked up the warm Florida sunshine; at night Capone took the boys night clubbing and then put them to bed with voluptuous showgirls from the night-club choruses.

On the morning of Tuesday, 26 June, Scalise, Anselmi, Burke, and Gibaldi were driven in Capone's bulletproof Rolls-Royce to the railroad station in Miami, where they boarded the Chicago-bound Southbound Express.

But when the train pulled into Knoxville, Tennessee, the four got off the train and carried their heavy suitcases to a Buick dealership. There they plunked down $2,040 in cash for a used, but low-mileage, black 1926 sedan. They put their suitcases into the trunk and drove directly to Brooklyn. They got themselves lodgings late that Saturday night in the Hotel Bossert.

For Mrs Bertha Kaufman that 1 July dawned with the promise that it was going to be a lovely Sunday: the bright sunshine, gentle breeze, and temperature heading into the low 80s, augered the perfect day she had prayed for. She was giving a reception for her thirteen-year-old son's Bar Mitzvah.

A few minutes before four that afternoon, the ladies in their party finery began gathering in the garden, which fronts along Forty-Fourth Street just east of Ninth Avenue. A knee-high row of privets separated the side of Mrs Kaufman's garden from the sidewalk and street it bordered.

A mile away, Frankie Yale was standing in front of the dresser mirror in his bedroom, trying to tilt his cream-colored Panama hat on his head at the precise, jaunty angle which pleased him. He was dressed as if he were going to the Easter Parade: a gray lightweight linen summer suit, white oxfords, and a four-carat diamond ring on the third finger of his right hand which was a gift from Al Capone. In addition, he was holding up his pants with a belt that Scarface had also given him, the buckle of which sported seventy-five diamond chips. Capone was in the practice of giving such belts only to those whom he respected and admired very much.

After Frankie had adjusted the Panama he walked from the bedroom to the living room, where his wife was nursing their year-old daughter Angelina.

'Hey, Lucy,' Yale called out. 'I gotta go now. You take care yourself, all right?'

'When you gonna be back, eh Frankie?' Lucy wanted to know.

'All I wanna do,' Yale said, 'is drive my damn car around and find out what else is wrong. You know I take it back to dealer tomorrow to fix the goddam windows . . .'

Yale had received delivery of the dark-coffee-colored brand-new 1928 Lincoln coupe a few days earlier, but the dealer had goofed. Frankie ordered the car bulletproofed. Great pains were taken in Detroit to put an inch-thick shield of armor on the body. But one detail had been overlooked: they hadn't installed bullet-proof windows. Frankie was due to take the car back to the dealer early the next morning to have that oversight corrected.

Frankie drove a few blocks to a Bay Ridge speakeasy on Fourteenth Avenue and Sixty-fifth Street with James 'Sam Brown' Caponi, who was driving the new 1928 Lincoln.

'Hey, boss,' Caponi said. 'This here car is terrific. Other than the windows being not bulletproof, I think it's perfect . . .'

'You might be right, Jimmy,' Yale said. 'But after we get a coupla drinks I want to drive it and see how I like the way she handle.'

At the bar, just after Yale and Caponi called for a second round of drinks, the phone rang. The bartender answered.

'Hey, Frankie,' said the barkeeper, 'it's for you.'

The voice on the other end was short, cryptic: 'something happened to Lucy . . . Come home quickly –'

'What happen to my wife?' Yale asked in panic.

'Just come home, right away.' The caller hung up.

Frankie dropped the phone and hurried out of the saloon for his car. Caponi fell on his heels and asked, 'Frankie, what happened – where ya going?'

'It's all right Jimmy . . . I gotta get home right away . . . You take it easy . . . I see you later . . .'

'Hey boss!' called Caponi, 'let me drive you –'

'No need . . . I handle this okay . . .'

The plans that Frankie Yale had outlined to test his new car's road worthiness that Sunday afternoon went awry. Now he was barreling toward New Utrecht Avenue on his way home to see what was wrong with his wife. Had he had the presence of mind to phone his house from the saloon, he would have learned from her that she was perfectly fine. But he became so uptight when he got the call that all his senses were dulled.

But not so dulled that when he stopped for a red traffic light, he didn't notice the black Buick sedan behind him. The car may not have disturbed Yale so much as its occupants: four men, two in the front seat, two in the back.

It shouldn't be hard to guess what must actually have flashed through Frankie's head as the Buick tailed him doggedly after the light changed. He turned the corner into Forty-fourth Street so sharply that he almost lost control of the car.

The Buick gained speed and was closing in.

In seconds, the Buick pulled alongside the Lincoln. Up ahead, children were playing kick-the-can in the middle of the street in front of 957 Forty-fourth Street. Suddenly the children saw the cars bearing down on them. Screaming, they scattered off the pavement to the safety of the sidewalks on both sides of the street. The cars tore past them.

The children's cries attracted the ladies at Mrs Kaufman's garden party, who turned to see what was happening. The Lincoln and Buick were now nose to nose, and suddenly there was a loud, ear-splitting blast. It was the explosion from the muzzle of a shotgun sticking out the front window of the Buick. The shot burst into the driver's side of the Lincoln and the man behind the wheel lurched forward.

In that same instant, there was another series of blasts, loud and steady, spewing from the muzzle of a weapon pointed out the back window of the Buick. The gun had an ungainly circular cylinder attached to its long barrel just in front of the trigger. The fire from that piece was an unrelenting *rat-tat-tat-tat*.

It was a sub-machine gun, and this was the first time in the history of the New York underworld that such a weapon had been used in a gangland killing. Until then, the sub-machine gun had been employed exclusively in Chicago's mob wars.

And though there were four assassins in the car that came abreast of Frankie Yale's Lincoln that Sunday afternoon, there has never been any question which of them triggered the deadly fusillade from the sub-machine gun. The man who squeezed off those bullets was Machine Gun Jack McGurn, who, as a youth of nineteen and known then as Vincenzo Gibaldi, was pushed into his career as a killer in Al Capone's gang by none other than Frankie Yale.

As Yale slumped over the steering wheel, blood pouring from a countless number of bullet holes in his head, face, neck, and upper torso, the Lincoln went out of control. It veered all at once to the right and mounted the sidewalk.

By now the children on the street and the ladies at the garden party were shrieking hysterically. The black Buick never slowed down as it roared toward the corner. There was a piercing squeal of tires, the car made a sharp right turn into Ninth Avenue and disappeared from view.

Meanwhile, the careening Lincoln skirted past the privets alongside Mrs Kaufman's garden and rammed into the stone stoops of the house at No. 923. The impact spun the car almost completely around and brought it smashing into the brick front wall of the house. The force with which the vehicle hit sprung open the driver's door and Frankie Yale's limp, bleeding body was catapulted out of the car. It landed on the sidewalk not far from the feet of the terrified women in Mrs Kaufman's garden.

As spectacular and gory as were so many of the killings that Frankie Yale had masterminded and pulled off, few matched the high drama and unique horror attendant upon his own assassination.

It was a virtuoso performance by the clique of killers Al Capone had sent, a performance that surpassed any extermination Frankie Yale himself had orchestrated in the many years of his career as the dreaded chieftain of the Black Hand gang.

Frankie Yale's funeral on Thursday, 5 July, was no less spectacular than his bloody career and violent death. It was a send-off of such splendour and magnitude that to this day it stands unmatched by any other gangland funeral.

The $15,000 silver coffin that carried Frankie's remains to his final resting place was borne from St Rosalia's Church to Holy Cross Cemetery aboard an open hearse with a podium.

Banks upon banks of funeral wreaths surrounded and covered the casket. Hundreds upon hundreds of floral arrangements were stacked aboard twenty-three flower cars. They led a cortege of one hundred and ten freshly simonised black Cadillac limousines and two-hundred and fifty passenger cars carrying many of the ten thousand mourners who turned out for the funeral through Brooklyn's streets. It was like the last ride for a head of state.

Ironically, these could not be arranged by Frankie's own funeral parlor, nor could he even be waked there. His director, Albert Balestro, the brother of the late Anna, one of the victims of the Stauch's Dance Hall shootout, didn't have anywhere near the expertise or facilities to handle the exequies in the proportions demanded for his late and greatly lamented boss.

So Balestro had entrusted the send-off to the Boyertown Funeral Home in downtown Brooklyn, which acquitted itself with such resplendence that all major gangland funerals held since have been cast in the mold of Yale's unforgettable send-off, though none have ever equalled its scope and size – or even remotely approached its sentimentality.

A special mourner was Denny Meehan's widow Peggy, who was shot the night her husband was killed beside her in bed. Standing at the corner of Fourth Avenue and Sixth Street as the cortege passed, Peggy Meehan stepped away from the crowds lining the sidewalk, darted into the street, and spat on the fifteen-thousand-dollar casket!

But perhaps the greatest single show of sentiment was exhibited by the round-faced man with the light brown hair, standing at graveside just as the casket was being lowered into its waterproof, airtight concrete vault. Tears were in his eyes and his lips were trembling as he stared sadly at the ribbon on the floral bed which he had ordered for the casket. It read:

WE'LL SEE THEM, KID ...

That was an oath of vengeance whose genesis even predates the Mafioso's ancient code of *omerta*.

But against whom was the vengeance sworn?

Or, to whom was he referring when the young man murmured, 'Frankie, Frankie, how anybody do this to you I don't understand ... such a waste, such a shame, so sad ... I wanna know who do this to you ...'

The heavyset man standing next to him and also wearing a black tie and black arm band on the left sleeve of his suit jacket, turned to the teary-eyed mourner and said, 'I feel so sorry for this poor fella ... my heart is all broke up. Come, we go. I can't stand no more ... this too much for me.'

Al Capone took hold of Machine Gun Jack McGurn's arm and led him away, followed closely behind by Fred Killer Burke, John Scalise, and Albert Anselmi, all attired very properly for that solemn occasion in deepest black mourning suits.

Chapter 21

Scarface Al Capone: King of the Underworld

Once Al Capone had eliminated Frankie Yale as an uninvited and unwanted partner in his liquor shipment operations, Scarface received the shipments in Chicago in the same condition they arrived on the rum-running cutters and off-loaded onto his trucks. James 'Jimmy' Crissali made certain that there were no more hijackings of the Big Guy's rigs.

Anthony 'Little Augie Pisano' Carfano had succeeded to the leadership of the Black Hand which Frankie Yale had abdicated so precipitately. And by now it had been four years since Don Giuseppe Balsamo had begun relinquishing his daily duties as the godfather. Although his counsel was still sought by Little Augie on matters relating to the gang's activities, Battista Balsamo was decreasingly looked upon as a vital cog in the Black Hand's operations. He had, by his own desires, turned himself out to pasture.

One thing was certain: Scarface's position as the czar of Chicago's underworld had totally solidified. The way he had managed to eliminate his rivals for leadership of the Windy City's rackets greatly enhanced his stake in the Midwest underworld, and he was now, in that year of 1929, the undisputed king of crime.

It was late 1930.

'I will withdraw my men from the work of seizing control of labor unions if I will be assured that I won't be bothered in the beer business in Cook County. I will give up on the charge of vagrancy if I have assurance that the charge will be quashed immediately. I will go to Florida and control my business from there.'

Alphonse Capone preferred not to label this statement an ultimatum, but a 'kingly message', to Chief Justice John P. McGoorty and other officials of Chicago's Criminal Court.

And indeed Capone was very much the king – of the underworld – with undisputed power and income beyond his wildest dreams, an iron-handed, cruel, and hard law violator who thought nothing of ordering the killing of friends and foes alike if they happened to be in his way.

Al Capone had become a legendary figure: Public Enemy Number One – and he was considered beyond the reach of the law as he reigned over the vast Chicago underworld and its monarchy of booze, vice, and racketeering.

Such was the status of this potentate of the three-hundred-million-a-year crime empire over which he ruled that it surprised no one when he delivered his 'kingly message' to Justice McGoorty. It was typical of Capone's boastfulness and bravado.

Even the Federal Government was powerless to act against this all-powerful potentate of the rackets world. When they asked Capone what his income was, he just grinned. He could convert his kingdom into an easy twenty-five million of cold cash anytime he chose, yet he didn't pay tax on a thousandth of that amount.

The story of Al Capone is a chronicle of violence and death – a nine-year war waged by a standing army of five hundred grim-faced hoodlums through almost the entire era of the roaring twenties, which elevated the Capone crime empire into its incredible position of power in the 1930s.

If there was one thing that established Capone's unchallenged dominance of Chicago's rackets it was the horrible carnage of the St Valentine's Day massacre of 1929. In one fell swoop, Scarface wiped out five of George Bugs Moran's top aides in the North Side gang and literally left his chief rival in crime a general without a staff.

The genesis of this extraordinary genius of the underworld was hardly indicative of the inordinate heights he would attain as America's most infamous gangster. Born in Brooklyn in 1899 of hard-working Italian immigrant parents, Alphonse was a clod in elementary educational circles. He managed to reach the fourth grade, but never saw the fifth.

A big, bulky, blockbusting youth who became a formidable street fighter, Al had one talent that gave promise of a decent future: he was a sandlot baseball pitcher. But lack of control prevented him from achieving his ambition to play in the major leagues.

He turned to the pool halls and alleys and became a gutter fighter. At age nineteen, he picked on the wrong guy, a merchant seaman, in a public dance hall; the seaman pulled a knife and sliced Al down the left side of his face from the tip of his eyebrows to the end of his square jaw.

No whiskers ever grew through this cyanotic scar, and Capone, ever vain about his appearance, made it a habit to shave three or four times a day and keep his face coated with flesh-colored talcum. He also promoted the legend that he suffered the wound with the army in France during World War I, but the truth is he never served a minute in the military.

Capone may not have risen from the level of gutter punk if it hadn't been for his friendship with Johnny Torrio, the torpedo-for-hire with the pop eyes and pursed mouth which made him look like he was always surprised. Fifteen years older than Capone, Torrio was a product of the tough East River gang in New York City in which he rose to leadership as a terrorist, a bomber, and killer.

It was easy to see why the then-boss of Chicago's early Prohibition Days crime cartel 'Big Jim' Colosimo would want Torrio to move to the Midwest's capital city and into a position of importance in the gang. The message came from his second cousin, who was married to Big Jim Colosimo.

Torrio soon saw the great potential that Chicago offered for a smart gang chieftain. Colosimo, in Torrio's view, wasn't smart. What was needed, the pop-eyed transplanted Brooklyn hood concluded, was organisation. As things stood, there were a half dozen loosely federated gangs in the city: Dion O'Bannion, the foppish little flower shop owner, George Bugs Moran, the Genna and Aiello families. Colosimo, of course, was top dog. But he had amassed so much wealth that his only desire now was to lay back and enjoy his ill-gotten riches. More than anything he wanted peace.

Not Torrio. He bided his time, waiting for the opportunity to move in. That opportunity came after Big Jim divorced Torrio's cousin and married a young and beautiful girl named Dale Winter. Torrio decided it was time to move in. He plotted the conspiracy with O'Bannion, Moran, the Gennas, the Aiellos, the Capone brothers, and other gangland overlords.

On the night of 11 May 1920, Big Jim sat at a table near the entrance of his gaudy café at 2126 South Wabash Avenue. A great diamond sparkled on his right hand as he deftly rotated a fork against a spoon, winding spaghetti. Next to him was a bottle of the best red wine in the house.

Jim didn't seem to have a worry in the world. He knew if things got hot, he had only to nod and Torrio, now known as 'Terrible John', and Al Capone, who had moved up as an enforcer in the mob, would be there in a flash with their gats ready to belch a deadly dose of lead at anyone Colosimo fingered.

After the meal, Big Jim seemed very content. He folded his hands over his paunch and surveyed his café. The orchestra had just finished the last number and was putting away its instruments; the bar was serving the last round. It was closing time.

'Well,' Colosimo turned to his manager, 'things look under control. I guess I'll take off and give the pleasure of my company to the bride.'

Jim got up and walked into the lobby. As he neared one of the phone booths there was a deafening roar. In the next instant his body heaved and convulsed, then tottered to the floor. Blood from a single bullet wound in his head formed an instant puddle of crimson on the white tiles.

The overlord of vice, the political boss of the district, the *padrone* of the Italians – Big Jim – was dead!

The question of who killed Jim Colosimo was never answered, although police hauled in nearly twenty mobsters for questioning, including Torrio, the Capone brothers, and Frankie Yale.

Torrio was now the boss and he quickly organised the leeches of iniquity into a massive, formidable organisation that became known as 'The Syndicate'. The operation spread out into the suburbs of Cicero, Stickney, Chicago Heights, Western Springs, and Melrose Park, among others.

In these outposts, what once had been quiet neighborhood speakeasies took on an entire new complexion. Gambling in the back and girls upstairs were introduced for a vast new source of income to Torrio's organisation.

But bootleg hootch was the biggest money-maker. The stuff the mob produced wholesaled for $5 a gallon and from each of a dozen or more stills that he operated the income came to roughly $1.8 million a year.

Torrio managed to get control of these outlets, many of them breweries built in the pre-Volstead Act days, by making deals with the mobs around town. Ruling gunmen of the smaller groups allied themselves with Colosimo's heir.

But the peace that Torrio sought to maintain by coming to terms with rival gangsters didn't work effectively. Although there was money aplenty for all, it seemed that many fingers were near triggers. Smaller crooks and some bigger ones thought they could make a killing by hijacking Torrio's trucks.

The net result was the opening of the beer murders, destined to take five hundred lives. It was the beginning of the Nine Years' War.

In 1922 Al Capone ran into his first serious encounter with police when they tried to get him for the murder of Joe Howard, a one-time petty criminal who ventured into hijacking and whose payoff was six bullets in the head.

The attempt to prosecute Capone was as futile as were to be many future efforts to pin killings on him.

Now that he was firmly entrenched as the Number Two man in The Syndicate, Al completed the Capone family migration to Chicago by sending for his mother, Theresa, and setting her up in splendid accommodations at 7244 South Prairie Avenue.

But Capone wasn't completely off the hook in Howard's murder. Word drifted into the State Attorney's office about some behind-the-scenes events that led up to the shooting. It seems that Jacob M. 'Little Jack' Guzik, the money handler for Torrio's mob, had argued with Joe Howard in a saloon, and that Guzik ran and told Capone.

Big Al went looking for Howard, found him in a saloon at 2300 South Wabash, and tried to tell him off.

'Listen, you fat, greasy pimp,' Howard is supposed to have said to Al, 'you ain't man enough to talk to me. Why every broad you've ever taken to bed laughs when she thinks about it. You're a stinking lover. You're not even potent, you pig ...'

Capone was never one to extend himself for accuracy with a gun, but in this case the autopsy on Howard's body showed unerring perfection.

A young Assistant State Attorney, William McSwiggin, saw the way Capone got off the hook with the police and Chicago District Attorney's office and he wanted to see Al swinging by the neck from the end of a rope. That was a statement that Scarface didn't like – and wouldn't forget. He swore he'd get McSwiggin.

By 1924 The Syndicate had Greater Chicago in its grip. Uniformed policemen were serving as guards against holdup men at the Mob's gambling joints and motorcycle cops were convoying the underworld's beer trucks to prevent hijackers from taking them.

The politicians also were in the Mob's hip pocket. Rarely did a politico rap the Mob in a campaign speech; rarer still did elected officials castigate the underworld.

During election time in the suburb of Cicero in 1924, the honest people of the community put up a reform ticket pledged to run the gangsters out of town. A reform movement poll watcher's statement tells the story:

I was walking from my home to my voting place when a car pulled up. Three men jumped out, and one of them hit me in the face with the flat side of a pistol. I came to in a basement with eight other reform people. All of us had been beaten. They kept us in the basement until the polls closed. I'm thankful they didn't murder us all.

Anthony J. Czarnecki, head of the Chicago Board of Election Commissioners, deputised one hundred Chicago policemen as sheriffs and sent them into Cicero to protect the citizens. Toward the end of the day of Mob violence, two of these cops, Sergeants William Cusack and William Riley, were on patrol in their cruiser when they spotted three suspicious characters near a polling place. They recognised two of them as Frank Capone and Charlie Fischetti, brother and cousin of Al Capone.

The hoodlums spotted the policemen. Fischetti ran into a vacant lot, tossed his revolver away, then put his hands over his head. Frank pulled two .38s, one in each hand, and fired away at the policemen. He emptied both guns at them, but only one bullet did any damage: the one fired by one of the sergeants through Capone's heart!

Fischetti was taken without trouble, while the other man disappeared. Asked who the other head-buster was, Charlie replied:

'Gee, I wouldn't be able to tell you that. I don't know him. He stopped us to ask for a match . . .'

What were they doing in Cicero, Fischetti was asked.

'Frank and I were thinking of opening up a restaurant out here, and we were looking for a location.'

Frank's funeral was a send-off such as none that Chicago had ever seen before. He was laid out in a $20,000 bronze casket and Dion O'Bannion sent three thousand rosebuds; as many as could be were strewn over the Capone floor to form a carpet and the rest were stacked on the lawn.

The mourners lined up for two blocks; among them were aldermen, police officials, judges, state legislators, and congressmen. The cortege to Mount Olivet Cemetery consisted of one hundred shiny black limousines and every important mobster in Chicago.

'It's a disgrace!' complained Assistant State Attorney McSwiggin. Al Capone vowed that this remark about his brother's final journey to the unknown would not go unpunished.

Al was also infuriated by a remark that the grapevine had credited to Dion O'Bannion during one of his drinking sprees with one of his sycophant gunmen, Louie Alterie: O'Bannon reportedly had said that Capone was a 'gutless wonder'.

On 10 November 1924 O'Bannion got it from Frankie Yale.

And then, with Hymie Weiss's mysterious disappearance and Torrio's own self-exile to Brooklyn, there was no one other than Scarface Al Capone to fit into the vacated Mob thrones.

Capone was the natural heir to the decimated crime empires that had been headed by Torrio and O'Bannion. Big Al stepped in and, with no opposition whatsoever, declared the separate mobs now were one, and anointed himself as the king.

Although technically Al Capone's residence was the family home, shared with his mother and other brother, Ralph, Scarface also established a suite with inordinately fancy appointments, at a Twenty-second Street hotel, and set up an apartment in The Hawthorne Hotel in Cicero.

There he could invite the youngest and best-looking heads among the coterie of prostitutes who worked for him in the nearby brothel capital of Stickney. Al's reputation as a ladies' man never amounted to much. What the late Joe Howard had said about Scarface apparently had some substance: he was a lousy lover. That was the talk among the girls who'd been called for command performances before their big boss.

But there was one girl, a pretty, petite, dark-haired Irish doll who would never have any unkind word to say about Al. She was the girl Capone married and who bore him his only child, Sonny. Mrs Capone was never seen in public, but to say that she didn't know about her husband's extra-marital infidelities is another thing. How could she help but know after Big Al had contracted syphilis?

Of all the forces of good which had tried to combat The Syndicate through its growth from infancy to giantism under the aegis of Colosimo, Torrio, and finally Al Capone, none was more persistent than the voluble Henry C. Hoover, a young Congregational minister.

The mobsters had slugged, clubbed, terrorised, and shot their way to triumph over the reformers in the previous year's elections, and they believed they had defeated the do-gooders permanently. But not the Rev. Hoover.

Each Sunday from his pulpit Hoover deplored the organised rackets of prostitution, gambling, bootlegging, and general corruption, as well as killing. Capone stole his way into a rear pew one Sabbath and listened to one of Hoover's fire-and-brimstone sermons. He left laughing.

On Kentucky Derby Day of May 1925, Hoover organised a vigilante group composed of American Legion posts, Kiwanis Clubs, Parent Teacher Associations, and varied church groups. They raided Capone's notorious Smoke Shop on the ground floor of the Hawthorne Hotel in Cicero, which was overflowing with the betting gentry on the bookies' biggest day of the year.

The raiders overturned gambling tables, tore racing sheets, scattered decks of playing cards over the floor, and demolished furniture. The flunkies in the place couldn't believe their eyes. Capone, who was upstairs, was summoned and he came tearing down to challenge the Rev. Hoover.

'Listen, Reverend,' Big Al growled, 'why don't you lay off me? If you let up on me in Cicero, I'll get out of Stickney.'

'No bargains!' Hoover thundered. 'We are going to destroy you and your kind!'

The minister and his vigilantes finally retreated, leaving the place a shambles. Capone would not forget this incident because in time it would come back to haunt him as no other single episode in his crime-scarred career.

Capone became a great sports lover and seldom missed the important prize fights or football games; he had eight box seats for all Chicago Cubs and White Sox games; he ate in the best restaurants and his ten-dollar tips had the waiters licking his boots.

Wherever he went Capone had a coterie of bodyguards as no mobster anywhere in the country could command. They were the meanest, deadliest torpedoes extant, among them Machine Gun Jack McGurn (Vincenzo Gibaldi) and George 'Shotgun' Ziegler, the college graduate and football hero who in time would leave

Capone's employ to toil for the frightful gang of Ma Baker and Alvin Karpis. Ziegler's alias was Fred Goetz: his superior intelligence and higher educational training earned him the nickname of 'The Brain'.

In 1926 Capone gave himself the kind of 'class' no mobster before him had acquired. He bought a big white stucco and stone mansion on Palm Island off a causeway from Miami to Miami Beach. This was his winter retreat. He had a twenty-foot-high solid wall built around the place. He installed an Olympic-size swimming pool and a tropical garden.

This was also the year that Assistant State Attorney McSwiggin, the prosecutor who vowed to see Al Capone hanging by the neck, met The Syndicate's violence in a most unexpected way. McSwiggin was a West Side youth who had worked his way through law school; he was the son of a veteran police sergeant.

McSwiggin had known gangsters along the West Madison Street section of Chicago, and he had even attended high school with several boys who later went into the underworld. On the night of 27 April McSwiggin made a surprise appearance in Cicero with four notorious gangland figures: Klondike and Mike O'Donnell and Doherty and John Duffy. Together they walked into John Madigan's saloon at 56134 West Roosevelt Road, where Klondike's beer flowed despite Capone's ultimatum that Madigan buy Al's brew or face the dire bottom line of having the joint closed permanently. Madigan stared in disbelief: the prosecutor was with the prosecuted!

After they had downed a few steins, the drinkers departed. As they stepped out on the sidewalk a terrifying *rat-a-tat* erupted. Madigan and the patrons in the saloon recognised the unmistakable clatter of machine guns. They ducked for cover.

One bullet after another ripped into McSwiggin. A burst caught Duffy and another tore into Doherty. The three went down. Duffy and Doherty tried to get to their feet – but another relentless stream of deadly .45s sliced them almost in half.

As the black limousine containing the three machine gunners barreled away, the O'Donnell's, who had escaped the massacre because they were not in the direct line of fire aimed at the other three, leaped to their feet from the sidewalk, picked up McSwiggin's body, and drove it to a prairie farther west.

Chicago was horrified by the assassination of its top crime fighter. The utter viciousness of the attack – more than two hundred bullets had been fired – indicated only one possible culprit: Al Capone's gang. A dragnet was spread for Capone, but he was nowhere to be found.

There could be no question that this was his work. For now Scarface had practically every important 'chopper' in gangland working for him. Besides Machine Gun Jack McGurn and Fred the Brain Goetz, the royal execution staff included such notorious triggermen as Claude Maddox, Tony Accardo, and Tony Capezio.

Sergeant Anthony McSwiggin, the slain prosecutor's father, was prostrate with grief, but not frightened to speak out against the man everyone suspected of the awesome crime.

'Al Capone killed my son,' McSwiggin said. 'I know – I have inside information from the gang.'

The furor among judges, prosecutors, police, and citizens of Chicago reached a deafening pitch. McSwiggin's death was called evidence of a super-government of criminals. And even as these charges were levelled, a communiqué was received from Capone dictating the terms under which he would submit to interrogation.

Authorities had no choice but to accept. They met Scarface in his armoured car parked on the Indiana-Illinois state line.

'Of course I didn't kill McSwiggin!' Big Al insisted. 'I liked the kid. Why should I kill him? The day before he was knocked off he was at my place and I gave him a bottle of Scotch for his old man.

'If I wanted to knock him off I could have done it then. I'm no squawker, but get this: I paid McSwiggin plenty and I got what I paid for! And I got a runout because some saphead copper was likely to take a shot at me just to get promoted.'

So Al rode away to freedom once more.

With the flow of gold running record high and profits hitting astronomical levels, Al Capone was soon bitten by the bug that had visited Big Jim Colosimo and Johnny Torrio while they were riding atop the heap of mob wealth: he suddenly decided to do away with the internecine wars.

There were still a few small-time mobs operating in pockets of the area where The Syndicate was not in total and absolute control. Now and then there were shootouts between Capone's boys and those minor rivals. The score was heavily in favor of Big Al's side, but he felt that even these occasional flare-ups should not occur. So he called a peace powwow with the various gang chiefs.

The gathering was in the Sherman Hotel. Gathered along the banquet board were Joe Saltis, grinning at his enemy, Spike O'Donnell; Frank McErlane watching Ralph Sheldon; Klondike and Mike O'Donnell, and others. The pieces were in the checkroom, in topcoat pockets, by the terms Capone laid out for the conference.

'Let us have peace!' said the speaker, authoritatively. 'Everybody must stay in his own territory and keep fingers off triggers: North Side for Weiss, Loop and South Side and West Side for Capone, Southwest Side for Saltis.'

Capone was speaking; the men-at-arms in the underworld heard – and agreed. There was going to be peace.

But as part of the agreement, Weiss and Vincent 'Schemer' Drucci demanded that Capone hand over Albert Anselmi and John Scalise, one-time Genna artillerymen who had deserted for Capone's ranks.

Capone's blue-gray eyes narrowed. 'Give you two of my best men for slaughter?' he roared. 'What'sa the matter, you crazy? I wouldn't do that to a yellow dog!'

Capone was talking to Tony Lombardo, one of his top henchmen, who was ordered to bring the king's reply to Weiss and Drucci.

Weiss was furious. 'So that's the way Capone wants to play,' he told Bugs Moran. 'I think we should teach Al a lesson.'

Not too long afterwards, Weiss and Moran were driving through Cicero and suddenly spotted Capone riding not in his bullet-proof limo but an ordinary sedan. They pulled alongside and let go with automatics. Bullets streaked past Scarface as he dropped to the floor and reached for his own rod. But he never got the chance to use it.

The car crashed into a parked coupe and the assassins were

gone. Capone's car had gone out of control because its chauffeur, Tony Ross, was drilled through the brain by the .45s.

Less than a week later, while Capone was dining in the Hawthorne Hotel Restaurant with two friends, eight cars stopped in front. The doors opened and several gunmen leaped out, dropped to one knee on the pavement, and poured a volley of lead from tommy guns into the front of the restaurant. The spray missed Capone and his friends, who dropped to the floor. The only casualties were a man and woman, slightly wounded on the street.

By the time the cops got there, the gunmen were gone and the glaziers were replacing the shattered windows of the restaurant. Capone was questioned.

'My guess is that some disgruntled customer who didn't like the food did it,' was his response.

On the late afternoon of 11 October, Weiss left a courtroom in the county building where he had been attending a trial for the murder of Mitters Foley, one of the town's lowlier hoods. With him were Patrick Murray and Sam Pellar, his henchmen; Benjamin Jacobs, an investigator for the State Attorney's office, and W. W. O'Brien, a lawyer. Together they drove to Superior Street enroute to Hymie's office above the flower shop where O'Bannion had been rubbed out. They stepped out of the car in front of Holy Name Cathedral and into a blistering fusillade of machine gun bullets.

Hymie Weiss fell clutching his chest. Above the clanging of a street car gong came more bursts of gunfire. Pellar and Jacobs toppled over, wounded. Murray also went down, dead.

The bullets had also taken their toll on the cathedral. The words 'At the name of Jesus . . .' were obliterated by a spray of bullets.

Little Hymie had hardly been put into the peaceful embrace of Mother Earth before Capone called another peace conference.

Al, absent from the fête, was represented by Tony Lombardo, who had succeeded Mike Merlo as head of the *Unione Sicilione*. Another Capone aide, Maxie Eisen, aided in setting forth the king's commands.

Drucci and his gang would have the entire North Side. The

South Side would be divided between Joe Saltis, Ralph Sheldon, and Spike O'Donnell. Klondike O'Donnell's gang was to share in West Side profits. Capone would handle most of the West Side, Cicero, and the greater part of the eastern section of the South Side, and the Loop.

'And, of course,' Maxie said sternly, 'the Big Fellow says there will be no more assassinations, no more rides. The hunting season on the boys in the beer rackets is hereby declared closed.'

There was a chorus of 'Okay!'

There were smiles and handshakes, everybody went away singing 'peace'.

But Schemer Drucci, now the head of the O'Bannion mob, didn't like to be told where to operate. He also felt that if he could succeed where Weiss and O'Bannion had failed – in rubbing out Capone – he could very easily become the king.

So he followed Al down to Hot Springs, where the Big Fellow had gone to shed some of his poundage, and in the tradition of O'Bannion and Weiss sent a few bullets Scarface's way. And as O'Bannion and Weiss had before him, he missed.

At election time police were given special instructions to keep the hoods away from the polls. And that was the idea when Sergeant Daniel Healy removed Drucci from a North Side street and rode him to headquarters for questioning. During the ride, the blast of a gun reverberated in the car.

Drucci was dead and Sergeant Healy was holding the smoking pistol.

'I killed him,' admitted Healy. 'He called me a punk copper and reached for my gun. I got it first.'

A coroner's jury freed Healy quickly. Now the third of the embattled North Side gang's chieftains had met sudden death. But this time Capone sat back nonchalantly and cackled:

'Well, that's one rap they ain't gonna pin on me.'

Below the surface, trouble was stirring for Capone. It wasn't the type of trouble he was accustomed to from his mob rivals: it was happening in Washington D.C., where President Calvin Coolidge decided on some drastic action against the mob invasion of Chicago. He appointed George E. Q. Johnson, a

Chicago lawyer, to be U.S. Attorney for the Northern District of Illinois – and to war on mobsters.

At the same time, Frank J. Loesch, a former army colonel and outspoken civic leader, rounded up a group of businessmen, bankers, and industrialists and with their contributions headed up a group known as the Secret Six. The organisation hired a crew of investigators with one objective in their sights: get Capone on a murder rap.

Simultaneously the FBI came into Chicago, headed by a young University of Illinois graduate, Elliott Ness. His orders were to harass and, if possible, to smash The Syndicate. With a crew of eager young agents, Ness was soon beginning to cost Capone and some of the other mobsters thousands of dollars a week in wrecked alcohol stills, confiscated beer shipments, and other similar damaging acts.

In Capone's humble opinion, no man was without his price. He sent an emissary named Short Pants Campagna to buy off Ness with $50,000 wrapped in a newspaper.

'Tell Scarface to shove it!' Ness told Campagna.

Meanwhile, a scheme had been devised by a branch of government that the underworld had never taken seriously: the Internal Revenue Service. For a good many years the IRS had been fighting a losing battle with gamblers, bookies, rum-runners, beer racketeers, and other operators in the shadow world of crime who paid little or no taxes on their enormous windfall profits.

All the agents could do was observe the business the mobsters didn't draw up on even rough estimates of the take. So the IRS would put the arm on some stooge of the big shot behind the racket. He'd fork over a few hundred dollars and Uncle Sam would be happy to have pocketed a small percentage of what was coming to him.

But that method didn't sit well with Arthur P. Madden, as the new head of the Intelligence Division in the Chicago office of the IRS. A veteran of government service and a genius at numbers (he could see instantly the kind of dough Capone was raking in from his many rackets), Madden decided to target in on the Mob's higher-ups. He decided to do a number on Big Al's brother Ralph – a testing of the waters.

United Press International, Inc.

Murder Inc.'s Arthur "Dutch Schultz"
Flegenheimer, 1934

Collections of the Municipal Archives of the City of New York

The body of Abe "Kid Twist" Reles after his
plunge from the Half Moon Hotel in Coney
Island, 1941

Frank Costello, 1946

Albert Anastasia at the Kefauver Hearings, 1951

Charles "Lucky" Luciano, 1958

Vito Genovese brought into Federal Court,
June 8, 1958

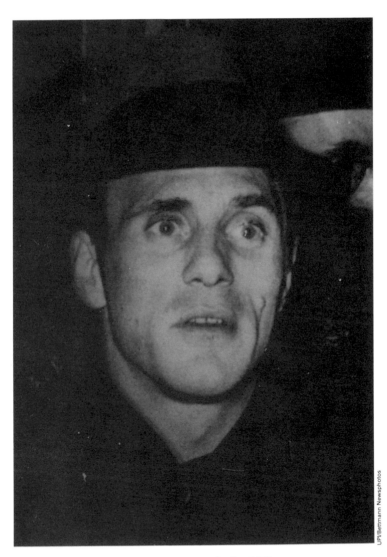

Joseph "Crazy Joe" Gallo, 1961

Carlo Gambino (center) at wife's funeral, 1971

John Gotti and fan, 1987

Madden harassed Ralph until he finally admitted a total income of $55,000 for the years 1912 to 1926. And having neglected to seek the benefit of his brother's guidance in this matter, Ralph signed some papers that showed he owed Uncle Sam a tax of $4,065.

But when it came to paying, 'Bottles', as Ralph Capone was known, pleaded poverty.

Couldn't he take it from the roll of $10,000 cash he carried in his pocket to stave off arrest?

'Listen,' he said. 'I'm broke. I can't even afford new shoes. Look at my soles, they are so thin that when I step on a dime I can tell you if it's heads or tails.'

How about the stable of racing horses? What if the government seized them?

'You can't do that to me!' he wailed. 'Those animals are old clods; they're ready for the glue factory. The only reason I'm keeping them is sentiment. Gee, I love those animals.'

He offered to settle for $1,000. No dice. He upped the offer to $2,500. The government agreed.

'But you'll have to wait until I can raise the dough,' he pleaded. 'I'm busted right now.'

Fine, said Madden, and the sworn statement of Ralph Capone's inability to pay was filed away. It was to prove in time a very damaging bit of evidence against Bottles.

Meantime, despite the vigorous efforts to bring gangland to its knees, The Syndicate purred on relentlessly. Law enforcement had little real effect on the overall operations of the underworld. At most, the wounds they inflicted were pin-pricks.

Chapter 22

The St Valentine's Day Massacre

The staccato explosions were too numerous and too steady to be the backfire of a car, even for those Prohibition Era days of 1929 when everything from hootch to gasoline was diluted for an extra buck of profit.

To Mrs Jeanette Landesman, wife of an investigator in the Chicago prosecutor's office, there was a distinct, unmistakable resonance in the crackling, bursting sound that seemed to leap from across the street and crash through her closed kitchen window.

'That's machine gun fire!' she exclaimed to herself, turning from her ironing board and hurrying to the window. From her apartment at 2124 North Clark Street, the scene outside seemed placid. Snow was swirling down on this wintry St Valentine's Day.

She could see nothing that suggested gunfire, yet there was something about the front of the S.M.C. Cartage Co. garage across the street that told her the shooting had occurred behind the grim tan brick façade. Surely the bark of bullets could mean only one thing: murder.

She threw her coat over her shoulders, and darted down the single flight of stairs to the street, only to be met by a man who shouted, 'Call the police – go back upstairs and call the police! There's been a killing!'

The man pointed to the door of the garage across the street.

Mrs Landesman raced back to her apartment and phoned headquarters. In less than two minutes, Sergeants Thomas Loftus and Fred O'Neill screeched to a stop in front of the garage, scrambled out of their car, and headed through the door.

In a mingled state of fear and curiosity, she followed the policemen into the garage. Suddenly Loftus and O'Neill stopped as if they had walked into a brick wall.

Mrs Landesman had only to catch a glimpse of the sight that petrified the policemen to make her turn on her heels and race back out to the street screaming at the top of her lungs.

Inside the garage, the bleeding bodies of seven well-dressed men were sprawled in a line on the floor next to a bullet-riddled wall. Blood flowed from their heads, their torsos, and their limbs, taking a downhill course along the inclined floor into the sewer drain.

In the utter silence of the incredible spectacle of butchery, the blood could be heard dripping like water into the catch basin.

'My God!' O'Neill gasped. 'What a massacre!'

'A massacre!' Loftus repeated. 'A massacre!'

Slowly both policemen regained their sensibilities and edged toward the victims to determine whether any could conceivably be alive.

The first victim's head was blown open as though by a blast from a cannon. The second, third, and fourth bodies were on their backs, their eyes staring sightlessly at the ceiling. The fifth corpse was in a kneeling position, the upper part of the body resting against a chair now glistening with a lurid crimson that had drained from his veins. He looked as though he might have been praying. The shreds of skin dangling from the cheeks and neck, exposing the broken bones and shattered teeth of the sixth body left no doubt of his fate.

'Hey!' O'Neill cried as he approached the seventh and last victim at the end of the row of bleeding bodies. 'This guy's alive! We've got to get him to the hospital!'

Loftus and O'Neill bent over the still-living form and whispered, 'Easy, lad, we'll get you fixed up.'

There was no response. Just a gasp for breath and a heavy choking cough caused by the syrupy substance filling his mouth – the blood gushing up from internal wounds.

As they picked up the body and carried it to their police car, Loftus and O'Neill were relieved to find that Captain Thomas Condon and a half-dozen uniformed patrolmen had arrived on the scene. Enroute to Alexian Brothers Hospital, O'Neill suddenly recognised the blood-covered face of the gasping victim sprawled on the back seat.

'Tom! That's Frank Gusenberg!' O'Neill half-shouted. Every Chicago cop knew him. Together with his brother Pete, he had put in many years of faithful service with the mob of George 'Bugs' Moran, yet another who didn't want to participate in the 'peace movement' Al Capone was endeavouring to foster. One of Gusenberg's big mistakes had been to attempt a number on Machine Gun Jack McGurn.

Even as Gusenberg was being rushed to the hospital, Lieutenants John L. Sullivan and Otto Erlanson of the Homicide Division were beginning to examine and identify the other bloodied victims.

'Body Number One,' Sullivan announced as Erlanson began writing, 'is Peter Gusenberg.'

Pete had been a criminal for about twenty-five of his forty years, with a record of burglary, robbery, and hoodlumism. He had done three years in the Illinois State Penitentiary at Joliet and another three years in the federal penitentiary for his part in the four-million-dollar Dearborn Station mail robbery in 1923. He was a natural for Moran's gang.

The officers removed $447 in cash, along with papers and letters, from Pete Gusenberg's pockets, pulled a large diamond ring from one of his hairy fingers, then carried the remains out on a cloth-covered stretcher to the morgue wagon at the curb.

As Sullivan and Erlanson shifted their attentions to the next body, other detectives searched the neighborhood frantically for anyone who could offer eyewitness testimony of what might have happened.

It was obvious that the massacre in the garage had been performed with tommy guns and shotguns. It was also clear to the authorities that the victims had been lined up against the wall, all seven of them, with their backs to the executioners.

But who were the killers? How many were there? How did they bring their victims into the garage? How did they get away?

And most importantly: why were seven men shot down in cold blood?

Jeanette Landesman, who had phoned the police and caught a brief, bone-chilling glimpse of the horror behind the garage walls, was one of the first to be questioned. She remembered something now that she'd forgotten to tell the sergeant she spoke to on the phone.

'Just as I got to the street – and before the man told me to go back upstairs and call the police – I saw a big automobile on the west side of the street. It started away slowly, and then put on a great burst of speed. It passed a street car on the wrong side and then I lost sight of it.'

The search for other witnesses continued. Meanwhile, inside the garage Lieutenants Sullivan and Erlanson stood over Dr Herman N. Bundesen, the Cook County coroner, who was examining the second body for a count on the bullet wounds.

'At least thirteen,' he said firmly, rising to his feet. 'It looks like they all died like dogs. They didn't have a chance.' Another detective pointed to the wall. 'They were peppered with machine gun bullets – look at the slugs in the wall . . .'

Lieutenant Erlanson stuffed his report paper in his pocket for a moment and pulled out a pocket knife and a clean white envelope. He stepped to the wall and dug seven .45-caliber slugs out of the plaster and dropped them into the envelope. Then he rejoined the process of identifying the victims.

'Body Number Two,' Sullivan called out, 'is Adam Heyer.'

Heyer, alias Frank Sneyder, was the owner of S. M. C. Cartage Co. which occupied the garage. He was also part-owner of the Fairview Kennels, the dog racing track which competed with Al Capone's Hawthorne Club. About thirty-five years old, Heyer had done a year in 1908 in Chicago's Bridewell Jail for robbery, then a stretch in Joliet in 1916 for his part in a confidence racket.

'Hey,' a detective who heard the name suddenly shouted, 'that guy's the brains of the Bugs Moran mob!'

'Yeah,' another responded. 'And I'll bet by the time John and Otto are through identifying these poor guys you'll find they all worked for Bugs. It looks to me like Capone really went to town on Moran's boys this time.'

Lieutenant Sullivan reached into the victim's right-hand pocket and took out $1,399 in cash.

All at once a detective burst through the door from the street and approached Captain Condon. 'We've just found a dame who says the cops did this! I think maybe you oughta talk with her –'

'What!' Condon shouted. 'This is incredible!'

The captain and detective rushed out to the sidewalk, across the street, and up the stairs to the apartment of Mrs Alphonse Morin. Her apartment had a number of windows that provided an unobstructed view of the garage across the street.

'I was standing at my window looking out,' Mrs Morin repeated her story to the captain. 'All at once I saw two men leaving the garage with their hands high over their heads.

'Two men who appeared to be in police uniforms were behind them, prodding them with revolvers. They all got into what looked to me like a big police car, and drove away. They went in that direction.' She pointed south.

Other detectives by now had interviewed other witnesses who contributed bits and pieces of information that began to form a general idea of the ingenious execution of the heinous crime.

Four, possibly five, constituted the executioners' party in the big, black sedan that looked very much like a Cadillac. One apparently stayed behind the wheel while his accomplices went into the garage and mowed down the enemy.

The question of whether three or four gunmen had wreaked such carnage was academic.

'With automatic weapons even two torpedoes could have pulled this job,' Coroner Bundesen suggested. 'One is out of the question,' the doctor went on, 'because Body Number Three is riddled with buckshot.'

As he examined the body, he pointed to the side of the face torn away by the impact of the blast, exposing jagged bones and shattered teeth. 'This was done with a shotgun,' Bundesen said, 'and from fairly close up.'

'Body Number Three,' Lieutenant Sullivan called out to his partner, Erlanson, 'is John May, the one-time safe blower.'

Father of seven children, in his mid-forties, May gave up his career in crime to toil in honest labor as a mechanic on the carting firm's trucks.

'It was just his tough luck to be here when the massacre took place,' Erlanson suggested. 'I guess those killers just didn't want any living witnesses.'

But at the moment there was a living witness. He didn't seem long for this world, yet he was holding up remarkably well in spite of several critical bullet wounds, and Frank Gusenberg was given a better than even chance to survive long enough to identify his killers the moment he came out of surgery.

Sergeants Loftus and O'Neill were standing outside the operating room waiting for the opportunity to question him. Nearby was another phone with an open line to the garage, which had now become the field headquarters for the police and coroner, as well as the State Attorney's investigators. Every facet of further development depended upon what Gusenberg had to say: he was the only one who could provide the names of the executioners and perhaps even the motive for the slaughter.

The grim task of identifying the remaining corpses continued uninterruptedly.

'Body Number Four is our old pal and buddy Albert R. Weinshank,' Lieutenant Sullivan said thickly. 'He was sure taken to the cleaners . . .'

This crack obviously was a reference to Weinshank's connections with the Central Cleaners and Dyers Co., a prestigious firm which Moran apparently had hoped would serve as his entry into the cleaning-dyeing racket and the opportunity to further expand his diversified underworld holdings and interests. As an inducement to align himself with the Moran mob, Weinshank had been given the financial backing of Bugs in the operation of the Salazar Club at 4207 Broadway – which also became an outlet for Moran's illegal booze.

'I count eighteen dollars in cash,' Sullivan said to Erlanson, who noted the figure in his report. Then Sullivan removed a diamond ring from the victim's slender, manicured left pinky and turned it over to his partner to log.

'And let's not forget this,' he added, handing a bankbook to Erlanson, who opened it and let out a loud whistle.

'Here's $42,580,' Erlanson exclaimed. 'And they say crime doesn't pay!'

'Holy mackerel,' Sullivan blurted as he pulled out the identification papers in the clothing of Body No. 5. The victim's head had been nearly blown off, the damage very definitely inflicted by the point-blank blast of a double-barrelled shotgun. Although the muzzles of the gun had been pointed at the back of the victim's head, the terrifying force of the lead pellets literally gouged away every identifying feature of the man's face.

The factor that prompted Sullivan to gasp in surprise was the name on the driver's license in the victim's wallet: Reinhardt H. Schwimmer, an optometrist with offices in the downtown section. He was not a mobster by any stretch of the imagination, yet paradoxically no Chicagoan of good repute had any closer ties with gangland figures than Schwimmer did.

He was the favourite optometrist of most Chicago gangsters, but that wasn't his only link with the underworld. Schwimmer was one of those psychological oddities that exist in the strange world of hero worshippers. They're called 'buffs'.

Schwimmer was a gang buff. He sought the society of hoodlums and racketeers for kicks, and he made repeated use of his association with them to brag to friends, 'I can get you bumped off anytime I want.' It was a joke, but there were many who didn't doubt that Schwimmer could have had anyone murdered for the asking.

'Well, he wanted excitement and he sure got it,' remarked Sullivan as he handed Schwimmer's wallet and papers to Erlanson. The coroner's men moved in, placed the body on the stretcher, covered it with a white sheet, and removed it to the body wagon.

'Here's the last one,' Lieutenant Sullivan droned, 'Body Number Six.'

The name read by Sullivan served to jolt every detective and patrolman within hearing distance: James Clark, brother-in-law of Bugs Moran with a long but unproven record as a killer. Clark, who was in his early forties, had done time for burglary and robbery in Illinois prisons, but in recent years had managed to escape arrest while serving as one of Moran's top henchmen.

Coroner Bundesen turned to the detectives and reporters gathered in the garage:

'Gentlemen, I wonder if we can clear the room. I want this scene of murder re-enacted for the benefit of the Coroner's Jury which will be here any minute now. Will some volunteer to be the execution squad? I'd like others to be the victims. We ought to rehearse this a little . . .'

Volunteers stepped forward and permitted themselves to be aligned along the wall as the gangsters had been before the drumfire of bullets whipped the life out of them.

Chief of Detectives Egan, who had studied the entire theoretical approach of the massacre as provided by his ace detectives, served as the voice of commentary.

'First,' he said, pointing to the door, 'they came in there, carrying machine guns and shotguns, two in police uniforms. Quite simple. The Moran outfit reasoned they were policemen, coming to see if they were carrying weapons. Otherwise, you can be sure the killers would have gotten no farther than the partition. They'd never have gotten that gang to line up any other way. Presumably, the men in uniforms entered first, to set the stage.

'The two probably said, "Stick 'em up! The place is pinched!" Well that was all right with the Moran hoodlums. They'd been arrested and jailed before. So they let the fake policemen disarm them.

'Outside the other two were likely getting the machine guns ready. They got the signal to come ahead. The machine-gunners stepped inside, took a few seconds to aim then "Let 'em have it!"

'They probably stood at either end of the garage, the one on the left sweeping his fire from left to right across the row of heads. The other tommy, aimed a little lower, moved right to left.

'Somewhere in the middle was the man with the shotgun, blasting at the lineup somewhat indiscriminately – and as you can see he managed to get two of them and almost blew their heads off.'

Egan pointed to the blood and flesh that was flattened against the brick wall.

'And that, gentlemen, is how we have now come to face the worst mass murder in Chicago history.'

'How do you explain what Mrs Morin told us, about the policemen shepherding two men with their hands up out of the garage and into the car?' asked Dr Bundesen.

'Very simple,' Egan replied. 'When the job was done, the two uniformed men had their two civilian-clad accomplices march out of the place to make it look to anyone on the street that an arrest had just been made, and that the gunfire they might have heard coming from inside was connected to the arrest.'

Now one principal question remained to be answered: which of Al Capone's mobsters – if indeed it was Scarface's work – pulled the St Valentine's Day Massacre?

The only hope for an answer would have to come from dying Frank Gusenberg, who by now had come out of surgery and was being questioned by Sergeant O'Neill.

'Come on, Frank,' pleaded O'Neill, 'everybody's dead – even your brother Pete. Tell me who did it.'

Gusenberg's lips began to tremble as they parted in a labored effort to speak. Finally the words came out in a whisper:

'I'm not gonna talk . . . get me a drink of water.'

Again and again O'Neill begged the gangster to identify the assassins; each time he was answered with an adamant refusal.

A doctor standing by checked the patient's respiration and pulse.

'He's getting weaker,' the doctor said, 'you don't have much time.'

'Frank, listen to me,' O'Neill pleaded once more, 'you've got to do this one good thing. Tell me who did it.'

Gusenberg coughed several times in what seemed like his last dying gasps. 'Sarge, cover me up,' he whispered. 'I'm cold.'

'You are covered, Frank, the blankets are on you.'

'I'm still cold, get me . . . another blanket . . . the hot water bottle is cold on my feet . . .'

His words trailed off. The chill Frank Gusenberg felt was that of death. And when his eyes closed and his head sagged into his chest, he became the seventh victim of gangland's bloodiest massacre of all time.

Even as the last 'easy' road to solution of the horrifying crime was blocked off by death, the outcry of business, civic, and reform associations in Chicago reached an unprecedented crescendo. The thunder of voices was an uprising against the ten years of gangland warfare which had turned the city's streets into shooting galleries as one mob after another fought for domination of the rackets.

But now the last remnants of Dion O'Bannion's mob had been wiped out. The warfare was effectively at an end.

Chicago, finally and at last, was Al Capone's – lock, stock, and barrel.

Chapter 23

The Last Days of Scarface Al

After the St Valentine's Day Massacre wiped out Bugs Moran's top lieutenant and ended virtually all of Capone's competition, Moran's destiny was to return to his original profession of armed robbery. He died in Leavenworth Federal Penitentiary while doing time for a post office heist.

And, although Al Capone was in Florida enjoying the fresh ocean breezes of Biscayne Bay at the time of the massacre, he was blamed for it. He bleated:

'Why do they blame me for something that happened when I was miles away? They accuse me of killing everything except the Dead Sea – and they'll get around to that eventually.'

He then headed to Philadelphia with Frank Rio for a conference with Max 'Boo Boo' Huff, the East Coast gambler who had a hand in the 1919 Chicago Black Sox baseball scandal.

Caught with time on their hands before the Chicago sleeper was due to depart, Al and Frank Rio dropped into a movie. When they emerged from the theater, they were accosted by two detectives who disarmed them of one .38-caliber revolver each.

The charge: carrying firearms.

Capone put up a big fuss and offered $50,000 to the lawyer who could square the rap for him. Philadelphia Safety Director Lemuel Schofield was willing to bet no mouthpiece would get Al off this hook. Schofield quoted Capone as pleading:

'Keep my gun, take me to the city limits, give me a kick in the behind and you'll never see me again. I wasn't doing any harm in Philadelphia . . . I'm tired of murders. I want to live in peace. I don't want to wind up dead in the alley with the cats looking at me.'

His whining and his wealth did Al no good. A tough judge put him and Frank into Eastern Penitentiary for a year. But the story that made the rounds after Al's incarceration was that he had gotten exactly what he wanted: to be put away in a safe place for a while so nobody would knock him off for the St Valentine's Day Massacre.

Even as Al Capone paid his debt to Pennsylvania society, the Chicago crime front was still very much under his control. His absence didn't affect the continuing growth of his underworld empire, nor did it bring a diminution in the number of killings.

Of all the crimes committed while Capone was in jail, none raised the ire of Chicagoans as much as the cold-blooded killing of *Chicago Tribune* reporter Alfred J. 'Jake' Lingle. As never before, the newspapers waged a relentless crusade against crime. They demanded Lingle's murder be solved and the stories day in and day out spurred authorities into unprecedented action.

A St Louis gunslinger, Leo V. 'Buster' Brothers, was nabbed and charged with the crime. He went to trial, and witnesses, including a Roman Catholic priest, identified Brothers as the killer. He was convicted by a jury which had serious doubts of his guilt. It recommended fourteen years in prison.

Like Capone, who took a year in the can in Pennsylvania, Brothers was more than happy to repose in the slammer in Illinois. Had he been freed, he would have been extradited to St Louis for murder. When he was finally released, two years later, he returned to face the murder rap. But by then the witnesses were all dead. He went free.

The cries about Lingle being a crusading reporter didn't appear in the newspapers for long. Not when the truth about

Jake finally leaked out. Jake, a $65-a-week reporter, was a member of The Syndicate! He had been on Capone's payroll and had amassed a huge fortune, including a $100,000 stock market account with Chicago Police Commissioner William Russell.

If Lingle was a friend of the Mob, why was he killed?

Because the Mob found out that the Internal Revenue Service had begun gathering evidence against Al Capone, preparatory to bringing charges of tax evasion, and Lingle, over the barrel on his own fraudulent returns, had plenty of evidence to offer against Scarface.

The IRS made a deal with Lingle: if he would tell all he knew about the Syndicate's operations and take, he would in return spare himself from prosecution – and also collect a 'finder's fee' of ten percent on every dollar of tax the government got out of Capone, by ordering Secretary of the Treasury Andrew W. Mellon to do everything in his power to put Capone in jail. And the only way it could be done was to nail him for income tax evasion.

The year-long investigation gave the government plenty of evidence to stand up in court, but because they were dealing with Capone – and because President Hoover was anxious to put Capone away – investigators proceeded slowly and cautiously.

By midsummer of 1930 – not long after Capone was released from prison in Pennsylvania – the murmurings about a possible income tax evasion case against him made Al jittery. With a lawyer from Washington, Al called on U.S. Attorney Johnson. After a two-hour wait, Al and his lawyer were admitted to Johnson's office. Capone wanted to reach a settlement.

Johnson took a pencil and drew a thick pad in front of Al.

'Now, Mr Capone,' he said, 'if you will list all of your sources of income starting in 1924, we can get underway at determining your tax liability.'

Al gulped. He deferred to his lawyer for the answer. The mouth-piece said his client was willing to cooperate – but. The 'but' was in the threat to Capone that would come if he admitted he made money violating Illinois gambling laws, the Volstead Act, and other statutes.

No, the lawyer said, Al wouldn't put himself on the spot. But, he suggested, Capone would be willing to concede that his income had run as high as $100,000 a year.

'Would he put that in writing?' Johnson wanted to know.

Capone would – and did.

Al thought he was off the hook. He sat back and waited for the government to submit a bill which would run no higher than $150,000. Then perhaps tearing a leaf from his brother Ralph's negotiations with the IRS, Al might also plead that he was pinched for funds and maybe Uncle Sam would settle for about $50,000.

Happy in the belief that he had beaten the government, Al went back to his domain. Now in the sophisticated 1930s and with the onset of the Great Depression, Scarface found other fertile territories to invade.

His eyes fell upon the International Brotherhood of Teamsters, Warehousemen, and Helpers, the union which in later years would come under the leadership of James R. Hoffa. For openers, Capone started on the Chicago Milk Wagon Drivers. He found peppery, white-haired Robert 'Old Doc' Fitchie unyielding to any proposition the Mob had to offer. Al had Doc kidnapped and held him until $50,000 was paid from the union treasury for his release.

A series of murders followed as Al tried to stick his greedy hands into the union movement. Then on 12 January 1931, a Federal Grand Jury indicted Al Capone for income tax violations for the years 1924 to 1929, inclusive.

Capone immediately got lawyers, politicians, and even bankers to plead on his behalf. He was willing to pay $215,083 which the government had figured he owed in back taxes – but could he be spared the indignity and agony of going to prison? Would Uncle Sam let him off with probation?

Absolutely not, U.S. Attorney Johnson said. Not even a light sentence. Capone would have to throw himself upon the mercy of the court – and in this case, U.S. District Court Judge James H. Wilkerson was not disposed to dispense mercy for a criminal like Capone.

'You cannot bargain with the United States Government,' the judge told Capone sternly. Capone looked at his lawyers in disbelief. The statement was to become one of the most oft-repeated quotations in the courts of the land, and to serve as an enduring memorial to Judge James H. Wilkerson.

The following September the trial got underway. The evidence stood up more solidly than U.S. Attorney Johnson had dared to hope. Not a witness backed down. Capone sat in the court glum and pale, glaring at those who boldly took the stand.

The most damaging of testimony came from the Rev. Henry Hoover, who had led the raid on the Smoke Shop in Cicero. He told the court that Capone admitted to him that he owned the shop. And the government presented records, however incomplete, which showed that the place pulled down tens of thousands of dollars a year.

Elliott Ness produced figures showing the quantity of hootch that had been produced in Capone-run stills, indicating income of at least fifty million dollars a year.

Another investigator who took the stand exhibited evidence that Capone's hotel bill ran as high as $1,600 a day; another document indicated that in one month alone Capone had bought $6,500 worth of choice steaks, pheasant, and other delicacies and had them delivered to his Palm Island estate.

The government's argument was that since Capone had spent such vast amounts of cash so freely he must have received it as income.

The jury retired to weigh the evidence and testimony. When it returned, its verdict was: GUILTY!

The sentence: eleven years.

America had won its most significant victory over the underworld. And there would be many more now that the ice had been broken against Al Capone.

As Al was led handcuffed to the train that would take him to Atlanta, he cursed under his breath at the three men named Hoover who had brought him to this desolate state of affairs:

There was the Rev. Henry C. Hoover, the fighting Congregational minister; FBI boss Edgar Hoover, who sent Elliot Ness into Chicago to war against the Mob, and President Herbert Clark Hoover, who started the avalanche of accountants tumbling down on Capone's head.

It was figures – not firearms – that were Capone's undoing.

From Atlanta, Capone was transferred to Alcatraz, known as 'The Rock', where he lived in constant terror of mob revenge. He survived: after doing seven years, six months, and twelve days, he was released.

He was a mental wreck when he came out. The syphilis he had contracted years before had gone neglected and now it had developed into paresis.

After treatment at Johns Hopkins Hospital in Baltimore, Capone retired to his retreat in Florida. Meanwhile, the Mob empire that Al had controlled had diminished. The repeal of Prohibition in 1933 ended the illicit beer and alcohol rackets. But there were other fields – particularly the unions – in which Al's successors made money.

Among those in whose hands the mob passed through the years were Frank 'The Enforcer' Nitti, Paul 'The Waiter' Ricca, and Tony Accardo.

On Saturday evening of 25 January 1947, word came out of Palm Island that Alphonse Capone was dead. Newspapers screamed his name in headlines for the last time.

Even in death Al couldn't be denied his place at the top of the list of this nation's most infamous criminals: Al Capone's name lives on today as though he were still alive. Every young hoodlum and punk and every top mobster in the country holds Al Capone up as a hero to emulate. There will probably never be another Scarface.

America won't allow it.

Chapter 24

The Castellammarese War

By 1930–31 Giuseppe Masseria was at the top of the heap in the underworld of Manhattan. Masseria, known as 'The Boss', the term by which he liked to be addressed, suddenly fell into odds with the Italian clique headed by Salvatore Maranzano, who hailed from another Sicilian locale, Castellammare del Golfo in the western part of the island.

Squat and fat, Joe Masseria was also vain. He believed the Old World ideology he brought to the New World in 1902, when he emigrated from Palermo, would make him the Mafia's Number One man.

During the years from 1910 to 1915 Masseria served the Mafia as a gunman. His reputation in the underworld zoomed in August 1922, when two torpedoes tried to kill him in an ambush, and he dodged the hail of gunfire, to emerge from his tenement apartment on Manhattan's Second Avenue to breathe the sweet air of a second life.

Then, seconds later, as Masseria began to believe he was no

longer a target for assassination, the racketing bark of gunfire exploded again. He was caught in a .48-caliber lead crossfire.

He again escaped the pulverising onslaught of bullets and made it to what he presumed was the safety of a men's hat shop. But he was not home free. One of his would-be assassins followed hard on his heels.

The gangster pursued Masseria to the back of the shop and took careful aim at Joe's head. He triggered off four quick shots as Masseria threw himself on the floor and again escaped the deadly fusillade of lead. An instant later, the gunman pegged two of his last bullets at the cowering Masseria – and once more missed. His revolver empty, the assassin flew the coop for parts unknown.

Joe Masseria lived to fight another day. And he did fight, reaching new heights of power after Frankie Yale's assassination. Yet the total power and control he sought over the city's underworld was denied him by the imposing presence of Salvatore Maranzano, who headed a particularly large faction of awesome gangsters from Castellammare.

Technically, Maranzano was under Masseria's command, but Joe the Boss was beginning to sense a disturbance in the ranks – that Salvatore was itching to break away and form his own Mafia organisation. Masseria tried to reinforce his hold over Maranzano by demanding a greater cut of the Castellammarese mob's take from the rackets it ran.

But Salvatore was in no giving mood – not when the men allied with him were tough, dedicated, ruthless Mafiosi – many of who would become the most dreaded underworld leaders in the years to come: among them, Thomas Luchese, Gaetano Gagliano, and the three Josephs: Bonanno, Magliocco, and Profaci.

Yet Masseria wasn't without his own big guns, torpedoes who themselves would one day be household names: Frank Costello, Carlo Gambino, Willie Moretti, Charles Luciano, Joe Adonis, and Vito Genovese.

After Maranzano sent word back to Masseria that he wasn't about to pay higher tribute, Joe the Boss declared an unannounced war on Salvatore's soldiers and proceeded to have several of them rubbed out.

The Castellammarese retaliated quickly. Among the earliest victims was Peter 'The Clutching Hand' Morello, one of Masseria's top triggers. As the killings continued on both sides, the conflict came to be known as The Castellammarese War. It raged for only a year – from 1930 to 1931 – but the toll was catastrophic in the number of underworld lives it took.

By July 1931, Maranzano had defected totally from Masseria's fold and counted five hundred soldiers in the underworld organisation he commanded. While Masseria still had more troops – in the neighborhood of nine hundred operatives – he had lost his stomach for continued warfare. So he sent out olive branches to Maranzano. But they were flatly turned down. Maranzano knew he was making Masseria hurt and that it was merely a matter of playing hardball with Joe before he either caved in or . . .

Two of Masseria's closest and most trusted *capos*, Genovese and Luciano, decided that Joe the Boss was no longer the leader he once was. He was losing his grip and, they feared, it was just a matter of time before the Castellammarese took over the fast-fading Masseria mob.

To protect their own hides – and to snatch leadership of Masseria's organisation for themselves – Genovese and Luciano went to Maranzano and proposed to give Joe the Boss a farewell luncheon at the Nuova Villa Tammaro Restaurant in Coney Island on 15 April. The eatery was owned by Gerardo Scarpato, a crony of Masseria's who had no ties to underworld activity other than to be their gastronomic provider extraordinaire.

In this instance, he exceeded the Mob's fondest expectations. The menu he prepared for the four distinguished diners consisted of cold and hot antipasto appetisers, minestrone soup, a seafood salad of calamari, scungilli, and shrimps; lobster fra diavola with accompanying pastas of linguine in marinara sauce and spaghetti alla Milanese. Choice imported Italian wines were also in evidence and a large selection of pastries, topped off with demitasse.

The luncheon guests arrived at about noon, a Wednesday. Masseria was overwhelmed at being taken to lunch by three of his top lieutenants – Genovese, Luciano, and Ciro Terranova, who at the time was known as New York's 'Artichoke King'. Terranova wore that crown because of his total domination over the distribution of the exotic vegetable. No table could have an artichoke on it unless Ciro first got his cut from its sale at the wholesale produce market.

The lunch went off swimmingly; it became even more liquefied during and after the main course, when *vino* flowed as though it were going out of style. Masseria couldn't believe the feast his boys had arranged for him. He could not imagine the trio was merely observing an ancient tradition of the Honored Society: fill the man with the best of food. But don't overdo it. You must leave room for the bullets.

It was close to 3:30 p.m. About an hour had passed since Genovese and Terranova had politely excused themselves because of 'business' they had to attend in the Bronx. After they left, Luciano called on Scarpato to fetch a deck of cards so he and Joe the Boss could play a game of 'Brisco Joe'.

After a couple of games, Luciano rose from the table.

'Don Giuseppe,' he said. 'I have to go to the bathroom . . . please you excuse me . . .'

'Oh, of course my good friend, Lucky,' Masseria replied. 'I will be right here when you return . . . and perhaps I give you another chance to beat me at cards . . . You may be more lucky next time . . .'

As Luciano left for the men's room Masseria found himself the only patron in the dining room. In the next instant four men wielding .38-caliber guns strode into the restaurant and unlimbered a fusillade at Masseria's back. Twenty-five bullets plowed into his head, neck, and back.

Masseria collapsed onto the table and turned the white tablecloth into a crimson lake with the blood draining out of his wounds.

When police reached the restaurant and searched for evidence, they turned up a playing card bearing the ace of diamonds.

It was still clutched in Joe Masseria's left hand – a sure sign that he would have won the next hand from Luciano. But luck ran out that day for Joe the Boss.

'How can I know what happened?' Luciano asked when detectives questioned him. 'I was in the men's room. I had to go; you know, after I eat big meal. I don't know nothing about what happen until I wash my hands. Then I hear noise. I come out right away and find poor Joe is dead . . .'

Gerardo Scarpato was also questioned. He, too, pleaded no awareness of what happened to Masseria until after the shooting. 'I was out taking walk,' he protested. 'How can I know anything . . .?'

Not long after he was interrogated by Coney Island precinct detectives, Scarpato no longer could prepare the kind of spreads he had done for Joe the Boss's last meal. Evidently he was put on the syndicate's 'drop dead' list, for his body was found stuffed in a burlap bag stashed in the trunk of a stolen four-door sedan abandoned near Brooklyn's Prospect Park.

According to legend, Scarpato became expendable because he was the only identifiable person – other than Luciano – in the restaurant that afternoon. Luciano and his subordinates didn't want to chance the possibility that the restaurateur might one day have a refreshing recall of memory and identify the only other person in Masseria's company that afternoon: Luciano.

Did Lucky Luciano order the hit on Gerardo? There are scores upon scorers of criminologists and students of this case who have arrived at that conclusion.

Barely two weeks had passed since Masseria's untimely death when the new head of The Boss's domain, Salvatore Maranzano, held a banquet in the Pelham Bay section of the Bronx. Virtually every gangster in New York, and Mafioso bosses from such distant domains as Chicago, Cleveland, Detroit, Kansas City, and other cities around the country, attended.

Few of his followers knew of Salvatore Maranzano's in-depth knowledge about the Roman Empire. He had studied extensively the rise and fall of Rome and greatly admired the feats of its legendary leaders. Maranzano envisioned himself as Caesar, transplanted in America as the emperor of all Mafia families in the country.

For openers, he decided to conquer the New York region before extending his rule to the rest of the country.

For the meeting, Maranzano had the hall decorated with crucifixes, religious paintings, and other assorted theological trappings that suggested a gathering of any group other than the *crème de la crème* of America's underworld.

After the banquet, Maranzano walked to the dais and gave the only address of the evening:

'Our Thing has been through some very hard times. It is now time to stop all the bickering, all the killings, and to organise into a strong association that nobody can hurt.

'What I am doing is dividing New York into five families: just like the Roman generals commanded Roman legions. There will be one Caesar here – that will be me. I will be the *capo di tutti capi* [the boss of all bosses] . . .'

Maranzano proceeded to name the *capos*, or leaders, of the five Mafia entities in the city and also picked their immediate under-bosses, or subordinates:

1. Gaetano Gagliano, with underboss Thomas 'Three Finger Brown' Luchese.
2. Charles 'Lucky' Luciano and his *capo* Vito Genovese.
3. Joseph Profaci and his brother-in-law, Joseph Magliocco, as his second-in-command.
4. Vincenzo Mangano and his brother Phil, picked as co-bosses – just as the first godfather, Don Giuseppe Balsamo, had decreed it should be. Phil, who was the Number One man in this family of dual leadership, chose Albert Anastasia to be the top *capo*.
5. Joseph 'Joe Bananas' Bonanno was given leadership of the last family designated by Maranzano. Bonanno's top *capo* became Carmine Galante.

Following this, Mafia leaders from all over the country pilgrimaged to New York to pay homage to Salvatore and his great mind that brought about this seemingly impregnable five-family rule over New York City Mafia activity – and which set the pattern for its ultimate expansion to vast areas of the United States.

One would think that Maranzano's remedies for the Black Hand operations were welcomed by all Mafiosi after having toiled for so long in the often-muddled Mafia ventures of the past rough, bloodied eras. Maranzano did enjoy a honeymoon with most of his subjects after he became the godfather. But it was only a brief excursion. Very soon a growing coterie of top-ranked Mafiosi began holding Don Salvatore Maranzano in far less favor than they had Don Giuseppe Masseria.

They began to see Maranzano as a power-hungry despot, much worse than his predecessor Masseria. Word spread rapidly that Don Salvatore had become aware of the growing animosity toward his rule and was planning wholesale rubouts of his top underworld aides to protect himself against the possibility of a 'palace rebellion' in which he'd suffer the same fate as he had inflicted on Masseria.

Maranzano's 'hit list' included Lucky Luciano, Vito Genovese, Vincent Mangano, and even Al Capone!

The new Caesar's greed now far exceeded Masseria's – or even Frankie Yale's, who had written his own death warrant by hijacking Scarface Al's liquor shipments. Maranzano was playing the dangerous game that Yale postured: holding on to liquor trucks seized from Luciano's and Genovese's rum-running operations during the height of the Castellammarese Wars.

He was also suspected of arranging the theft of merchandise from his own gangs and pocketing the proceeds amounting to tens of thousands of dollars. This suspicion grew out of an awareness that Maranzano had appropriated the more than $100,000 collected at the 'unification' banquet in the Bronx. The money was tossed by the gangsters at the conclave into kitties set up on tables in tribute to Don Salvatore. The custom in the Black Hand always has been that when a leader is so honored with monetary rewards, he shares them with his soldiers. But Maranzano's underlings received not a penny of that loot.

Among those who were most livid over how the self-anointed godfather was conducting his underworld domain were Luciano and Genovese – and they decided something had to be done. They quietly began plotting for Maranzano's overthrow, and, like most Mafia changes of leadership, it would not be bloodless.

Luciano and Genovese won over such fervently loyal Maranzano supporters as Joe Bonanno and Joe Profaci. But Don Salvatore got wind of the developing treachery. On 9 September 1931 he made it known that he planned to eliminate the bosses he feared. Maranzano revealed his decision to a man who had worked for him as chauffeur and bodyguard since ascending to *capo di tutti capi*.

His words were not known until 1962 during the sensational United States Senate hearings into the workings of organised crime by the bodyguard/chauffeur himself, Joseph Valachi, the most celebrated canary in Mafia history. Valachi, who almost did away with the term Mafia by supplanting it with the then-briefly popular phrase 'Cosa Nostra', quoted Maranzano:

'Joe, I hear you're wondering why you didn't get a piece of the take from the banquet. Don't worry, you'll get your share – and more. But we are holding onto the money right now because we have to go on the mattress again [i.e., a major war is about to be fought].

'You see, I'm not hitting it off with that bastard Luciano and his underboss Genovese. We gotta get rid of them before we can control anything . . .'

Valachi said Maranzano ran off a list of others whom he felt had to be killed as well: Al Capone, Willie Moretti, Frank Costello, Joe Adonis, and Arthur 'Dutch Schultz' Flegenheimer, one of Luciano's many non-Italian associates in the rackets.

In his testimony, three decades after it happened, Valachi admitted he was overwhelmed by what Maranzano told him.

'Gee, I wanted to say, who wants to control everything? You got to remember that it's just a few months since we are at peace. All I wanted to do was make a good living. But naturally, I dared not say anything.'

Maranzano went on to tell Valachi:

'I am having one last meeting with Luciano and Genovese tomorrow around three o'clock . . .'

But the godfather didn't inform Valachi he had arranged for Luciano and Genovese to be 'surprised' in his real estate offices at 230 Park Avenue. The assassin was to be Vincent 'Mad Dog' Coll, a psychopathic killer who hired out for executions and was now only months away from his own extermination because he was a gunman gone so berserk that all the underworld feared him.

Chapter 25

The Rise, the Reign, and Fall of Charles 'Lucky' Luciano

Salvatore Maranzano arrived at his Park Avenue office behind Grand Central Terminal. To go beyond this building motorists have to traverse a snake-like roadway through the bowels of the high-rise office building and exit on Park Avenue South.

Maranzano kept these offices to hold the law off his back while he wheeled and dealed as America's foremost Mafia chieftain.

For the first time, Maranzano had no armed bodyguards surrounding him in these offices. He had been tipped off that the NYPD was planning to stage a raid any day now to check out the legitimacy of his real estate enterprise and to look for any evidence that might link him to the illegal ventures of which he was suspected.

He told his protectors to stay away that day not only because he was expecting the lawmen's visit but also because he didn't want them to interfere with Luciano's and Genovese's rubouts he had scheduled for that afternoon. But he did have one last

307

card up his sleeve to protect him from the worst scenario: a .38-caliber Colt automatic, for which he had a license.

When five men walked into the office that afternoon at two o'clock, not long after he finished lunch, Don Salvatore had no reason to suspect the badges the quintet flashed on their arrival were not of the NYPD.

On their arrival, Maranzano rose from his desk, walked to the door, and greeted the visitors with welcoming arms. For weeks he had rehearsed the scene. He told himself over and over: 'Don't get rattled when the cops come. Stay loose. Act as if nothing was happening . . .'

Don Salvatore may have been put out because the cops had barged in at that late hour – just before Luciano and Genovese were to arrive for their lethal sendoff. But he knew the lawmen would find no incriminating evidence against him if they chose to search his offices. So he didn't feel intimidated. He felt confident the 'bulls' would be out of his office before 3:00 p.m., when he had scheduled Lucky's and Vito's double rubout.

All at once Maranzano sensed something amiss. Three of the men remained in the receptionist's office while two entered his quarters and shut the door. He had no way of recognising who the two 'detectives' were, yet Don Salvatore must have suddenly realised they were not representatives of the law. He reached desperately into his desk drawer for his gun. It was a futile effort.

Sammy 'Red' Levine moved in on Maranzano and in one swift motion pinned his arms behind his back. In that same instant Abe 'Bo' Weinberg pulled a knife from under his jacket and plowed it into Don Salvatore a half-dozen times. But Maranzano refused to be floored by the stab wounds in his neck and stomach. He made one last effort to reach for his .38 – and that's when Levine drew his own .38 and unlimbered four bullets into the Mob boss. Those slugs finished the job.

The two assassins high-tailed it out of Maranzano's office to the three accomplices standing guard in the reception room.

'We did the number on the fuck!' Levine shouted. 'Let's get the hell out of here!'

The five members of the killer team then took off. Instead of taking the elevator, they took the stairs down and, when they reached the lobby level, streaked for the exit. They were brushed on their elbows by another gunman on his way into the building on a mission.

He was Vincent 'Mad Dog' Coll who was on his way to carry out Salvatore Maranzano's urgent assignment – the assassination of Lucky Luciano and Vito Genovese in Maranzano's offices.

By the time the killer reached Maranzano's offices and discovered the man who hired him for a double execution was himself the victim of a rubout, Coll didn't have to execute anyone that afternoon.

Lucky Luciano had done much more than beat Salvatore Maranzano at his own game of entrapment and murder: he had rid himself of the biggest obstacle in the way of his daring master plan to alter the entire structure of the Mafia's corporate structure not only in New York but the entire country.

Luciano knew that Maranzano's assassination would antagonise all of his old-line Mafia friends not only in New York but in the entire country. He feared that they could form a coalition which would substantially thwart his effort for a takeover of the underworld organisation. So he decided that something had to be done to put down the so-called 'Mustache Petes' – the hardline Mafiosi from the old country who had been in Maranzano's fold.

Within twenty-four hours of Maranzano's dispatch into eternity, about fifty other 'Mustache Petes' across the entire country were killed. It was the fulfilment of Luciano's decision: kill all the old-line bosses at once.

It was the most extensive orgy of assassinations ever in the history of the Mafia in this country. It came to be known as The Night of the Sicilian Vespers – Lucky Luciano's greatest single strike. Overnight he became the lord and master of America's underworld!

And he had a bright and fresh set of ideas on how the Mafia should operate.

He was born as Salvatore Lucania in 1897 in the small Sicilian town of Lercara Friddi near Palermo. His father Antonio was an energetic, thrifty laborer in the nearby sulphur pits. When nine, Salvatore emigrated with his parents to America and settled in one of the country's toughest locales, Manhattan's Lower East Side near the shadows of the Brooklyn Bridge.

The tenement district teemed with thousands of recent immigrants living elbow to elbow in squalor and poverty. The locale soon became one of the city's centers of vice and crime. Young Lucania's parents both worked at menial jobs for long hours and had little time to attend to their son. Left to his own devices, Salvatore attended classes in elementary school with less and less frequency until he became a dropout. Then he drifted into a life of crime.

At fifteen he was a petty thief, a knife-wielding member of a street gang, and a runner for a drug peddler. At sixteen, he was nabbed delivering a parcel of heroin, was convicted, and sentenced to six months in jail. When he was released, he joined the Five Point Gang which was the terror of Little Italy around Mulberry Street.

From that day on, Lucania was on his way. His assignments in mayhem and other assorted illegalities were carried out so effectively that he came to the notice of *capo* Giuseppe Masseria. By the early 1920s Salvatore Lucania became Giuseppe Masseria's chief of staff. Though small, and with delicate hands and feet, Salvatore was nevertheless totally qualified to be Masseria's underboss: he was quick of mind, always hard in his decisions, and a thinker.

After he had engineered Maranzano's robust rubout, Lucania – who now began to call himself Charles 'Lucky' Luciano – rose very quickly to a *capo Mafioso* of the first order. And he soon devised a plan that would organise the New York Mafia gangs into a nationwide syndicate that would ultimately control virtually all the rackets in the United States.

But before embarking on it, Luciano realised he had to work out a system of coexistence with some non-Italian gangs in New York who were messing for the spoils of racketeering. The White Hand was a dead issue, but not so the Jewish boys in Brooklyn who started out as the Amboy Dukes – because they came from Amboy Street in Brownsville – who were now shaping into a gang that would become known as Murder Incorporated.

Sammy Red Levine and Abe 'Bo' Weinberg, who did the number on Salvatore Maranzano, were members of Murder Inc.

Luciano had not only struck a deal for a working arrangement with Murder Inc.'s head man, Louis 'Lepke' Buchalter, the dominant force in the city's Garment Center rackets, but with a whole host of other non-Sicilians who were of the Jewish persuasion: Meyer Lansky, boss of New York gambling operations, and Longy Zwillman, who controlled most of New Jersey's rackets. Another infamous underworld power in Luciano's 'National Syndicate', as it came to be known, was Benjamin 'Bugsy' Siegel, one of the chief executioners for the infamous Murder Inc. mob, who was destined to follow Horace Greeley's advice given to young men in an era when no movie colony existed in Hollywood. Siegel, with cunning and wile, ascended the ladder of crimedom until within a few short years he was truly the mahatma of the West Coast underworld.

Siegel, who was born in Brooklyn and grew up in the poverty and despair of Manhattan's East Side slums, soon moved into a $250,000 mansion, then came to have an elbow-rubbing friendship with, among others, Jack Warner, Clark Gable, Gary Cooper, George Raft, and Jean Harlow. His was now a life of combined ease and adventure in one of the nation's most lucrative crime fiefdoms.

In time, Bugsy would spread his influence into Las Vegas, build its first casino-hotel, The Flamingo, and become known as the father of the gambling capital.

Luciano's was the very first effort to organise a racketeering combine and take virtually total control of criminal enterprises nationwide. The prospect of huge economic dividends was received enthusiastically by all members of the combine from one coast to the other.

By 1935, Luciano was the most dominant Mob leader the United States had ever known. He had made Al Capone's rule over Chicago gangland look like a kindergarten. He directed his vase empire like a potentate of a legendary kingdom. His base of power was seated in New York's world-famed Waldorf Astoria

Hotel, where he was registered as a year-round resident in a sumptuous suite under the name of Charles Rose.

No gambling enterprise, no dock racket – whether it was protection, pilfering, or loansharking – and no Garment District extortion operation could be conducted without his sanction, nor unless an ironclad agreement had been reached beforehand for his very substantial cut of the action.

Not only did Lucky Luciano have unchallenged clout in the underworld as no boss before him, but he also commanded virtually total political protection from the traditionally corrupt Tammany Hall, the infamous Manhattan political clubhouse that controlled City Hall, wielded enormous influence on Capital Hill in Albany, and was owed the unswerving allegiance of judges and elected officials it had handpicked for their jobs in smokey backroom congresses.

Those same judges, elected officials, and chieftains from the Hall could always be found in the morning at sessions Lucky held in the fashion of conclaves called by noblemen or kings.

By the beginning of 1935, Luciano, architect of the Mafia's reorganisation, had reached new pinnacles of power because he had sought – and received – the cooperation of many thousands of 'associate' members of every race, creed, and national origin. Later, William David Kane, a member of the FBI's Criminal Intelligence Squad, would say:

'There are Mafia associates with Boston Irish twangs and Memphis drawls; there are blacks and Mexican Americans, Jews, Syrians, Poles, and St Louis Germans who do the Mafia's bidding.'

But none did the Mafia's bidding as thoroughly and convincingly as Murder Inc., a syndicate whose membership was comprised almost exclusively of Jews. The awesome and widely feared bloody-handed cartel of killers became known as the 'Kosher Nostra'.

While its hierarchy was top-heavily Jewish, it no more depended solely on the sons of Abraham to do its dirty work than the Mafia relied upon natives of Italy and their American-born offspring to shoulder the entire operation of their organised lawlessness. Names such as Albert Anastasia, Philly Mangano,

Louis Capone, and Frank 'The Dasher' Abbandando are mixed like ingredients of a Greek salad with such Hebraic names as Louis Buchalter, Mendy Weiss, Benjamin 'Buggsie' Goldstein, 'Pittsburgh' Phil Straus, and, of course, Benjamin Siegel, 'the Bug'.

The Mafia's and Murder Inc.'s marriage was a union that all at once eliminated costly and complicated inter-Mob warfare. For the first time big crime machines worked together, not only locally but on a national scale, sprouting an epidemic of organised thievery and butchery. And the beauty of it all was that the gutter rats could avoid treading on each other's toes.

Gang murder was put on an organised, assembly-line basis. Operating like a modern big-business enterprise, Murder Inc. was retained as official mobile executioner, the chief hatchet man being an arrogant, self-glorying gang leader named Abe 'Kid Twist' Reles.

Though Bugsy Siegel itched for an opportunity to 'go where the action is' and be triggerman for this ring of killers for hire, Lucky Luciano overruled him. 'I've got bigger things planned for you,' he told Siegel.

Lucky made the Bug one of his chief lieutenants, leaving the dirty work to Kid Twist and his lethal ratpack.

Luciano appointed Buchalter to command the gang, while Anastasia was selected to ride herd over Reles and his underling killers. Albert became known as 'The Chief Executioner'.

The new pattern of organised crime soon bore the fruits of its endeavors. Murder Inc. responded to calls from every corner of the country in the performance of its hideous and incredible services: contract murders that sustained the rackets in all of the nation's industrialised cities.

In a decade of its existence, Murder Inc. was credited with committing no fewer than one thousand contract killings!

But by this time, Siegel was long gone from the New York scene and Murder Inc. was well on its way to dissolution and its members off to long-term penitentiary incarceration – and, for some, execution in Sing Sing Prison's electric chair.

While he was enjoying unprecedented euphoria as the country's top crime boss, Luciano was suddenly overcome by the same disease that had afflicted his predecessors: greed.

Perhaps it was because of his early years' experience as a thug on the Lower East Side. Besides a thief and narcotics runner, he'd been a messenger and solicitor for brothels. He had learned well about the way prostitutes were handled, the way they worked. So he organised a ring of call girls that soon were giving him an income greater than all of his gambling, narcotics, extortion, and other rackets could yield.

At their peak, Luciano's brothels housed more than two hundred madams and more than one thousand call girls paying tribute into his coffers – an annual gross of $10 million. But this income wasn't enough for Lucky. He began over-charging the madams for the cost of doing business; they, in turn, took it out on the girls, who were left with all-too-little take-home pay. When there was even a very first failure to ante up to Luck's enforcers, the madams and girls were subjected to brutal beatings and slashings.

Soon the girls began to rebel. But high up in his Waldorf Towers suite, Lucky had no awareness of what was happening on the street. He had a low esteem of the women who were his white slaves. 'Whores is whores,' he'd say. 'They can always be handled. They ain't got no guts.'

Luciano would soon learn differently. His big mistake was that, despite how little he thought of them, he had all too many of them in his company constantly. And because he also regarded them as 'dumb broads', he sometimes let his guard down and permitted them to listen in on his phone calls dealing with his various underworld activities.

Several of the women in his entourage – Nancy Presser, Mildred Harris, and Cokey Flo Brown, among them – weren't stupid and weren't gutless. They all had excellent memories.

In 1935, at the height of Luciano's and the Mob's dominance over the underworld, New York City reformist groups clamored for action against organised crime. Although the municipal government was run by an audacious and totally honest Mayor, Fiorello H. LaGuardia, he was powerless to effect a crackdown on such an elaborate and complicated machine like Luciano's Mafia organisation.

A special grand jury was impanelled to investigate, but suddenly decided the incumbent District Attorney of New York County wasn't performing as he should be. A clamor was raised for a special prosecutor. The plea was heeded by Governor Herbert H. Lehman, who then drafted a vigorous young lawyer in the U.S. Attorney's office of the Southern District in Manhattan.

Thomas E. Dewey, who would later succeed Lehman as Governor, then bid twice for the Presidency of the United States as Republican Party challenger to Franklin D. Roosevelt in 1944 and Harry S. Truman in 1948, fired his opening round at operators of the numbers game. Not long after, he trained his sights on the wholesale white-slave traffic run by Lucky Luciano. For now, Dewey didn't want to get involved in the godfather's involvements in narcotics and other rackets. He felt he had enough evidence on Luciano as a vice lord to nail him good and hard.

Not long after Dewey began his probe, Dutch Schultz, at a meeting with Luciano and several gang overlords, suggested that Prosecutor Dewey had to be killed. Luciano didn't turn cartwheels over the idea, but consented to let Anastasia case Dewey and return with a plan on how to assassinate him.

Anastasia dutifully prepared all the details and reported back. But the high counsellors of the Syndicate decided they wanted Thomas Dewey to live, because if he were killed the public wrath would be far more devastating than the harassment the special prosecutor was likely to wage against the Mob.

Schultz didn't agree. He said he'd send his own killers after Dewey. With that, the Syndicate called in Bugsy Siegel. Luciano himself addressed him.

'Go figure how we can get rid of the Dutchman,' Lucky told the Bug.

Siegel scouted the one-time Prohibition Era's beer baron and determined from his lieutenants that Schultz planned to have dinner at his favourite eatery, the Palace Chop House in Newark, New Jersey, on the night of 23 October 1935.

That night at about 8:20 p.m. Dutch, together with his henchmen, Lulu Rosenkrantz, Abe Landau, and Otto

'Abbadabba' Berman, arrived at the Palace. Minutes later, the racketeer's wife, Frances, walked into the restaurant wearing a glittering velvet gown and a silver-fox cape around her shoulders.

But the Dutchman wasn't pleased to see her. 'I'm too busy,' he apologised. 'Run along and see a movie. I'll meet you here at eleven-thirty.'

An hour and a half later, about 10:00 p.m., Dutch Schultz had finished his late supper and sat smoking a cigarette. At that moment, the front door of the Palace Chop House opened and two strangers entered. One of them ambled up to the bar in a very businesslike manner and muttered to the bartender, 'You'd better duck, boy!' The guy behind the mahogany didn't have to be told twice. He dropped to the floor.

Meanwhile, Lulu Rosenkrantz, Abe Landau and Abbadabba Berman were huddled in a whispered conference at another table. As he puffed his cigarette, the Dutchman paid little heed to what was going on around him. Suddenly the newcomer standing at the bar turned, pulled a .45-caliber automatic from his coat pocket, and opened fire.

The fusillade of slugs found its target.

Dutch Schultz fell face forward on the table; Lulu Rosenkrantz, Abe Landau, and Abbadabba Berman lay on the floor in pools of blood. The scene was faintly reminiscent of the St Valentine's Day Massacre in Chicago six years before.

Only Dutch Schultz was alive; his three henchmen died instantly.

Later, as the Dutchman lay dying on his hospital bed, authorities tried to extract from him the names of the torpedo and his pal who did him in. But the gangland killer kept to the code of the underworld.

'I didn't see nobody,' he said.

Dutch Schultz perhaps knew then, as the police would learn in time to come, that his execution had been ordered by the New York Syndicate, Murder Inc. It could not have been easier.

Earlier, when Bugsy Siegel had returned to Luciano and reported the findings of his intelligence assignment on Schultz, Lucky summoned Albert Anastasia and ordered him to 'take care' of Schultz at the Palace Chop House.

Anastasia summoned two of his deadliest gunmen, Charlie 'The Bug' Workman and Mendy Weiss. The New Jersey mob, run by Abe 'Longy' Zwillman, provided a driver familiar with the roads and highways around Newark for the getaway car.

The three Murder Inc. exterminators rendezvoused with Zwillman and the driver he was supplying in the Riviera Hotel in Newark early that evening. While Anastasia remained with Zwillman, Workman and Weiss were driven by Zwillman's wheelman to the Chop House and performed their extermination.

It couldn't be called a perfect job because Schultz wasn't killed immediately. But he didn't have long to go, for twenty-four hours after he had been brought to the hospital, Arthur 'Dutch Schultz' Flegenheimer succumbed to his wounds.

A little-reported facet of this rubout was Bugsy Siegel's role in Schultz's actual killing. After Lucky Luciano had dispatched Anastasia, Workman, and Weiss to New Jersey, he called in the Bug.

'Benjy,' directed Lucky, 'you take a couple of boys and go out there to Newark. Don't get mixed up in this deal unless Tony's guys mess it up – you just make sure the Dutchman don't get away.'

So Bugsy, accompanied by Harry Teitelbaum and Harry 'Big Greenie' Greenburg, went to Newark and waited in their parked car a short distance from the restaurant as a 'second line of defense'.

But the trio never had to unholster their guns, for the 'first team' did the job with the sort of thoroughness that made Bugsy smile. It made Luciano smile, too.

Lucky was happy that Thomas Dewey would live on. Luciano would also live on. Luciano would also live to rue the day that he saved the prosecutor's life. Yet it was a good thing that he had.

Newspaper headlines were soon screaming about 'Racket-buster' Tom Dewey as he mounted his offensive against organised crime, which had begun with the intensive probe of the numbers games and other rackets and moved on to the wholesale white-slave traffic, as well as the other underworld involvements, run by Lucky Luciano.

Dewey went after the Waldorf-Astoria's permanent tenant, Mr Rose, with a vengeance. He zeroed in on the great *capo* with an offensive that enlisted the very people Luciano never imagined could harm a hair on his scalp.

The intimidated and terrified prostitutes and their pimps dribbled so loosely at the lips that Dewey blotted up all the evidence needed to obtain indictments that led to prosecution.

At the trial in Manhattan's General Sessions Court, the women Charlie Lucky thought such harmless 'whores' were supremely convincing witnesses and convinced the jury of his deep involvement in white slavery. Though Dewey could also have prosecuted the crime czar for drug trafficking and the many other rackets he was involved in, he prosecuted only on the one crime – because it was the easiest to prove and, because of the severe public indignation it aroused, was likely to draw the greatest sentence.

The jury found Luciano and his henchmen guilty of sixty-two counts of white slavery. When he appeared before judge Philip J. McCook for sentencing, Lucky found himself facing a time bomb. Judge McCook riveted a narrow gaze on the cool, immaculate godfather and proceeded to ream him out:

'You are one of the most vicious criminals that has ever been brought before this court. It is the sentence of this court that you serve thirty to fifty years . . .'

The judge probably believed he was imposing the equivalent of a life sentence.

But there was no way McCook could know that Lucky would play a significant and patriotic role for the United States in World War II, which would drastically shorten the term of punishment Luciano began serving in 1936 at the State Penitentiary in Dannemora, the maximum security prison on the Canadian border that's dubbed 'the Siberia of New York's penal system'.

Chapter 26

From Luciano to Genovese to Costello – and an Intimate Glimpse into Yet Another Underworld Hit

Lucky Luciano's successor was Vito Genovese, a natural heir since he had served so closely and faithfully for the top don. He filled Luciano's empty shoes as acting head – until such time that Lucky, still very much in charge from prison – could name his permanent 'successor'.

Genovese had the reputation of not ever letting anyone or anything stand in his way either in his lawless business life or his lawless private life. A chilling example of how the new mob

chieftain comported himself on the domestic front was in his
encounter with beautiful Anna Vernotico in 1932. Vito fell in
love with her on sight but his romance was hindered by another
man: Anna's husband Gerardo Vernotico.

As a practicing Roman Catholic, Anna could not divorce her
husband and marry Genovese. Only a parting by death could free
a spouse of this religion to marry again. So Vito arranged for
Gerardo's early departure from the conjugal bed. The cause for
this premature cessation of the Vernotico's marriage was attested
to very persuasively by the family doctor on the death certificate
he signed: 'Natural causes . . .'

Two weeks after Gerardo Vernotico was laid to rest amid a
cascade of tears, Vito became the widow Anna's new ''usban'.

But on the business front, Genovese finally met someone who
could stand in his way and not flinch. Thomas E. Dewey, now
fresh from his stirring prosecution of Lucky Luciano, leveled his
sights to Don Vito, whom he called 'the new King of the
Rackets'.

Being targeted for his racketeering activities didn't bother
Genovese so much as the disturbing rumor that authorities were
gathering evidence against him and other underworld biggies for
a 1934 murder.

The murder of Ferdinand Shadow Boccia occurred ostensibly
for two reasons. One was that Vito Genovese and Mike Miranda
(a consigliere in the Lucian Family) had set up a rigged card game
and money machine swindle that netted them some $150,000.
Boccia was told he would receive $65,000 as his share of the
proceeds. But he didn't receive it and began to complain.

The second reason for his execution was that Boccia was
suspected of having held up the liquor headquarters of Anthony
'Tony Bender' Strollo. That was even more unforgiveable than
shooting off his mouth about being done out of his cut from the
counterfeit card game take.

Bender, who was also believed to have been an influence in
Gerard Vernotico's untimely death, was quite close to Vito
Genovese. In fact, he was best man at Genovese's wedding to the
widow Anna Vernotico – a favor which Don Vito reciprocated
when Tony Bender himself became a married man.

However, Vito was as yet out of reach of law enforcement agents because of what happened in the year that followed Luciano's incarceration.

Feeling the hot breath of racket-buster Tom Dewey on his neck – and fearing possible prosecution for the crime of murder that could send him to the electric chair – Genovese went on the lam. A few months later, he surfaced in Italy with two suitcases crammed with $750,000. The long green would serve to give Don Vito a fresh start in the land of his birth.

With Charlie Lucky gone, and then Vito, I must say it was a shock to all of us . . .

Joseph Valachi

With Luciano and Genovese both reluctant departees, the family they left behind had to have a new leader. So their *capore-gima*, Frank Costello, became the acting boss – although not an eager one.

Costello wasn't the common gutter-rat Mafioso who makes it to the seat of power by brawling with and murdering his rivals until he sits on the throne. He let his brain do the talking for him, and that made him more effective than any of his predecessors.

He was a corrupter of politicians, a master fixer. While Luciano enjoyed close alliances with the Tammany Hall sachems and could count on them for favors, he was not the pure virtuoso greaser that Frank Costello had become when he was enshrined as the Luciano Family caretaker – a role that also entitled him to all the rights and privileges in the National Syndicate that by now was firmly entrenched in all forty-eight states.

Costello was destined to become the country's most visible and best known gangster – the first of his breed to ever make *Time* magazine's cover. The consummate fixer, Costello could do more for gangland with one phone call or having lunch with the right party than a half-dozen hit men with blazing muzzles.

In his takeover, the dapper, well-organised Costello came on as a kingpin who didn't want to be involved in the family's day-to-day operations. He had his own vast enterprises, legal and illegal, which he didn't wish to neglect. His most important venture of all was gambling: he had virtually complete control of that from New York to Los Angeles.

Because of their new leader's remoteness, the underbosses in the Luciano Family were able to take much greater control of the organisation's illicit activities than they were ever allowed to have in the past.

While the Luciano Family flourished in America and benefitted increasingly from the gusher of profits yielded by its far-flung criminal enterprises, Vito Genovese wasn't doing badly in Italy. With that $750,000 nest egg he took with him when he fled New York, Genovese started a number of small rackets in his homeland – but none flourished so much as the one in black market activities that began during World War II after the U.S. Army emancipated Italy from its former ally Germany's yoke.

Orange C. Dickey, a former special agent for Army Military Intelligence in Italy, learned of Don Vito's deep involvement in the black market while tracking the trail of missing army supplies: blankets, clothing, and foodstuffs, particularly sugar. The stolen stores which made their way to the black marketeers were sold for exorbitant profits to the ill-clothed, ill-fed hapless natives of the war-ravaged nation.

Dickey's tracking of black marketeers took him to an Italian who controlled these illicit activities in the Naples and Nola areas.

'I am questioned many times by many agents from Criminal Investigation Division,' the black market profiteer told Dickey. 'But nothing happen in those cases because I have friends in the Italian courts and in Allied Military Government ...'

Who are the friends, Dickey wanted to know.

'One is come sometime ago from America. You know his name – Vito Genovese.'

Dickey was stunned.

'What connection does he have?'

'He is interpreter for the Military Government in Nola. And is very big with Italian government ...'

Dickey pursued this disclosure further and determined that no sooner had Genovese set foot on Italian soil than he made it his number-one priority to ingratiate himself with dictator Benito

Mussolini by contributing heavily to the Fascist Party. For that, he was rewarded with the *Commendatore del Re*, the highest Italian honor that can be conferred on a civilian.

Other sources revealed to Dickey that, besides being the conduit in fixes between black marketeers and authorities, Genovese had his hand very much in racketeering both in Italy as well as the U.S. In fact, Dickey determined, Don Vito was still giving orders – along with Luciano from Dannemora – on how the Family should be run. Since Costello preferred to be a passive leader, it didn't concern him much that his two former bosses were still the powers behind his throne.

Agent Dickey moved in on Genovese and arrested him on 27 August 1944, on charges of black marketeering. But no action was taken in the courts over the next nine months. Genovese's influential legal battery succeeded in obtaining one postponement after another until Dickey threw up his hands.

He had been cognisant for some time since undertaking the investigation that Genovese was a suspect in Ferdinand Shadow Boccia's eleven-year-old murder. By now, a grand jury sitting in Manhattan had indicted Genovese *in absentia*, along with the homebound henchmen believed to have taken part in the hit: Mike Miranda, Gus Frasca, and George Smurra.

Thwarted so often in his endeavor to have the Italians prosecute Genovese as a black marketeer, Dickey went to his superiors in the Criminal Investigation Division and convinced them that there was a better way to give Vito his come-uppance. His plan was approved and on 14 May 1945, the army agent boarded an American ocean liner in Naples with Genovese in tow and sailed for New York. Dickey was going to deliver the fugitive from a murder rap to newly re-elected New York County District Attorney Frank S. Hogan. Hogan had first been elected in 1941 after his predecessor in that office, Thomas E. Dewey, declined to run for re-election.

Chapter 27

Thomas E. Dewey: A Racket-Buster without Flair or Flamboyance . . . But with Lots of Clout

The greatest moment in Thomas Edmund Dewey's life came late on Election Day, the first Tuesday of November 1948. The *Chicago Daily Tribune*'s eight-column banner headline read:

DEWEY DEFEATS TRUMAN

But that wasn't the way that year's Presidential race turned out. Harry S. Truman, who succeeded to the office in 1945 upon the death of Franklin Delano Roosevelt, wasn't given a Chinaman's chance to win the election for a second term. All polls indicated a runaway victory for Dewey, despite a universal concession that he was cold and colorless.

Because he believed the polls that had him so far in front of his Democratic rival, Dewey refused to roll up his sleeves and take on Truman, who had launched a 'Give 'Em Hell' campaign that saw him travel thirty-one thousand miles and deliver more than three hundred and fifty speeches which ripped the Republicans to smithereens at every whistle-stop.

When the ballots were tallied, 24,179,345 went to Truman, 21,991,291 fell into Dewey's column. It was the greatest upset in Presidential elections ever. The margin of defeat was 2,188,054, fewer than when Dewey first bid for the Presidency four years earlier. Then, FDR, elected to an unprecedented fourth term, outpolled his GOP rival from Owasso, Michigan, by 3,596,219 votes.

There was little in Dewey's background when he was appointed Special Prosecutor in New York County to suggest he would be the national figure he became. He was thirty-five years old at the time and it was ten years after his graduation from Columbia University School of Law.

A descendant of pre-Revolution stock, Dewey's family tree included a grandfather, George Dewey, a charter member of the Republican Party and a third cousin of Admiral George Dewey, the hero of Manila Bay.

Before young Tom's father died in 1927, he had served as GOP county chairman, postmaster of Owasso, and editor and publisher of a weekly newspaper, *The Owasso Times*.

As a youngster, Dewey did chores around his father's newspaper office. At thirteen, he acquired the agency that distributed several weekly and monthly magazines. He hired several other boys to help him build up sales. From his savings and a month's salary from work on a farm, Dewey paid for his first year at the University of Michigan, from where he graduated in 1923 with an A.B. degree.

Because of an excellent baritone voice that led his college glee club for two years, he won the Michigan state singing contest, placed third in a national contest, and headed for New York for voice training.

In Percy Rector Stephens's singing school Dewey met his future wife, Frances Eileen Hutt, a grandniece of Jefferson Davis, the President of the Confederacy.

They were married 26 June 1928, and had two children, Thomas Edmund Jr and John Martin Dewey. But their father never pursued singing as a career after arriving in New York. Instead, he enrolled in law school, finished the three-year course in two years, graduated in 1925, then toured England and France with a college chum in a battered automobile.

On his return to New York, Dewey took a job in a Lower Manhattan law office and was making $8,000 a year by 1931. Just then, U.S. Attorney George Z. Medalle, who headed the Justice Department's Southern District office in Manhattan, appointed Dewey his chief assistant in charge of fifty-two other lawyers. He was then twenty-nine.

A Republican, Medalle resigned as prosecutor in 1932 after Democrat FDR was elected President. Medalle had just started prosecuting the trial of infamous beer baron Irving 'Waxey' Gordon for income tax evasion.

Dewey took over in the trial, won a conviction, but chose not to continue in the office during a Democratic administration. He returned to private practice and made a reputation as a trial counsel with unusual ability. By then he was pulling down $75,000 a year.

A year later, for a salary less than half that, Dewey accepted appointment from Governor Herbert H. Lehman as Special Prosecutor to go after the gangland overlords like Lucky Luciano and Vito Genovese.

Even as Dewey was nailing the lid on Luciano's coffin, a disturbing groundswell of rumors reached Bugsy Siegel's ears: the racket-busting prosecutor was probing into his background and that one major point of interest which had seized Dewey's attention was Bugsy's 'perfect' alibi after mobster Tony Fabrizio's murder – that the Bug was hospitalised at the time of the killing.

Although Siegel was deeply concerned over having that alibi blown apart by the Special Prosecutor, that worry paled beside the distressing news that now reached him: Dewey was cooperating with newly elected Brooklyn District Attorney William O'Dwyer, who had vowed during this campaign to decimate Murder Inc., which he charged had committed no fewer than two hundred murders in the New York area alone.

But Bugsy could take some comfort in the knowledge that Dewey had also tried to crack the combination of that infamous pack of exterminators without success. His main target, Lepke Buchalter, had not only managed to escape prosecution for murder but even succeeded in saving the hierarchy of the kill-to-order corporation by silencing the prospective witnesses. Dewey couldn't proceed against Murder Inc. because his witnesses, to a man, had had their lips sealed by the onset of rigor mortis and the ravages of body decomposition.

But by early March 1940, the scene in Brooklyn had changed alarmingly. For when Bugsy Siegel awakened that morning in his outsize bed in California he felt terrifying seismic shocks, caused not by a fissure in the San Andreas fault but by the news on the radio.

District Attorney O'Dwyer – a future Mayor of New York and Ambassador to Mexico – had suddenly caught himself a canary!

The name, when it came over the air, sent Bugsy to the bathroom. It was none other than that arrogant self-glorifying ratpack leader, who was raised to respectability and to a position of high trust by the mob when they appointed him chief hatchet man for Murder Inc.: Abe Reles!

'That rotten scum bag!' Bugsy shouted into the phone to his brother-in-law, Whitey Krakower. Krakower was cooling it in his hideout in New York's Delancey Street after the rubout of Harry 'Big Greenie' Greenberg, who had been associated with Lepke in the garment rackets but had fled to Canada when Dewey launched his probe into Murder Inc. By spring of 1939, Big Greenie was running short of American dollars in his lair in Montreal and he penned a request for cash to the New York bosses. The language of the note conveyed an implied threat that if he didn't get $5,000 right away he might well blow the whistle on Lepke and the entire Murder Inc. hierarchy.

Strategically, this was a very bad move on Big Greenie's part. It made him a marked man.

Mendy Weiss, now the acting boss of Murder Inc., decreed that Greenberg had to die. He dispatched a very trusted lieutenant, Allie 'Tick Tock' Tannenbaum, to dispose of Big Greenie. But Allie – a skinny, nervous sort – the black-sheep son of a respectable Catskill Mountain hotelman, couldn't find his quarry.

Big Greenie, leery, fled Montreal and headed for Hollywood. At least that was the information Allie brought back after his failure to encounter his intended victim in Canada's largest city.

'Okay,' Mendy rasped exasperatedly, 'let Ben handle it.'

The word went out to Siegel.

'It's a contract,' he was told. 'But we are sending you help.'

Nervous Allie Tannenbaum was dispatched for the job a second time. But in a last-minute switch of plans, Bugsy himself decided to do the number on Greenberg to cover himself with personal glory and raise his stock with the mob. The assassination went off without a hitch. Big Greenie had bought a morning paper and was sitting in his car reading it. Suddenly there was a burst of gunfire, and the man who was going to blow the whistle on Murder Inc. sprawled over the front seat of his car, very dead.

Los Angeles police, faced with the first big-time killing orchestrated by the Syndicate in their city, went through the motions of an investigation but got nowhere.

Ben Siegel could relax. This rubout was like so many of the others he performed – very antiseptic. Nothing at all, simply nothing in the way of evidence or clues to point the finger of suspicion at him or anybody else. In fact if the medical examiner hadn't been so positive that the five holes drilled into Big Greenie's ugly face were caused by lead, he might have attributed the death to mosquito bites.

Bugsy Siegel became even more unnerved in his conversation with brother-in-law Whitey Krakower after the exchange on the phone about Kid Twist Reles turning squealer.

'All the shit's flying here,' Whitey murmured into the mouth-piece. 'The DA's also got Tick Tock and a couple of others in protective custody. I think they're singing . . .'

Siegel slammed the receiver into the cradle and reserved a seat on the 2:00 p.m. United Airlines flight to New York.

Although Siegel tried to keep his arrival a secret, District Attorney O'Dwyer wasted no time clarioning his awareness –

and great concern – not only about Siegel's presence in New York, but also the almost simultaneous arrival of Isidore Bernstein, an ace triggerman from Detroit's Purple Gang.

'Those men are here for business,' O'Dwyer said ominously. 'We expected out-of-town triggermen to arrive and we've been looking for them. Bernstein is a top-notch triggerman. There are other run-of-the-mill triggermen here from out of town and we know them. They are here to shoot down those who stand in the way. They won't get far in Brooklyn.

'Siegel is here because the leaders of the Brooklyn mob, the top men who should have taken over, have fled to cover. Siegel will try to restore order, calm jittery nerves, guide things until the heat is off. He will be a field director and, with Bernstein, mark out those who must go . . .'

Besides Reles, Tannenbaum, and Sholem Bernstein (no relation to Isidore from the Purple Gang), Myer Sycoff rounded out the singing quartet of 'contract' killers. All of them were holed up in a remarkable 'pigeon coop' called the Half Moon Hotel on the boardwalk of Coney Island. Their whereabouts, of course, was a carefully guarded secret; yet the underworld had somehow gotten wind not only of the hotel but the floor they were occupying: the sixth.

As freely as the prosecutor's witnesses were talking, none of the crimes that Bugsy had committed in New York held an immediate appeal for O'Dwyer.

Kid Twist, for example, spilled what he knew of Siegel's rubouts of Tony Fabrizzio and other New York hoods; but Reles's knowledge of these particular killings was mainly second-hand, and corroborating witnesses were lacking. Even when Reles told what he knew of Bugsy's role in Big Greenie's Hollywood rubout, it was hearsay.

Moreover, what interest could the Brooklyn District Attorney have in a crime that occurred three thousand miles away? Didn't he have enough problems trying to pin some of those more than two hundred local murders on the suspected rubout artists in his own jurisdiction?

Yet O'Dwyer faced a dilemma with Bugsy. So far as Siegel was concerned O'Dwyer had not an iota of court-admissible evidence

329

to prosecute the Bug in New York – not even for spitting on the sidewalk. However, in his passel of informers, oddly enough, he had a witness who could, in O'Dwyer's view, help send Bugsy Siegel to California's gas chamber.

That witness was Allie Tannenbaum, a participant and eyewitness in Greenberg's killing. Allie said he was prepared not only to testify that he trailed Big Greenie up to Montreal, but that he later followed him out to Hollywood to do him in, only to have the Bug make the murder his own personal production at the last minute. Allie further told his interrogators that Frankie Carbo, Champ Segal, and Whitey Krakower all had active roles in the crime.

It now became incumbent upon District Attorney O'Dwyer to flash this electrifying news to his counterpart in Los Angeles, District Attorney Buron Fitts, who about three years earlier had a brief but futile encounter with the Bug in an attempt to pin a gangland murder on him. Now Fitts had something more to work with: evidence of how the mysterious murder of Harry Greenberg was committed. And by whom.

And that distinguished gentleman of Hollywood, Benjamin Siegel, could now be fingered legally as a prime suspect in that killing.

Secretly and with elaborate precautions, Kid Twist Reles and Tick Tock Tannenbaum were spirited by O'Dwyer's heavily armed sleuths out of the Half Moon Hotel and flown to Los Angeles to tell the grand jury what they knew about Harry Greenberg's demise. No stories were published on this secret journey to the Coast, for O'Dwyer wanted his two pigeons back whole to help him hammer the lid shut on the coffin he was building for the Murder Inc. criminals.

Reles and Tannenbaum apparently told convincing stories, for the Los Angeles County grand jury returned an indictment on 16 August 1940, naming Siegel, Frank Carbo, and Harry Segal as Greenberg's killers, charging each with one count of murder.

Whitey Krakower wasn't included in the indictment because the grand jury hadn't been made aware of an unfortunate experience Bugsy's brother-in-law had suffered back there on Delancey Street on Manhattan's Lower East Side.

It happened just a month before on a typical hot July night when most of the populace residing in the sweltering tenements had come out into the street for breaths of fresh air. Whitey was no exception. He brought a chair from his furnished room out to the stoop, sat down, and gazed at the street, teeming with children playing games while their elders lazed about.

A typical mobland rubout. A car with New Jersey plates cruised by and a gunman opened fire. He aerated Whitey's body with five well-aimed bullets.

Meanwhile, a scandal of inordinate proportions loomed in Los Angeles, where it was discovered that Bugsy Siegel, instead of being lodged in the Los Angeles County Jail without bail pending his trial for Greenberg's murder, was cavorting on the outside, visiting nightspots, enjoying all the privileges of a free man.

The scandal cost District Attorney Fitts his bid for re-election and ushered in a new prosecutor, John Dockweiler. One of his first orders of business was to huddle with D.A. O'Dwyer, who came to L.A. to explain why a representative of the Coast prosecutor's staff, who went to Brooklyn a week earlier, was unable to discuss the testimony they were to give with Reles and Tannenbaum.

Assistant District Attorney Vernon Ferguson and two detectives were told that Reles was suffering a stomach ailment and Tick Tock was running a fever.

O'Dwyer's trip west had a purpose. It was rooted in his reluctance to let Reles and Tannenbaum out of his jurisdiction because he wanted them nearby to help in the prosecution of Murder Inc.'s other assassins being held in custody in Brooklyn.

O'Dwyer wasn't yet suspected of grandstanding for City Hall and the Mayor's seat, for 'Little Flower', Fiorello H. LaGuardia, was still ensconced there.

On the surface, it was said O'Dwyer didn't want to chance sending Reles and Tannenbaum to Los Angeles for the trial because he didn't believe any amount of protection the law provided these squealers on their road trip would be enough to save them from gangland's guns. They were much safer staying in their Coney Island lair and starring in his own production, O'Dwyer reasoned.

No sooner had O'Dwyer arrived in Los Angeles and conferred with the new prosecutor than the expected happened. The indictment against Bugsy and his cohorts was dismissed.

The reason given by the two District Attorneys at a joint press conference was that under California law (a law that was also very much in force in New York), the testimony of an accomplice or accomplices in a crime must be given independent corroboration at the trial. And inasmuch as the authorities had no other witnesses of the crime, they didn't have a case.

Of course, both Brooklyn and L.A. officials knew at the time the grand jury was asked to indict Bugsy, they had no witnesses other than the participants. And they certainly knew that Big Greenie wasn't going to take the stand and accuse his killers – not with all that aerating his body got.

It was all an exercise in futility.

Bugsy Siegel was a free man!

By now, Tom Dewey had made his mark on the underworld and left a rich legacy behind as he moved onward and upward from prosecutorial duties in New York City to the Governor's Mansion in Albany – and to his two unsuccessful efforts to gain residence at 1600 Pennsylvania Avenue.

Dewey had come a long way since those early days of his appointment as Special Prosecutor. Underworld leaders in the beginning ridiculed him and looked upon him as a 'Boy Scout'. They had a change of mind after he obtained the conviction against Lucky Luciano.

In the two years of his incumbency as Special Prosecutor, Dewey smashed rackets in the restaurant, laundry, garment, trucking, and other businesses. He brought convictions against seventy-two underworld operatives. Only one gangster among all those he prosecuted was acquitted.

Dewey was destined to make one more headline in his dealings with gangland, and that would come at a time when his duties as a prosecutor had been left far behind and his concentration centered on such gubernatorial achievements as bringing about reappointment of congressional and legislative districts in the state, placing New York on a pay-as-you-go policy for capital construction, increasing state aid for education, and establishing the first state commission to eliminate religious and racial discrimination in employment.

After finishing this third term in Albany, Dewey went into private practice with a law firm that counted among its clients some of the world's most distinguished names. And he was also instrumental – as a close personal friend of Richard M. Nixon – in influencing legislation on the national level.

He died at the age of sixty-eight of heart failure on 16 March 1971, in Bal Harbor, Florida.

Chapter 28

The Half Moon Hop; A Very Last Word on How Abe Reles Really Died

In 1941 Whirlaway won the Triple Crown by sweeping the Kentucky Derby, Preakness, and Belmont Stakes. He was the fifth horse to achieve that singular honor in the history of thoroughbred racing.

Bugsy Siegel had won one crown that year, but it didn't appear likely he'd gain another. His freedom from entanglements with the law didn't last long. The Federal Government was suddenly on his back. He was asked to saddle up on a Pullman and ride back to New York.

The rub this time was that the feds wanted The Bug to tell a grand jury all about how he harboured Lepke Buchalter during the latter's disappearing act. But Bugsy played it cool and stayed away. No subpoena was issued for him at first.

Then, on 17 April a team of federal marshals descended on Bugsy's mansion on Delfern Avenue, knocked on the portal of the huge thirty-five-room house, and put manacles on the resident's wrists.

'What's wrong?' he asked. 'I paid my income taxes . . . what are you guys doing to me?'

The arrest was based on a New York indictment alleging that Siegel conspired to harbor Buchalter while Buchalter was a fugitive from a drug rap. Although Lepke was now safely back in Leavenworth, the government wasn't about to let The Bug off the hook for diddling with them during their nationwide search for the missing mobster. The marshals took Bugsy before United States Commissioner David Head in Los Angeles.

'How do you plead?' Head asked.

'I don't know nothing about hiding anybody,' Bugsy groaned.

'How do you plead?' Head repeated.

'Not guilty,' Siegel sighed.

The commissioner ordered the prisoner held in $25,000 bail, which was posted promptly. Siegel walked out of the hearing room whistling. He was to remain free until the government could go ahead with extradition proceedings that would return him to New York to stand trial in Federal Court.

On the day of Siegel's arrest in Hollywood, a rather revolting development was unfolding at the penitentiary in Leavenworth. The man Bugsy was accused of hiding out was being given his walking papers. But when the bewildered Lepke Buchalter passed through the prison gates into the bright sunshine and fresh air of freedom, he found a couple of District Attorney O'Dwyer's men waiting for him.

They had a warrant for his arrest: the charge was murder.

That was why the government was so willing to let Buchalter off from doing the rest of his time on the dope rap that got him sent to the Big House. Because if by chance he – and a number of other Murder Inc. killers – should be convicted, society would have in some small measure been avenged. For that would mean death in Sing Sing Prison's electric chair.

Bugsy Siegel was casting a wary eye in the direction of Brooklyn at this moment. That thing the government grabbed him on – harboring fugitive Lepke – was a minor disturbance, so far as The Bug was concerned. He could beat that rap with his daughter Millicent defending him, and she was then only in the fifth grade. But this Brooklyn stuff was another matter.

If Abe Reles, Allie Tannenbaum, Myer Sycoff, and Sholem Bernstein took the stand at Buchalter's trial, who could say but what they might spill? Bugsy knew for sure that they could tell enough to put Lepke away fifty times over – and that they also could spill enough to have Siegel executed. Indeed, The Bug was also quite certain his worries about going to California's gas chamber weren't over yet, either.

For District Attorney Dockweiler was already going through the motions of impaneling a grand jury to take a fresh look at the Harry Greenberg extermination. This development, coupled with what was going on in Brooklyn, was very disturbing to Bugsy.

First, Bugsy decided he had to settle a score with the Los Angeles prosecutor. What a hell of a nerve he had re-opening the investigation, after Siegel plunked $30,000 into the District Attorney's political campaign kitty and helped elect Dockweiler!

Siegel was never much of a letter writer, but he knew how to put together a composition of vituperation and venom. That's exactly what he did, and when Dockweiler got the letter he almost knocked the marbled columns of the courthouse over in his haste to get an explanation.

'Who the hell took Siegel's dirty money?' Dockweiler asked his campaign manager.

'Well, we were a little shy of funds and every little bit helped . . .'

'Back! Back!' screamed the prosecutor. 'Give it back! Every damned cent goes back!'

And back went the $30,000 to Siegel – just in time, too. For Siegel's mounting legal problems augered a very big fee for his defense by famed Hollywood lawyer Jerry Geisler.

Bugsy's next courtroom appearance came on 29 May, when Commissioner Head called him back for the extradition proceeding. The Bug only put up token defense against being sent to New York. He really wanted to go so he could get away from the heat

Dockweiler was putting on him with the Big Greenie assassination inquiry.

Now, somehow, the course of events for Bugsy and Lepke seemed to be moving in tandem. For at the very moment Head wrote out Bugsy's cross-country ticket, Buchalter was taken, handcuffed, to Kings County Court Judge George W. Martin for arraignment on a charge of murder.

Burton Turkus, the assistant prosecutor who had unearthed most of the evidence that was credited to O'Dwyer, his boss, had nailed Buchalter and two other Murder Inc. killers for the 1936 slaying of Joseph Rosen, a former garment trucker who was standing in the wings as a witness against Lepke's underworld activities.

Buchalter's attorney expressed outrage in court that his client was indicted at all. Why, Brooklyn had absolutely no jurisdiction over Lepke, the attorney argued. Certainly not at a time when Louis was serving a fourteen-year sentence in the penitentiary at Leavenworth! Send him back to Kansas and let him pay penance – full penance – for being a dirty dope peddler, he told the court.

A smiling Judge Martin turned his gaze from the lawyer and settled his attention on Buchalter.

'I will hold the defendant without bail,' Martin intoned. 'Trial tentatively scheduled for 14 July.'

The Los Angeles Grand Jury that had been conducting the new inquiry into Big Greenie's killing reaffirmed the action of its 1940 predecessors in linking Siegel and Frankie Carbo with the crime. But the jury discreetly omitted the other participants – Champ Segal and Harry Krakower (who were beyond prosecution) – from any mention in the indictment.

It appeared that Bugsy's murder trial might not come off much before Christmas or the New Year, if then, and there was ample time for Siegel to prepare for his defense out west – without the advice and counsel of Jerry Geisler.

For even better than the roar of a great mouthpiece in the court was the absence of a silenced squealer's lips.

It was Wednesday, 12 November. A strong wind from the black, dismal sea was blowing. The night was cold. The temperature had dipped to just above freezing.

It was 3:00 a.m. now and one of Abe Reles's police guards, Detective James L. Boyle, one of six policemen on the midnight to 8:00 a.m. tour guarding Kid Twist and the other three canaries in Suite 620 at the Half Moon in Coney Island, was brewing himself a cup of coffee. Suddenly he turned away from his chore and saw Reles standing before him.

'Hey, Kid,' Boyle asked, 'wanna cup of coffee?'

'No thanks,' Reles replied, then turned and disappeared into Room 623, one of the ten rooms in Suite 620.

It was a lovely suite. The view was of the Atlantic Ocean and the seemingly endless stretch of white sandy beach of America's foremost shore playground.

The rest of the early morning hours passed quietly, it seemed.

But at 6:45 on that mist-shrouded morning, the phone on the hotel manager's lobby desk began jangling. The manager answered. The caller was William A. Nicholson, secretary of the local draft board. Nicholson was a guest at the hotel, occupying Room 123, five floors down and directly below Room 623, where Reles was staying.

Nicholson had just awakened and looked sleepily out his window, which had a view of an extension roof over the hotel's ground-floor facilities. And what he saw jarred him fully awake.

He saw the body of a man with crisp black hair garbed in a gray suit with a blanket and sheets all around him spreadeagled on the gravel-and-tar papered roof. His white shirt was opened, exposing his bare chest and abdomen, and the fly on his pants was unbuttoned.

The manager had only to hear from Nicholson to guess what probably had happened. Without even going to view the body, he phoned Suite 620 and talked with Detective Boyle. Boyle slammed the receiver down and dashed into Reles's room.

It was empty.

The untimely death of Abe Kid Twist Reles at the tender age of thirty-three was mourned by his wife, Rose, and their two children, and by William O'Dwyer and Burton Turkus. Elsewhere the Kid's demise was greeted with a chorus of cheers.

Among those raising their voices in jubilation were Lepke

Buchalter, Louis Capone, Philip 'Little Farvel' Cohen, Mendy Weiss, Harry 'Pittsburgh Phil' Strauss, Harty 'Happy' Maione, Frank 'The Dasher' Abbandando and, in particular – Benjamin 'Bugsy' Siegel!

Reles's death seemed to signal the end of the Brooklyn District Attorney's seeming determination to smash the mass murder machine. But nothing was farther from the truth.

With Tannenbaum and the other witnesses warbling their accusatory arias, O'Dwyer and Turkus went forward with their prosecution of Murder Inc. Eventually Buchalter, Weiss, and five of their murderous associates were sent to the electric chair. Other confederates were given long jail terms.

Murder Inc. was finally and at last out of business – or at the very least had been forced into bankruptcy. For the organisation, as it was constituted then, was no longer functioning with its original board of killers. Yet the pattern and frequency of killings that followed in the years since tends to indicate the techniques introduced by that band of mass murderers have not been supplanted by any greater technological advances.

Co-author George Carpozi Jr talked to Burton Turkus in 1965, a quarter century after Kid Twist's death.

Sitting behind a large, neat desk in a Madison Avenue skyscraper law office, Turkus puffed on his favourite bole pipe and related:

'Reles had murdered more than a dozen men and knew the technique, motive, and/or perpetrators in countless other killings. He was the most valuable bric-a-brac which law enforcement has owned to date.

'In the history of crime there never was an example of a crime complex and organised lawlessness equal to what Murder Inc. represented. It was a national ring with international connections, put together on the lines of a cartel. But that pattern continues right to this day . . .'

Turkus cited the major killings in the preceding twenty-five years:

'Charles Binaggio is slain in an open political clubhouse in Kansas City . . .

'A detective lieutenant in Chicago, Bill Drury, is eliminated on a September day in 1950 for becoming "too nosy" . . .

'Philly Mangano, an original Murder Inc. staff gunman, is dropped into a Brooklyn swamp in 1951 with three bullets in his head . . .

'Willie Moretti is silenced in New Jersey the same year . . .

'Albert Anastasia is publicly gunned to death in a Manhattan barber shop in 1951 . . .

'Augie Pisano, along with a woman companion, is a "hit" in Queens in 1959 . . .

'And that's to mention just a few in the box score that makes it brutally evident the pattern is still in use despite Murder Inc.'s breakup.'

Turkus was asked how severely his efforts to prosecute Murder Inc. were damaged after Reles's death.

'The silencing of Reles was a body blow to the investigation,' Turkus admitted. 'Thereafter everything ground to a halt; but Reles nonetheless had bequeathed a priceless heritage to a society and law enforcement, the blueprint for the only way the organised crime complex or syndicate can be successfully attacked – through a break from within its own ranks . . .'

Did Turkus have any new theory on how Abe Reles might have died?

The former prosecutor shook his head from side to side.

'The theories all have been exhausted,' he answered.

He was referring not only to the official investigative groups that concluded Reles died in a plunge while trying to escape from the sixth-floor room, but even to the suggestions made by Joe Valachi to the Kefauver Senate Investigating Committee that one of the cops guarding him pushed Reles to his death.

'The police threw him out,' said Valachi.

Yet one of the special grand juries impaneled to investigate all the circumstances of his death concluded:

'Abe Reles . . . fell to his death as a consequence of his attempt to escape from his room . . . He fell to an extension roof five floors below his room . . . His body was found nine feet from the building with two sheets partly entwined about him. They were knotted together and a length of wire was tied to one end.

'Just beneath the window of Reles's room was a steam radiator with the steam valve, a length of wire which extended from the bushing to the edge of the windowsill. This wire was of the same type as that tied to the end of the bedsheets.

'It is most important to note that the piece of wire attached to the end of the bedsheet was, for the purpose of our investigation, scientifically tested by the Federal Bureau of Investigation in its crime laboratory at the request of the District Attorney. The findings of the FBI showed that the free end of the wire attached to the sheets entwined with Abe Reles's body was unquestionably broken by tensile stress sufficient to pull it apart. Abe Reles, who was an unusually strong and agile man, weighed between one-hundred and sixty and one-hundred and seventy-five pounds. The FBI ascertained that this wire would not support a weight of one-hundred and sixty pounds. Its limit of stress was one-hundred and thirty pounds ...'

With his bad stomach and all, if Kid Twist hadn't lived so high on the hog and had dieted down to 130 pounds, might he have made it?

Burton Turkus shrugged and smiled sardonically at the question. 'But none of that happened, did it?' he asked.

The grand jury went on to conclude that the wire wasn't cut by a tool, that it simply broke from a weight hanging from it 'in excess of one hundred and thirty pounds.'

As Reles's descent was reconstructed, the jury suggested that Abe was trying to make his way like a human fly from his room to Room 523 directly below, which was unoccupied.

'The latch of the window [of 523] was pulled over about one-quarter of an inch and had to be moved before the window could be opened. A half-screen on the outside of the window was raised to within six inches from the top of the upper half of the window. This was not its usual position. On the stone windowsill of Room 523, scratches were observed, as were marks of scraping on the paint of the window frame ...'

The conclusion was that Kid Twist had made it okay with the bedsheets and wires down to the fifth floor, a distance of ten feet 'and one-quarter inch', as the jury noted. Perhaps that quarter inch made all the difference for the acrobatic kid. For, after that, the distance to the pebble-covered extension room below was another forty-two feet 'three-quarters inch'.

The medical examiner's findings also were noted by the grand jury:

'Reles died of a fractured dislocation of the fourth and fifth lumbar vertebrae, ruptured liver and spleen and hemo-peritoneum [hemorrhage in the abdomen] ... There were no bullet wounds, stab wounds or any other marks of violence on his body ...'

The Kid didn't need any other marks or wounds. What he suffered was enough to spread glee over gangland.

Bugsy was ecstatic. He was now looking forward to his trial, scheduled for mid-January 1942. Even the promise by District Attorney Dockweiler of Allie Tannenbaum as the state's star witness didn't lessen Siegel's enthusiasm for the courtroom fray.

The Bug knew – as Geisler knew – that no judge would let a trial run for long on the uncorroborated testimony of an accomplice. And the probers, hard as they had tried, could find no single credible witness for the upcoming trial.

With Reles out of the picture – or window – the case was even weaker than before. At least Reles could have testified that Mendy Weiss, acting on Lepke Buchalter's instructions, ordered Big Greenie's murder. With Kid Twist in the witness chair and not being truly a participant in the actual crime, only in its planning, the prosecution had a fighting chance.

But now their case was a great big zero. And Bugsy knew it.

As the day of Siegel's trial drew near, Allie Tannenbaum was hustled out of the Half Moon, and with a cordon of lawmen guarding him, trekked westward not by plane but train, because O'Dwyer decreed it was a much safer way to transport the witness.

It was a waste of taxpayer's money – those in New York and those in California.

The prosecution was an exercise in futility and Bugsy Siegel reached fulfillment as Superior Judge A.A. Scott interrupted the proceedings just after convening court the morning of 5 February 1942, and declared:

'I do not think the State has proved its case . . . The indictment is hereby dismissed . . .'

The highlight of the trial was a blistering cross-examination of Allie the Tick Tock by Jerry Geisler, who put on a grandstand show to earn that $30,000 Bugsy got back from District Attorney Dockweiler's campaign chest. Jerry could have gotten the dismissal without asking Allie a single question, but by merely turning to the judge after direct examination was completed and asking to have the case thrown out.

Frankie Carbo also beat the rap, but he was later caught in the clutches of the law for other heinous criminal acts and was imprisoned for a long stretch.

Though Murder Inc. went into a Chapter 11, the National Crime Syndicate, as Burton Turkus put it, remained very much in business.

And Benny Siegel's abiding loyalty and hard industry – coupled with the widely circulated suspicion that he had some kind of hand in Reles's death – were properly rewarded with expanded power and jurisdiction.

The Bug rose to the status of a top echelon director of the nationwide crime cartel, ruling gangland with other surviving members of the Big Crackdown such as Frank Costello, Joe Adonis, Longy Zwillman, Willie Moretti and Charles 'Lucky' Luciano, who still wielded power from his cell in New York's Clinton State Prison at Dannemora – and would continue to do so even after Governor Tom Dewey would perform his final act in underworld business.

22 June 1947. After a night on the town during which he gorged himself so that every inch of space in his cavity was filled with food, Bugsy Siegel returned to his palatial home, loosened his necktie, sighed with contentment, lay on the couch of his living room, and picked up the previous day's *Los Angeles Times* which he'd dropped on the table earlier without reading. Now he wanted to catch up on the news.

In the more than five years since he emerged unscathed from the Biggie Greenberg murder case, The Bug had travelled several light years into the future. He was now the proud owner of the fabulous Flamingo Hotel, which he built from the ground up as Las Vegas's first gambling palace. He had begged and borrowed money from scores, if not hundreds, of sources to finance the project.

Shortly before Christmas of 1946, with workmen still crawling about putting finishing touches in place, the garish, spectacular Flamingo flung open its doors for business.

It was a glittering premier in true Hollywood style. Bugsy had gone into hock for almost all of the $5,500,000 it had cost to build.

But none of his partners, neither the mobsters nor the legitimate businessmen and bankers, could fault Bugsy at the grand opening. The gaudy hotel-casino was an instant smash as planeload after planeload of Hollywood celebrities was shuttled to its glittering environs.

As the weeks and months passed, Siegel felt increasing pressure from his debtors. They were screaming for repayment of their loans. Now he had to battle against time to get out of the red. He begged, borrowed – and stole!

He held out a commission on a big Mexican drug deal that he'd handled. That antagonised the Mob and got him marked as a double-crosser, a label that Siegel had never worn in all his years as a criminal.

As his antagonism and quarrelling continued, Frank Costello and Meyer Lansky, by now the two biggest gambling syndicate bosses in the land, became totally disenchanted with Bugsy, for he was no longer the cool cucumber they had admired and respected during so many years of amicable relationships.

Just as Bugsy began to catch up on the news in the *Los Angeles Times*, at about 11:00 p.m. that night, a gun blasted thunderously seven times from the terrace window a few short feet away. Siegel slumped on the flower-patterned divan awash in his own blood that covered his face like a mask.

Neighbors who heard the shots at that late hour called the police. But by the time the first contingent of cops arrived, there was no need for an ambulance. Bugsy Siegel was very dead, and, as the autopsy later showed, he was drilled to death by three accurately fired bullets to his head.

The killer left no clues as to his identity, and the case was never solved.

One of the most credible theories in the underworld about how Bugsy met his demise dealt with a meeting that had been held in Havana, Cuba, a few weeks previously. It was a Syndicate summit attended by the hierarchy from all of the U.S.A.'s crime families and presided over by the chief justice of organised crime's supreme court – Charles 'Lucky' Luciano.

The situation in Las Vegas had become an unnerving crisis, and in a way the conclave in Havana, a solemn, full-dress gangland gathering, was a tribute to The Bug's standing in the Syndicate. The Mob bosses had journeyed to their Caribbean rendezvous to roast him. For they had soberly concluded that their colleague had gone haywire – and could find no alternative but to decree that he must be eliminated.

Siegel had not only been holding back on the take from the Mexican narcotics deal, but was also skimming the profits at the Flamingo's gaming tables – a totally unforgiveable act.

The meeting in Cuba, along with the sighting of a number of Eastern torpedoes in the Los Angeles-Hollywood-Beverly Hills area, as well as Las Vegas, in the days preceding the execution, tended to lend a measure of credibility to the theory that Siegel's killing was commanded by Lucky Luciano himself.

How could Luciano, who was sent to 'Siberia' to do up to fifty big ones, have been in the Caribbean capital city only ninety miles off the Florida coast – but more than 1,200 miles distant as the crow, or a plane, flies from Dannemora?

Chapter 29

The Untold Story: Why and How Tom Dewey Gave Lucky Luciano a Walk

Few, if any, lawyers in the nation's history can lay claim, as George Wolf could, of having represented so many of the country's most notorious gangsters – Costello, Schultz, Luciano, Anastasia, Torrio, Genovese, and Chicago's infamous Fischetti brothers – among many other big-name mobsters.

Though Frank Costello may seem to have been Wolf's principal client because of the wide publicity generated by their frequent court appearances, and especially on the celebrated televised Kefauver Senate hearings in Washington, the truth is that this veteran of more than sixty years of courtroom combat had been involved in the fortunes of scores upon scores of other notorious figures.

In 1974 co-author George Carpozi Jr met with George Wolf in his residence on Manhattan's East Side to lay the groundwork for the lawyer's biography. At the time, Wolf was eighty-three and had been retired a mere four years from more than six decades of courtroom combat.

Among the many cases Wolf recounted with all their revelatory, startling, even shocking detail was his secret deal in 1945 with Governor Thomas E. Dewey on behalf of Charles 'Lucky' Luciano.

In George Wolf's view, Thomas E. Dewey was a poor trial lawyer, yet was able to get convictions against some of the most notorious criminals when he was Special Prosecutor and District Attorney because of the staggering amount of preparation he invested in each case.

One of the most notable convictions was against Lucky Luciano. Although Luciano had committed every crime in the books including murder, authorities had never been able to gather the evidence to prosecute him. Finally, in 1936, Dewey brought him before the bar of justice on ninety counts of compulsory prostitution. Many legal experts to this day believe the charges were trumped up, Wolf said. Nevertheless, Dewey obtained his conviction and Luciano – to Dewey's utter amazement – was sentenced to a term of thirty to fifty years in prison.

In early 1943, while serving his first term as governor of New York, Dewey was visited in Albany by Luciano's trial lawyer, Moses A. Polakoff, who announced his intention to make a motion before the trial judge for a reduction of sentence.

'Who is going to make the motion?' Dewey asked Polakoff.

'I am,' the lawyer answered.

'You're out of your mind, Moe,' Dewey responded.

'Judge McCook can't stand your guts. You've got to get someone else to make the motion.'

Polakoff asked Governor Dewey if he could suggest anyone.

'Of course I can,' Dewey said. 'It should be George Wolf because Judge McCook respects him highly.'

Polakoff called on Wolf, bringing the bulky volumes of the court reporter's trial transcript of Luciano's case. He told Wolf what he wanted him to do.

'I don't like the smell of the case,' Wolf told Polakoff.

'But Tom Dewey directed me to ask you to handle it,' Polakoff replied.

'Then I've got to talk to Tom and get it from his own lips that my appearance in this case isn't going to hurt me,' Wolf said.

Wolf saw Dewey. 'What kind of a case can I make for the reduction of Luciano's sentence?' Wolf asked. 'He received the maximum penalty under the law and I don't have a thread of new evidence to spin into my argument before McCook.'

Dewey smiled. 'But there is new evidence,' the Governor said. 'Lucky, you see, helped our army's landing in Sicily ... he contacted Vito Genovese and some other people over there and they gave Major Murray Gurfein [later to become a U.S. District Court Judge for the Southern District of New York] information for military intelligence about Italian and German troop displacements there. Without Luciano's assistance, our troops may not have been able to land in Sicily.'

Wolf agreed to take up Luciano's cause. He saw Judge McCook. Major Gurfein was summoned to the judge's chambers. He confirmed what Wolf claimed about Luciano's 'patriotism' to the U.S.

McCook was pleased but not about to be the one to give the boss of bosses of the underworld his freedom. 'I am thoroughly satisfied ... that the defendant did make an effort towards helping the government,' he said. 'And taking into consideration and with all due respect to your eloquent plea, Mr Wolf, I have decided to presently deny the motion. However, if you will get Governor Dewey to commute his sentence and arrange for his deportation – because we don't want men of his caliber in this country – we can get around the matter that way.'

Wolf went to Dewey. 'Well,' Dewey smiled, 'so long as Judge McCook suggested that, I'll make the necessary arrangements.'

A few weeks later, Dewey commuted Lucky Luciano's sentence and Luciano went back to his homeland. 'A job well done as usual,' Dewey said to Wolf.

There have been many versions of the significance of Luciano's contribution to the Anzio beach landings. The main point is that when Luciano agreed to aid his adopted country in that World

War II effort, the navy asked for Lucky's transfer from far-distant Dannemora to the equally secure but more accessible Great Meadows Penitentiary just north of Albany.

Every few weeks a team of naval officers in civilian clothes, accompanied by lawyer Moses Polakoff, pilgrimaged to the prison and conferred with Luciano. Over a period of months, Lucky, who had been given carte blanche to communicate with sources in Sicily through the Mafia underground which penetrated Italian-German security with the same ease that their counterparts in America infiltrated the rackets.

In time, reams of data began to flow about Italian shore fortifications and troop displacements, the location of gun batteries and anti-aircraft artillery, and other military intelligence. Church Street, in turn, forwarded this material to Washington. It was shaped into a neat package that carried all the information the invading U.S. Troops needed to land effectively in Sicily and to suffer far fewer casualties than would have been inflicted without Luciano's help.

On a dreary, freezing February evening in 1946, a phalanx of Bureau of Immigration & Naturalisation uniformed agents escorted Luciano up the ramp of a creaking Liberty ship, the SS *Laura Keene*, which had seen its best days transporting troops across the Atlantic during the war years. She was docked at a Hudson River pier besides such venerable super-liners as the *Ile de France* and *Queen Mary*.

Clark Gable, Jack Benny and Mary Livingston, and Cary Grant were billeted on the French Lines flagship; John Wayne, former Ambassador to England, Joseph F. Kennedy, and other dignitaries were sailing on the *Queen*. Their pier-side send-offs paled in comparison to the salutes the *Laura Keene* experienced that night.

Limousines by the score pulled up dockside, and from their plush interiors stepped out a procession of the Syndicate's top echelon to bid a fond farewell to Lucky Luciano, their beloved *compare*. Their bodyguards carried baskets of fruits, wines, champagne, caviar, cooked lobster, and other gastronomic delights. They were lugged into the ship where a huge banquet table groaned under the enormity of the spread.

Those in the bon voyage party weren't aware of the terms which freed Lucky – that he was being exiled to Italy for life and was never to re-enter the U.S. again. In fact, arrangements had been made with Italy's post-war government to deny Luciano passport privileges for travel to any foreign land for the rest of his life.

Unaware of those arrangements, his Mafia pals toasted Lucky with such platitudes as:

'Here's to you, Lucky, we gonna see ya back real soon . . .'

'Hey, they no can keep a good man down . . . You showed them, Charlie . . .'

And on it went. In the cheering section were the luminaries of the National Syndicate that Luciano organised: Frank Costello, Albert Anastasia, Meyer Lansky, Joseph 'Socks' Lanza – and even Vito Genovese!

The *Laura Keene* tooted her croaky whistle a few minutes before midnight. His gangster pals stood on the pier waving and shouting their goodbyes as Lucky Luciano started on his way to Italy to a new life – but hardly the obscurity American authorities had mandated and presupposed.

In the aftermath of Bugsy Siegel's murder, authorities got wind of Lucky's presence in Havana – barely sixteen months after his deportation from America. Officials in Washington were outraged that Luciano could have eluded his Italian watchdogs and made his way to the U.S.'s closest 'foreign' neighbor, only a half-hour's private plane ride from Florida.

The State Department put extreme pressure on the Cuban government to get rid of this undesirable visitor, and President Grau San Martin ordered him out of the country.

Charles Lucky Luciano lived another fifteen years until 1962, when he died of natural causes in Naples.

He took many secrets to the grave – but one of the most puzzling was how he made his way back to Cuba and whether he, in fact, had given the order to ready Bugsy Siegel's body for the grave.

Chapter 30

Vito Genovese Is Back and Wants Frank Costello's Scalp

The ship bringing Vito Genovese back to New York departed Naples on 14 May 1945, and he had only one custodian on the six-day sail: Agent Orange C. Dickey.

During the nine months that Genovese was locked up in the jail in Nola, he had been beseeched almost daily by Dickey to come clean, admit his part in black marketeering, and settle for slap-on-the-wrist punishment – provided he named names of the major traffickers in the theft of stores from U.S. military installations.

True to the code of *omerta*, Genovese maintained a deafening silence. He wanted no part of a plea-bargain. He reasoned that sooner or later, with no concrete evidence to convict him at a trial, he'd be given his freedom.

But never in his wildest imagination could he conceive that Dickey would pull a Pearl Harbor on him by arranging for his deportation to face the charge of murdering 'Shadow' Boccia. It was only then that Vito squirmed and cowered.

'During one of my visits to his cell,' Dickey was to say, 'Genovese offered me a $250,000 bribe to turn my head and say none of the things I was trying to pin on him were true. Of course I turned him down flatly . . .'

On the ride from the prison to dockside to board the ship, Genovese protested violently.

'You can't do this to me!' he squealed. 'I offer you money . . . you want more? I give you anything you want . . . just don't take me back to New York!'

But no sooner had Dickey escorted Genovese to the first-deck cabin they were to share on the crossing than Vito's stance took a 180-degree turn. He became passive and seemed, suddenly, to relish the prospect of returning to his adopted country – even if he was the central character in a drama that could strap him in Sing Sing's electric chair.

'You know, Orange,' Genovese rasped. 'I gotta hand it to you. What you're doing for me is the biggest favor anyone do to me . . .'

During the crossing Genovese talked freely to Dickey.

'While he never admitted his complicity in the black market rackets, he was more than anxious to talk about his activities in organised crime.

'He spoke freely about the work he'd done in labor disputes – particularly as a strike-breaker. He said he was almost always able to convince the strikers that they'd be much better off leaving the picket line and returning to work . . .'

Genovese bragged that if friendly persuasion failed, he could always bring in strike-breakers who would crack heads to convince those in the walkout that it wasn't healthy to remain away from their jobs.

'I make plenty money doing this,' Vito said. 'I also make plenty money by working for the companies as labor-management mediator. You gotta play both ends against the middle . . . you understand why I say?'

When the ship docked at the 47th Street pier on the Hudson, Dickey finally returned the cuffs to Vito's wrists. When they descended the gangplank they were met by a team of NYPD detectives, who took custody of Genovese and whisked him downtown to the Police Headquarters Building on Centre Street.

There he was fingerprinted, mugged, and tossed into a cell to await arraignment in the morning in General Sessions Court, where the sitting magistrate ordered him held without bail.

But his lawyer, George Wolf, soon managed to obtain his release for the not-so-modest sum of $100,000, which the defendant had no problem putting up. In fact, it was backed by funds out of Vito's petty cash drawer.

Actually, holding the Crime Kingpin was a farce. How could he ever go on trial?

How, after one of the key witnesses in the case against Genovese and Mike Miranda, who conspired with Vito to set up Boccia for the rigged card game, was murdered?

How could District Attorney Frank Hogan ever give a second's thought to prosecuting Genovese, Miranda, and the others named in the indictment – Gus Frasca and George Smurra – when a second witness died under the most mysterious circumstances?

That key prosecution witness was put in protective custody to prevent a repetition of the first witness's fate. To make certain nothing happened to the second witness, Hogan provided him with around-the-clock guards. But then the witness had a chronic stomach ailment and was taking a liquid medicine to keep the condition in check. One day after he took a spoonful of the medicine, the witness collapsed and died almost instantly. An assistant medical examiner who performed the autopsy and toxicological analysis cleared up the mystery of how the witness died after taking just a spoonful of a medication for his stomach ailment:

'We found enough poison in his stomach to kill eight horses . . .'

There was now no way the blind lady balancing the scales of justice could have an opportunity to weigh the fates of Vito and the other accused killers.

Certainly not after District Attorney Hogan saw the futility of it all and asked the court to dismiss the indictment.

* * *

Vito Genovese, Mafia godfather, was free once more.

But he'd been away from the scene for about eight years – after having served barely twelve months as The King of crime, Tom Dewey had frightened him into exile and the scepter of Vito's undisputed leadership over the National Syndicate had been passed to Frank Costello.

So there was no way Genovese could demand his old job back. A takeover wouldn't work because Frank Costello had come a long way in the leadership of the Luchese Family that Vito had abdicated eight years ago. Despite his hands-off policy in overseeing the Luciano-Genovese Family day-to-day operations, Costello's leadership had resulted in handsome income for most members of the family. Genovese sensed that a takeover to restore his old dominance would take months, perhaps years.

He decided to bide his time. He would first have to win a following. And to that end, he went to his old soldiers and, one by one, tried to win them over.

Valachi had a bead on the situation:

'It was easy to see that sooner or later there was going to be trouble. Vito was building up to something. We just had to wait for him to make his move . . . Everyone was getting nervous.'

Genovese's first move was to attack one of Costello's most vulnerable lieutenants, Willie Moretti, an overseer of the rackets for the Luciano Family in New Jersey.

Moretti was one of the most well-liked leaders in the underworld – but there was one problem. He had syphilis, and it appeared it was affecting his brain. He'd discuss matters in public that no self-respecting Mafioso leader would dream of talking about, but the mob tolerated his lapses because he'd been Frank Costello's chum since childhood. They didn't dare move in on Willie.

But Genovese convinced the *commissione* that Moretti had to be hit. 'If tomorrow I go wrong,' Genovese argued, 'I would want to be hit so as not to bring harm to Our Thing . . .'

On 4 October 1951, Willie Moretti was enjoying a leisurely lunch in his favourite dining spot, Joe's Restaurant in Cliffside Park, New Jersey. A team of gunmen, headed by John 'Johnny Roberts' Robilotto, sauntered into the eatery. Moretti's recognition of the visitors came too late. Even before he could fathom what their presence meant, they opened fire and committed the 'mercy killing', as it came to be called.

Moretti's death was a giant step on the way to taking over from Costello. Now the Luchese Family began to wonder how many more maneuvers Vito would have to execute before he succeeded Costello.

'It seemed like everything got messed up when Vito came back,' Valachi said. 'At least with Frank Costello life was nice and peaceful. Then [with Genovese back] it's one rumor, then another . . . To tell the truth, I didn't want to talk to anybody no more. I was afraid to hear what the next thing was, and I'd get in trouble for knowing it . . .'

What Valachi meant was that while Costello was still running the family, a growing number of Mafiosi were grumbling over the fission in the ranks. They were wondering how much longer Costello could hang on as boss.

He held on for six more years.

The late evening of 2 May 1957 was a cool night; a slight breeze was wafting across the landscape as Costello, returning from dinner at a fashionable East Side restaurant, entered the lobby of his apartment building at 115 Central Park West. He had no awareness of the gunman lying in the shadows of the lobby.

No sooner had Costello walked but a few short steps toward the elevator than a voice cried out:

'Hey, Frank! Turn around and look at me! This is for you!'

A single shot rang out from a handgun and struck Costello in the head. Then the gunman fled from the building to a waiting car across the street, which barreled away, tires squealing.

But Costello was still alive. In a daze, he staggered to the doorman and mumbled, 'Someone tried to get me . . .'

Seeing blood trickling from Costello's head the doorman hurried to a phone and dialed the police, who conveyed the Mafia overlord to nearby Roosevelt Hospital.

After his head wound was patched Costello was quizzed by detectives who wanted to know who committed this horrendous act.

'I got no idea who would do this to me,' Costello said straight faced. 'Do you got any idea?'

Once again the underworld had gotten away with settling one of its own disputes – although in this instance it had failed miserably to do away with its target.

Although he played it cool in his response to questions posed about the attempt on his life, Costello was badly shaken. He called a meeting of the Mafia hierarchy and announced his retirement.

After biding his time for so many years, Genovese had finally returned to his zenith. He was back to where he'd been for that brief short period in the 1930s between Luciano's imprisonment and his own exile in Italy to avoid the murder rap that threatened to take him out of circulation for too many years of his life or to end it with a sentence to the electric chair.

Not satisfied with regaining the throne of the Luciano Family, Genovese now began to look out of the corner of his eye at the leadership of the Mangano Family that had fallen to Albert Anastasia. Genovese never could stomach Anastasia, perhaps the most ruthless killer in Mafia history.

What happened to Vincent and Philip Mangano to enable Albert Anastasia to take over?

The Manganos had been powers in the Mafia from the day in 1924 when Don Giuseppe Balsamo finally decided to step down and turned the reins over to Vince and Phil. But they did not assume roles as true leaders of the Mafia family until they were anointed as such by Salvatore Maranzano in 1931, when he declared the end of the Castellammarese War and set up the five Mafia family structures in the New York region.

Twenty years had passed and the Manganos had been running one of the tightest households of any organised crime family in the land. But they had an Achilles heel: Albert Anastasia. Though 'The Enforcer', as he came to be known, was a Mangano Mafioso, his association with the family in the early years had been strictly one of membership. He was actively engaged in other great underworld works, such as running Murder Inc.

But when Assistant District Attorney Burton Turkus broke up that gang of killers, Anastasia's endeavors as 'The Enforcer' were consigned to a power base that was rooted in the Mangano

Family structure. True, he went out on 'assignments' to kill for the other families, but his orders always came from either Vince or Phil Mangano, his nominal bosses.

After about ten years of being a second banana to the Mangano Family leadership, Anastasia decided he'd had quite enough of the runner-up role and took steps to take over the leadership.

The date was Wednesday, 18 April 1951. Philip Mangano stepped out of the bright noonday sun into Joe the Bootblack's Shoe Shop on Brooklyn's Sackett Street, near Columbia, to place a bet on a horserace. Just then a man dashed into the store and told Phil he was wanted around the corner on Union Street, not far from the clock.

Mangano apparently knew and trusted the two men, for he went with them in their car. At ten o'clock the next morning his bullet-riddled remains were found in the swamp grass of Brooklyn's Bergen Beach.

The autopsy showed he had been slain with three .45-caliber bullets, all of which had gone through his brain and made it look like a soufflé on the medical examiner's gurney.

Under normal circumstances, Vincent Mangano would have ordered a search for his brother's killers, spent a quiet period in mourning, then returned to the helm to lead his mob onward and upward. But this was no normal circumstance.

With the discovery of Philip's body, messengers bearing the sad tidings journeyed to Vincent Mangano's headquarters at the City Democratic Club on Clinton Street, between DeGraw and Kane. But Vincent wasn't there. Nor was he there the next day, the day after that, nor all of the days that followed into that year's Kefauver Hearings in Washington. By then no one doubted that Vincent had suffered the same fate as brother Phil, but that his remains were nowhere to be found.

'Who killed Phil Mangano?' a questioner asked Joe Adonis Doto, a lieutenant in the Mangano family who'd been summoned for his testimony at the nationally televised hearings.

'It was not a gangland murder,' replied Adonis. 'I think Phil was killed by a jealous lover. His pants were off when they found him. This would mean a crime of passion . . .'

Albert Anastasia was asked the same question. His response echoed the mournful requiem at Frankie Yale's funeral by Al Capone and the killers who had taken the Brooklyn mobster's life:

'I knew Phil and Vince Mangano like brothers for the past thirty years,' Anastasia said. 'I liked them like brothers too . . . You ask me now who killed Philipo? I don't know who would want to kill such a fine man . . .'

Anastasia had finally reached the throne room. Now he was the king. It had been a long and tedious climb from his humble beginnings as a street thug.

Albert Anastasia had observed his nineteenth birthday in Sing Sing's death row after he and a pal, Giuseppe 'Joe' Florino, another smalltime hood, were convicted for the murder of a longshoreman who threatened to blow the whistle on Albert and Joe for pulling a $95 holdup of James Fallon's jewelry store on downtown Brooklyn's Myrtle Avenue.

Fallon was a boyhood pal of Pegleg Lonergan, then a growing power in the White Hand gang. Lonergan enlisted George Tirello, a longshoreman employed by an Irish-owned stevedoring firm, for which he was roundly despised by his fellow Italians. Lonergan crossed Tirello's palm with a crisp $100 bill and whispered, 'See if you can find out who held up Jim Fallon's jewelry store.'

Tirello would have made a great detective. By keeping his ears open at a couple of waterfront cafés, he learned that two young men were trying to sell hot jewelry. His instincts took him to Robert Corn's Jewelers on Columbia Street – the gemologists with the landmark clock on their sidewalk. Tirello didn't learn the names of the two bandits at Corn's, where they had tried without success to sell their loot, but from Nat Sissler of Cheap, Cheap Nat Sissler's Bargain Store.

Sissler had been in Corn's store when the two bandits were turned away by the owner. When they left, he followed them out and bought a handsome diamond ring from them. When Tirello spotted the ring on Sissler's finger, he grabbed the merchant by the scruff of the neck and demanded to know where he got the sparkler.

'I bought in the city ... on Canal Street,' the proprietor squirmed.

'You lying bastard!' screamed Tirello. 'You bought that from the two guys who tried to sell the stuff they stole to Corn!'

Further persuasion by the longshoreman elicited the names of the two jewel thieves: Albert Anastasia and Joe Florino.

'How come you know their names so easy?' demanded Tirello.

'Because Joe's girlfriend, Margie Ferrara, shops here a lot, and they come in with her sometimes ...'

As luck would have it, Tirello found his quarry the next day – meeting under the clock on Columbia Street. They were waiting for Margaret Ferrara to come out of the matinee performance at the Happy Hour Theater, across the street.

Tirello walked up to them.

'Hey, you fuckers ... I think I'm gonna turn you in for pulling the heist at Fallon's,' the dock worker snapped. 'But ...'

He let his words drift into a brief silence. His brain was churning. He had made a quick $100 from Pegleg Lonergan to turn up the two holdup men, but there was no promise of further reward from the Irish mobster. Now, however, having cornered Anastasia and Florino, Tirello figured he could make himself a hefty piece of change with a shakedown.

Not so. Albert and Joe turned on Tirello and began punching him silly. Just then Margie Ferrara walked out of the theater, saw the fight across the street, and ran over screaming. The distraction caused Anastasia and Florino to let their guards down. Tirello all at once exploded with flailing fists that caught Anastasia and Florino on their respective jaws.

As they stumbled backwards, Anastasia and Florino both pulled pistols and began firing. Albert fired twice but his bullets ricocheted off the sidewalk. Joe's didn't: all three slugs plowed into George Tirello's chest. He fell to the sidewalk, dead.

'Come on, let's get the hell out of here!' Florino screamed, grabbing Margie's hand and running, hard on Anastasia's heels.

Although there were dozens of passers-by who witnessed the rubout, police of the Hamilton Avenue stationhouse found not one who was willing to make a statement. This was not the first gangland killing under the Corn Jewelry Store clock – and wouldn't be the last.

The date was 26 May 1920.

On 29 May 1920 Joe Florino was arrested for George Tirello's murder.

On 30 May 1920 Albert Anastasia was arrested for his part in the killing.

On 26 May 1921, after a lengthy jury trial and a guilty verdict against both defendants, General Sessions Judge James C. Van Siclen asked if Anastasia and Florino had any last words to say before sentence was passed.

The five-foot-seven, 165-pound Anastasia stood defiantly before the bench, arms intertwined across his chest, and glared in silence at the judge. Florino, at five-feet-nine and 190 pounds, offered a great contrast. He spoke for forty-five minutes.

'Your honor,' he began in a raspy, tear-choked voice. 'I am innocent . . . I was framed by that dirty woman . . . She lied to you on the stand. You see, after I tell her I no break up with my wife and no leave my three children, she tell me to my face: 'Joe, I'm gonna put you behind bars . . . You gonna fry . . .' That's the true story, your honor . . . You don't think I was wrong to not leave my wife and children for that tramp, eh Judge?'

Indeed, Margaret Ferrara did in Anastasia and her boyfriend. It was very poor judgment on Florino's part to have had words with Margie just after she had witnessed the murder under the clock, and to tell her very bluntly that he was through with her.

That rejection was the only reason the cops were able to make such fast arrests in the case despite the almost total lack of clues and the stone wall of silence by people who had ringside seats at the fight and fatal shooting on the Columbia Street sidewalk.

Judge Van Siclen sentenced Anastasia and Florino to die in Sing Sing's electric chair. But Frankie Yale wouldn't allow it.

His elbow-rubbing acquaintanceship with Supreme Court Justice Francis McQuade was enough to win Anastasia and Florino a reversal of their conviction, grant a new trial (on a legal technicality), and order the condemned men's release from Death Row.

The fact that Judge McQuade was a silent partner in a Havana gambling casino and that he counted Lucky Luciano, Dutch Schultz, Meyer Lansky, and Vincent and Philip Mangano as friends had nothing to do in his decision to spring the killers. It was purely a legal decision.

There was no second trial. No need to have one after Margie Ferrara took a powder. Where she went, few people knew. It was some place out of state. Her whereabouts didn't become known to the mob until about five years later. She was kidnapped from her home in Connecticut and taken to New York.

Her body, with twenty stab wounds, was dumped on the sidewalk in front of Albert Anastasia's old apartment house in Brooklyn.

Albert Anastasia was on top of the heap in that year of 1951 after the power of Vince and Phil Mangano passed to him. And he remained in that dominant position for much of the early and mid-1950s. But the crown he wore was shaky, for Vito Genovese never quite felt comfortable with The Enforcer in charge of the Mangano Family.

Genovese wanted to do to Albert Anastasia what he had done to Frank Costello. He began to plot in mid-summer of 1956.

Chapter 31

Now Genovese Aims for Albert Anastasia's Scalp

One reason Vito Genovese wanted Albert Anastasia eliminated was the disturbing reports that were reaching his ears.

'Hey, Vito, you know what I hear?' asked Thomas Three Finger Brown Luchese at one of their luncheon get-togethers in Little Italy. By now Luchese was riding high as boss of one of the country's top five crime families. One of the most respected members of the ruling commission, Three Finger Brown (so named because those were all the digits he had on one hand) mentioned a name that knotted the pit of Genovese's stomach.

'All right, all right, Tommy, stop da bullshit,' a solemn-faced Vito responded. He had just returned from his lawyer George Wolf's office on a legal matter that had upset the mob boss no end. We'll return to that juristic situation shortly . . .

'I'm not kidding you, *paisan*,' Luchese snapped, 'that's the fuckin' truth – that madman Anastasia ask Frank Costello to come back and take over from you –'

The report devastated Genovese. He sprang into action at once.

What better plan could any Mafioso devise than the one that Genovese blueprinted in his brain: enlist the services of Albert Anastasia's own Number Two man – Carlo Gambino – to give The Enforcer the royal sendoff?

Nothing pleased Carlo more than to hear from the Luchese Family's big caretaker that he wanted him to succeed Anastasia as the boss of the mob Albert inherited from the Mangano brothers.

'I cannot tell you how honored you make me feel, Don Vito, that you ask me to do this for you,' responded Gambino in a voice choked by the tears he was holding back.

There was a long period of silence as Carlo tried to overcome his emotions. Then he finally let the words roll:

'Don Vito, this is certainly a very special thing you ask me to do for Our Thing. How good of you to call on me for this favor. I cannot tell you what it means to make this a family affair for my family.'

Translation: It was to be a family affair in more ways than one because Luchese's daughter was married to Gambino's son, Thomas; it was to be a family (i.e. Mafia) affair because, with Anastasia no longer among the living, Carlo would ascend to the crime family's leadership.

A further inducement from Genovese to Gambino:

'My dear Carlo, I want you should understand one thing. When Don Albert is no more, you are gonna be the big cheese. But you will not only rule your family but I will put you in for some of the profits from my own operations. How do you like that?'

Gambino was ecstatic. This was an offer no self-respecting Mafioso with ambitions to attain greater heights in organised crime's hierarchy could refuse.

'I accept your proposition and will execute it to your complete satisfaction,' Gambino replied.

The plot was also shaped so as to simultaneously abort Anastasia's ambitious scheme to restore Costello to the Luciano Family driver's seat. Anastasia wanted Costello back not only because they were *paisans*, both hailing from Reggio, Calabria, but also because in Frank Albert he had a leader he could manipulate around his little finger.

But the assassination would not involve killers from either Gambino's or Luchese's ranks. They would put the contract into the hands of one of the original five-family bosses, Joseph Profaci.

Now in his twenty-sixth year as head of his crime household and running a tight ship at all times, Profaci parceled the Anastasia rubout to a crazy triumvirate of killers who relished carrying out the work that Murder Inc. no longer was into: the Gallo brothers, Joseph 'Crazy Joe', Larry and Albert 'Kid Blast'.

The Gallos, together with a mean, ugly torpedo named Joseph 'Joe Jelly' Gioelli, comprised the cream of the Profaci army's hit squad. They killed only on orders handed down personally by the man himself, Joe the Boss. But they didn't use their guns with such gusto because they had all that much love in their hearts for Profaci. They did it because, first and foremost, they relished their line of work and, secondly, were exercising the cardinal rule all assassins must follow if they're to get away with their deeds: the fewer who know about the contract, the better for the triggers.

In going after Albert Anastasia, the Gallos could be forgiven if they wanted to break with that tenet for just this once. For it would be a huge feather in their respective hats if word got out that they exterminated The Enforcer, mobdom's most feared chieftain.

Albert Anastasia had no reason to change his daily routine on 26 October 1957, when he left his mansion behind the sprawling high walls of his property in Fort Lee, New Jersey and headed in his new Oldsmobile over the George Washington Bridge for Manhattan's busy midtown.

Squatting in the back seat of the 1956 four-door luxury sedan, Anastasia looked like a Wall Street broker or banker being driven to his office. It was his custom to catch up on the news by reading the morning newspapers enroute to work. He was totally confident that he would reach his destination at Seventh Avenue and West 55th Street in one piece, because his chauffeur was also his personal highly trusted bodyguard, Anthony 'Tough Tony' Coppola.

More often than not Anastasia ribbed Coppola about his nickname, because Albert had a brother who also bore that sobriquet: Anthony Anastasio (spelled differently by 'Tough Tony's' choice), who headed the International Longshoremen's Association in Brooklyn and was 'caretaker' for Albert's interests in the borough's waterfront rackets that once were the domain of Frankie Yale, then passed on to the Mangano brothers, and finally to Anastasia, who was now in supreme command.

Anastasia's destination – the Park Sheraton Hotel – previously known as the Park Central, had been home and headquarters for the celebrated gambling kingpin, Arnold Rothstein, until he was murdered in his posh suite.

There are confused accounts of how Anastasia entered Grosso's Barber Shop on the first floor of the hotel. One story has Anthony Coppola accompanying Albert into the shop, another has Tough Tony dropping off The Boss at the hotel entrance, then driving to a parked garage before taking a 'convenient' stroll for the next few minutes.

A third version is from the lips of Virginia (last name unknown), who appeared on Geraldo Rivera's TV show in 1987 and reported that a man she knew only as 'Squillante', was with Albert when he entered and 'hid behind a chair when the shooting broke out . . .'

There were two notorious Squillantes in mobdom in those years and both of them, Jimmy 'Jerome' and Vincent, were knee-deep in the festering stench of the garbage collection rackets. Whether one or the other was with Anastasia on that day of reckoning, no one has said for certain.

Anastasia walked into the barber shop, hung his overcoat on the clothing rack, and slipped into the fourth chair. 'Haircut,' he commanded to barber Joseph Bocchini, then squiggled further back in the chair as the man with the comb and scissors covered his customer's expensive imported Italian suit with a protective barber's white drop-cloth.

The Enforcer was just beginning to get his trim when the barbershop door flew open and two men with scarves covering their faces surged in, pulled guns, and shouted to boss Arthur Grosso, behind the cashier's counter: 'Keep your mouth shut if you don't want your head blown away!'

Taking long, determined steps past the first three chairs, the invaders stopped at the fourth, raised their guns, and unlimbered a cacophonous round of bullets in the back of Albert's head. With the first burst, Anastasia leaped out of his chair and made a frantic grab at his assassins. But he ended up shattering the mirror. He had become so disorientated by the volley, which had inflicted only what were deemed minor wounds, that he went after the killers' reflected images.

Now the gunmen fired again and again and Anastasia finally crumpled to the floor, carrying with him a shelf full of hair tonics, pomades, and other tonsorial accoutrements.

As he lay writhing in a semi-prone position, one of the gunmen took dead aim at the back of Anastasia's head and fired a single last bullet into it.

The particular gunman was described as 'stocky like a barrel . . . about five-feet-seven.' That could have been Joseph Joe Jelly Gioelli. But no one knew what to make of the other assassin who was said to have 'dirty blond hair'.

The gunmen made quick tracks out of the shop and headed into the bowels of the earth via the BMT subway stairs at the corner. In their flight, they discarded their weapons. One was found immediately in the entryway of the barbershop, the other was retrieved a while later from a trash can in the subway station.

Besides a very dead mobster, the executioners also left behind a legacy of atrocious marksmanship which could by no stretch of the imagination qualify them as bonafide professional killers.

The autopsy on Anastasia performed by Dr Milton E. Helpern, New York's world-renowned chief medical examiner, revealed that of the ten shots fired at the victim, only five hit their target and four were hardly a credit to the triggerman's purported reputations as killers. One bullet struck Albert in the left hand, another plowed into his left wrist, one struck him in the back, and one other grazed his hip.

Anastasia would have lived to continue as leader of his family had it not been for that tenth and final shot that went through his brain and ended his misery.

The killers were never caught.

Without so much as a fanfare from a single trumpet and with not a single foot of red carpeting laid out before him for his coronation, Carlo Gambino sat in Albert Anastasia's empty throne and took over the powerful Mafia family whose influence under The Enforcer was nationwide. There wasn't a second's thought given to the possibility of Gambino assuming the title of *capo di tutti capi* that Albert had vacated so precipitately.

That distinction tentatively went to Vito Genovese, who was trying to do for himself what Don Salvatore Maranzano had done for himself when he organised the National Syndicate: be anointed as 'Boss of all Bosses'!

Don Vito wasted little time preparing for his coronation. He took a commanding lead by calling a gangland 'summit' at which the Syndicate bosses would act upon a set of crucial issues confronting Our Thing. Genovese set the agenda for that conference:

- Explain to the Syndicate why he was justified in his attacks on Costello and Anastasia which took both out of their respective family leadership.
- Institute a wholesale purification of Our Thing's membership to do away with all unreliable, untrustworthy Mafiosi.
- Prohibit further Mafia memberships to unworthy Italians or other ethnics deemed unreliable. For it was learned that Anastasia had been pocketing $50,000 a throw for commissioning young Italian hoods into the Mafia for 'made-status', which entitled them to full participation – and profit-sharing – in all Syndicate-sponsored activities.
- Adopt an organisation policy against continued dealings in narcotics because of proliferating crackdowns by local authorities – but especially by the Federal Government. Genovese's bottom-line recommendation was that the Mob abdicate its still-dominant role as the world's leading trafficker in narcotics.

• The last item on the agenda for the gang conclave was the selection of the *capo di tutti capi* (boss of all bosses), which Genovese had slotted for himself.

Vito intended to call the meeting in one of Chicago's major hotels, but was prevailed upon by Buffalo underworld ruler Stefano Magaddino to take advantage of the pastoral surroundings of his lieutenant Joseph Barbara's estate in the quiet hills of Apalachin.

That was when New York State Police Sergeant Edgar D. Crosswell broke up the party just before Barbara could head up the coals on the barbeque and arrested the Mafiosi en masse.

The delegates were hauled off to holding pens so swiftly that they never got a chance to cast ballots on Vito Genovese's agenda.

The disaster at Apalachin wrought devastation on Don Vito's plans to take over as Boss of Bosses. But he had a far more serious problem on the home front.

The lovely woman he took for his wife, Anna, whose first husband he had killed to win her hand in marriage, was all at once no longer the lovely woman he once knew.

Anna Genovese may well have been living in the lap of luxury, but to hear her tell it, it was a brutal way to live because of the way her husband treated her.

Anna threw fabulous parties, regarded diamonds as one of the essentials of life, ordered clothes as though she were a buyer for Lord & Taylor, and in general spent money as if the key to Fort Knox belonged to her husband.

On the other side was Vito's cruelty to contend with, rooted mainly in his unfaithfulness to Anna. He publicly flaunted her own girlfriends as his mistresses – and beat her when she complained.

Finally a time came when her plaints were answered by Vito with a threat to kill her. She went to Frank Costello, who spoke to Genovese.

'But it didn't do any good,' Anna was to say in court – after Costello advised Vito to hire a good lawyer.

'Can I have your mouthpiece?' Vito asked.

'Sure, but only for your divorce case – nothing else, all right?'

Attorney General Wolf came into the picture. He was defending Genovese against Anna's suit for separate maintenance and an exorbitant demand for alimony based on her audit of property she claimed her husband owned:

- Their home in New Jersey's Atlantic Highlands, which was purchased for a modest $75,000 but which Vito enhanced with $100,000 of improvements to the structure itself.
- Genovese also plowed another $250,000 into the house for furnishings, including Oriental vases, gold and platinum dishes, Italian statues, teak furniture from the Far East, and marbled staircases and fireplaces.
- Anna had several closets full of furs that cost up to $20,000 and an assortment of gowns that cost from $300 to $1,000 each.
- Vito never paid less than $250 for a suit, $350 for overcoats, $35 for shirts, and wore $60 shoes.

'We lived very high,' she told the court. 'Money was no object.'

Anna spoke very much out of turn when it came to chronicling Vito's business affairs.

'All the time Vito was in Italy and I was here in the United States,' she testified, 'I kept his books for everything from the Italian lottery to all his other businesses.

'He was making at least forty thousand dollars a week . . .'

The guillotine lowered on the Mafia overlord. Almost at once the Internal Revenue Service took pad and pencil in hand, did some hasty computations, then hit their old Victor adding machines which preceded by a score or more years the advent of computers.

But by either method of calculation, the figures would add up to the same total: more than $30 million of income – none of which Don Vito had reported for taxes.

As federal agents prepared their documents to do to Vito Genovese what the government had done to Al Capone a quarter century before, the investigation veered in another direction. The

369

feds figured they could do a better number on Vito in terms of penitentiary time by going after him as a drug trafficker – the very business he was looking to abandon.

This turn in direction came after a small-time heroin trafficker, Nelson Cantellops, a Puerto Rican doing five years on a drug conviction in Sing Sing, suddenly summoned federal narcotics agents to the prison to apprise them of what he knew about Genovese. It boiled down to this:

Soon after he emigrated to New York from the islands, he began to encounter some important drug traffickers and became a runner for them. Before long, he was conveying bags of heroin for Guiseppe 'Big John' Ormento, a Genovese *capo*, and for James 'Jimmy Doyle' Plummeri, a *capo* with the Luchese mob in East Harlem.

Because he was so proficient in his assignments, Cantellops claimed, he was soon into doing errands for Rocco Mazzie and Natale Evola, two of Genovese's top lieutenants – and then with none other than Don Vito himself!

Cantellops then flew a sortie over Genovese that left the feds gape-mouthed and so incredulous that they subjected Nelson to a battery of lie-detector tests, grillings under hot light bulbs, and a whole assortment of other interrogations. He came out positive in every test. His story:

'One day I was in car with Mazzie, Evola, Ormento, and Plummeri when Genovese come up and he give orders that his boys take over the narcotics distribution in the Bronx . . .'

Cantellops was hauled before a Federal Grand Jury in Manhattan. In July 1958 Genovese and twenty-three others in his mob were indicted for conspiracy to traffic in drugs. Trial was scheduled for the spring of 1959.

Meanwhile, Vito Genovese was becoming shell-shocked on the domestic front by the cannonading of his estranged, divorce-seeking wife and her demand for a magnanimous alimony settlement. She had visions of getting thousands of dollars monthly from an understanding judge.

Much of the testimony during the trial was side-splitting.

'A woman named Elizabeth was on the phone. She spoke in Italian and asked Vito if I was still there. When he told her that

I didn't leave yet, Elizabeth became angry and asked Vito what I was waiting for.'

Anna's lawyer asked her if this was the woman Genovese wanted to marry.

'No,' she replied. 'This was another woman . . . Vito becomes infatuated very easily.'

While Vito laughed during this phase of her testimony, he was to wince a while later when Anna testified about how her husband pulled down forty thousand a week from the Italian lottery alone – and a whole bunch of other money from his other rackets.

'He owns it!' were Anna's words in describing her husband's connection with the lottery operation.

At a later time, Genovese was to reflect on Anna's suit in divorce court:

'Ah, women. They're a puzzle – a big puzzle. This woman lived with me for twenty years when she left. Then she puts the blast on me. She testified I was a gangster. That's when all my trouble started.'

Though Anna laid bare her husband's wealth for all the world to know, she suddenly retrenched in her endeavor to get a handsome settlement from Genovese. She startled the courtroom by saying:

'All I want is three hundred and fifty dollars a week and fifteen hundred dollars in counsel fees. But I want you to know my husband is a millionaire many times over.'

The judgment of the court was that Genovese pay Anna $300 a week and the counsel fees she requested.

Because of the limitation Frank Costello had set on his lawyer's services to Vito Genovese – to represent him only in the divorce action and in no other area of legal entanglement – one could say that the man who would have been Boss of Bosses won the battle but lost the war.

'You done good by me,' Vito thanked George Wolf. 'With another lawyer, I might have ended in the poorhouse.'

But for his trial in the Federal Courthouse on the narcotics charges Genovese did indeed end up with a different lawyer.

At that trial Vito was convicted along with fourteen of the twenty-three other indicted mobsters (nine of them flew the coop

371

to avoid prosecution) and was sentenced to fifteen years in prison.

One would think that Anna Genovese must have lived a charmed life for not having been buried in the wet concrete of a deep foundation being poured for one of Manhattan's many skyscrapers rising one after another in those days. But Vito chose the old Mafia slogan: 'Always kill a brother for revenge.'

The 'brother' Genovese designated for a hit in order to get even with Anna was close friend and confidante Steve Franse, in whose care Vito left his wife when he high-tailed it to Italy to avoid prosecution for murder.

Clearly, Franse had fulfilled Anna's bedroom urges over the years of her husband's absence. In fact, over the years following his return to the States, Vito had no question in his mind that Anna and Steve were still carrying on their relationship. But Genovese was forgiving, for, after all, he himself was into extra-marital machinations in a great big way.

Joe Valachi himself provides us with the rundown on the way the number was done on Steve Franse:

'He was lured to the restaurant that I owned. The two hit-men Genovese gave the contract to were waiting there. They threw this rope around his neck and pulled it tight till his eyeballs popped out of his head. At the same time they beat the hell out of him.'

Hours later, Franse's body was found in the back seat of his car abandoned on the Bronx's Grand Concourse.

Though by now Vito was safely tucked away from society in the penitentiary, he'd gotten his long-range revenge on Anna by depriving her from spending her remaining years with the only other man in her life whom she loved.

Vito Genovese had served almost ten years behind the big wall and was looking forward to a parole hearing that would have turned him out into the fresh air of freedom.

But that day never came. Vito Genovese died in prison in 1969.

Chapter 32

The Gallo-Profaci War

After Vito Genovese's incarceration in 1959, a period of incomparable ineptitude befell his family's organisation. The ruling hierarchy of Gerry Catena, the underboss, and the *capos* – Tommy Eboli and Mike Miranda – seemed totally incapable of asserting themselves into any form of strong leadership.

Worse, direction that had been coming from Charlie Luciano's exile in Sicily to the ruling body after Genovese's imprisonment seemed to bear no fruit, although his advice and counsel over the trans-Atlantic telephone lines did help to keep the family organisation together. Then came the day in 1962 when word was flashed to the states that Lucky Luciano had died in Naples of a heart attack.

With Genovese in prison and Luciano dead, the family headed for bad times. Men who took over the top slots couldn't rule with the kind of force Vito and Lucky had exercised. Those left to command – Jerry Catena, Tommy Eboli, and Mike Miranda – lacked either the stature or power to lead others.

Only one Mafioso among all others was deemed to have the qualities for leadership not only of his own family but as the nation's godfather, the overseer of the National Syndicate: Thomas Three Finger Brown Luchese.

373

Luchese had all the qualifications to be a ruling Mafia chieftain from the Atlantic to the Pacific. He had run his own family over the years with total efficiency and effectiveness. His was a model after which other crime families patterned themselves.

But Tommy Luchese was in his sixties and had neither the desire nor stamina to undertake such a role. He was content to manage his own family and rake in the take from the Mob's illicit and 'legitimate' businesses.

Luchese, who had always rated high in the councils of the Syndicate, might have recommended his own son-in-law's father, Carlo Gambino, to be the godfather. But Gambino wasn't ready for that role. He had just recently assumed the leadership of his own family after arranging Albert Anastasia's barbershop exit and had a lot of housekeeping chores ahead of him.

There were two other family heads who had enough clout to merit consideration for the top job. But both Joe Profaci and Joe Bonanno were encountering increasing difficulties managing their own families.

Profaci, whose organisation of some two hundred and thirty men was the smallest of the five families, was beginning to have big headaches in keeping his soldiers contented. That was because of Joe's hard-nosed Old World ways that made him, in the eyes of his underworld army, a tyrant.

Long after the other family bosses had ceased the practice of collecting tribute from their underlings, Profaci continued to demand twenty-five dollars a month from all his subordinates. Ostensibly these moneys were held 'in escrow' to pay members' legal fees when they were jammed by the law or to ease the anguish of a soldier's family were he to meet an unfortunate accident.

Another of the policies Profaci brought with him from Sicily was the imposition of a payoff from his soldiers, based upon a substantial percentage of their income from the operation of their own rackets. While all such Mob-run businesses were protected by the family, other bosses made no such demands on their men. But they received 'voluntary' tribute from their soldiers, which was given to them 'out of respect'.

What grated most against his men was that Profaci affected a lifestyle contrary to the modest ways other bosses carried on. Joe was making money hand over fist. He was one of the nation's leading distributors of olive oil and tomato paste. He was a millionaire many times over and lived in a showcase mansion on Long Island and a three-hundred-acre estate in New Jersey that included a hunting lodge.

Profaci might have offered his services to run the Syndicate had it not been for the beginnings of rebellion in his family's ranks, spurred by the three Gallo brothers – Larry, Albert, and Joey, who by now, along with Joe Jelly Gioelli, were openly claiming they had fulfilled the contract on Anastasia.

The Gallo brothers had grown up in Brooklyn's Bath Beach section and from their adolescent years were constantly in trouble.

Joey was the meanest and toughest of the brothers. He grew up wanting to be like movie gangster George Raft. He would stand on streetcorners flipping a half dollar and talk without moving his lips. He also affected the black shirt and white tie of Richard Widmark in the film *Kiss Of Death*.

Joey earned his nickname, 'Crazy Joe', when he was twenty-one after being arrested for a heist. He was declared mentally incompetent to stand trial and was given a walk after agreeing to receive psychiatric counselling. But no one in the Mob ever mentioned his nickname in his presence. They were too frightened of Joey.

The Gallos first came into the spotlight in 1957 when they were summoned before the McClellan Select Committee on Improper Activities in the Labor Management Field to tell about their juke box rental racket. Not only did they supply the record coin machines for hefty monthly fees, but also organised a union of repairmen – Teamsters Local 266. What was illegal about it was that the Gallos and their enforcers compelled restaurants, taverns, and other renters of their jukeboxes to use their repairmen exclusively or be picketed.

The committee heard nothing from the Gallos; they took the Fifth Amendment. However, Crazy Joe didn't leave Washington without uttering the memorable line after balking at questioning in the office of the committee's chief counsel, Robert F. Kennedy: 'Nice carpet ya got here, kid. Be good for a crap game.'

* * *

It was in early 1960 that the Gallos and two other soldiers, Joe Jelly Gioelli and Carmine 'The Snake' Persico, joined forces to stage a revolt against Joe Profaci's oppressive rule. This decision followed a rather significant assignment they carried out for the boss: bump off a short, fat-faced policy banker, Frank 'Frankie Shots' Abbatemarco, who was holding back some of the take for himself.

Although the Gallos, along with Joe Jelly, were credited with filling Frankie's head with lead, they got no respect from the man for whom they performed this deed. They expected the least Profaci could do was to give them a piece of the action in gambling or loan-sharking or drug trafficking in Brooklyn's East New York section, which had been Abbatemarco's territory. Instead, Profaci carved up the region among relatives and friends.

That was the last straw for the Gallos and their co-conspirators. Joey Gallo, so tight-lipped on Capitol Hill, was far looser of tongue when he was heard speaking on a phone that had been bugged by the NYPD's Central Intelligence Bureau.

Someone in the room was overheard saying to Joey, 'Frank Costello has Louisiana . . .'

'Who gave Louisiana to Frank Costello?' Gallo roared. 'Eisenhower gave it to him? Any man who is strong enough to take something and hold it, he owns it. If he is not strong enough to take it and hold it against all comers, nobody can give him Louisiana or any place else.'

Later, the CIB's Frank Salerno, considered one of America's foremost law enforcement experts on the Mafia, met Joey Gallo on a Brooklyn street and tried to pump him for information. Salerno knew by then that Profaci's troops were in revolt. He asked why. Although Joey was not specific with names, Salerno was certain that Gallo was bad-mouthing Don Joseph Profaci:

'Some old *compare* Greaseball come over from Italy and Moneybags put up fifteen G's to open a grocery store for him. The delivery boy in the store stole the business right out from under his nose and he goes bankrupt, and Moneybags backs him a second time . . .'

Throwing his hands up in disgust, Joey ranted on:

376

'Me, I can't even run a crap game. Why? Ya need a college education to run a crap game? When you want somebody hit, we're good enough. But not good enough to come to the house.'

The time was at hand for the uprising.

It might have been a bloodless coup had it not been for the American system of justice. Joe Profaci and his underboss and brother-in-law, Joseph 'The Fat Man' Magliocco, were among twenty of the Apalachin conclave's delegates convicted in Manhattan Federal District Court for obstruction of justice because they refused to come clean on why the mobsters were in convention. But the convictions were reversed on appeal, thus dashing the hopes the Gallos and the other revolutionaries had of taking over after Uncle Sam had placed Profaci and Magliocco in a federal penitentiary.

Adopting Joey Gallo's credo of 'Any man who is strong enough to take something and hold it, he owns it,' the insurrectionists decided to take and hold. What they grabbed were the family's top leaders; Joe Profaci's brother-in-law Magliocco; Joe's brother, Frank Profaci, and two powerful aides and bodyguards, Salvatore 'Sally the Sheik' Mussachia and John Scimone.

The Boss was also targeted for abduction but he'd been alerted about the conspiracy. He high-tailed it to a Florida hideout. Meanwhile, the hostages were holed up in separate Manhattan hotel rooms under heavy guard for the following two weeks.

Finally a line of communication opened between the Gallos and Profaci. Don Joseph agreed to negotiate the Gallos' demands for a piece of the empire by placing them before the National Commission.

Albert and Larry Gallo went for the proposal but Joey and Joe Jelly turned thumbs down. Joey bellowed:

'You kill one, you tell them you want one-hundred G's in cash as a good faith token. Then we sit down and talk!'

The dispute became so heated that Larry slapped Joey to silence him, then put him on a plane for California to spend some time cooling off.

Meanwhile, the Commission took up the dispute but couldn't reach a decision. Even if it found the complaints against Profaci's rule justified, it couldn't possibly render a verdict against him. For that would open a Pandora's box in the ranks of organised crime. Every dissident group in every family would demand a better deal – and the whole Mafia structure would be in danger of collapsing.

The counsellors on the ruling Mafia court declared that this was an internal family dispute that would have to be worked out by Profaci and the dissidents. The Commission did make two rulings: one, there should be a truce until a solution is reached; two, other families must not get involved in the dispute.

The truce begun in early 1961 was uneasy. Profaci made it so by undermining the Gallos and their young Turks. Don Joseph lured the younger defectors, one and two at a time, over a period of months until he had enough of them to make an offer they couldn't refuse:

'Knock off the Gallos and I'll make it worth your while . . . I'll give you a nice piece of the action . . .'

Even as the dissenters wooed back to Profaci's camp laid plans for ways and means to kill the Gallos, Joey eased the burden on their shoulders: he got himself arrested for extortion.

On the night of 11 May undercover cops sprang a trap on Joey. He'd been harassing the owner of several taverns and a check-cashing service to buy $40,000 worth of stolen liquor for a bargain $25,000. After weeks of negotiations and many middle-of-the-night threatening calls from Joey, the businessman agreed to meet him in one of his gin mills.

The cops were seated nearby and heard Joey's answer when his victim asked for 'just a little more time to make up his mind'. Joey Gallo cracked:

'Sure. Take three months in the hospital on me.'

The sleuths stood up from the adjoining booth, spreadeagled Joey against a wall, frisked him, and put the cuffs on him.

No sooner was he booked on the extortion charge than he was out on bail. Later, a Kings County Grand Jury indicted him. But before he stood trial, a great deal transpired in the simmering Profaci-Gallo feud. It was destined to erupt into war despite the Commission's edict that both sides do their utmost to resolve their differences without a public airing.

20 August 1960 was a day to remember in the Gallo-Profaci War.

That Saturday Joe Jelly Gioelli went deep-sea fishing, a passion of his. His car and Joe himself disappeared for what we must now consider was forever. Because all we know is the only evidence of Joe Jelly's outing on the Atlantic was his coat, wrapped around a dead fish, dumped from a car in front of a popular Brooklyn Gallo hangout.

That same day, Profaci unlimbered a second volley against his revolutionaries. He sent his own bodyguard, John Scimone, into a meeting with Larry Gallo. Scimone implied to Larry that he was joining the Gallos in the insurrection against Don Joseph. It was a ruse. But that was not the bottom line.

The truth bore on the arrangement Profaci had worked up for Scimone's meeting with Larry Gallo. Scimone had called the oldest Gallo brother earlier and asked him for a get-together. 'Why don't you and me meet tonight in the Sahara Lounge?' John said.

'Oh, sure, I'll be glad to meet you there,' Larry Gallo responded. They agreed to be at the restaurant on Brooklyn's Utica Avenue at 5:00 p.m. – an hour before the restaurant opened for dinner.

Larry Gallo was already at the bar when Scimone arrived with what he had promised would be an olive leaf. Larry had been offered rich rewards from Profaci even during the negotiations, but all he received from emissary John at this meeting was a hundred-dollar bill.

'Hey! What kind of shit is this!' demanded Gallo when Scimone crossed his palm with the century note. 'This is no fuckin' good!'

Scimone seemed nervous. Or at least was acting out the part. 'Hey, *paisan*, please excuse me . . . I gotta go to the toilet . . .'

Before Profaci's emissary disappeared from view, Larry Gallo felt a horrendous tug around his neck. It was a thick rope that one of two men who suddenly loomed behind him had looped around his throat. One of the would-be garrotters was Carmine The Snake Persico Jr, whom Larry Gallo himself had trained to be an underworld hit man. But by now, Junior had been won over to the Boss's cause and was performing just what Profaci wanted him to do: make Larry hurt so badly that he would lure his two brothers into an assassination trap.

'Call them! Call them!' Persico screamed at Larry.

The rope was so tight around Gallo's neck he couldn't utter a sound. All he could do was shake his head side to side in refusal. The rope was then pulled so taut that it caused Larry to defecate and urinate in his pants.

By now Larry had been dragged behind the bar for the coup de grace. But then his would-be assassins were interrupted, before they could administer the hit, by a police sergeant who walked in to have a chat with the bartender. Seeing the blue uniform and gold shield, Persico and his partner, joined by Scimone, dashed out a back door and headed to their car out front.

The patrolman, who was the sergeant's driver, spotted the trio and tried to stop them. But he didn't. He was stopped instead with a shot to the face.

Meanwhile, in the bar, the sergeant found Larry Gallo barely alive.

'Who did this to you?' the sergeant asked.

'Never saw them,' Gallo rasped.

On that same day, two other young torpedos won over by Profaci's promises of a better deal tried to do in Joey Gallo, but he eluded them. Hours later a friend of Joey's, using his car, was shot as he was driving near Idlewood Airport in Queens.

Now the Gallos and their followers knew they were in for some deadly warfare. While screaming at Larry and Albert with admonitions that they should have listened to him and killed a Profaci soldier or two to make their point, Joey took refuge with them in two brick-faced tenements at 49 and 51 President Street, near the Brooklyn waterfront. They were in friendly territory; their grandmother lived nearby and their father, Albert Gallo Sr, volunteered to live with them and cook their meals. All together there were some thirty Profaci family defectors in residence there, all having vowed to wage a war of attrition against Don Joseph's significantly larger forces.

Surrounded by mattresses as buffers against gunfire and for sleeping and a large store of food, the renegade mobsters prepared to stay holed up there and battle against Profaci's mob. Now and then they ventured out of their lair and engaged Don Joseph's soldiers in mortal combat. But it was a lost cause. Profaci's men were knocking off the Gallo forces by a three-to-one ratio.

In early December of 1961, after he'd been convicted and failed to appear for sentencing, police broke into the hideout, took Joe in tow, and hauled him off to begin serving the seven-to-fourteen-year prison sentence for extortion imposed by the court.

Early in 1962 Joe Profaci suddenly took sick. His condition deteriorated week by week until, on 6 June, he died. His successor was his brother-in-law, Joseph Magliocco, who proved immediately to be a weak, vacillating leader. The two remaining Gallo brothers on the Profaci family roster couldn't accept him. And the Commission also refused to approve Magliocco as Boss.

The war continued, but more Gallo soldiers than Profaci loyalists dropped in the hail of gunfire that erupted sporadically over the Brooklyn landscape.

Magliocco sought out Joseph Bonanno to intercede on his behalf and gain him the acceptance he needed from the Syndicate to rule his late brother-in-law's family. Bonanno wanted a price: a share of the Profaci Family's income. Magliocco agreed to the deal. But Bonanno couldn't swing it. The Organisation wanted no part of Magliocco as a family ruler.

In the midst of this turmoil Magliocco took sick and died before the end of 1963. Now suddenly the path was opened for a takeover of the family by a *caporegime*, a young ball of fire named Joseph Colombo, who had just passed his fortieth birthday and had enough savvy to convince Larry and Albert Gallo that the mantle of leadership in the Profaci Family should be handed to him.

With a personal appeal to Carlo Gambino, Colombo made it. He promised that he'd never be a threat to the leadership of New York's other Mafia families. Nor would he even try to occupy Profaci's place on the National Commission; thus making it possible for a deserving Mafia leader from another part of the country to be seated and help broaden the Commission's geographic influences in the nation.

Colombo didn't reach the pinnacle of acceptance just like that. He had been involved earlier in a plot that had been hatched by Joe Bonanno after Profaci's death. Joe Bananas suddenly seemed to envision himself as the Boss of All Bosses and wasted little time laying the groundwork to achieve that goal.

He decided he was going to eliminate all the Bosses who stood in his way: Luchese, Gambino, Buffalo's Stefano Magaddino, and even Los Angeles leader Frank DeSimone. He approached Magliocco, then only less than a year from death, and swayed him into his fold with promises of rich rewards after the takeover. Magliocco was so enthused that he agreed to handle the contracts for the New York murders – Luchese and Gambino. He then summoned Colombo and ordered him to do the two numbers.

But Colombo looked upon Magliocco as a loser and promptly went to Gambino with a complete rundown on the plans worked up by the man who'd taken over Joe Profaci's leadership. Gambino called an emergency session of the Commission, which included Luchese, Philadelphia Boss Angelo Bruno, and Chicago's Momo Giancana, among others.

Gambino's tidings greatly upset the Commission heads because they stirred unhappy memories of the violent internecine warfare of the 1920s and early 1930s, as well as the bloody episodes inspired by Vito Genovese in recent times when he had Frank Costello shot and Albert Anastasia assassinated.

The overlords summoned Magliocco to face the Commission. Trembling and in tears, the man who would be king suddenly was pleading for his life. The leaders sensed that Magliocco lacked the internal fortitude to have conceived of the plot to murder the leaders – most likely hatched by ambitious Bonanno – and they spared Joe's life. They fined him $50,000, stripped him of the leadership he had taken over from his brother-in-law, and let him go home to die within a few months of a heart attack.

Joe Colombo was then richly rewarded. He was anointed as boss of the Profaci family – and at the same time acknowledged as the youngest Mob leader and Syndicate member in the country.

Now the National Council turned its attentions to Joseph Bonanno. He had to be dealt with for plotting those hits against Luchese, Gambino, Magaddino, and DeSimone.

But Bananas, who had wide and varied interests that ranged from legitimate garment manufacturing to a nationwide narcotics operation, was nowhere to be found. He abandoned his outposts in Brooklyn and Long Island, the Midwest, Arizona, Canada, and the Caribbean and went into hiding in California.

Bonanno ignored two successive summonses to appear for trial before the Commission. This infuriated the Bosses. They decided on drastic action.

Chapter 33

The Banana War: Joe Invents the Unique Bunk-Bed Coffin – the Ultimate Wrinkle in Getting Rid of Bodies

It had been a year since Profaci's death catapulted Joseph Colombo into The Boss's seat.

And much had happened between 1962 and 1963 to negate the suggestions that either of the two Josephs – Bonanno or Profaci – were viable candidates for the powerful role the now-imprisoned Vito Genovese abdicated in the National Syndicate.

While Joe Bananas didn't lose control over his family the way Profaci had, he had suffered other indignities between 1962 and 1963 that cut deeply into his credibility as a top don. Not only had he backed the wrong side in the Profaci-Gallo War, he also lost two of his closest allies, Profaci and Magliocco.

Moreover, nothing hurt more than the disgrace he suffered in the plot to become Boss of all Bosses by killing the four Mafia family leaders – Luchese, Gambino, Magaddino, and DeSimone. Bonanno was now facing a trial similar to the one that exiled Magliocco into retirement and made him pay a $50,000 penalty for handling Colombo contracts for hits on Luchese and Gambino.

In many ways, Bonanno had begun to self-destruct several years earlier when he became consumed with the idea that he could reach out beyond the territorial limits of his underworld empire which was largely New York-based. For more than thirty years Bonanno had ruled his family with ruthless efficiency. Since 1931, when Salvatore Maranzano established the five-family crime concept in New York and made Bonanno, then 26, the youngest of the bosses, Joe's star had been in the ascendant.

His boys were loyal to him – and forever grateful. For he insisted on efficiency, efficiency, efficiency. So much so that the family profits from narcotics, policy-making, and trucking, among many other ventures, were always extremely high. And so was morale.

Bonanno was also an innovator. He improved dramatically on the long-established practice of burying victims of hits in concrete or littering streets and empty lots with their corpses. He invented a foolproof way to dispose of dead bodies. The idea came to him because, in addition to all his other enterprises, Bonanno also operated a funeral parlor in Brooklyn, which was a cover for his illicit activities as well as a way of avoiding the Internal Revenue Service.

His brainstorm was the 'bunk-bed coffin': a remarkably constructed bi-level 'casket for two'. Mourners visiting Joe's funeral home to pay last respects to a loved one lying with hands folded across the chest in an open coffin, could not possibly see the body that lay beneath the one they were looking at.

But it was there: the victim of a gangland execution being given a decent burial. But a most illegal one.

Bonanno solved the problem of the extra weight the second body added to the coffin by sending muscular pall-bearers to do the honors.

It was this sort of cunning that propelled Joe Bonanno to the top as a crime Boss that merited the highest admiration and respect of the other underworld leaders. But his success ultimately fired a megalomania that led him to broaden the perimeters of his underworld territory beyond all reasonable bounds.

He pushed his family into regions the Mafia had neglected completely, or that were under weak leaderships. Bonanno made his moves into upstate New York, Canada, Arizona, Colorado, then California.

The Commission didn't encounter much flak when Bananas sent his troops into the Grand Canyon and Centennial States, but it was something else when Joe made his expansionist moves in the Empire State and Canada, then the Golden State.

In the Buffalo area, Bonanno's incursion didn't sit easy with Stefano Magaddino, who was boss of his own family. Stefano's territory included all of greater Buffalo, virtually every locale of New York's Northern Tier, and parts of Canada. Magaddino didn't squawk too loudly when Bonanno established outposts in Albany, Rochester, Utica, and Syracuse, among other upstate cities. But when he crossed the border, Magaddino shrieked: 'That son of a bitch is planting flags all over the world!'

Yet the outrage that Stefano Magaddino felt about Bonanno's invasion was nothing compared to his feelings when he learned Joe Bananas had him in his sights for a lower-level bunk-bed coffin accommodation. Stefano couldn't believe that his one-time close friend from Castellammare del Golfo would do that to him.

'How could he dare do this to his own blood cousin!' Magaddino cried as he headed straight to the Commission to file his complaint along with a demand for a hearing. His request was honored by the ruling Mafiosi – but Bonanno, now holed up in a California locale, twice ignored the call for a trial.

And Frank DeSimone, head of the Los Angeles crime family, who was also earmarked for a hit, lodged the second major complaint against Bonanno.

There were numerous other ways that Bonanno had offended the Mafia; had stepped on toes that generated cries of outrage from the Mob bosses. In his book, *Honor Thy Father*, Gay Talese paints a clear portrait of the growing concern about Banana's weird and unorthodox behaviour:

Ever since the unfortunate gathering on Apalachin, the elder Bonanno [by now son Salvatore 'Bill' Bonanno was also an underboss] avoided meeting in groups with other dons . . . On the occasions when his organisation was represented at meetings with other organisations, it was never Bonanno himself who attended but rather one of his captains . . . He believed that the Commission was now composed of confused men and he did not intend to follow their dictates, having lost faith in their collective judgment. When they should have had the foresight to maintain ultra-secrecy, such as immediately following Albert Anastasia's death in 1957, they had foolishly scheduled the Apalachin meeting. And when they should have demonstrated unified strength, such as ordering the rout of the Gallo brothers for leading a revolt against their boss, Joseph Profaci, in 1960, the Commission had voted to do nothing.

Bonanno assumed the alias of J. Santone during the more than two years of his self-imposed exile. Yet he still ran his far-flung criminal empire without missing a beat. Son Salvatore was a capable understudy, but much of the strength in keeping the troops working and in a contented state of mind fell to the lot of capable underbosses such as Carmine Galante, Frank Labruzzo, Gaspar DiGregorio, Paul Sciacca, Natale Evola, Philip Rastelli, and Joseph DeFillipo. All of them remained loyal to Bonanno because he had ruled so well for so many years and done so much good for them.

In mid-1964 Bonanno slipped off to Canada, where he was finally seen for the first time. Again the Commission was implored to act against Joe. The request came once more from his cousin, who was now feeling Joe's hot breath on his back from just across the Niagara River.

Finally, the Syndicate bosses called for a meeting with Bonanno at the home of Thomas Eboli, the *consigliere* of the Genovese Family, who lived in Englewood Cliffs, New Jersey. At the same time 'Sam The Plumber' DeCavalcante was asked to mediate on behalf of the bosses with Bonanno. Why DeCavalcante was chosen as go-between is a mystery that persists to today.

Again Bonanno ignored the summons from the Syndicate and took steps to make a new start in his new hiding place. He filed papers with the government for Canadian citizenship. Ottawa not only denied the application but hauled Don Joseph to the border under armed guard and turned him over to the U.S. Immigration and Naturalisation Service. Since there were no outstanding warrants against Joe, INS agents simply let Bonanno make his way to New York City.

He arrived there the afternoon of 20 October 1964, a Wednesday, just after twenty-three members of a Federal Grand Jury were seated in Manhattan to investigate organised crime. Joe was subpoenaed to give testimony the next morning. He had been advised beforehand by his lawyer, William Power Maloney, not to ignore the summons. Joe arranged to have dinner that night with Maloney and other attorneys in his firm in a Manhattan steak house to review the testimony he'd give before the jury in the morning.

Bonanno had no way of knowing at that point what was happening behind the scenes in regard to his status in his own family and the Commission.

On the day he crossed the border from Canada and headed to New York City, the Syndicate bosses formally stripped Joe of his membership on the Commission. At about the same time one of his captains, Gaspar DiGregorio, a member of the Bonanno Family from almost its inception, pulled out of the organisation. DiGregorio was best man at Bonanno's wedding and also was Salvatore 'Bill' Bonanno's godfather.

What brought about those decisions by DiGregorio was word from Bonanno that the family's next don would not be his loyal and dedicated *paisan* Gaspar but his son Salvatore. DiGregorio's decision was reached largely at the urging of his brother-in-law Stefano Magaddino, the Mafioso leader from Buffalo who'd been marked for death by his cousin Joe Bonanno.

The Commission's ouster of Bonanno triggered DiGregorio into an attempt to take over the family. But Gaspar wasn't able to effect the coup that easily. The majority of the Banana's mobsters remained loyal to the old guard and threw in their lot to young Bill's leadership.

This was the start of The Banana War.

During the dinner with his lawyers that evening of 21 October, an unidentified man joined the diners at the steak house. Apparently Bonanno knew him for he spoke with the man constantly. During the meal, the man twice left the table and returned.

On one of his absences from the table, the man left the restaurant, walked out into a rainstorm, and made a call from a corner phonebooth. Following dessert and after-dinner drinks, Bonanno called for the check, paid it, and shook hands with the assembled guests. Then he and Maloney walked out, hailed a taxi, and headed for Maloney's apartment building at Park Avenue and East 37th Street.

The unidentified man followed Bonanno and Maloney out of the steak house, summoned a cab for himself, and had the driver rush him down to Park and 37th. He hopped out of the cab and stood in a doorway out of the driving rain, waiting for the taxi carrying Maloney and Bonanno to pull up in front of the lawyer's apartment house.

As the cab came to a stop at the curb, the mystery man signaled to two men seated in a car at the corner. They jumped out and rushed over to Bonanno just as he stepped out of the taxi. One of the duo pulled a gun and pointed it at Bonanno's head and commanded in a harsh voice:

'Come on, Joe, my boss wants to see you!'

As Bonanno got into the abductor's car, the gunman turned to Maloney when he made a brief surge towards his client in an apparent gesture to save him from his fate, and fired a bullet at his feet that hit the sidewalk and ricocheted harmlessly.

Although there'd been many such kidnappings of Mob figures over the years, the taking of Joseph Bonanno still remains the most notorious of all – because it had commanded so many of the tabloids' big black Page One headlines for an endless period.

In time it was learned that Stefano Magaddino was the abductor and whisked Joe to a lodge in the Catskill Mountain area, where he convinced him that there was no good reason left for him to run the Mob – that the reign of leadership must go, not to son Bill as Joe had decreed, but to the *capo* whom the Commission ruled should take over: his good *compare* Gaspar DiGregorio.

It took the better part of six weeks for Bonanno to capitulate. Before he was released, he had to give his solemn word to Don Gaspar that he would never return to Mob activity again – and especially not to get mixed up any further in the territory that belonged to the Buffalo boss.

Upon his release Joe dropped from sight. He was believed to have sought refuge in Haiti, where dictator Duvalier gave him a piece of the action in the country's gambling enterprises.

Nineteen months later – on 17 May 1966 – Joe Bonanno reappeared. Wearing the same clothes he had on the night of his disappearance, he walked into Manhattan's U.S. District Court in Foley Square, went into the courtroom of Federal Judge Marvin E. Frankel, and said in a clear voice:

'I am Joseph Bonanno. I understand that the government would like to talk to me.'

Indeed the men from the Justice Department did. He was booked on the spot on standing charges filed after he had vanished – obstruction of justice. Bonanno was freed on $150,000 bail, walked out of the court, and made tracks to his old haunts determined to retake his old organisation from Gaspar DiGregorio, whom the Commission had installed as his successor.

The Banana War was in full swing long before Bonanno's dramatic reappearance. The dissension in the family's ranks was horrendous. It was virtually impossible to tell who was a Bonanno loyalist or a follower of the new boss imposed upon the Mob by the Council. The Bonanno faithful had come to the conclusion that if they couldn't be led by Joe himself, then they wanted son Bill to be their main man.

The sides had split sharply, and had to arm themselves, preparing to turn the streets into bloody alleys as the Gallo-Profaci War had done. The family as it had existed so successfully over the decades seemed about to be torn asunder.

Adding immense tension and annoyance to the gang's woes was the government's probe into the Bonanno Family's activities. Underbosses and soldiers were constantly being summoned before the grand jury for testimony. But the prosecutors from the U.S. Attorney's office were being driven up the walls of the courthouse because they couldn't tell apart the players loyal to Bonanno and those who swore allegiance to DiGregorio without a scorecard.

The newspapers started calling the dissension 'The Banana Split'.

Five months before Bonanno returned from his West Indies hideout, son Bill was approached by DiGregorio's lieutenants waving an olive branch. They wanted a 'sitdown' in order to reach a peaceful solution of the ongoing mess. Bill agreed to meet the emissaries at the home of a relative on Brooklyn's Troutman Street.

But young Bonanno was totally apprehensive about Di-Gregorio's intentions. He had had the experience of working against his rival for some two years now, and his godfather never once indicated he was willing to mediate the dispute.

Could it be that DiGregorio, now sixty-three years old, was tired of running the Mob – and especially tired of being followed and harassed by authorities? Did he want to give young Bill the wherewithal to take over the Mob and reunite it into the once-thriving organisation it had been.

It was possible. But uppermost in Bill's thoughts was the possibility that he was being set up. It had happened to his father – so why couldn't it happen to him? Of course Bill knew of his father's whereabouts, knew that he was safe, and knew that he'd be coming back soon to try a takeover.

Bill couldn't help but wonder whether the DiGregorio side had heard Joe was planning a return and decided to discourage him from coming back by doing a number on young Bill.

With such concerns, Bill headed for his rendezvous with DiGregorio's people prepared for anything on the freezing night of 28 January. He brought with him several of the gang's top gunmen. They were met by a cacophonous roar of rifle and shotgun fire from the windows and stoops of the Troutman Street tenements.

Bill and his buddies threw themselves behind parked cars, unlimbered their own weapons, and returned the fire. For several minutes, the bullets and shotgun pellets filled the air. Then all went deathly still as police sirens were heard in the distance. Both sides withdrew and made their respective ways to safe refuges. Young Bonanno took a circuitous route to his home in East Meadow on Long Island. Later that morning Bill phoned one of his *compares* and learned that the police had found discarded weapons on the street, but no casualties.

Over the weekend Bill tried to learn what progress the police probe was making into the shootout, but caught nothing on radio and TV broadcasts nor saw anything in the newspapers.

On Monday he made his move to revenge himself on his godfather, Gaspar DiGregorio, and sabotage his leadership in order to regain total control of his father's family. He phoned a reporter on *The New York Times* who had been in frequent touch with Bill for stories about his father, and gave him chapter and verse about the trap set for him.

Authorities had kept the whole incident under wraps, so when the reporter phoned it caused them unease. They were hoping to get leads on who the participants were before their chances of doing so were blown by the newspaper headlines. Compelled to admit that there was a shootout, the *Times* published the story under the headline:

GUN FIGHT LEAVES
POLICE PUZZLED

The story went:

A gang shot up a Brooklyn street Friday night, leaving behind seven guns of various kinds, bullets imbedded in buildings, and a mystery that had police still puzzled yesterday after questioning more than a hundred persons in the neighborhood.

Although residents of Troutman Street between Knickerbocker Avenue and Irving Avenue heard more than twenty shots around 11:00 p.m., detectives and patrolmen who rushed to the scene from the Wilson Avenue station house, six blocks away, found no victim and not a single bloodstain nor has any complainant appeared.

Detective Lieutenant John W. Norris discounted rumors yesterday that the shootup may have been a skirmish between Mafia factions seeking to take over the underworld 'family' of Joseph (Joe Bananas) Bonanno.

'If this was meant to be a professional job, they need a refresher course in shooting,' Lieutenant Norris said. 'It doesn't have the earmarks of organised activity. It doesn't make sense the way they abandoned all those guns. In all my twenty-three years in the police I've never seen such an erratic action.'

The *Times* story generated bigger headlines and far more detailed accounts of the shootout in the tabloids the next day. Within hours the Brooklyn District Attorney's office launched an intensive investigation to get the bottom line on the Troutman Street shootout. Since they already knew that this couldn't have been anything else but a confrontation between the opposing forces trying to grab exiled Joe Bonanno's leadership, the D.A.'s men zeroed in on the top two combatants – Gaspar DiGregorio and Bill Bonanno.

Both lived on Long Island: Bill in Nassau County's East Meadow and DiGregorio fifteen miles away in Suffolk County's West Babylon.

When a team of the District Attorney's detectives went to DiGregorio's house to bring him in for questioning, his family said wasn't there. The lawmen didn't buy that line and stuck around. Within an hour an ambulance pulled up in front of the house and DiGregorio was taken out on a stretcher. It was claimed he had suffered a heart attack. That cut no ice with the cops. They served him with a subpoena even as he was being put into the ambulance.

The D.A.'s sleuths had no success catching up with Bill Bonanno. He didn't surface until the D.A.'s grand jury investigation of the shooting had ended – without a finding because none of the more than one hundred neighborhood residents questioned about the gunplay could remember anything about that night.

DiGregorio's failure to do away with Bill Bonanno was exacerbated in that it attracted all that unwanted publicity. The Commission came down hard on him; they booted him out of the family's leadership. The job was turned over to tough Paul Sciacca.

But the crown on Sciacca's head was shaky. No sooner had he been enthroned than Joe Bonanno was back. Now the bloodletting began. In two years the toll of dead mobsters was to reach a pitiful total of nine, with another two probables since they had vanished and never reappeared, and four wounded.

One of the first victims was the leader of the ambush on Bill Bonanno, who was ambushed himself. He escaped death but was gravely wounded.

The Bonanno torpedoes weren't done. They hit their stride in 1966 when they invaded the Cypress Gardens Restaurant in Queens and blew away three henchmen who had sworn allegiance to Sciacca.

In September 1966, a meeting was held by some of the Mafia's highest leaders: Carlo Gambino, Santo Trafficante, Joseph Colombo, Tommy Eboli, Michele 'Mike' Miranda, Carlos Marcello, and seven other major underworld leaders. They met in La Stella Restaurant, also in Queens, to discuss Joe Bonanno: should he live or die?

No decision was reached that night. The restaurant was raided and police, who called this meeting Little Apalachin, arrested all the participants. After their release on bail the following day the Commissioners met again and decreed that Joe Bananas must be eliminated.

But Joe, still churning along with a mind of his own, saw the handwriting on the wall and hied off to his home in Tucson, Arizona, where early in 1968 he suffered a mild heart attack. Joe sent word back that his health prevented him from ever trying to make a comeback; that this was his retirement notice.

But some didn't buy the line. They arranged to have Joe killed when he visited his close friend and neighbor, Pete Licavoli, the Syndicate's Detroit leader. They planted a bomb in Pete's garage. Another bomb was detonated on Bonanno's patio, while a third delivered by a messenger to the front door had been so poorly packaged it never went off.

Bonanno wasn't kidding when he said he wasn't coming back – especially not after those bomb incidents. He remained permanently ensconced in Tucson while son Bill went into early retirement in San Jose, California.

The once-mighty Mob that Joe Bonanno ran for more than thirty successful years in racketeering and gangsterism had fallen on bad times.

Sciacca proved he wasn't the man to run the family and in 1970 was compelled to step down, making way for a leadership that went to a troika: Natale Evola, Joseph DeFilippo, and Philip Rastelli. But three heads proved they weren't anywhere the match of the one that reposed between Joe Bonanno's shoulders.

The Commission finally anointed Natale Evola as the *de facto* don.

The Bonanno experience told the underworld in clear and unmistakable language that it didn't dare defy the Commission. Yet in time there would be other family bosses who'd venture into this perilous area of confrontation against a leadership that, it would seem, is always in a win, win, win situation.

Chapter 34

The Colombo-Gallo War

Joseph Colombo, who took over the leadership of the Profaci Family in 1963, commanded very little respect as a boss even though the Commission had given him its benediction. Mafiosi from the other families couldn't understand how the Syndicate had picked Colombo to head the family that Joe Profaci had almost run into the ground.

What was needed to strengthen Profaci's mob was a tough, arrogant, no-nonsense leader. But at the time there were only two others in the Profaci Family ranks considered to be viable candidates: Salvatore Mineo and Joseph Yacovelli. Yet neither was strong enough for the role. For that matter, neither was Colombo.

Then why was he picked?

Joe was whom powerful Carlo Gambino wanted. Carlo's Family was thriving under his aegis. Profaci's wasn't. It was weak at the top and morale among the soldiers was at its lowest level ever – especially since they had waged the bloody, costly war with the Gallos. In Colombo, Gambino had a man who was a veritable slave to him, and in effect that gave Carlo control of two families. New Jersey's boss, Sam The Plumber DeCavalcante, was recorded on FBI wiretaps in a conversation with his underboss Frank Majuri:

'I told you,' Sam opened the dialogue, 'I was surprised when I heard he was in there. I never would have made that guess.'

'What experience had he got?' DeCavalcante wanted to know. 'He was a bust-out guy [smalltime hood] all his life.'

A time eventually came when even Carlo Gambino became distressed with Joseph Colombo. It wasn't the way he was running his mob but how he was all at once coming to the defense of the Mafia as no member of the underworld society had ever done before.

This was now the advent of the 1970s and the growing public consciousness of the secret Italian society was due not only to the Kefauver hearings and the McClellan disclosures through Joe Valachi, but also to Mario Puzo and Gay Talese, among other writers, about the members and activities of the Mafia or La Cosa Nostra.

With *The Godfather*, first the book then the movie, followed by *Honor Thy Father*, which told about the life and times of Joe Bonanno and his son Bill, the public was viewing everyone with an Italian name as a probable member of the underworld society. If your name ended in a vowel, you were in the Mafia.

By now, with Gambino's strong support, Colombo had revived his family and was sitting on top of the heap. His mob had a firm control of gambling in Brooklyn and Queens, they were raping Kennedy International Airport of stolen cargo, they were shafting New York State by smuggling tax-free cigarettes from the South, and were reaping riches from numerous other rackets.

Joe himself was living in the lap of luxury that even the extravagant Al Capone never dreamed could have existed: he owned a fashionable home in Brooklyn, a country estate with his own private horse track, swimming pool, and all the other trappings of the wealthiest legitimate American barons of big business.

But there was one rub and it grated on Colombo's thin Italian hide.

'They ain't giving me no respect,' was the plaint of this Mob boss who was now reading and seeing too many Mafia books and movies and becoming so obsessed by the low esteem Italians were held in that he decided to try and change that concept.

To the amazement – and chagrin – of the Commission (and all others in organised crime), Colombo founded the Italian-American Civil Rights League to counter the bad image that was being imposed on Italian-Americans in general. But this was a ploy that Colombo worked up to take law enforcement agencies off the Mob's back.

Joe organised the league just after the FBI arrested his son, Joseph Jr, on a charge that he had melted down dimes, quarters, and half-dollars and made them into ingots that were far more valuable for the silver than the face value of the coins in monetary use. His reasoning in establishing the League was not only to play upon the grievance of all respectable Italian-Americans who resented the Mafia label but to use the organisation as a coercive force against the Federal Government from harassing the Mob.

As it turned out, his own son's arrest was a case of the Justice Department moving too precipitately in a case where evidence was, at most, threadbare. The government's chief witness cracked on the stand and admitted he had lied when he named young Colombo in the plot. The charges against Little Joe were then dropped.

Colombo thought that if he could focus on the public's growing sensitivities to ethnic bias he could meld a relationship in people's minds between anti-Italian feelings and the increasing crackdowns on the Mafia-run organised crime gangs. The bottom line: sell the public the idea that law enforcement is discriminatory and make them believe that it's all a civil rights issue – it'll give the mob some breathing room to operate.

What Colombo had done in 1970 was not a new concept. Twice before Italian-Americans had organised themselves into fraternities to foster a better image of themselves and thwart further embarrassing reflections of themselves as Mafiosi.

During the 1960s the Federation of Italian-American Democratic Organisations was founded by New York City Congressman Alfred Santangelo. The immediate purpose was to get TV's popular show *The Untouchables* off the air because what Elliott Ness was doing to savage the Chicago Mob was giving Italian-Americans a weekly black eye in prime time.

The organisation is said to have been covertly initiated by the Mob, but it stayed behind the scenes and never let their hand show. The producers and network refused demands by the FIADO to take the show off the air. So an Italian-American boycott was organised against the program's sponsor, Chesterfield Cigarettes. In less than a year, Liggett & Meyers caved in and withdrew its commercials. The show's demise followed soon – as did a fadeout of the FIADO.

By 1970 it seemed that the Italian-American Civil Rights League was going somewhere. By rushing off to a courthouse wherever and whenever a member or members of organised crime were busted, by rallying with sandwich signs bleating protests, and generally causing commotion after every arrest, Joe Colombo won a large following. He became a folk hero of sorts; the late night as well as morning talk shows rolled out the red carpet for Joe to show before the cameras and cry about the terrible way Italian-Americans were being treated by the law.

On 28 June 1970 Colombo held his first Italian Unity Day rally in Columbus Circle, on the southwestern fringe of Central Park. Thousands showed up and the IACRL seemed to be on its way as a force in influencing sympathy and sentiment for his cause.

One of Colombo's most notable achievements was in having the words 'Mafia' and 'Cosa Nostra' dropped from *The Godfather* script. There were numerous other gains:

- Attorney General John N. Mitchell agreed that the Justice Department no longer would refer to gangsters as members of the Mafia or the Cosa Nostra.
- FBI Director J. Edgar Hoover consented to a demand that Italian-sounding names would not be allowed in the TV series, 'The FBI', to which the bureau had given its official imprimatur.
- Italian jargon like, 'Whatsa matta, hey *walyo*?' and 'Whose gonna say *souza*?' became taboo in TV scripts, as did 'Mama

mia, datsa soma spicy meatballs' in the popular TV commercial.

While he had won the affections of hordes of Italian-Americans who had had their fill of the unflattering Italian-American attitudes and were pleased with the progress the Mafia boss had made in gaining respect for them, there was no comparable admiration for Joe Colombo in the Mafia hierarchy. To the Mob, he was an unwanted press agent straight out of the pages of *What Makes Sammy Run*. He was dubbed the 'Mafia's Sammy Glick'.

The feverish activity that Colombo engaged in to draw attention to the Mafia worked well for him, but he was losing further favor elsewhere. For all the gains he had made in garnering respect for Italian-Americans, he accomplished the one thing the Syndicate had not wanted to happen: the focus of public attention and awareness on the Mafia.

Colombo was making the other family bosses look like second-class citizens by the way he was commanding media attention. All America was looking upon Joseph Colombo as the underworld boss, above all other Mafia leaders, who was going to end Italian-American discrimination. He was also the heroic figure of the ground-breaking 1970 Italian-American Unity Day, which was being prepared for a repeat performance.

The date for the second annual Italian Unity Day was scheduled for 28 June 1971. But this one was not being received with the same enthusiasm as the first rally. Carlo Gambino took the lead in seeing to it that the second affair did not have the rousing success the first one did.

He sent out word that soldiers were to stay away from the demonstration. Moreover, Brooklyn longshoremen couldn't take the day off (with pay), as they had done the year before, to attend.

Then came the tipoff that Joe Colombo should have realised meant the end of the line for him. His league's chief organiser, Joseph DeCicco, suddenly tossed in his resignation. He used ill health as an excuse.

Another underworld big wheel, Tony Scotto, son-in-law of the late Albert Anastasia and nephew by marriage to Brooklyn dock boss Anthony Anastasio, sent word he wouldn't attend the second gathering as he had the first.

During this time that the bosses were withdrawing support from Colombo's league, one of his most dangerous enemies, Joseph Gallo, was released from prison. Imprisoned when Colombo had arranged an end to the Gallo-Profaci War and taken over Joe's family, Crazy Joe was still seething. For he had not been consulted about the peace terms when Colombo reached accord with his rivals in the Gallo mob for peace.

Crazy Joe wasn't willing to adhere to the terms of the 1963 treaty, not only because it had been signed without him but because of the disarray in which his once-strong organisation was now wallowing. With older brother Larry having died of cancer in 1968 and younger brother Albert not demonstrating his brothers' qualities as a Mob leader, Joe was furious about the current state of affairs his gang was in. Its status was hardly equal to the five established crime families that were organised in the early 1930s and were still thriving.

Whether Carlo Gambino, now without question the ruling Mafioso of the country, and the Commission which he headed, decided to act against Colombo isn't known. Yet the rate at which the big wheels from the 1970 rally were washing their hands of the 1971 affair clearly indicated orders were coming from somewhere on high to 'cool it'.

This much was certain: with Joey Gallo back on the street, tensions between the Colombo and Gallo forces mounted quickly.

Despite the withdrawal of an increasing number of top-ranking underworld figures, Colombo tried to make the best of a deteriorating situation by using the only tools at his disposal to get his way: threats and muscle. His soldiers invaded Italian neighborhoods, ordered shopkeepers to close for the day and to post signs announcing the time and place of the rally. Just as soon as Colombo's emissaries departed, Gallo gangsters and those from other families entered the shops and warned merchants not to attend the rally and to take the posters down. Several of Colombo's advance men returned to the boss with news that they were roughed up by Crazy Joe's torpedoes and tossed out of the neighborhoods they were canvassing.

But Joe Colombo could not be dissuaded from staging the demonstration.

28 June 1971, a Monday, dawned oppressively hot. It didn't deter the tens of thousands of Italian-Americans and other ethnic groups from showing up at Columbus Circle. True, the crowd was somewhat smaller than the previous year, but it still had an enthusiastic and festive air about it.

The same could be said about Joe Colombo and his body-guards as they arrived in a chauffeur-driven limousine that discharged them in the middle of the crowd. It seemed everyone rushed the gang leader to shake his hand and shower him with praise for his efforts on behalf of Italian-Americans. Joe looked like a politician on the campaign trail as he thrusted his clenched fists high over his head and saluted the crowd's welcoming cheers.

Colombo looked as though he had hardly a care in the world. If the snubs and backbiting of the leaders and subordinates from the other families had gotten to him, he surely didn't betray any sign of it. Nor did he seem concerned about his safety, for he moved through the throngs in a jubilant mood, his face frozen in a perpetual smile.

In an instant Joe Colombo's face was transformed into a blood-spattered mask of horror by three rapidly fired shots from a 7.65 caliber gun in the hand of a black man who, until a second or two before, had a camera in one hand and was pretending to be a newspaper photographer.

As Colombo crumpled to the pavement, the explosion of bullets brought undercover police detectives on the run from their places in the mass of humanity. But by the time they reached the shooting scene, they had at their feet two unmoving bodies lying in two separate pools of blood.

The assassin never had a chance to have his day in court. He was meted instant Mafia justice by Colombo's bodyguards who filled his body with so much lead that several policemen who jumped on the killer to keep him pinned wasted their energy. He was killed instantly.

Meanwhile, Colombo was lifted into a gurney, wheeled into an ambulance, and sped to Roosevelt Hospital. He was barely alive. He'd been struck in the head and neck at point-blank range and it took several hours of surgery to remove the slugs.

This was the beginning of several months of hospitalisation for Colombo. But when he was finally discharged and sent home for what was loosely termed 'convalescence', everyone knew that Joe would never make it back to lead his family.

The damage to his brain was so extensive that he was reduced to a vegetable. He would remain in that state for several years until his death.

Meanwhile, no official motive could be associated with the would-be killer's attack on Colombo. The name Jerome A. Johnson meant nothing to authorities, although they and many of Colombo's followers fixed it firmly in their minds that the attempted execution was masterminded by Crazy Joe Gallo.

Giving some credence to that belief was an awareness that while doing his stretch, Gallo had befriended a number of blacks in the Big House and even organised a civil rights unit for them. Thus it was entirely possible Joey had cultivated friends who were able to enlist the services of a gunman in the black community who couldn't be connected to him for the hit on Colombo.

Of course the New York Police Department tossed Joe on the grill and, of course, he insisted that 'I don't know who would want to do such a terrible thing to such a nice guy like my good friend Joe . . .'

So far as the keenest watchers of Mob activity viewed the situation, it wouldn't matter whether or not Joe Gallo had ordered the shooting. He was bound to be fingered as the architect of Colombo's demise as a Mob boss because it was to Gallo's advantage to have that other Joe out of the way.

Crazy Joe knew this full well and made himself as scarce as he could on the street. He hid out in a flat in Manhattan's West 14th Street with his wife, expecting bloody warfare to break out between his renegade band of Mafiosi and the Colombo combine. Except for some close but insignificant brushes, the expected Colombo-Gallo War never materialised. At least not during the rest of 1971 and into the beginning of 1972.

By mid-January 1972, after more than six months in virtual hibernation, Joe Gallo was fed up with the hermit's dreary life and emerged from his self-imposed exile. He did a complete turnabout. He returned to many of his old saloon hangouts and branched out to other classier places he'd never been to before, such as Sardi's, the renowned Times Square restaurant that was a magnet for the showbiz crowd for many years, and Elaine's, newly heralded as the in place for the literary cognoscenti.

He also attended Broadway openings, playing bridge and chess, discussed literature and the classics, and gathered about him a circle of the most unlikely friends with no connections whatsoever to the underworld, among them, playwright-producer-director Neil Simon, actress Joan Hackett, and actor Jerry Ohrbach and his wife Marta, who was to recall at a later time that Joey was always talking about 'going straight'. Meanwhile, law enforcement officials adamantly insisted that Crazy Joe was as deeply entrenched in the front lines of racketeering as ever.

But Carlo Gambino also could have said as much, for the crazy man had aroused anger in the Boss of Bosses as no one ever before. Gambino could forgive Joe Colombo's 'stupidity' for starting the well-intentioned Italian-American Civil Rights League. After all, Colombo was still Carlo's very obedient servant, his lackey, and never, never would Joe have ever dared do the deeds Gallo and his gang were doing now.

And pulling them on, of all people, Carlo Gambino.

In mid-March 1972 Gallo was summoned for an audience with the Boss of Bosses.

'I want you, wise guy, to cut the shit out,' Carlo began. 'For too long now I let you give me screwing but you not gonna get away longer . . .'

'What the fuck are you complaining about, grandpa,' Gallo interrupted angrily. 'Tell me . . . what the fuck's bugging you . . .?'

Gambino sucked in a long breath and screwed his face into a scowl.

'I'm tell you to stop musclin' my operations in East Harlem. I want you keep your dirty hands off the business I got there with drugs . . . And I don't want you screw me no more on the other things I got going in my territory . . .'

They didn't call him Crazy Joe Gallo for no reason. This was the moment he earned his name – in spades. Leaping to his feet with a loud, ear-piercing Indian war cry meant to be a derisive putdown of the Big Man, Joey bent at the waist and leaned his torso forward until his face was almost touching Gambino's face, now masked by utter astonishment.

'Do you know what I have to say to you, old fart?' Gallo thundered, his saliva showering Carlo's stunned countenance. 'I tell you to go fuck yourself!'

Then Crazy Joe spat into Carlo Gambino's face.

As *Time* magazine commented on the incident: 'If that act seemed foolhardy, it was nevertheless typical of Gallo, who never had the sense to play by the rigid rules of the brotherhood.'

Crazy Joe Gallo could now be counted among the walking dead.

But you'd never believe his days were numbered from the way he hopscotched around town, dropping in on Jerry and Marta Ohrbach in their Greenwich Village place to chat about the autobiography the actor was going to write for Joey, and being seen on the street and nightclubs with a youngish woman who certainly wasn't his wife.

Shortly after he came out of his 14th Street hibernation, Joe divorced his wife. And, as he approached his forty-third birthday, he began to keep company with pretty, affable Sina Essary, a divorcee, who toiled days as a dental assistant and spent nights hobnobbing with the hoi-polloi in Crazy Joe's company.

On or about 12 March, Gallo made two more significant turns on his peripatetic trek as a mobster and social climber.

He had not only invaded Carlo Gambino's Harlem haunts for a cut of the booty, but also was taking dead aim at a number of the rackets that had been controlled by Carmine The Snake Persico. Carmine was no longer running his businesses because he had been sent to the federal penitentiary in Atlanta to do fourteen years for hijacking.

Then Joey married Sina Essary and adopted her ten-year-old daughter as his own.

By now Gallo had made himself prey for an open season on himself. Yet no one was quite able to lure Joey into a trap or an ambush.

The evening of 7 April was like most others of the past three months, following Joey's emergence from hiding. It started out for Joey, Sina, his sister Carmella, and his bodyguard Pete 'The Greek' Dipioulis with drinks, dinner and the early show at the Copacabana. This was a special occasion: Joey's forty-third birthday.

After a round of other nightspots that lasted until nearly 3:00 a.m., Joey and his party made their way downtown in a limo piloted by Dipioulis to Umberto's Clam House on Mulberry Street in the heart of Little Italy.

The pre-dawn breakfast they had come to eat was hardly down their gullets when, at precisely 4:00 a.m., four men with drawn pistols entered through the side door and made their way toward Gallo's table.

He did not see them, for his back was toward the door. But Sina and Carmella, seated on the opposite side, caught sight of the intruders and their eyes opened wide in horror. Seeing their reaction, Joe wheeled around and glared at them. For an instant, all four men stopped in their tracks. But then one moved toward Gallo.

'You son of a bitch!' he screamed as all four gunmen, as well as Joey's bodyguards, began firing. Some two dozen shots were fired in little more than a minute. In the end, only Joey suffered lead poisoning. He was hit by two bullets in the restaurant and one more – the coup de grace – after he staggered out and collapsed on the sidewalk.

The gunmen escaped in a waiting getaway car. Seconds later a police cruiser came to a screeching stop in front of Umberto's. The patrolmen were attracted there by Carmella's hysterical cries.

Gallo was beyond aid when he was brought into the emergency room of Beekman-Downtown Hospital.

At his funeral three days later, sister Carmella stood in front of the casket and cried to her unhearing brother:

'The streets are going to run red with blood, Joey!'

And they did. Later that day, a Colombo *capo*, Gennaro Ciprio, was slain gangland style. Over the next few days, four more underworld figures were blown away. The killings continued uninterruptedly for several weeks – until the toll reached a dozen dead mobsters.

By now the Gallo gang was quaking in their boots. Albert Gallo, 'my do-nothing brother', as Crazy Joe called him, had taken command of the men in his mob and barricaded them in apartments on President Street, almost directly opposite the flats in which they'd taken refuge during the three years of the Gallo-Profaci War of the 1960s.

From his President Street lair Albert Gallo asserted himself as the leader his brother didn't think he would ever be. He issued contracts for hits on three top *capos*: Alphonse 'Alley Boy' Persico, the imprisoned Snake's brother, and Joe Yacovelli, both the Colombo Family, and Nick Bianco, a Mafioso from the New England regime of Raymond Patriarcha who was in the forefront of negotiating the pact that ended the Gallo-Profaci War a decade before.

However, the new war between the Colombo and Gallo factions couldn't be settled at a conference table because Carlo Gambino didn't want peace to come until the two sides had decimated and destroyed each other. In fact, the Gambino Family was supplying guns and ammunition to the warring families.

The rationale was simple: the more of each other they kill, the fewer Carlo would have to contend with when he moved in to take control over the families.

Gambino stepped closer to that goal less than three months after Gallo's rubout when Thomas Eboli, one of the trio of underbosses who inherited the Vito Genovese Family in 1969, was gunned down on a Brooklyn Street. That left Gerado Catena and Michele Miranda as surviving leaders of the clan. But with Catena arrested, tried, convicted, and now imprisoned for racketeering, and Michele Miranda at seventy-eight too old to do anything about it, Gambino had yet a third Mafia family under his thumb.

There were two more to go.

Thus began the killing of other Mafiosi to scare those remaining tribes – the Luchese and Bonanno Families – to come under Gambino's rule.

The Luchese Family got the message first and fell in line immediately after leader Carmine Tramunti came to the conclusion that he wanted no further truck with Gambino. Not very long after, the head of the Bonanno family, Natale Evola, along with Philip Rastelli and Joseph DeFilippo, also let Carlo Gambino know they were perfectly willing to play 'fair and square' in his ballpark.

By now Carlo Gambino had become so all-powerful that none of the other families across the length and breadth of the U.S.A. could challenge him.

And thus he became the Mafia's new *Capo di tutti Capi* – Boss of All Bosses – the first since Salvatore Marango, who was assassinated in 1931.

A new era in the American Mafia and organised crime had begun.

Chapter 35

The Nixon Administration and the Mafia

But even Carlo Gambino could not completely control and direct the affairs of another vast underworld venture: the International Brotherhood of Teamsters, the nation's oldest and largest labor union. Yet his grip was on the throttle.

Thirteen years later, in 1986, a special Presidential Commission was to find that the Teamsters 'have been firmly under the influence of organised crime since the 1950s'.

Those in the know considered that conclusion laughable, for it had never been a secret what the Teamsters were all about. Not only were they 'under the influence of organised crime', but they were also involved in a pact with the Mafia, whose top leaders had for many years pulled the strings in the operations of America's most corrupt labor union.

Nothing in the Teamsters' fetid record kept them from moving forward with sure and steady steps in gaining both size and strength during a time when many other unions had sunk in bureaucratic torpor. Even as scandal after scandal confronted them, the Teamsters reached new heights of power in the labor movement.

As the union's membership climbed to more than two million, it counted among its newcomers thousands of police officers across the country and other distinguished bodies of the labor force who lent the union's tarnished prestige a gilt-edged quality.

At the top reposed James R. 'Jimmy' Hoffa, at once the most engaging and most baleful of all the union's leaders – a character straight out of *The Godfather*.

Hoffa had been a Teamsters' Union official for many years, with his home base in Detroit. During those years, rumors of his ties with organised crime abounded. Despite that reputation, he was elected president in 1957. As president of the Teamsters, he was a two-fisted leader who'd run afoul of the law only after he had run the union for a decade.

He wasted little time establishing the Mafia imprimatur on the Teamsters.

'Everybody has his price' was the credo by which Jimmy Hoffa managed the union. That policy resulted in payoffs for some and promises of political support or special favors for others. He kept no bank accounts, drew no checks, and when he traveled he carried an attaché case that contained up to $500,000 in cash.

'Don't forget the case,' Hoffa admonished his aides when entrusting the bag to them on his speech-making outings or at contract negotiations. But his greatest impact over the years that he ran the union was on Capitol Hill.

Each month of every one of the ten years he steered the Teamsters steamroller through the nation's Upper and Lower Houses, some of Hoffa's most trusted intimates would enter the offices of the representatives and senators who were on the union's 'friendship rolls' and plunk down a large manila envelope on each of those lawmakers' desks.

'Here's your copy of the magazine,' Hoffa's emissaries said. Indeed, that month's issue of *International Teamster* was in the envelope – but so were $500 to $1,000 in crisp legal tender of $50 or $100-bill denominations.

The practice received a severe setback in the late 1950s after televised United States Senate hearings on illegal Teamster activities. The legislators were so shaken by the disclosures of bribes to government officials and others that many balked at taking any more of Hoffa's money – at least not in their Washington offices in full view of their staffs.

As the Teamsters' influence with Congress decreased, one Hoffa stooge told of having walked into an office that had been on his monthly rounds for years and placing the envelope on the representative's desk.

'What's this?' demanded the congressman, his face a scowl.

'It's this month's *International Teamster* magazine,' the emissary said with a knowing wink.

'Out!' the congressman roared. 'I want nothing whatsoever to do with the Teamsters! Get out of here!'

When Hoffa heard about the snub, he shook his head in disgust.

'Why didn't you leave it anyway?' he reprimanded the emissary. 'The bastard would have taken it just as he always has!'

While congressmen and senators were becoming increasingly reluctant to remain on his payroll, Jimmy Hoffa exhibited no unease about ripping off his own membership for millions of dollars every month. Jimmy Hoffa had a fertile, creative mind that led him to devise a scheme that came to be known as The Money Machine.

Hoffa put this machine together by rounding up four hundred and fifty thousand Teamster members in twenty-two states who were asked to cough up from four dollars to twenty dollars a month, depending on the contributor's average monthly salary. They let Jimmy assess those fees on his promise that when they grew old and gray they would retire on a nice fat pension.

But Hoffa didn't find any fun in raking in all that money and letting it sit in escrow in some bank account yielding a puny four percent interest until it came time to distribute it to the retirees. He worked up a scheme by which he'd first keep people who paid into the fund from collecting their pensions, and, second, invest in enterprises that yielded the highest possible returns. Trouble was, they'd have to be illegal ventures to bring the kind of rich profits Hoffa anticipated.

The Money Machine was labelled 'The Central States, Southeast and Southwest Areas Pension Fund'. In its basic operation, it was legal. But it quickly lost all semblance of legitimacy when the machine was thrown into high gear.

The gimmick the inventive Hoffa came up with rested on two basic rules contributors to the fund had to abide by: no one collects a pension if more than three years have passed without having made a contribution toward retirement, and each of the four hundred and fifty thousand members must keep records proving the required monthly contribution had been made.

How the fund actually worked is to this day one of the great mysteries of Jimmy Hoffa's rule over the Teamsters. Perhaps the most detailed information about the way the fund functioned came from successful federal prosecutions in New York City that were launched when the present New York District Attorney Robert Morgenthau was the United States Attorney for the Southern District of New York.

An undercover agent – Herbert Itkin – provided details about ten percent kickbacks made to middlemen on a number of large loans. Itkin discovered that David Wenger, the fund's accountant, received half the dirty money, then split his cut with Hoffa.

The other half of the kickbacks went to the foundation on which the Teamsters was built – the Mafia! The principal recipients of these New York payoffs included labor racketeer John 'Johnny Dio' Dioguardi's brother and underworld big, Salvadore Granello.

Who were the beneficiaries of those loans?

The money went to finance gambling casinos run by organised crime figures in Nevada and to gangland investors in various resort enterprises in California and Florida.

The Money Machine also churned out big-buck loans for various businesses that employed Teamsters. One firm was the Bally Manufacturing Company, makers of pinball machines. This was a sweet-heart of a deal for at least two of the company's stockholders – Frank Fitzsimmons and William Presser.

Fitzsimmons just happened to be Jimmy Hoffa's chief underling in the union and Presser was a power in the Ohio Teamsters as well as a pension fund trustee.

Later investigations turned up evidence that the fund had invested heavily in high-risk enterprises such as motels and bowling alleys and in speculative real estate deals. Many of these ventures failed and the fund was the loser on these investments. Yet Hoffa and those who nursed the fund continued to rake in the money.

The time was rapidly approaching for Hoffa to take a fall. His reckless ways with The Money Machine were going to help bring about his arrest, conviction, and imprisonment for pension fraud, bribery, and jury tampering. Hoffa's most brazen act in managing the fund was the arrangements that allegedly enabled Allen Dorfman, son of an Al Capone associate, to be the conduit for hundreds of dollars in pension reserves that wound up in so many of those shaky real-estate ventures operated by gangsters and stock swindlers.

Dorfman remained in that role – his official title was the Central States 'insurance agent' – until Hoffa was sent off to serve his time in the federal penitentiary at Lewisburg, Pennsylvania. Then Dorfman took over as the head of the pension fund, yet on the largest decisions he had to await word from Hoffa at the prison.

This arrangement fell through after Frank Fitzsimmons was shunted into the $200,000-a-year Teamsters' presidency by Hoffa, who wanted his close ally to be the union's caretaker while he was in jail. But Fitzsimmons rejected Hoffa's guidance the first week Jimmy was in jail. Hoffa's lawyers went to him to change his ways but he turned them away. 'Don't bother me. I don't want to hear it!' he told them. Shortly afterward, Dorfman followed Fitz's lead and refused to consult with Hoffa on pension fund matters.

Hoffa vowed that a day would come when he'd be released from prison, return to the helm of the Teamsters Union, and again manage those hundreds of millions of dollars in trust that flowed into high-risk ventures controlled by the Mafia.

It all began in 1962 when a Federal Grand Jury in Nashville, Tennessee, indicted the Teamster president for violating federal labor laws. A mistrial was declared after reports of jury tampering.

Over the next two years an investigation overseen by Attorney General Robert Kennedy sought to ferret out what happened at that trial. The probers hit paydirt and Hoffa was indicted anew, found guilty, and sentenced to eight years in prison for jury-fixing with an additional five years for fraud and conspiracy in the handling of the union's benefit fund.

However, Hoffa's appeals were not exhausted until 1967. And only then did he surrender and begin serving his time at Lewisburg Penitentiary.

By the time he had done half of his sentence. Hoffa used a ploy on President Richard M. Nixon, who always had been an ally of the International Brotherhood of Teamsters.

Hoffa agreed to say that he was retiring as Teamsters' president and renouncing any and all ambitions to regain a seat in the union organisation's ruling councils. Nixon commuted Hoffa's sentence and made him a free man.

The terms of the release of America's most corrupt labor leader had a string attached to it: Hoffa must not meddle in Teamster Union activity before March 1980, when his thirteen-year-sentence would expire. But Jimmy wasted precious little time trying to unseat Fitzsimmons, whom Nixon had once described as 'my kind of labor leader . . .'

While still in the midst of his efforts to regain the presidency, Hoffa left his home in the Detroit suburb of Marion on a sweltering August day in 1971 – and has not been since.

Was he murdered?

Ex-Teamsters warhorse Dave Beck, who handpicked Jimmy Hoffa as his successor for the union's presidency in 1957, said in 1978:

'The Mob murdered him. But I don't know who . . .'

There has been a persistent rumor in the years since Hoffa vanished, that his probable assassin was New Jersey crime czar and labor racketeer Anthony 'Tony Pro' Provenzano. But Hoffa's murder was never officially tied to him, though Tony Pro was indicted, prosecuted, and incarcerated for other killings.

Perhaps Hoffa was slain and his corpse ditched on a roadside that has since become a paved rest area for those many thousands of truck drivers Jimmy robbed in his years at the helm of the Teamsters.

Frank Fitzsimmons's leadership of the Teamsters lasted until 1981, when he died of cancer. He was succeeded by Roy L. Williams, the union's vice president who was elected despite a federal indictment that hung over him for union abuses and widespread reports that he was linked to organised crime.

Williams finally was convicted in 1982 when found guilty of conspiring to bribe a United States Senator and defrauding the union's Central States Pension Fund. He was sent to prison.

Jackie Presser, son of William Presser, one-time head of the joint council in the Cleveland area who had been dispatched to prison to do three separate stretches, was elected the union's president.

Three years after Jackie Presser was made head of the Teamsters, a Federal Grand Jury came along and indicted him for embezzlement and racketeering in a union local.

Once again things didn't look too well for the Teamsters' hierarchy.

But there were worse scandals that kept encircling them.

'What I mean is you could get a million dollars . . . And you could get it in cash. I know where it could be gotten . . . We could get the money. There is no problem in that . . .'

Those words were spoken by Richard Nixon on 21 March 1973, in a conversation with White House Counsel John Dean while discussing the Watergate burglars' demands for huge sums of hush money. But when the transcript of that tape-recorded conversation was disclosed a year later, some reporters speculated on what the President was really thinking. And it remained one of the myriad mysteries that were never cleared up in the wake of the Watergate investigation.

When that scandal broke, the first ugly, indeed horrific, words that flashed before some people in the Justice Department was that there'd been a huge Mob payoff.

One of the first thoughts that occurred to a member of the Justice Department's probers was that Nixon, in his tape-recorded conversation, was talking about a secret cash fund that had been raised by racketeers hooked up with the Teamsters.

According to a *Time* magazine article of August 1977, the Department of Justice believed, and a later FBI inquiry substantiated, that the purpose behind the largesse may well have been that the $1 million the President spoke about was intended as a payoff for the Administration's cooperation in preventing Jimmy Hoffa from wresting the union presidency from Nixon's favourite labor leader, Frank Fitzsimmons, a staunch Nixon supporter.

But why should Nixon have sprung Hoffa and then, according to the FBI findings, exerted every effort in his power to knock him down?

An article appearing in *The New York Times* on 11 November 1977, discloses that Hoffa felt that Nixon was pressured by his buddy Frank Fitzsimmons to commute Hoffa's sentence. Fitzsimmons was unhappy over the power Hoffa was wielding over the Teamsters from behind prison walls and could see the handwriting on the wall: within a year or two Hoffa would be parolled after doing minimum time. Then he'd be out on the street and wooing the Teamster rank and file, as well as many of its officers, to put him back in the presidency. Fitzsimmons decided to end the suspense. He wanted Hoffa's comeback to happen as soon as possible – thus his appeal to Nixon to give Hoffa his walking papers, the sooner the better. Nixon is said to have signed the documents hurriedly.

Moreover, when Fitzsimmons approached Nixon for a deal, he came with a handful of requests, besides Hoffa's commutation.

Fitzsimmons also told the President that electronic surveillance of Chicago Mafia chieftain Anthony Accordo and other mob figures had to cease at once. They didn't want the Justice Department monitoring their conversations about the Teamsters' membership pension funds.

According to information the authors were privileged to see in FBI reports, two leading union figures, Tony Provenzano and his muscleman Sal Briguglio, were the likely culprits in the payoff plans.

It all began when Mafioso chieftain Accardo met the union's top honcho, Fitzsimmons, in early January of 1973, at a plush Spa resort hotel in California, which Jimmy Hoffa and the

Teamsters' retirement fund partially financed a few years previously. Tony told Fitz that he was well aware of his friendship with Nixon, and laid it on the line to him.

Three of Nixon's aides – John Ehrlichman, H. R. Haldeman, and John Dean were at the hotel that very day.

Nixon was staying that weekend at his retreat in San Clemente. Close enough, in fact, to be able to give Frank Fitzsimmons a lift on Air Force Once when the Presidential plane took off from California for Washington that late Sunday afternoon.

On the flight, we're told, Fitzsimmons said to Nixon: 'Mr President, I know you've been in touch with the gentlemen I met earlier today at my hotel [Ehrlichman, Haldeman, and Dean]. I don't believe they told you what we're prepared to pay for the request I put on the table.'

Fitzsimmons then went on:

'You'll never have to worry about where the next dollar will come from in any future campaign you're involved in, nor after you leave the White House.'

Nixon is said to have turned to Fitzsimmons and stared him down for the last word on what reward the labor leader would offer for the favors the Mafia was asking of him. The response allegedly was:

'We're going to give you one million dollars up front, Mr President . . . and then there'll be more that'll follow to make certain you are never left wanting.'

Within thirty days every demand Fitzsimmons had put before Nixon's three top aides was granted. All probes into the Mafia and Teamsters were scuttled, the wiretap on Accardo and other mobsters were rescinded, and arrangements were made to spring Hoffa.

Meanwhile, according to government informers, Provenzano and Briguglio were engaged by the Mob to handle plans for the payoffs. The first instalment came due in early January 1973. It was a $500,000 cash payment that the FBI believes was handed to Charles Colson, who handled the administration's dealings with the Teamsters, or his emissary, in Las Vegas on 6 January 1973.

The timing was crucial. For just a few months before, Watergate burglar Howard Hunt, who had become a loose cannon in the Administration, was pressuring his lawyer, William Bittman, for the money he'd been promised for his continued silence.

Bittman had a meeting with Colson on 3 January. Later, Colson told Dean: 'Bittman came at me like a train.' There is striking evidence that such a payoff occurred.

The FBI found hotel records showing one of Provenzano's couriers was in Las Vegas on 6 January 1973.

Then, too, there's Colson's White House calendar that Watergate probers obtained in 1974. For reasons not clear either then or today, Colson had blank pages for the weekend of 6 and 7 January – a phenomenon that didn't occur on any other weekend in all his years at the White House.

The calendar provided a significant clue that the FBI believes filled the gap on what happened that untelling weekend: Colson spoke with Fitzsimmons on Monday, 8 January.

What did they discuss? Colson was later asked by the FBI.

'Gee, I just can't remember what I talked about with Fitz,' he replied. 'And I certainly know nothing about any Teamster payoff . . .'

The FBI first went after Dean, then Ehrlichman and Haldeman, who were in prison after the Watergate scandals. Finally, the G-men targeted former Attorney General John Mitchell, also in jail by then for his role in the Watergate coverup.

'How can you ask me if I dropped the investigations into the Teamsters union and those other organised crime cases because the President was bribed to do that?' Mitchell asked in high dudgeon.

'The inquiries were aborted because we finally decided none of the cases had merit . . . that there simply wasn't enough evidence to prosecute . . .'

According to a *Time* magazine article, the FBI had planned to question Nixon about the purported payoffs but never went through with it.

The mystery has lain on the Justice Department's back burner for more than ten years. And now Rudolph W. Giuliani is about to give it a second, and without a doubt, far more comprehensive investigation from behind the desk he occupies in the United States District Attorney's office for the Southern District of New York.

Giuliani is bringing the Teamsters' top leadership – some twenty-three people – to court and trying to strip them, in a civil suit, of their positions in the union.

At the same time he will ask a federal judge to appoint a trustee to supervise the union's affairs until such time as the rank and file can vote for new officers who are free of the taint of corruption and influence of organised crime.

In our interview Giuliani would not say on what grounds beyond a civil action he will prosecute the Teamster bigwigs. But if he delves into the union's criminal activities, then it's quite likely that more will surface about the Nixon Administration's relations with the corrupt and crooked leaders who misguided the Teamsters through the years.

Chapter 36

The Mafia's Hold on the U.S.

It has wielded not only an influence but, in many instances, control over a very large area of New York's industry and commerce – which also means America. The five crime families had it in their power, if they so conspired, to paralyse the city by halting the movement of every car, cab, bus, truck, train, ship in the harbor, and passenger and cargo plane. Until Uncle Sam cracked down with:

THE COMMISION TRIAL

Who owns New York?

According to the Mob, they do.

With their control of many areas of commerce and industry over the people in the city's five boroughs and millions more in surrounding suburbs, the underworld could shut down literally thousands of retail and wholesale businesses in a drastic and prolonged crackdown on the metropolis.

Such a stoppage could affect the area's supplies of food, clothing, furniture, pharmaceuticals, and hundreds of other goods.

The underworld could also close off hundreds of services, such as laundering, dry cleaning, linen supply, knife-sharpening, catering, window cleaning, and many more.

The Mob has exerted its influences over thousands of businesses in the city through a huge conglomerate of subsidiaries which have dealt in every conceivable aspect of commerce. The Mob's hands – or its millions of dollars – have touched a very significant portion of the goods and services the average New Yorker requires in a twenty-four-hour day.

And where its hands or its money hasn't touched the region's multi-billion-dollar industrial and commercial businesses, its influence has done so to a discernible degree.

Among the instruments the Mob has had at its disposal are racketeering, extortion, union corruption, murder, and strong-arming. The orders to commit these illegalities that have kept the Mafia at the pinnacle of this vast criminal kingdom are handed down by The Commission – the board of directors who have arbitrated Mob disputes, divided territory, authorised new members, and directed major gangland murders since that ruling body was established in 1931.

It took nearly half a century before law enforcement agencies finally united in 1980 to strike a mortal blow against the Mafia. Yet nearly six more years passed before enough evidence was gathered to assure a successful prosecution that would lead to the dramatic decommissioning of the Commission's top leadership.

The investigation carried out by a vast, well-constructed joint organised crime task force, comprised of hundreds of FBI agents, New York City Police Department detectives, and prosecutors from U.S. Attorney Rudolph W. Giuliani's office in Manhattan was unique in that its mission was to penetrate deep into organised crime families by employing bold and heretofore untried undercover operations, leaning on new legal strategies which enlisted the cooperation of rival law-enforcement agencies, using sophisticated court-approved around-the-clock surveillance equipment, and utilising the latest computer technology. All together, these tools resulted in the arrest, indictment, and conviction of eight Mob leaders who sat at the very apex of the Mafia's criminal empire.

* * *

Until that day in 1980 when he declared war on the Mob, Attorney General William French Smith had no precedent to fall back on in the Justice Department's long history of battling the nation's most ferocious criminals. While his predecessors had fought organised crime, almost all other efforts to penetrate the inner chambers of the Mafia, with the exception of the mild successes of Robert F. Kennedy, were frustratingly unfruitful.

Law enforcement had spent billions of dollars trying to stem the tide of underworld infiltration and domination of our airports, docks, garment industries, cigarette trade, trucking services, produce and food business, labor and union federations, garbage and refuse carting, and scores of other legitimate enterprises, but those efforts were almost always total failures.

Authorities also spent billions in the battle against illegitimate organised crime operations. Yet gambling, narcotics, pornography, prostitution, murder-by-contract, hijacking, robberies, embezzlements, burglaries, and strongarming were in healthier states than ever when Attorney General Smith committed himself to war on the Mob.

On the waterfront

The Mob has owned it because it has controlled and influenced all activity on the piers, from dock workers to shipping companies, through extortion, bribery, theft, labor racketeering, fraud, shylocking, gambling, skull-cracking, and murder.

The Mob has also held a paralysing grip on the International Longshoremen's Association, a labor union infiltrated so deeply by organised crime that its thirty thousand members in the New York Metropolitan Area alone have been bled for millions of dollars in tribute. It all started in the roaring twenties after the ginzo-mick war put the Port of New York and its six hundred fifty miles of waterfront under Mafia domination. Now the Mob's tentacles are deeply embedded in such other Atlantic and Gulf Coast ports as Boston, New Orleans, Charleston, Mobile, and Miami.

THE MAFIA'S HOLD ON THE U.S.

Yet conditions in the New York region were, as always, the worst, because New York's is the biggest and busiest harbor.

At the airports

The Mob owns Kennedy, La Guardia, and Newark.

And authorities are so disorganised that their conception and planning of an attack against gangland's control over the airports bears no semblance of a unified assault on mobdom's forces that are bleeding the airlines and the public for several billions of dollars a year.

Statistics bare nothing about the true extent of air freight thefts at Kennedy, LaGuardia, and Newark. The stats are routinely doctored by some airlines to conceal the real losses.

The practice has existed since the Mob first moved into Kennedy – then known as Idlewild International – in the 1950s under the aegis of John 'Johnny Dio' Dioguardia and Anthony 'Tony Ducks' Corallo. The Mafia's influence and control spread like a cancer to LaGuardia, then Newark, almost immediately.

The Mob's control over Kennedy – the nation's largest air freight center – is total; the more than four million tons of cargo, worth $50 billion, passing through the airport each year is at its mercy.

Three of New York's five families – Genovese, Gambino, and Luchese – have been fleecing the airline and public through an array of illicit as well as ostensibly legitimate ventures.

Their airport specialities are hijacking, robbery, labor racketeering, loansharking, and gambling. An even greater threat to the stability and economic well-being of the air freight industry in these locales is the Mob's increasing acquisitions of trucking firms hauling cargo to and from the airports.

Not only could the Mob shut down Kennedy Airport at will, but they have also gained considerable power at the airports of Philadelphia, Boston, Miami, Detroit, Dallas-Forth Worth, Denver, Los Angeles, and San Francisco.

The airlines are petrified by the Mob, yet adamantly veto genuine offers for legal crackdowns that would emancipate them from its influences and astronomical financial losses. The airlines even tolerate the indiscriminate employment of criminals and ex-cons in the cargo facilities and flatly turn down offers to endorse proposals to institute screening systems to keep undesirables off their payrolls.

At the cigarette counter or machine

The Mob owns this business, too.

The Bonanno, Colombo, Gambino, and Luchese Families have been the biggest wholesalers of regular, king-size, mentholated, and filtertip cigarettes from top to bottom, not just in New York, but in such high-tax-per-pack states as Maine, Connecticut, New Jersey, Pennsylvania, Ohio, Illinois, Wisconsin, Minnesota, Arkansas, Tennessee, Alabama, Florida, Texas, Arizona, and Washington.

Law enforcement officials estimate organised crime's involvement in illicit cigarette bootlegging and sales is grossing the Mob $2.5 billion annually, netting it $1 billion – about two-thirds the profit realised by America's six biggest tobacco companies – and cheating the states with the highest imposts on smokes for that very same $1 billion in tax revenues.

The bootlegging and sale of cigarettes in New York City alone nets the four crime families some $500 million a year from sales – money that should be pouring into the city's and state's tax coffers.

It all began in 1965, when cigarette taxes were doubled by New York State from a nickel to a dime. That opened a corridor for contraband, untaxed cartons of cigarettes. The Mob supplanted the average citizens – or 'buttleggers', as they were called – who were saving about $1.50 on a carton by bringing their own up from North Carolina, a practice that escalated to the point where 'buttleggers' would smuggle cartons for family and friends. The Mob stepped in to turn buttlegging into a wholesale operation that borrowed techniques from its bootlegging days of the Prohibition Era. They used trucks, autos, campers, vans, buses, and even planes to haul their illicit cargoes to New York.

The practice soon spread and encompassed all the other states that taxed cigarettes. The marketplaces were inundated with untaxed butts. Legitimate wholesalers and subjobbers experienced a precipitate decline in business – and still suffer from it today. The tools of the Mafia's trade are stolen and counterfeited tax stamps, organised hijackings which regularly feed their lines of distribution, and intimidation of the legal distributors until they buy the underworld cigarettes.

The clothes we wear

The Mob owns the garment industry.

More than the power it exerts on the waterfront, greater than the control it flaunts at the airports, and to a far broader extent than its domination of the cigarette industry, organised crime commands almost total reign over the forty square blocks of New York City's Garment District.

It runs every level of the apparel industry, from absolute ownership in large garment manufacturing firms to silent but sovereign partnerships in other dress houses; from jurisdiction in the cutting and trimming rooms to the movement of the lowly sidewalk coaltrack pushers; from delivery trucks to the many other critical services from carting to money-lending.

No other area of organised crime activity in the city commands the presence and involvement of so many of the most notorious underworld figures as the Garment District does.

At least two dozen firms on New York's Fashion Avenue (a.k.a. Seventh Avenue) are either owned or controlled by organised crime figures, while more than three times that number are known to be managed by Mob associates holding substantial pieces of the action just short of all-out dominance.

Organised crime's take from the city's clothing center – a $12 billion-a-year industry employing more than two hundred thousand – profits not only from 'legitimate' investments, but also from a score and more of illegal activities such as loansharking, theft of union pension fund loans, phony payrolls, extortion, hijacking, shylocking, gambling, and protection rackets.

Beyond the Mafia's ownership and operation of clothing firms in the Garment Center, its members also have other, far-reaching, interests: they run trucking companies that bring in the raw bolts of cloth and then, after the cutting and stitching, deliver the finished garments to their destinations at shipping depots, freight terminals, and airports.

Loansharking is the next most profitable racket on Seventh Avenue. In what is perhaps the most unique feature about the underworld's grip on the district, the Mob works in an almost perfect atmosphere of co-existence with its victims.

Undoubtedly, the circumstances so singular in the Garment Center allow for this. For instance, a dress manufacturer already in hock, as most are quite often in this seasonal business, has just turned out a line of dresses. He expects to make a killing when the buyers around the country – department stores, mail order houses, retail chains, and independents – send payment for the goods they bought. But that won't begin happening for at least thirty days. So the manufacturer's immediate problem is meeting the payroll and paying for gas and electricity, phones, insurance, and other expenses. His application for the bank loan is turned down – he's too much of a risk. So he turns to the loanshark, whom he meets in his office as he would a buyer from Saks Fifth Avenue.

'So, you're up against it, eh?' the loanshark smiles.

'Yeah,' the dressmaker replies. 'I need fifty big ones . . .'

'Okay, Nathan, you're good for it. I'll have it on your desk tomorrow morning.'

'Thanks, Joey . . . thanks . . . You saved my life.'

It will be Nathan's life if he doesn't come up with the 'vigorish' or 'vig' – slang for interest – on time all the time.

The interest? Could run anywhere from three to five percent on the dollar. How does that compare with the interest banks charge?

A bank may charge thirteen percent interest annually on a loan. But the Mob's interest is charged weekly.

Thus, the borrower of $50,000 must come up with $2,500 every seven days for the shylock, who becomes an enforcer if the creditor should falter on his payment. The Mob doesn't care about getting back its principal. All it wants is the vigorish. Because if the dress manufacturer encounters a problem in collecting for his new line, he rides along the $2,500 interest payments for as long as he's in the hole.

In a mere twenty weeks the Mob has gotten its money back and every week after that the $2,500 weekly extortion is gravy. Through it all, the businessman always still owes the Mob the principal of $50,000.

Organised crime has never been known to have patience with slow or delinquent payers. Unsightly weed-grown lots, the waterways around the city, and many of its concrete highways hold the remains of borrowers who failed to exonerate their indebtedness to the Mob.

But it's infinitely more likely that a garment manufacturer will never meet the fate of, say, a Brooklyn dockworker or a Kennedy Airport employee who has welched on a loan. The business on Seventh Avenue has something to offer the Mob in lieu of repaying the loan: he has his business to turn over to them.

And that's mainly why so many organised crime figures have come to be such renowned principal owners and partners in so many dress and suit firms.

The food we eat

The Mob owns the food industry.

There's hardly a bagel sold in New York – or most other cities in the United States – that isn't made, traded, or touched by organised crime.

No visitor to the Big Apple can buy a Kosher salami, frankfurter, or other provision proclaiming rabbinical approbation that isn't produced, sold, or handled under some area of Mob control.

There's hardly a butcher shop or supermarket whose cuts of meat haven't passed through the underworld on the way to the store. And if the Mob didn't sell the meat out of one of its 'legitimate' fronts or deliver it in one of its trucks, then the beef, lamb, or pork shipment was hijacked and sold to the outlets through wholesale stolen-meat fences.

427

The city's renowned Fulton Fish Market underwent massive rehabilitation during the 1970s and 1980s; its once-decrepit buildings and ramshackle East River piers along Manhattan's Lower East Side were rebuilt or restored to their original look that reflected the grandeur of Little Old New York. The biggest influence in the facelift came from the recreation of the old waterfront further downtown that is today's highly popular South Street Seaport, an expanse of shops and restaurants that have replaced the eyesore buildings that existed incongruously for all too many years alongside the glamorous financial district of Wall Street.

But one aspect of real life in the Fulton Fish Market hasn't changed. The Mafia is still the great white killer shark who rules over every single catch of the sea filling the myriad wholesale fish outlets that line the famed marketplace.

Not one lobster, nor a pound of haddock, no clam or oyster, absolutely no creature that has been trawled from the deep and hauled to shore enroute to a home dinner table or a restaurant is immune from the clamp of the Mob's claws. They control, as we've already cited, the longshoremen who unburden the ships of their perishable cargoes.

'You don't wanna pay this week?' a tough-talking 'collection agent' asks the skipper of the fishing boat.

The slightest hesitancy in answering the question could cause a work stoppage – and the captain may as well dump his catch back into the sea. Because if he doesn't Health Department inspectors will be there to slap him with a summons for the stink he's making with his dead and rotting fish.

The Fulton Fish market rackets began in the 1920s and reached the public's awareness in the 1940s and 1950s when the extortionate practices of Mafia chieftain Joseph 'Socks' Lanza triggered headline stories on the way he was choreographing the underworld's stranglehold on the freshwater fish business.

'Joe Zox', as his intimates knew him, had total control of the Fulton market. No fish could be unloaded unless he was paid $10 tribute from every arriving vessel. No stall could do business with the buyers unless there was a 'contract' with Lanza to pay him a percentage of the day's take. Moreover, no truck could leave from the city-owned facility unless Joe Zox's palm was crossed with $50.

Although Lanza's rule over the Fulton market was interrupted twice – in the 1930s and again the 1940s – with prison sentences for racketeering, he managed in both instances to maintain control until his death. But that did not end the Mafia's rule over the fish business. It is as solidly entrenched in the Fulton market today as it's ever been.

Then there are the many varieties of knives used in the food trade.

No blade that splits a bagel in a knoshery or restaurant, no cutting tool that slices a salami or pastrami in a deli; no hacksaw, cleaver, or boning knife in the hands of a butcher, restaurant chef, or fish market clerk is immune from gangland's touch. Whether the Mob sold or didn't sell these tools to their users, it has a voice, to whatever extent, in the sharpening of those tools. Even if the grinder is not even remotely connected to a crime family some part of his income ultimately must make its way to the Mob, because organised crime controls the cutlery grinding business – lock, stock, and grinder.

In many of its operations involving meat processing, organised crime has been known to incorporate in their frankfurters and other ground-meat products meats never intended for human consumption.

Many New Yorkers can still recall with fondness a day in the distant past when they feasted with relish on provisions provided by the Merkel Meat Company, which had the best reputation for quality meats. A day came when Merkel sold its business to Sheldon Lokietz, who bought it with his father Norman's money. Norman became Merkel's president and Sheldon began to use inferior products in his franks, wursts, and other provisions.

Young Lokietz hooked up with a meat wholesaler linked directly to organised crime and to the wholesale purveyors of horsemeat, as well as beef and pork intended to be fed to animals on mink ranches.

These products were provided by a packing house in Utica, New York, which specialised in the purchase from local farmers of dead or dying animals: cows, horses, sheep – all uninspected and never intended to be for human fare.

From Utica, the meats made their way to a processing firm on Manhattan's West Side run by organised crime associate Charles Anselmo. His credentials for the wholesale meat business were gathered from long experience in loan-sharking.

Anselmo quickly convinced Sheldon Lokietz that none of Merkel's hundreds of thousands of faithful customers would ever taste or sense the difference if the diseased meat were substituted in the firm's franks and other ground-meat products.

Lokietz had just one hurdle to cross before distributing the defective meat products to Merkel's outlets: Department of Agriculture inspectors. Lokietz bribed them to certify the inferior meat products his firm was packaging.

Using variations on these tactics, the underworld succeeded in putting a stranglehold on the kosher provisions industry, too. In fact, until the State Investigation Commission blew the cover a large number of kosher provision firms were carrying organised crime figures on their payrolls. This way of life for those firms coincided with the sudden rise in popularity and resulting high profits of the kosher provisions industry.

The Mob also has the upper hand over the garbage and refuse collection business. No one, without the Mafia's blessing, can become a carter.

Nor can anyone go into the New York Metropolitan Area's multi-million-dollar sex-oriented industries – the X-rated movie theater operations, massage parlors, peep shows, and the many other pornographic and vice rackets – before first passing muster with the Mafia and agreeing to pay regular tribute for the privilege of being a part of the sex mill that the crime lords control not only in New York but in virtually every city in the rest of the country.

Certain other rackets, such as the construction industries and hotel, restaurant, and tavern businesses, were – and still are – the

Mafia's biggest money-makers. But they also were to be the Mob's Achilles Heel.

The long, searching investigation of the five families and their ruling council, The Commission, resulted on 26 February 1985 in a fifteen-count indictment against nine defendants: the five bosses or acting bosses and four other high-ranking family members. They were accused of participating in the decisions and activities of an underground conspiracy in which the Commission regulated the 'Mafia's criminal activities ranging from loansharking and gambling to drug trafficking and labor racketeering; authorised murders of Mafia members, including the 1979 assassination of Carmine Galante, four other specific killings and an attempted murder, and carried on a multi-million-dollar extortion scheme, described as 'The Club', which dominates the concrete industry.'

The five bosses named in the indictment were Anthony 'Fat Tony' Salerno (Genovese Family), Paul 'Big Paul' Castellano (Gambino), Anthony 'Tony Ducks' Corallo (Luchese), Philip 'Rusty' Rastelli (Bonanno), and Gennaro 'Jerry Lang' Langella (Colombo).

Castellano, known at times as 'Paulie', 'Mr Paul', and 'Big Paul', was assassinated in Times Square before United States District Attorney Rudolph Giuliani finally brought the criminals before the bar of justice. The four other indicted members or associates of the Commission were Aniello 'Mr O'Neill' Dellacroce (Gambino Family under-boss), Salvatore 'Tom Mix' Santoro (Luchese underboss), Christopher 'Christie Tick' Furnari (Luchese *consigliere*), and Ralph Scopo (Colombo member and president of The Concrete Workers District Council, Laborers International Union of North America).

Aniello Dellacroce died of natural causes on 2 December 1985, ten months after he was indicted and nine months before the trial's launch. In his place was another boss who was named in a superseding indictment: Carmine The Snake Persico (Boss of the Colombo Family).

An unusual prosecution team was structured by Giuliani. He designated Assistant United States Attorneys Michael Chertoff and Jon Savarese from his office to prosecute the defendants, and added a third member to the team, Kings County (Brooklyn) Assistant District Attorney John Gilmore Childers, who was cross-designated as a Special Assistant United States Attorney for this trial. Childers had contributed mightily to the joint task force investigation that led to the indictments of the eight Cosa Nostra Commission defendants and his expertise was viewed as a big plus for the prosecution.

The evidence at the trial established that the defendants, as members of the Commission, regulated the relationships between and among Mafia families. The prosecutors also showed that the eight top-ranked men oversaw the Mafia's criminal activities ranging from loansharking and gambling to drug trafficking, and that they carried on a multi-million-dollar extortion scheme upon New York City's ready-mix concrete industry.

The government set out to prove before Federal Judge Richard Owen and the jury of seven women and five men at the trial that: the Commission established a massive extortion and bid-rigging scheme called 'The Club', involving construction contractors who poured concrete at building sites, and each of the defendants, except Rastelli, was personally involved in controlling the allocation of the pacts to pour concrete on construction jobs where the value of the concrete contract exceeded $2 million; the Commission designated the contractor who would make the successful bid on any given contract. And the Commission enforced the rules of 'The Club' with threats against the disobedient contractors to cause their supplies of cement to be stopped – which they could enforce because truckers are all members of the scandal-ridden Teamsters Union, which takes its orders from the Mafia.

The nuts and bolts of the prosecution's case also dwelled on the Mob's most abhorrent acts: committing murders. The lawyers set out to convince the jury that the Commission resolved the leadership dispute in the Bonanno family and with other Mafia families by sanctioning the executions of Bonanno Boss Carmine Galante and underbosses Leonard Coppola and Giuseppe Turano, as well as other killings.

During the thirty-four days of trial testimony, the government brought in more than eighty witnesses and introduced into evidence one hundred and fifty tapes that left no doubt the Commission was engaged in each and every act its members were accused of committing.

Hard solid evidence was shaped by ledgers and journals which clearly demonstrated that bribes and payoffs were made by firms who had paid amounts ranging from seven hundred to twenty-nine thousand nine hundred to insure that they would be permitted either to make concrete deliveries or to pour the mix once it reached a building site.

The most shocking part of the trial was reached when the prosecution divulged the payoffs some of New York's most prestigious restaurants were making to the Mob. Prosecutors Chertoff, Savarese, and Childers demonstrated to the jury, with the use of charts, the amounts of the bribes and who made them:

DATES	RESTAURANT	AMOUNTS
1975 to 1982	Sherry Netherland and 781 Fifth Avenue	$7,500 per year
1978 to 1981	Café Ziegfeld 227 W. 45th Street	$25,000 plus $2,000 per month
1983 to 1984	Ciro's One Lincoln Plaza	$25,000
1983 to 1984	Kenny's Steak Pub 565 Lexington Avenue and Kenny's Steak Pub 221 W. 46th Street	Amount unknown

The restaurant workers, it was found, were also made to pay tribute to the Mob.

The trial was highlighted by the refusal of Carmine Persico to be represented by an attorney. He served as his own counsel, and in the views of many, did a commendable job in his defense. He concluded the proceedings on his behalf when, in summing up, he pleaded with the jury: 'Please don't send me back to prison simply because I am a member of the Mafia . . .'

His plea fell on deaf ears. Persico was found guilty, along with all the other defendants who had paid astronomical legal fees to their lawyers for their defenses.

Anthony Salerno, who also received one hundred years and a $240,000 fine – the same fine also assessed against Persico – will be one hundred seventy-five years old before he walks into the bright sunshine of freedom.

The one who got off the lightest was Bonanno soldier Anthony 'Bruno' Indelicato, thirty-eight, who was found guilty of only two racketeering counts, was given fifty years and fined $50,000.

The bustup of the Commission leadership precipitated a cascade of encomiums for the people who prosecuted the case. But even more significant was the torrent of predictions on how the convictions dealt a blow so devastating to the Mafia that it might well never recover.

This was the most successful use yet of the 1970 Racketeer-Influenced and Corrupt Organisations statute, known as RICO. This law provides stiff penalties for a pattern of criminal activity, and prosecutors had begun using it, together with expanded applications of wiretaps and undercover surveillance, as the keystones of their assaults on the Mob.

'This is not the old prosecution that takes out one guy at a time like a wolf picking off the sick and the lame,' commented Robert Blakey, the Notre Dame University law professor who helped draft the law in 1970. 'We just took out the heads of the herd. The herd can't hold together without leadership. The herd's very rationale is called into question by these convictions.'

Adding more voice in the aftermath of the Commission's convictions and ostensibly life-long sentences that should obviate the possibility the eight top Mafiosi will ever return to rule, came the predictions of law enforcement officials that the jailing of these leaders had created turmoil in the Mob as younger, less experienced hoods jockeyed to move up.

'It creates a power void in the hierarchy of organised crime,' offered New York FBI Agent-in-Charge John L. Hogan. 'Now we have underlings who are not as seasoned, who haven't got the contacts, who don't have the experience to manage as well as their predecessors. They're new to the career path, so to speak. That makes it easier to get to them.'

Ronald Goldstock, head of the New York State Organised Crime Task Force, agreed, although he didn't believe the Mafia was ready for interment.

'The Commission will continue to exist,' said Goldstock. 'But it will be new people, none of whom have worked together. So their ability to negotiate and to oversee will be weakened. They will be less likely to rule effectively.'

United States Attorney Giuliani, who coordinated and supervised the investigation that led to the prosecution and conviction of the dreaded eight members of the Commission, said: 'This was the precise way in which Congress intended the RICO statute to be used. It was intended to be a powerful weapon against criminal enterprises, such as the Commission.

'The sentencing of organised crime's top bosses sends an emphatic message that the heinous and brutal crimes committed by the Mafia will not be tolerated and that those who lead the Mob, no matter how powerful or seemingly untouchable, will be brought to justice and appropriately punished.

'These extraordinary sentences are well justified for these defendants who exploited others and who threatened the integrity of civilised, lawful society. Law enforcement will remain dedicated to conducting more investigations and more prosecutions aimed at all forms of organised crime until such vile criminal forces are permanently crippled.'

Rudolph Giuliani will be the first to tell you that we'll not be able to eliminate all the elements of organised crime. Yet, he predicts that the harder law enforcement hits them, the more the Mob is hurt, and the less organised and powerful they'll be.

It wasn't surprising that Giuliani and his team of prosecutors went right back to their arsenal and requisitioned some new artillery to fire at the Mafia in what had been an altogether far-too-long ongoing war with the law in another courtroom.

Chapter 37

The Pizza Connection; Hold the Pepperoni, Heavy on the Heroin, and Thick on the Dough

The battle had begun 30 September 1985, in the courtroom of United States District Judge Pierrê N. Leval with a jury in attendance. By 20 November 1986 the Commission Trial, which had started in August, was over and the eight Mafia bosses convicted and sentenced. Yet after fifteen months the trial of twenty-two Mafiosi involved in the world's most complicated heroin trafficking case was still going on, guided by United States District Attorney Giuliani's words:

'This case represents the first time in history that the Sicilian and American Mafia have been brought to justice for the large-scale narcotics trafficking they have inflicted upon the United States.

'This court is presented with an historic opportunity: the chance to break the control of the Mafia over international drug trafficking.'

Indeed it had been. And the trial went to great lengths to break the Mafia's hold on the drug trade. The judge, jury, and courtroom spectators were to be shocked first by the murder of one defendant, Gaetano Mazzara, a former restaurant owner accused of being a heroin supplier, who was found slain inside a plastic garbage bag on a Brooklyn street on 3 December 1986, during the sixteenth month of the trial, and then by another hit which shook up not only the judge, prosecution, and defense but, most importantly, the defendants, and yet again by the testimony of Tommaso Buscetta, who told all that has ever been told on how one is groomed and prepared to be a Mafioso.

Tommaso looked like a fashion plate in his blue blazer, gray slacks, pale blue shirt, and dark blue tie. He was a soft-spoken man who had come to New York from his native Italy to help bury the Mafia.

No underworld figure since Joe Valachi had laid bare so many secrets of the Mafia. Buscetta was born into a Mafia family. His father and grandfather before him were members of the Sicilian secret society, and until a bloody Mafia war broke out in Sicily two years earlier this fifty-seven-year-old gangster was on top of the heap in organised crime.

Yet he helped launch the sensational multi-billion-dollar 'Pizza Connection Case' which involved an international drug ring that operated across the United States from hundreds of Mafia-controlled pizza parlors and which commanded the big black headlines of the American press for more than three years.

Tommaso Buscetta was thirteen years old when the schools were closed in his hometown of Palermo. World War II had broken out; the Allied bombings began in 1940.

Buscetta hid in bomb shelters and managed to stay alive with his family as first the Germans, then the Allies, bombed and strafed the city continually.

After the war, Buscetta did nothing to further his education. But it came as no surprise when, at age twenty-one, he was summoned to serve the Sicilian secret society.

'I didn't make out any application to become a member,' Buscetta explained. 'I was called, I was invited. I was first approached and then, during the course of these approaches, I was asked one day whether I could on some future days go to some place for a meeting. And there I found four people and they had me take the oath.'

He called the oath-taking 'ridiculous', then described the ritual:

'I was given a saint [a holy card with a prayer that's nominally carried in wallets by the religious] and then my finger was pricked. I had to rub the blood from my finger onto the saint and set fire to it and I had to say the oath.

'After having gone through the process I had to pronounce the oath whereby I was to say that if I should betray the organisation my flesh would burn like the saint.

'I was then taken to the boss and I was introduced to him and was warned that I should never appear or present myself by myself.'

The boss was Gaetano Filippone, and the conversation was very brief:

'He gave me his good wishes, which was a bad auger and he urged me to always be very discreet,' recalled Buscetta.

Although his father and grandfather were Mafiosi, Buscetta didn't yet know how the organisation was structured. The oath of silence, *omerta*, prohibited anyone from talking about it to those outside. But once Buscetta broke ranks with the Mafia, he revealed the secret details of the crime kingdom and how it was structured.

'The organisation was divided up into families. The group was called families because we are or we were brothers. These families adopted the name of the village where they were located or of a small town where the family was located.

'The family consisted of a *capo*, or boss; *sotto capo*, or deputy boss; *consigliere*, or counsellor; *capo decine* [soldier's superior], and *soldato*, or soldier.'

As a beginner, Buscetta naturally was given the lowest ranking: soldier. As such, he soon learned about his duties and responsibilities within the organisation.

'There is not a great deal of difference between a soldier and a boss,' Buscetta pointed out. 'The only difference lies in knowing how to deal with people during a conversation. Some people speak better and some people speak not so well.

'And, as in everything, there has to be a boss. But there is no difference between the boss and the soldier as to dignity or conduct of the man.'

His responsibilities, Buscetta conceded, were limited in the beginning. And there were many rigid rules that he had to abide by as a Mafioso.

'I was reminded to behave in the appropriate manner, to be silent, not to look at other men's wives or women, not to steal, and especially, at all times, when I was called, I had to rush, leaving whatever I was doing.'

He was further instructed on how to pass information to others:

'By voice. Nothing is written in the Mafia,' he stressed.

Then there were his commitments as a 'Man of Honor', as Mafiosi refer to one another. 'There are many such obligations,' said Buscetta. 'The main ones are the maximum silence, secrecy also between husband and wife or brothers, and no leak of information from the Mafia to the outside.

'There was another thing. A person of the Mafia could abstain from talking, but when he talked, he had to tell the truth. Should he not tell the truth, then he may be subject to expulsion or death.'

One of Buscetta's most harrowing experiences as a Mafioso occurred when he became involved in an extra-marital affair – a strict no-no according to the Cosa Nostra constitution.

Buscetta revealed what punishment he had coming to him for his infidelity to his wife, Cristine:

'I had done some things which, under the Mafia rules, one was not to do, namely, betrayed my wife. My *capo decine* told me that I had violated one of the basic rules imposed upon a man of honor and I was subjected to suspension.

'That meant you cannot participate in any more meetings with Cosa Nostra people. You cannot participate in Cosa Nostra activities for six months. Then I was taken back.'

Buscetta left himself open for one more suspension, in the mid-1950s, when he was arrested for smuggling cigarettes into Sicily. He was caught in this misdeed in a locale far removed from Palermo, and that constituted a serious violation for a Man of Honor.

'When a person has to leave or go far from the city,' Buscetta said, 'he has to ask for permission from his *capo decine*.'

But Buscetta neglected to inform his overboss about his extra-curricular activity in crime. Thus the suspension. But he wasn't punished because of the illegality he was caught committing:

'I was not reprimanded for engaging in cigarette smuggling, but because I had been arrested and taken out of the city, and there had been publicity about this,' he said. 'This is something which must be avoided.'

Despite his twin setbacks brought on by cheating on his wife and getting caught committing an unauthorised crime, Buscetta's rise up the ranks of the Mafia was swift. So much so that in the late 1960s Tommaso was dispatched to America to do his dirty work under orders from the Sicilian Boss of Bosses Gaetano Badalamenti – the friend and ally he would one day betray from the witness stand when the spectacular Pizza Connection drug-trafficking case broke wide open.

For more than ten years following his arrival in the United States, Tommaso Buscetta was the Mafia's biggest honcho in illegal crime activity in the country – until he was snared in a $200-million heroin-smuggling conspiracy with nineteen other Mafiosi.

He jumped bail, fled to Mexico, then made his way to Brazil, where he organised pizza parlors as fronts for the drug ring in the country's myriad cities. The system was an exact carbon copy of the pizza parlor operations set up in the United States by Carmine Galante and Carlo Gambino.

Galante and Gambino were the pioneer importers of the old-line Mafiosi, known now as 'the Zips', who were brought here to restore a semblance of order in the American underworld run by Italians and descendants of Italians no longer able to run the underworld with the efficiency and profitability as the old bosses had done.

Many of the newcomers were set up in pizza parlors in scores of cities around the country so that Galante, Gambino, and the numerous other Mafia leaders who dealt in drugs, especially heroin, could wash their dirty money through those eateries.

The operation continued for about a dozen years – until a grand jury returned indictments against thirty-eight defendants on 19 April 1984. But only twenty-two were in court on 30 September 1985 when United States District Attorney Rudolph Giuliani and Assistant United States Attorney Louis Freeh appeared in the United States Courthouse in Manhattan's Foley Square for the start of a seventeen-month-long trial that would be the longest-lasting federal prosecution in history.

One of the no-shows later came forth to stand trial but was murdered before he testified, another was suspected of having been executed, and the others, for the most part, had fled to Switzerland and Italy, among other places.

The defendants were charged with taking part in a Mafia scam that distributed vast amounts of heroin and other narcotics, using the pizza parlors as fronts to wash the money. They had sent $10 million in profits to secret Swiss bank accounts.

The case hinged on these sets of facts and was predicated on developments that grew out of an investigation by the Organised Crime Drug Enforcement Task Force program, which was created by President Ronald Reagan and Attorney General William French Smith in 1983.

The OCDETF, whose goal was the destruction of major drug trafficking organisations, was comprised of agents from the FBI, the United States Customs Service, Drug Enforcement Administration, Internal Revenue Service, Bureau of Alcohol, Tobacco and Firearms, as well as personnel from the United States Marshall's Service and United States Attorney's Office.

The trial was well into its eighteenth month when one of the remaining nineteen defendants was gunned down on a busy

Avenue of the Americas between Eighth and Ninth Street in Greenwich Village.

Pietro Alfano was walking with his wife Maria, carrying bags of groceries they had just bought from a supermarket, when two men hopped out of a red Chevrolet in the middle of the block and one of them pulled a .38-caliber revolver and fired at the Pizza Connection defendant.

As Alfano, struck by a fusillade of bullets in his back, collapsed on the sidewalk, the gunman turned and, for no apparent reason, shot a bystander, thirty-one-year-old Ronald Price.

The gunman and his accomplice escaped, one taking a cab and the other fleeing the scene in a blue van. The victims were taken to nearby St Vincent's Hospital, where Alfano was found to have been struck by three bullets in his back and Price by one in the buttock.

The shooting prompted defense lawyers to plead for a mistrial the next morning in a tense courtroom session surrounded by tight security and with the jury sequestered in its deliberating room.

'It is impossible for us to proceed in the atmosphere of fear, intimidation, and chill that permeates this courtroom,' defense lawyer Michael Kennedy told Judge Leval. 'I feel it personally.'

Kennedy headed Gaetano Badalamenti's defense, which had been implying in summations that the rival New York group of defendants tried to lure Badalamenti out of the protective custody lair into which he was placed after being extradited to New York from Spain, so he could be murdered in order to close the books on the Mafia heroin war that had begun in Sicily several years before.

Another defense lawyer, Joseph Benfante, complained to the judge that the summations suggested some of the defendants had tried to 'set up other defendants in the case for a hit'.

Before the proceedings drew to a close, Judge Leval ordered the jury sequestered until the end of the trial and warned them that they were not to read newspapers or tune in to television or radio stations reporting on the case.

The next day authorities raided the homes of Frank Bavosa, Philip Ragosta, and Giuseppe Amico, awakened them, and brought them in on charges of shooting Alfano and the innocent pedestrian. The FBI arrested them without having to do much additional leg-work other than what it had already done: the G-men were on the trio's back since 30 November 1986, the date they had begun to stalk Alfano each day he left the courthouse after the trial proceedings had ended.

The FBI said the trio was paid $40,000 for the botched hit, ordered because of the factional split among the defendants.

The jury required only six days of deliberations to reach a verdict on 2 March 1987; they found all seventeen guilty.

Despite his deep involvement in the Pizza Connection on three continents, Tommaso Buscetta was not a defendant in the case. He was merely the prosecution's star witness.

How had Uncle Sam grabbed Buscetta out of South America and brought him to New York to testify?

Tomasso Buscetta's days in Brazil came to an end when the law caught up to him and deported him to Palermo, where he was wanted in a gangland war rubout of seven policemen and three bystanders. It was deemed of far greater importance to Brazilian authorities that Buscetta be returned to Italy rather than the United States because of the severity of the crimes in his homeland.

While he expressed no regrets for his role in spilling the blood of ten innocent people, Buscetta was given good reason to go into deepest mourning when the war between the Corleone and Greco Families broke out: he lost seven relatives, including two sons, a nephew, a son-in-law, and a brother-in-law in the bloodletting that left an estimated one thousand dead and forever changed the face of the Mafia.

It was then that Buscetta, to spare himself from the firing squad, offered to turn canary. Because of his testimony at the Mafia trials in Italy, 366 Mafiosi were arrested.

When the curtain came down on his performance there, Tommaso agreed to do an encore in New York.

Buscetta consented to his extradition on only one condition: that his wife, Cristine, and young son, Tommaso Jr, be protected. There was never a question that Tommaso was, first and foremost, concerned about his wife's and son's safety. After the loss of his first two sons and five other relatives in murderous rubouts, Buscetta wanted to take no chances with the lives of the two people who remained closest to his heart.

The family was placed under extraordinary guard.

Cristine and young Tommaso were brought to the United States after Buscetta's extradition papers were prepared, and were sequestered with him in a heavily protected hideaway in the New York area.

When he finally was escorted by United States Marshalls into the Federal Courthouse and summoned to the witness stand, nothing about the murder and mayhem Buscetta accused the defendants of committing was as startling as his picture of life in the Mafia.

Buscetta held the spectators and jury in rapt attention as he described the ritualistic life in the Mafia. But when he was questioned about Badalamenti, Tommaso was a dud.

'I never saw nor did he speak to me personally,' replied the Mafia turncoat. 'Nor did I see him dealing with others in drugs. I was certain he was not working in drugs . . .'

Assistant United States Attorney Richard Martin was stunned by the response. Buscetta went on to explain that because Badalamenti was a deposed Mafia boss, it was unlikely that he could have participated in drug activities in the United States.

It remained for the government's other most significant witness, Salvatore Contorno, also an admitted Mafioso, to set the record straight. He positioned himself as a drug trafficker who had known Badalamenti for more than ten years and had worked closely with him.

'What position did Badalamenti hold at the time you met him in Sicily?' prosecutor Martin asked.

'Mafia boss,' Contorno replied and explained to the jury that the defendant headed the Sicilian Mafia's Cinisi Family.

The prosecutor then wanted to know whether Badalamenti held any other Mafia position at the time.

'Head of the Commission,' the witness answered.

'That's the top level of the Mafia where the orders are given,' Contorno continued, referring to the commission of Mafia leaders in Sicily.

Martin then asked Contorno about Buscetta.

'I met Tommaso in the prison in Palermo several years ago,' the witness replied. 'He was introduced to me by other Mafiosi as *lastesa cosa*.

'That he was a member of La Cosa Nostra, that he was a man of honor, like me.'

Contorno, unlike Buscetta, spoke not a word of English and an interpreter translated his testimony that was given in Sicilian.

One revealing disclosure by Contorno was that pizza parlors in Italy weren't fronts for the drug traffickers. They used other businesses, 'like in Milan', where they export powdered milk.

'Those places are fronts to do the drug trafficking . . . and they [Mafiosi] have to invest a lot of money in the operation . . .'

Then he offered gratuitously: 'They were all men of honor and you have to have capital to get into it . . .'

Those 'men of honor' were the link with the men of honor now on trial for using pizzerias in the United States to conceal drug trafficking and money laundering.

Meanwhile, there was the high drama outside the courtroom – for example, the murder of Gaetano Mazzara, whose body was found in a plastic garbage bag.

He was killed just before he was scheduled to take the stand and testify in his defense when he disappeared. A Pizza Connection bigshot, Mazzara was later found shot and beaten on the Brooklyn waterfront. His legs were fractured, an X-shaped cut had been gouged in his scalp, and his tongue was lacerated by what appeared to have been the prongs of pliers in what was determined by the medical examiner an effort to tear it out.

At the sentencing, the sixty-four-year-old Badalamenti and Salvatore 'Toto' Catalano, forty-six, were handed the stiffest punishment – forty-five years and $1.5 million fines.

Buscetta and Contorno are now ensconced in the safety provided by guarding United States marshalls and living some-where in America under assumed names with their loved ones.

Thus came to an end the Mafia operation that left a trail of thousands of hours of wiretapped conversations, thousands of surveillance photos, and evidence that was followed from hundreds of pizzerias and other drops from Long Island clear across the country to scores of cities where the Mob sold $1.6 billion worth of deadly heroin from grocery bags and shoe boxes, then through the pizzerias funneled its ill-gotten gains to some of Wall Street's largest brokerage firms before it was routed one last time to the safety of banks in Zurich, Berne, and other havens.

Among all of the major Mob trials that the Justice Department prosecuted in the several years of its major crackdown on organised crime, the Pizza Connection went farthest in exposing the Mafia's innermost secrets and operations.

The Mafia may never be the same.

Chapter 38

The Giuliani Offensive: How the Prosecutor Who Likes to Get the Bad Guys Goes and Gets Them

Hammer-fisted Rudolph W. Giuliani is the toughest law-enforcement officer Uncle Sam has ever fielded in the war against the Mob.

His name and the power he has exerted as United States Attorney of New York's Southern District against organised crime strikes terror in every underworld figure from the far reaches of Maine to the outermost precincts of Hawaii.

But to his wife, syndicated television news anchorwoman

Donna Hanover, Rudy is a 'soft, tender, incurable idealist with a lot of romance in his soul'.

Rudy Giuliani admits he enjoys seeing the New Year in with his wife cuddled in his arms and listening to opera on the stereo. His idea of a night on the town is taking Donna dancing. And his favourite relaxation is playing tennis or snorkelling in the waters of the Virgin Islands or St Martin.

Tell that to Paul 'Big Paul' Castellano, the Mafia's seventy-one-year-old top Boss of Bosses, and head of the dreaded Gambino Family – now the largest and most feared Mob organisation in the nation.

For years Big Paul and his underboss, Aniello Mr O'Neill Dellacroce dominated the restaurant, food distribution, entertainment, garment industry, jewelry, construction, and sanitation rackets.

By 1986, Big Paul and Mr O'Neill, who with a mere nod had brought extortion victims to their knees for tribute, were themselves buckling from the burden of Giuliani's grand jury indictment, which threatened to put them and their powerful underworld organisation out of business for good.

With the seventy-three-year-old Anthony Fat Tony Salerno also out of circulation, the family once headed by the late Vito Genovese was in disarray, as was the Luchese organisation and the Bonanno bunch, with their respective leaders, Tony Ducks Corallo, then seventy-three, and Rusty Rastelli, sixty-seven, booted into prison.

Giuliani was himself forty-two years old in 1986 when he was beginning to skin the Mafia's hide. Before coming to New York he had been the Associate Attorney General in the Justice Department in Washington, D.C. – and the scourge of the Cocaine Connection between Columbia and the Florida Keys. His relentless crackdowns snared scores of smugglers in the government's net.

The fearless Mob-buster who was making so many Mafiosi say their prayers had himself wanted to be a missionary priest. He also had it in his mind at one time or another to be a doctor.

Giuliani was destined to be a kid with street smarts to go in tandem with his high intellect. His father, Harold, owner of a tavern in Brooklyn, Rudy's birthplace, taught his only child to box when he was two years old. Although his father used rough language, he also possessed a curious mind. Unfailingly, the elder Giuliani made it a point to bring home at least three newspapers a day and carry on conversations about local and world events as well as politics.

The Reverend Alan J. Placa, a Roman Catholic priest on Long Island and Rudy Giuliani's lifelong friend, pinpointed the father's strongest suit: his hatred of organised crime.

'Harold Giuliani felt people were prejudiced against him because he was Italian,' Father Placa explained. 'But he didn't get angriest at the prejudiced people. He hated Italians in organised crime for giving all Italians a bad name.'

Father Placa remembered that sometime around 1965, when Rudy was not long out of college, father and son were going over a list of appointments to the Supreme Court when the elder Giuliani expressed dismay over the dearth of Italian names.

'It's up to your generation to do better,' Harold Giuliani said to his son. Just at that time Giuliani was on his way to his law degree at New York University. He finished at NYU in 1968 with honors, which brought him a prized clerkship with United States District Court Judge Lloyd F. MacMahon.

Ironically, his first case was defending the judge on a traffic rap. MacMahon wanted to fight the ticket but Giuliani convinced him otherwise.

'Your own daughter, who was riding with you, says you ran that red light, your honor . . .' Giuliani said.

The judge pleaded guilty and in the years since he has unfailingly chided his former protégé: 'Rudy, I will always say you lost your first case.'

In 1970 Giuliani was appointed an Assistant United States Attorney in the office he now heads and has put on the map not only for its prosecution of the Mafia but also for being in the vanguard of the government's crackdown on municipal corruption, Wall Street insider trading, and business and tax fraud.

'That first year I tried many cases,' Giuliani recalled. 'I remember waking up on my birthday and being unable to remember the last Saturday morning I'd had off.'

The horrendous hours left him so little time to be with his first wife that the marriage went on the rocks. When Rudy then took Donna Hanover for better or for worse he vowed he would never allow his work to interfere with his conjugal harmony.

By the time he was thirty years old, Giuliani was the Southern District's third-ranking prosecutor.

'They kept giving him better cases to try, and if they didn't give them to him, he took them,' recalled attorney and close friend John N. Gross.

Giuliani was the key prosecutor in two early cases that captured headlines. He was one of the main men in the police corruption trial that subsequently shaped the scenario for Robert Daley's bestseller *Prince of the City*, which Sidney Lumet later made into a movie, and he also sent Representative Bertram L. Podell to jail after a dramatic bribery trial that was highlighted by Giuliani's merciless cross-examination. So devastated was the congressman that he ended up poking out the lenses of his eyeglasses with a finger just before pleading guilty.

Giuliani was on his way – to Washington. Judge MacMahon, who'd observed Rudy's prosecutorial successes, recommended his former law clerk to good friend Harold Tyler after President Gerald Ford appointed Tyler Deputy Attorney General. Tyler recalls his first encounter with Giuliani:

'I was giving a talk at the United States Attorney's office. All the guys and girls were there, and I see this eager-looking guy in the front row eating up every word I was saying. And I said, that's got to be Rudy Giuliani.'

Giuliani had arrived in the nation's capital and his new post with scores of criminals' scalps hanging from his belt. After two years as a hard-hitting Associate Deputy Attorney General in the Justice Department, Giuliani followed Tyler to New York and private practice. Tyler, a Republican, left Justice after Jimmy Carter defeated President Ford in the 1976 election, and convinced Giuliani, a Democrat-turned-Republican, to do the same.

Tyler got Giuliani a partnership in the corporate firm of Patterson, Belknap, Webb & Tylor. Only thirty-two then, Giuliani was appointed temporary head of Aminex, a coal company in receivership. In a few short months he put the firm back on its feet.

After four years he returned to Washington where he became the Number-Three man in the Justice Department under Attorney General William French Smith. After another round of successful prosecutions, Giuliani was named by President Ronald Reagan to the office of United States Attorney in charge of New York's Southern District, the largest and most important branch of the Justice Department's offices in the fifty states and Puerto Rico.

That was in 1983. And since then, Giuliani has compiled the most formidable record of criminal convictions this country has ever known:

Organised crime

The Colombo Family: In one of the earliest cases to use the Federal Racketeer Influenced And Corrupt Organisations Act against an underworld crime family's entire leadership, nine members of the Joseph Colombo Family were convicted in June 1986 on charges of labor racketeering in the restaurant and construction industries. Chief defendant was the family leader, Carmine Persico, who was later found guilty of being a member of the Mafia ruling council.

Pizza Connection: The Prosecutor wove together his organised crime and drug investigations into the sensational case related in the preceding chapter that led to the seventeen-month trial in which seventeen defendants were convicted of distributing tons of heroin and cocaine through a network of pizzerias across the country.

The Commission: After another lengthy trial, eight organised crime leaders were convicted in November 1986 as members of a national ruling commission of Mafia families who, prosecutors charged, coordinated activities, resolved disputes, and often ordered executions. The strategy for this prosecution was devised by Giuliani and it resulted in convictions of top members of the Colombo, Genovese, Luchese and Bonanno Families with sentences from forty to one hundred years.

Municipal corruption

Stanley M. Friedman: The Bronx Democratic leader was nailed in a scandal involving New York City's Parking Violations Bureau. The RICO law was employed by Giuliani, who led the trial team in New York's most significant prosecution of a corrupt political figure in ages. Friedman and three co-defendants were convicted and he was sentenced to twelve years' imprisonment.

Mario Biaggi: A Bronx military contracting firm purporting to employ minorities sought favors in Washington for preferential treatment. The involvement of Congressman Mario Biaggi, a former highly decorated cop with the New York Police Department, led to his own indictment and that of his son, Richard, former Borough President Stanley Simon, and four other men. Convicted earlier in another case handled by the Organised Crime Strike Force, Biaggi was again found guilty in this case, along with all but one of his co-defendants and faced a long prison term.

Bess Myerson: Miss America of 1945 and New York City's former Cultural Affairs Commissioner was indicted with her lover, Carl A. Capasso, a wealthy sewer builder, and former State Supreme Court Justice Hortense Gabel. Myerson was accused of hiring Judge Gabel's daughter in a municipal job for which Capasso received a substantial reduction in her mother's courtroom of his alimony payments. Giuliani got them on mail fraud charges.

Double Steel: A Sting operation named 'Operation Double Steel' involved an agent posing as a steel salesman who went to a procession of municipal employees in a position to negotiate the purchase of steel products. He made offers to one hundred and six such officials and one hundred and five of them accepted his bribes to do business with him. The one hundred and sixth turned down the offer – he wanted more money! A total of fifty-eight persons were busted in the scam.

Insider trading

Wall Street: Giuliani's most spectacular bust, other than the Mafia characters he went after, was that of Dennis B.

Levine, the former investment banker who pleaded guilty and implicated a bigger target, arbitrager Ivan F. Boesky. The prosecutor unravelled, with the help of the Securities and Exchange Commission, an insider-trading scandal of historic significance. Although some of his cases fell through when indictments were dismissed, Giuliani went right back to the drawing board and began mapping a new assault on the Financial District's crooks.

Business and tax fraud

Marc Rich: A major commodities trader, Marc Rich was one of Giuliani's first major tax fraud cases. Rich pleaded guilty and paid $200 million in fines from two of his companies. The government contended the companies concealed more than $100 million in taxable income from oil trading. Rich and his partner, Pincus Green, fled prosecution and became fugitives in Switzerland.

Edward A. Markowitz: A Washington promoter, Markowitz turned out to be one of the biggest tax defrauders in history. He pleaded guilty to creating $445 million in false income-tax deductions for wealthy investors, such as entertainment celebrities Woody Allen, Dick Cavett, and others. Although they were not accused of wrongdoing, the stars were subjected to audits and payment of back taxes.

Don King: The promoter who staged the Mike Tyson-Michael Spinks world heavyweight bout that Tyson won with a first-round knockout, proved too elusive for the prosecutor's offensive in the bout Giuliani waged against King on charges of evading payment of income taxes on hundreds of thousands of dollars drawn as cash advances against King's company receipts. King claimed he didn't know he was failing to pay taxes. Although King got off the hook his associate and girlfriend, Constance Harper, didn't escape conviction. She was found guilty of income tax evasion and was sentenced to a year and a day in prison.

Charles A. Atkins: The young co-founder of an umbrella organisation for limited partnerships, and two associates who, as

THE MAFIA

Giuliani said he found, had created more than $350 million in fraudulent deductions for tax shelter investors.

'I began to see what I had to do after I read Joe Bonanno's book,' Giuliani says, referring to *A Man Of Honor*, Bonanno's autobiography.

The narrative recreated detailed workings of the Mafia in earlier years. Giuliani and his assistants culled hundreds of hours of already existing FBI surveillance transcripts on the Mafia, reviewed past Senate hearing data, and compiled a complete tapestry of what existed on charts.

Giuliani received help from Ronald Goldstock, head of New York State's Organised Task Force, who offered the federal prosecutor access to tapes that recorded conversations on a bugging device secretly planted in the Jaguar of a Mob leader. The analysis of that evidence launched Giuliani into a declaration of war on the Mafia.

After his encounter with Goldstock, Giuliani flew to Washington in September 1983 to meet with Attorney General Smith and FBI Director William H. Webster, and proposed:

'This chart tells us where the members of organised crime are operating, what they're into, and what they're raking in. I want to borrow [FBI] agents in these fourteen cities to pull together anything and everything they can come up with on the operation of the Mafia high commission.'

Smith and Webster gave Giuliani their blessings and put him together with several hundred G-men. After he briefed the agents, they went off on their probes. Sixteen months later, the evidence was in – and the indictment followed.

The biggest Mafia bust of all time happened and Rudolph Giuliani had done it. Caught in the vise were some of the biggest Mafiosi of all time: Paul Castellano, Antonio Corallo, Anthony Salerno, Gennaro Langella, Philip Rastelli, and many others.

'I don't see any significant differences between today's Mob and yesterday's,' he says. 'Perhaps they're a little more American-ised than the old timers were, but they run the gamut of people who were around thirty years ago.

'Some may be sophisticated. Others may put on a front of respectability, yet others are total animals who act like animals.

By and large, they are all murderers. They destroy human life to make their living in the illicit ways they do. To me, people like that don't change very much over the years.

'I'm an Italian-American. I'd like to see the whole Mafia ended as any kind of influence on America.

'It has unfairly hurt large numbers of Italian-Americans, and the best way to ensure it can't harm them in the future is to participate in its destruction.'

Years ago, as pointed out earlier in this narrative, Dutch Schultz decided to kill racket-buster Thomas E. Dewey, but the Mob instead killed the underworld beer baron because they thought murdering the prosecutor would put too much heat on them. Giuliani was asked whether he had thoughts that he might be targeted for a mob hit.

'It's the one decision of theirs,' he responded with a laugh, 'that I probably agree with: it's a mistake to kill a prosecutor. The whole world will fall in on them then.'

Giuliani has other thoughts about threats against the lives of prosecutors:

'I believe by speaking out that it helps discourage the Mob. It tells them that we can't be intimidated. I can't talk to the Mob directly, but I assume they read newspapers and watch television. It gives me the opportunity to say to them:

'"We know that you are making threats, but it won't deter us."'

Organised Crime
Has Changed

Where have you gone, Vito Genovese, Vito Genovese, oh where have you gone, dreaded Vito . . .?

Even though the Mafia's hold on integral industries across the country is still extensive, there is little question that it has been greatly undermined by The Giuliani Offensive.

Since Vito Genovese died in prison in 1969, ten years after his incarceration for pushing drugs, his mighty crime empire, in the hands of acting boss Gerado Catena, under-boss Thomas Eboli, and *consigliere* Michele Miranda, has just about disintegrated.

Since Eboli's assassination in July 1972, things have grown progressively worse for the Mob. The nominal head of the Genovese empire, Anthony Fat Tony Salerno, is behind the big wall doing one hundred years after being convicted for racketeering in the 1986 'Commission' Trial, as were the godfathers who headed the other four most-feared crime families in America.

Carlo Gambino's heir, Paul 'Big Paul' Castellano, was killed in front of Sparks Steakhouse, on Manhattan's East Side on 16 December 1985.

But before the last echoes of gunfire faded, John Gotti, who was a gutter hood of nineteen at the time Genovese was sent to prison, became, at the age of forty-five, the new Godfather.

Many people, both inside the Mob as well as in the law enforcement community, suggest Gotti prepared the menu for Big Paul that afternoon.

In any case, John Gotti took over the remnants of the Gambino gang and proceeded to do to it exactly what the successors to the other crime families did: he took it downhill. Yet he succeeded in one respect where all the other new bosses had failed: he beat the rap in the lengthy Brooklyn Federal Court trial that ran for seventeen months and ended on 13 March 1987. Gotti was prosecuted on charges of operating a racketeering ring for eighteen years.

Increasingly looked upon as the Godfather of the 1980s, he was brought to trial with six co-defendants who, with Gotti, could have been sent away for forty years. But the jury of six men and six women found them not guilty. It was a stunning defeat of the government; the first setback since the Justice Department began its crackdown on organised crime.

This was the Mafia that once was. The old images now seem like a caricature: the aging dons living behind high-walled estates, taking part in the shadowy world of secret rituals, swearing vengeance on their enemies, dispatching hit men to end the lives of rivals. It was the stuff of novels and movies – and it was all real.

But in the past few years the bosses and underlings of organised crime have been buffeted by the onslaught of federal crackdowns. A procession of turncoats and government agents which has infiltrated the Mafia's inner sanctums has crippled its leadership and inflicted damage that was never deemed possible just a few years ago.

The underworld's most intimate secrets of how it operates have been laid bare as at no time in the past. Today the Mafia is divided by an old and new generation, and is torn asunder by different ideals. The new breed Mafiosi, native Americans for the most part, are no longer willing to live and work by the standards of a bygone era. They want to be underworld yuppies with their hands in the corporate glitz of the 1980s.

The Pizza Connection and the Commission Trials decimated the Mafia hierarchy. Such pressure from law enforcement agencies also is forcing the Mob to change some of its management techniques. Commission members are now reluctant to gather in large ceremonial 'sitdowns' to settle their territorial disputes. The FBI has made such extensive use of wiretaps and electronic bugs that sitdowns are no longer a preferred way of getting together to discuss business. Even lunches and dinners in restaurants are going by the wayside. More and more, bosses are using couriers to pass along their directives.

But one thing stays unchanged: the culture of organised crime. Mob members call each other 'Wise Guys', and so-called Wise-Guy rules define a strict code of conduct. For example, a member who vouches for someone who may in time betray the organisation takes the hit – usually before reprisals are taken against the stoolie. Also, a fixer taking a payoff for the job must produce exactly what he promised the Mob; he can't offer excuses or refunds.

Those are only two of the many old values that are still in vogue. Many of the others have been put on the back burner, because of the new 'elitist' Mafiosi. The Mob has finally begun to go back to the old ways that were so successful over the decades.

The transformation is being performed by Sicilian-born thugs who are being brought to the United States in droves. The movement was begun in the 1970s by Old World bosses like aging Carlo Gambino and Stefano Magaddino. Hundreds of Sicilian Mafiosi have since been secretly slipped into the United States over the Canadian and Mexican borders to revitalise the crumbling new-breed Mafia with Old World blood.

In describing what was happening, Long Island's Nassau County District Attorney Denis Dillon, who headed the Organised Crime Strike Force in Brooklyn before becoming a state prosecutor, remarked:

'I can't tell what's going on in their minds, but it seems that the old bosses don't feel that the second-generation Italians are good enough. The Mob is having discipline problems and those aliens will do the Mob's bidding because that's the way they were disciplined in the old country.'

In the beginning, a lot of the discipline was enforced by Sicilian Mafia executioners like Tommaso Buscetta, who was brought into this country and given carte blanche to enforce the toughest rules on the five families of New York's Metropolitan Area. In the time since, some nine hundred to one thousand Sicilian Mafiosi, many of them fugitives from Italian police, have been smuggled not only into New York, but Chicago, Cleveland, Kansas City, Las Vegas, Los Angeles, San Francisco, and other Mafia strongholds.

Called 'Zips', these imported Mafiosi have been solidifying their positions in the crime families across the land. With the urging of top Mafia elders, they have been taking on street activities such as policy, loan-sharking, hijacking, extortion, trucking and garbage rackets – as well as many other operations.

These illegal-immigrant Mafiosi have also undertaken the role of hitmen for the Mob – and are showing their increasing mastery in the way they carry out assassinations. They never leave clues behind. One of the first hints that the Sicilian killers were at it here turned up in the silencer-equipped 'grease gun' found near the body of Thomas Eboli. Were there fingerprints on the gun? Not if you consider it was probably fired by one of the illegals who could hardly be expected to have a rap sheet in the United States.

The aliens' success in gradually taking over from the young turks is largely attributed to the fact that they are given wide leeway in operating in the territories where the young, American-born members of organised crime have been firmly entrenched. But the foreigners have distinct advantage over their domestic counterparts: they have no police records in this country, no Social Security numbers, no draft cards, no fingerprints or photos on file, and no childhood friends, disenchanted wives or jealous neighbors who could run to the cops of the Internal Revenue Service.

These imported recruits are just what Old World Mafiosi are

about: serious, no-nonsense, hard-working racketeers and killers. Most importantly, they toil anonymously. You won't find them being interviewed by Ted Koppel on *60 Minutes* or helping Al Ruddy make *The Godfather* or talking to Gay Talese so he can write *Honor Thy Father*, or to Nicholas Pileggi for his *Wise Guy*.

'It's a new ballgame,' says Arthur Grubert, former Assistant Chief Inspector of the New York City Police Department's Intelligence Division. 'Authorities are now losing track of Mob operations. New arrivals are taking over more and more of the street operations.'

The infiltration has now reached what one official described as 'an invasion of epidemic proportions'. The first visible signs of the influx surfaced about fifteen years ago when police began noticing that illegal immigrants were repeatedly turning up in narcotics cases, robberies, and homicides. Early case in point:

Rosario Gambino, a cousin of Mafia chieftain Carlo Gambino, was arrested in Brooklyn for threatening a policeman in an attempted extortion case. The investigation turned up records that showed he had been deported from the United States as an illegal alien and somehow made it back here. The lawmen had no idea when or how Rosario had re-entered the country. He was given the boot again. Yet for all we know, he might again be among us.

Not all imported Mafiosi are immune to arrest. They get tripped up despite their penchant for secrecy and undercover maneuvers.

Sicilian aliens were caught up in two major narcotics cases. One involved more than $1 million in cash found in the walls of drug leader Louis Cirillo's home. The other involved the seizure of a suitcase containing $965,000 that belonged to a Sicilian who had joined the Gambino Family.

The Gambino Family also figured in a multi-million-dollar counterfeiting scheme that was run exclusively by illegal aliens. They dealt in the falsification of every conceivable documents from passports to drivers' licenses.

When they initially were imported into the United States, the Sicilian Mafiosi were employed almost exclusively as hit men. Today that has changed. The aliens increasingly have been taking over the street business from the young American-born hoods. And the latter are crying a blue streak of complaints.

One café operator who found himself paying protection money to the 'Italianos', as they're called, shook his head in dismay as he drew the picture:

'Hey, here I was doing a nice business with no bother from the local Wise Guys. Sure, they come in and they eat and they walk out without pay. You expect that. But they leave you alone. You do a nice business, so what's a few meals on the cuff. I give to the cops all the time anyway . . .

'But these foreigners come here and they are pushy like you can't believe. They put me down for $100 a week for 'fire insurance'. I tell them I got fire insurance with Globe. But they tell me Globe no pay for incendiary fires . . .

'I can't believe this. The local guys used to laugh at them in the beginning. They dressed too sharp. They had pointy patent leather shoes. They had longer hair. They used to wear their jackets over their shoulders. The local guys used to let them alone. They had their own cliques and own clubs. You could see they were mean and they were the kind of Wise Guys you don't want to mess with.

'I watched and I saw what made them click. They were great schemers. They were also great manipulators. They might start by selling jewelry [stolen] out of the back of a little pizza joint. Pretty soon they're doing errands for some big guys – seeing about this, taking care of that, talking to each other in *Scidgie* [Sicilian dialect] and always scheming and earning.

'They're hungry. You turn around for a second and they got a cousin in there with them, and now you got two on the block. Today, the local guys are scared of them. There are no rules with the Greasers – all right, so they are called Zips. But no matter what name you wanna give them, they got the okay. When they started out, they started nice and easy. But now they don't ask no more, they demand . . .'

With the approval of the top Mafia bosses, who felt their control slipping as more and more of the new breed became obstreperous and resentful of orders, the immigrants were given even greater

461

latitude to operate. They were even allowed to shake down the home-grown shakedown artists themselves.

That was because bosses like Gambino believed that was the only way to force their organisations back to where they belonged.

An example is Joseph Colombo, who promised he would 'eliminate all complaints about the way we run the family ... [and] I promise to spread the bread around . . .' and who, as soon as he had taken over the reins became a much-too-visible force when he picketed the FBI for cracking down on Italian-American mobsters and campaigned for other causes. He brought nothing but woe upon the Mob. By the time he was assassinated, two-thirds of the five thousand men identified as Mafiosi by the Senate's McClellan Committee in the early 1960s were either in jail, under indictment, or dead. And the American-born hoods promoted to replace these fallen gangsters proved to be inept to the extreme. And that opened the way for the Invasion of The Zips from Sicily.

Respect for one another in the Mafia – a cardinal rule of the old-line Mafiosi – had undergone dramatic erosion during the 1960s and 1970s, but most especially in the early years of the 1980s. That point was brought vibrantly to life by Aniello Dellacroce, the late Gambino underboss, in a secretly recorded 1985 dressing down of an underling who had gone over his head to the boss about some matter:

'I'm through with you,' Dellacroce scolded. 'You understand? I don't want to say hello to ya. Twenty years ago, youse woulda found yourself in some fuckin' hole someplace . . .'

'You're right, Neill,' the now-contrite underling replied.

'You know what I mean?' Dellacroce persisted. 'But things change. Things change now because there's too much conflict. People do whatever they feel like. They don't train their people no more. There's no more – there's no more respect. If you can't be sincere, you can't be honest with your friends – then forget about it. Ya got nothing.'

The old Mafia bosses who've survived the dramatic changes over the years are today very much like tired corporate executives. They face each day with increasing weariness and feel like tossing in the towel.

In another wiretap recording made at Genovese boss Anthony Salerno's hangout, he and Tony Ducks Corallo bemoaned a headstrong young mobster who was disrespectful to Fat Tony:

'I don't know what to do,' Salerno complained. 'I swear I don't.'

'And you have to run downtown yourself when you want something done?' Corallo said.

'No,' protested Salerno. 'I'll retire. I don't need that. Listen, Tony, if it wasn't for me, there wouldn't be no Mob left. I made all the guys. And everybody's a good guy. This guy don't realise that. I worked myself – Jeez, how could a man be like that, huh?'

He said the underling had even called him 'Fat Tony' to his face.

'I know the way he talks,' Corallo commiserated. 'Shoot him. Get rid of them. Shoot them. Kill them. But you can't go on – it's disgusting . . .'

The Mafia's wounds largely have been inflicted from within.

Undercover agents posing as thieves and thugs have infiltrated the once-impregnable Mafia – and have provided considerable information on murder contracts, leadership conspiracies, and even the everyday life in the Mob. Among the countless tidbits of intelligence they gathered was the one that the Mafia never works on Mothers' Day.

And by using the lure of a witness-protection program and the threat of lengthy prison sentences, authorities have succeeded in persuading Mafiosi to break the once-sacred code of *omerta* and testify against their former friends.

And, of course, there's the extensive use of modern electronic eavesdropping devices and surveillance techniques, all made possible by the Racketeer-Influenced and Corrupt Organisations Act.

While the trials of the past few years have left the Mafia leadership and a number of its most lucrative rackets in disarray, organised crime is far from being a dead issue. It continues to harvest enormous profits from its myriad enterprises, and even the most optimistic law-enforcement officials are not prepared to say that the Mafia's death knell has been rung.

United States Attorney W. Giuliani, who has dispatched more Mafiosi to prison than any prosecutor in history, has high hopes that the attacks mounted against the Mafia the last couple of years are having a telling effect. Yet he cannot predict how the new emerging leadership will reconstitute itself and what course it will chart to gain access to the numerous long-established rackets and drug-distribution networks that have been crippled by local and federal lawmen.

'This has been the Mafia's worst year,' Giuliani says of 1988. 'We keep making gains and they keep getting moved backward. If we take back the labor unions, the legitimate businesses, eventually they become just another street gang. Spiritually, psychologically, they've always been just a street gang.'

Thomas L. Sheer, head of the FBI's New York office and an expert on organised crime, views the present situation in another light:

'The government of the Mob, the ability to make secret agreements and set up spheres of influence, has been weakened. The families have been driven apart . . .'

One thing is certain. The American-born hoods are no match for the Zips, who bring the customs of the old country to these shores. The domestic hoods can't help but agree that they have been overexposed in the media and are altogether too long under surveillance, which easily subjects them to ready identification, so that it's become almost impossible for them to remain active without being detected.

'How can I operate?' one young American Mafioso complained to a detective. 'They're making moves about me right here on my own block . . .'

This same domestic hood takes a measured glance at the Sicilian Mafiosi who are streaming into the country to restore old-fashioned values into the Mafia. He observes:

'The Greasers can work like hell because a guy like – let's call him Sonny – has to lay back. Sonny's so hot he can't even buy the paper without risking a bust by the cops or feds. He's compelled to hold back and let the Greasers take the cream and give him a little bit.' You don't have to call him Sonny. His name is John Gotti, a perfect example of an altogether overexposed Mafioso boss. At his prosecution with the other Mafia defendants, hours of tapes gleaned from bugs planted at the home of Gotti lieutenant Angelo Ruggiero and videotapes of traffic at a Mob social club were played, making very public the workings of today's Mob.

Also at the trial was James Cardinali, a thirty-seven-year-old ex-Mob errand boy, who called Gotti the finest man he'd ever met. Cardinali's pedigree included five murders, narcotics ripoffs, pistol-whipping a priest, and drug abuse.

With immunity for four of the murders he admitted he committed, Cardinali told the jurors that Gotti explained the wonders of crime between trips the witness made to the bank with the big boss's money.

In the days of the old-time bosses this testimony would never have reached any hall of justice. Ruggiero and Cardinali would have disappeared into the wet concrete of the Long Island Expressway's retaining walls during its widening project – Angelo for letting himself get bugged, James for blabbing to authorities. Neither would have lived to see the inside of the courtroom.

The same can be said about fifty-six-year-old Dominick Lofaro, a gambler who turned witness after he was nailed with enough heroin to send him away for life. He struck a bargain with the feds. He wore a hidden recorder and taped Gotti discussing gambling activity and picked up other mobster voices praising Gotti as a 'hoodlum's hoodlum'.

Throughout the trial, Gotti laughed, sneered, or muttered Wise Guy retorts whenever prosecuting Assistant United States Attorney Diane Giacalone addressed the court. Each morning, he changed out of jail garb (he was held without bail in the federal penitentiary during the entire trial) and donned tailored suits, handsewn shoes, crisply-pressed shirts. He sat at the defense table looking more like a law school scholar than a high school dropout. During recesses, he fussed over his co-defendants' dress, straightening ties, adjusting collars. He was confident and cocky.

Evidently the jury liked what they saw in this dapper Mafia godfather. They gave him a walk.

Gotti's troubles are not at an end. He faces yet another trial. But even if he wins again, the chances are that he'll be a loser, because the ever-growing number of Sicilian Zips will exercise increasingly greater influence over the five crime families in the New York region. Overexposed men like John Gotti may have a very short-lived future in the new order, which is really the order of the old.

But how far will these Sicilian Mafiosi go in restoring the old values and resurrecting the crumbling foundations of the Syndicate?

A number of law enforcement officials are expressing the belief that the Mafia's days as the overlord of organised crime are numbered; that the Zips cannot save the families from going down the tube.

They're saying it's just a matter of time before the new arrivals become as well known to police as their American *cugini*. Immigration and Naturalisation Service officials are already compiling dossiers on some of the newcomers. And the New York Police Department is shaping a special 'Mafia Hit Squad' of cops from Sicilian descendants who've already begun translating hours of tapes from the dialect preserved on as-yet-untranscribed wiretaps.

Yet the recruiting goes on as though a bright, promising future lies ahead for the Mafia. By fashioning a team from the Old World, the bosses are following in the 1980s what worked for them a half-century ago and even up to very recent times.

They are conscripting hometown Mafiosi whom they see as having been molded in their own image. They are anxious to turn over their secret society to these men who speak their dialect, still believe in their codes, and don't want to pull a Johnny Torrio.

It was Al Capone's rapacious mentor who launched the migration from their Chicago base to the western suburbs in 1923. Gambling and gunfire soon rocked once-sleepy Cicero at the Windy City's perimeter. It's lethargic City Hall fell to the Syndicate in an election that killed four and wounded forty.

After Prohibition, a primmer breed of businessman-thug moved to Oak Park and River Forest, stately towns renowned for their Frank Lloyd Wright architecture.

While suburbia is a grand locale to bring up the kids and to have a three-bedroom split-level and a barbeque pit, that's not what the old-line bosses ever wanted. They were content to live out their lives in crowded tenement houses in decrepit neighborhoods.

Well-manicured lawns, carefully trimmed shrubs, trees, peace, and quiet were never intended to be the Sicilian Mafioso's way of life in these United States.

The godfathers' new recruits will tell you that, if you care to ask them. Provided, first, that you can find them.

Acknowledgements

The authors wish to acknowledge with profound thanks contributions to this work by individuals, historical, and reference sources, without whose valuable advice, guidance, and assistance the book would not have been possible. Our deepest appreciation goes to:

U.S. Attorney **Rudolph W. Giuliani** of New York's Southern District for insight and observations on the operations of Organised Crime, and to his wife, broadcast journalist Donna Hanover, for details about their life together that shape an intimate portrait of the couple away from the maddening daily swirl and bustle of the prosecutor's office and the television newsroom.

U.S. Attorney **Raymond Dearie** of New York's Eastern District and such other able officials in that office, including Assistant U.S. Attorney **Edward McDonald**, head of Brooklyn's Federal Strike Force Against Organised Crime, his predecessor, **Thomas P. Puccio**, as well as Special Attorney of the Organised Crime Strike Force **Douglas Behm**. Their help in making available public records on Mafia operations in racketeering and drug trafficking was invaluable.

Ralph F. Salerno, retired member of the New York City Police Department and one of America's foremost authorities on organised crime. He supervised the investigation into Joe

Valachi's testimony for the McClellan Permanent Senate Sub-committee, served as the only police officer on President Johnson's Organised Crime Task Force, on a presidential commission looking into campus unrest and campus violence, and as an organised crime consultant to the House Select Committee on Assassinations looking into President Kennedy's murder. Mr Salerno gave co-author Carpozi a thorough indoctrination into the inner workings of organised crime when together they wrote an eight-part serialisation for the *New York Post* entitled 'The Mob's Deadly Hold on New York'.

Queen's District Attorney **John Santucci** for his complete and enthusiastic support in enabling the authors to gather material on the Mafia's illicit activities in his borough, but especially for information about the mob's involvement in rackets at Kennedy International Airport.

Nassau County District Attorney **Denis Dillon,** not only for insights and interpretations of underworld operations in his jurisdiction, but for his recollections and remembrances of his own battles with the Mafia when he headed Brooklyn's Federal Strike Force Against Organised Crime.

Lieutenant **Remo Franceschini** of the Queens District Attorney's Squad, for his always-generous assistance in providing information not only about underworld activity in his own jurisdiction but far beyond the county's borders to as far-off places as Florida.

Antoinette Giancana, daughter of slain Chicago organised crime kingpin Sam 'Momo' Giancana, who roundly denied the story that Mrs Judith Exner Campbell had been a go-between for President Kennedy and her father plotting the assassination of Cuba's Fidel Castro, and that they were involved in other Mob business (author Kitty Kelley and Mrs Exner reportedly shared $100,000 from *People* magazine for this uncorroborated story in the publication).

George Wolf, known as the 'Mobster's Mouthpiece', who contributed the untold details in this book (Chapter 29) of why and how New York Governor Thomas E. Dewey released America's Number One underworld leader, Charles 'Lucky' Luciano, from prison and arranged for his deportation to Italy.

Also counsel to mobsters Frank Costello, Arthur 'Dutch Schultz' Flegenheimer, Albert Anastasia, and Johnny Torrio, Wolf further gives us a humorous but penetrating insight into another client Vito Genovese, in a surprising divorce proceeding.

Burton Turkus, Assistant District Attorney of Kings County, who virtually single-handedly broke up and prosecuted America's most infamous gang of killers, Murder Incorporated. Mr Turkus wrote the first definitive book on the gang after his retirement, *Murder, Inc.*, published by Manor Books in 1951. Mr Turkus was instrumental in providing co-author Carpozi with many insights into the working of this infamous mob that slew on order, but he contributed even more extensively to the inside story of how the gang's informer, Abe Reles, met his death in a mysterious plunge from Coney Island Hotel.

Mickey Cohen, the notorious West Coast Mob chieftain, who made co-author Carpozi privy to heretofore untold tales about gangland operations he headed out of Los Angeles and Hollywood. Mr Cohen was once the subject of an exclusive three-part series Carpozi wrote about the gangster for Hearst's *New York Journal-American*.

Senator **Estes Kefauver** (D. Tennessee) who conducted the Senate hearings into organised crime in the early 1950s and provided material that enabled the authors to write the Introduction for this book.

And most especially to:

Librarian **Christopher Bowen** and the Reference Department of the *New York Post*.

Head Librarian **Faigie Rosenthal** and the Reference Department of the *New York Daily News*.

The authors are also indebted for the information that helped guide the path this work took to these highly regarded books and their scriveners:

Organised Crime in America, by Gus Taylor, the University of Michigan Press, 1962.
The Green Felt Jungle, by Ed Reid and Ovid Demaris, Simon & Schuster, Inc., 1963.
The Valachi Papers, by Peter Maas, G. P. Putnam's Sons, 1968.

The Crime Confederation, by Ralph Salerno and John S. Tompkins, Doubleday & Company, Inc., 1969.

The Brotherhood of Evil, The Mafia, by Frederic Sondern Jr, Farrar, Straus & Giroux Inc., 1969.

Capone: The Life and World of Al Capone, by John Kobler, G. P. Putnam's Sons, 1971.

Honor Thy Father, by Gay Talese, World Publishing Co., 1971.

Recognition also is given to the editors of *New York Magazine* for the special 1972 edition of their publication entitled *The Mafia at War*, which excerpted significant passages from several important books on organised crime. That publication featured contributions by such distinguished writers about organised crime as **John Kobler, Peter Mass, Nicholas Pileggi, Ralph Salerno**, and **Gay Talese**.

And special thanks to Reed Sparling, books editor of STAR magazine, whose advice and counsel were given to his colleague, News Department Editor George Carpozi Jr, the co-author as the text for this book was shaped day by day over the lengthy period of its production.

To all these invaluable resources, Will Balsamo and George Carpozi Jr extend heartfelt gratitude.

The authors also very specially wish to extend, together, an immense note of thanks to New York's CBS-TV's newscaster **Chris Borgen** for teaming them up in 1976 which resulted in their joint effort for a book entitled *Always Kill A Brother*. As a result of that first association, Balsamo and Carpozi collaborated more extensively on this volume.

And the authors wish to thank Sergeant **Thomas Krant** for his always-total cooperation, along with the NYPD's Academy Museum which provided invaluable information about organised crime in the realm of guns and photos.

The authors wish to express their thanks to Ronald Deliso and Frank Cascella for their help in translating certain words from English to Italian.

Then, too, one very final salute must go to Kenneth Cobb of

the City of New York Department of Records and Information Services lodged in the Municipal Archives, for his tremendous resourcefulness in providing the authors with editorial and photographic information that helped put this book all together.